George Oliver

History of the Masonic Persecutions in different Quarters of the

Globe

George Oliver

History of the Masonic Persecutions in different Quarters of the Globe

ISBN/EAN: 9783337397074

Printed in Europe, USA, Canada, Australia, Japan

Cover: Foto ©ninafisch / pixelio.de

More available books at **www.hansebooks.com**

HISTORY

OF

MASONIC PERSECUTIONS

IN

Different Quarters of the Globe,

WITH AN INTRODUCTORY ESSAY;

AND

MASONIC INSTITUTES,

BY VARIOUS AUTHORS.

WITH AN

INTRODUCTORY ESSAY AND EXPLANATORY NOTES.

BY THE

REV. GEORGE OLIVER, D. D.,
Author of
"THE HISTORICAL LANDMARKS," "HISTORY OF INITIATION," "STAR IN THE EAST,"
ETC., ETC.

NEW YORK:
MASONIC PUBLISHING AND MANUFACTURING CO.,
432 BROOME STREET.
1867.

CONTENTS.

PAGE.

Introductory Essay on the Usages and Customs of Symbolical
    Masonry in the Eighteenth Century. By the Editor.   .   1

CHAPTER I.

A Detection of Dr. Plot's Account of the Freemasons   .   . 21

CHAPTER II.

An Apology for the Free and Accepted Masons   .   .   . 52

CHAPTER III.

An Impartial Examination of the Act of the Associate Synod
    against the Freemasons   91

CHAPTER IV.

An Account of the Sufferings of John Coustos in the Inquisition
    at Lisbon. Written by himself   114

CHAPTER V.

A Vindication of Masonry from a Charge of having given rise
    to the French Revolution. By Stephen Jones, Esq .   . 116

CHAPTER VI.

The Misrepresentations of Barruel and Robison exposed. By
    W. Preston, Esq.   185

CHAPTER VII.

Persecutions of Freemasonry now in Operation   .   . 203

THE HISTORY

OF

MASONIC PERSECUTION.

MASONIC PERSECUTION.

INTRODUCTORY ESSAY

ON THE USAGES AND CUSTOMS OF SYMBOLICAL MASONRY
N THE EIGHTEENTH CENTURY.

BY THE EDITOR.

" The Scalds exclaim, with miserable frown,[1]
Masons repair? they'd sooner pull it down.
A set of ranting, roaring, rumbling fellows,
Who meet to sing old rose and burn the bellows.
Champagne and claret, dozens in a jerk,
And then they say how hard they've been at work.
Next for the secret of their own wise making,
Hiram and Boaz, and Grand Master Jachin!
Poker and tongs! the sign! the word! the stroke!
'Tis all a nothing, and 'tis all a joke.
Nonsense on nonsense! let them storm and rail,
Here's the whole history of their mop and pail;
For 'tis the sense of more than half the town,
Their secret is—a bottle at the Crown!"

MASONIC PROLOGUE.

" You shall not go out to drink by night, or if occasion doe happen that you must goe, you shall not stay till past eight of the clock, having some of your fellowes, or one at the least, to beare you witness of the honest place you were in, and your good behaviour, to avoid scandall."
—ANCIENT CHARGES.

" I wish the reader to take notice, that in writing of this book, I have made myself a recreation of a recreation; and that it might prove so to him, and not read dull and tediously, I have in several places mixed (not any scurrility, but) some innocent harmless mirth; of which, if thou be a severe sour complexioned man, then I here disallow thee to be a competent judge; for divines say, There are offences given, and offences not given, but taken."—IZAAK WALTON.

FROM the habits and usages of any society or body of men may be gathered a tolerably correct idea of their relative qualities, and the tendency such an association

See Masonic Institutes, p. 247.

possesses to promote the happiness and prosperity of its
members. The eighteenth century was distinguished by
the existence of numerous local institutions, which peri-
odically congregated together different classes of society,
for divers purposes, the chief of which appears to have
been the amusement of a vacant hour, when the business
of the day was ended. Few of these ephemeral societies
aimed at a higher flight. Some met weekly, while the
members of others assembled every evening. Each profession and calling had its club, and in large towns the
trade of every street was not without its means of thus
killing the evening hour.

Such societies embraced every class of persons, from
the noble to the beggar; and, whatever might be a
man's character or disposition, he would find in London
a club that would square with his ideas. If he were a
tall man, the tall club was ready to receive him; if
short, he would soon find a club of dwarfs; if musically
inclined, the harmonic club was at hand; was he fond
of late hours, he joined the owl club; if of convivial habits, he would find a free and easy in every street;[2] if
warlike, he sought out the lumber troopers;[3] if a buck
of the first water, he joined the club of choice spirits;
and if sober and quiet, the humdrum. If nature had
favoured him with a gigantic proboscis, an unsightly

[2] A celebrated tavern, called the Coal Hole, was famous for midnight
gossiping. Here the most celebrated comedians entertained their
private friends in a series of convivialities after they had delighted the
town. Here, too, certain painters, poets, sculptors, musicians, and other
ingenious men, who preferred late hours, a smoky room, and hilarity, to
the sober comforts of domestic life, wasted the night in glorious independence, fearless of the frowns, and tears, and curtain-lectures which
might await them at home.

[3] The Lumber Troop is till in being, and is held at "the Falcon," Fetter Lane. Grant says that there have been many members of distinction
in the ancient Lumber Troop, who have, in most cases, joined it from a
pure love of fun. Prince George of Denmark, the consort of Queen
Anne, was a Lumber Trooper, and so was Hogarth, the prince of
humourous painters. In fact Hogarth joined the Troop with the view
of forwarding his professional business. Some of his best subjects were
selected from Troop Hall. John Harrison, of Bell Yard, Temple Bar,
an eccentric personage, who kept a tobacco shop, and went to all the
meetings of the Troop with his pockets stuffed with tobacco, which he
sold in retail to the Troopers, is supposed to be the character whom
Hogarth represents in his Modern Midnight Conversation, as leaning
over the parson when challenged to drink a particular toast.

protuberance on his shoulders, or any other striking personal peculiarity, he would have no difficulty in finding a society to keep him in countenance.

One great characteristic of the age may be named—there were no temperance societies; and the name of a teetotaller was unknown. All these associations had one common purpose,—they were equally addicted to drinking and smoking, and seldom parted sober; for their usual motto was, "Another pot, and then! What then? ANOTHER!"[4]

A few of these institutions, however, must be exempted from this sweeping censure. The kit-cat, the beef-steak, the literary club, and others, were frequented by the nobility and gentry, and though they indulged in convivialities which would not be tolerated in our more temperate days,[5] it would be too much to say that the members of these aristocratic societies never exceeded the bounds of decorum. But the truth and beauty of a picture consists in the development of shade as well as

[4] Even in this state, instances are on record where drunkards were more sensible than those who were sober. The following anecdote is told of a poor woman who, labouring under temporary derangement, hung herself in her own house. As soon as her husband was aware of her situation, he set off in search of a medical man, leaving his wife suspended by the neck, and giving strict injunction that she should not be meddled with till he came back. In consequence of the alarm, a number of persons were collected together, amongst whom was a man more than half seas over. He bawled out "Why don't you cut the woman down?" When several females immediately replied, "You drunken brute, would you put a finger on her when her good man is gone for the doctor?" The toper nevertheless cut her down, but too late to save her life.

[5] Even Erasmus, according to Fuller, (Hist. Cam., p. 87) when he resided at Queen's College, Cambridge, often complained of the thin potations of that seminary. "The ale," he said, "was raw, small, and windy." Erasmus seems to have been attached to good wine, and to have been at first ill-satisfied with his fare at Cambridge. He tells his friend (Epist. viii., p. 16) that he did not intend to remain long at Queen's College; that he did not like the ale, and the wine to be procured there was not much more to his taste; and he ends by requesting him to send him a cask of the best Greek wine that could be procured in London. His friend procured him a constant supply; but on one occasion, when Erasmus had drank out one barrel before the other arrived, as a bit of a hint, he returned the empty cask, with a note to the following effect: "I return your cask, which I have kept by me empty rather a long time, that I might at least have the pleasure of enjoying the smell of Greek wine." Fuller further certifies that in his own time the scholars had the same complaint, and he assigns this reason for it,—"the brewers, having prescription on their side for a long time, little amended it."

I*

light and colouring; as in the Roman paintings, the
vices were placed beside the virtues, that the latter
might appear more brilliant by the contrast; and therefore it must be admitted that, like the frequenters of the
lower clubs, they would sometimes extend their potations to a point which made them rather unsteady in
their movements;[6] yet, as this was an exception to a
rule, it became a source rather of merriment and good-
humoured raillery, than of regret; although Prior says:

"——————— 'Twas rage, 'twas noise;
An airy scene of transitory joys;
To the late revel and protracted feast,
Wild dreams succeeded, and disordered rest."[7]

[6] " What would our fastidious teetotallers say to the following eulogium
on brandy by a reverend prelate——Theoricus Episcopus Hermenensis in
Romanula juxta Bononiam? He recommends it to be taken before meat
as well as after, because it " sloweth age, it strengtheneth youth, it
helpeth digestion, it cutteth phlegm, it abandoneth melancholy, it relish-
eth the heart, it lighteneth the mind, it quickeneth the spirits, it cureth
the hydropsy, it healeth the strangulary, it pounceth the stone, it ex-
pelleth gravel, it puffeth away all ventosity, it keepeth and preserveth the
head from whirling, the eyes from dazzling, the tongue from lisping, the
mouth from maffling, the teeth from chattering, and the throat from
rattling : it keepeth the weason from stifling, the stomach from wam-
bling. and the heart from swelling; the belly from wirtching, the guts
from rumbling, the hands from shivering, the veins from crampling, the
bones from aching, and the marrow from soking."
[7] The grave Dr. Johnson was a club man, but he studiously avoided a
personal exposure. He said, "when I drink wine, I scorn to drink it
when in company. I have drunk many a bottle by myself; in the first
place, because I had need of it to raise my spirits; in the second place,
because I would have nobody to witness its effects upon me." (Boswell,
vol. iii., p. 39, Ed. 1820.)   Boswell, however, tells us that at an earlier
period he was a gourmand, and sometimes drank a bottle of port after
supper at the Mitre. " We had a good supper," says he, " and port wine,
of which he then drank a bottle." (Ibid, vol. i., p. 396.)   Indeed, Johnson himself was heard to say, "some people have a foolish way of not
minding, or not pretending to mind what they eat. For my part, I mind
my belly very studiously, and very carefully; for I look upon it, that he
who does not mind his belly will hardly mind anything else." " I never
knew," adds Boswell, " any man who relished good eating more than he
did.   When at table he was totally absorbed in the business of the moment; his looks seemed riveted to his plate; nor would he say one word,
or even pay the least attention to what was said by others, till he had
satisfied his appetite; which was so fierce, and indulged with such in-
tenseness, that, while in the act of eating, the veins of his forehead
swelled, and generally a stong perspiration was visible; for Johnson,
though he could be abstemious, was not a temperate man either in eating
or drinking." (Ibid, vol. i., p. 464.)

But in that age Bacchus was the lord of the ascendant, and all classes of society were but too happy to offer sacrifice to him. In my younger days I have been witness to many illustrations of this propensity, which, I may also add, so far from being esteemed disgraceful, were considered meritorious, and he who could swallow the greatest quantity of wine was esteemed the most delectable companion, particularly if his bibulous superiority were accompanied with that universal letter of recommendation, the capacity to sing a good song.

There was, however, one society in that period, which, if it did indulge its members with the enjoyment of decent refreshment, had a standing law which provided against all excess; declaring that "they ought to be moral men, good husbands, good parents, good sons, and good neighbours; not staying too long from home, *and avoiding all excess.*" This society was Freemasonry; the exclusive character of which excited the envy of all other periodical assemblies of convivial men; and produced a series of objections, which have been embodied in the Motto to this Essay, which forms part of a prologue written in the year 1765. Freemasonry was said by these captious individuals to be a mere convivial society;[3] and the existing clubs and coteries which embraced the common design of mutual entertainment by the song, the toast, the merry tale, and the cheerful glass, without any pretensions of a superior character,

---

[3] We will give the defamer every latitude he desires, and for a moment admit that Masons did enjoy themselves at their public festivals. Were they alone in the practice of good living? Read the following document, which is a detail of the provisions that were consumed at a single episcopal dinner, holden at York in the sixth year of Edward IV., and say no more that Masons were either gourmands or drunkards. It included 300 quarters of wheat, 300 *tuns of* ale, 100 *tuns of wine, a pipe of hipo-* cras, 104 oxen, 6 wild bulls, 1000 sheep, 304 calves, as many porks, 400 swans, 2000 geese, 1000 capons, 2000 pigs, 400 plovers, 100 dozen quails, 200 dozen ruffs and rees, 104 peacocks, 4000 mallards, 200 cranes, 200 kids, 2000 chickens, 4000 pigeons, 4000 rabbits, 200 bitterns, 400 herons, 200 pheasants, 500 partridges, 400 woodcocks, 100 curlicus, 1000 egrittes, 500 bucks and more, 4000 cold venison pasties, 1500 hot venison pasties, 1000 parted dishes of jelly, 3000 plain ditto, 4000 tarts, 3000 cold custards, 2000 hot custards, 600 pikes, 800 breams, 12 porpoises and seals; with salmon, sturgeon, whitings, eels, mackerel, barbels, trouts, lampreys, turbot, brill, ling, tench, crabs, lobsters, &c., &c., in unnumbered abundance; and spices, sugared delicacies, and wafers, "plentie." (See Leland's Collect. vol. vi., p. 2.)

were piqued and annoyed at the assumption of superior privileges which distinguished the masonic fraternity; and therefore they vented their indignation and spleen by ridicule and contumely.[9] It cannot be supposed that the above charges were invented by the Mason who wrote the lines. The passage was merely introduced into the prologue to show how perfectly ridiculous and unfounded they were, and how much they were despised by the fraternity at large. The opinions existed notwithstanding in all their force, and their operation was boundless amongst those who were determined to use every effort to cry the institution down.

But the members of our sacred order met together for other purposes than those of conviviality, although moderate refreshment was not denied at the termination of the grave labours of the lodge, when the brethren responded to a call from the south. The objects which were avowedly pursued in the lodge, were the study and investigation of science; mutually communicating lessons of morality, and practising the exercise of brotherly love, that the fabled reign of Astræa might be restored, and truth and justice prevail in the lodge, and from thence be extended to society in general.

> "————Nec verba minacia fixo
> Ære legebantur; nec supplex turba timebant
> Judicis ora sui; sed crant sine judice tuti."—Ovid.

The world gave Freemasonry credit for some other usages, of which the Brethren were perfectly innocent; but they were too gross to excite even a momentary annoyance. They were charged with the practice of forbidden arts; as, for instance, "raising the devil in a circle;"[10] although the use they made of his infernal majesty does not appear; but from hints scattered about in other places we may surmise that it was for the purposes of divination, the discovery of hidden treasures, and other illegal designs, which were more openly avowed in the innovations of continental Masonry. We find mention made of "a red hot poker" being used to inflict an indelible mark of initiation on the unfortunate

---

[9] See Masonic Institutes, p. 8.
[10] See Euclid's letter in Anderson's Const. Ed. 1738, p. 227.

candidate,— 'the shirt of an apprentice," and some other absurdities, which it will be unnecessary to name,[11] because there are no persons at the present day so weak as to believe that we practise magic, divination, or alchymy, at our private meetings;[12] although the charge was revived in 1824 by a writer in the London Magazine, who contends that the Rosicrucians and the Freemasons are one and the same body; that the former being "alchymists, cabalists, and dealers in the black art," it was evidently intended to be understood that the Freemasons of the present day use the same delusive practices.

These absurd charges, however, were widely disseminated and implicitly believed in the eighteenth century, and several books were written to prove their truth.[13] And one enthusiastic anti-mason went so far as to introduce them into a sermon, which he published, under the forbidding title of "Masonry the way to Hell; a sermon wherein is clearly proved, both from reason and from

[11] Scots' Mag. 1755, p. 133.

[12] These practices in the eighteenth century do not appear to have been considered disreputable. Weishaupt, the founder of Illuminism, boasts of them as so many proofs of his virtuous character. He says : " I have gone through the whole circle of human enquiry. I have exorcised spirits, raised ghosts, discovered treasures, interrogated the cabala—*hatte Loto gespielt*—I have never transmuted metals. The tenor of my life has been the opposite of everything that is vile ; and no man can lay anything to my charge."

[13] The author of the Freemasons' Lexicon, however, asserts that on the Continent, until the year 1780, there were to be found, here and there, Freemasons' lodges, in which alchymy was practised. Although it never formed any part of the science, yet there were a few men to be found, and amongst them Freemasons, who employed themselves as alchymists; who, if they could not make gold in the crucible, knew how to make it, in considerable quantities, out of their credulous dupes. A Freemason is directed to study the wonderful and stupendous works of nature ; not that he may be enabled to make gold, but that he may prepare himself, by comparing the beautiful effects produced by apparently the most simple means in the hands of nature, to duly reverence, worship, and adore nature's God. Notwithstanding the rapid strides towards perfection which modern chemistry has made, it is yet far from being able to trace the manner in which nature composes the various metals, to trace their growth and their produce, until they are converted into gold or silver, and thus to be able to imitate the process. The labours of the alchymist are therefore nothing but a blind groping in utter darkness ; and he is entangled in a labyrinth of ignorance, delusion, and deception, from which he does not know how to extricate himself.

scripture, that all who profess the mysteries are in a state of damnation." Such assertions, how wild and unreasonable soever they may now appear, found believers, and would constitute a powerful obstacle to prevent Freemasonry from being considered the instrument of unalloyed good.

Any trifling irregularities amongst the Brethren would tend to give effect to the defamatory reports which were circulated against the institution; for if individuals could be found who could indulge in excesses foreign to their masonic duty in the lodge, they would not pay very great respect to it beyond the walls; and hence the most injurious surmises would find confirmation in the indiscretions of these semi-masons. If they slighted that ancient charge which directed them to be " cautious in their words, carriage, and motions, that the most penetrating stranger may not be able to discover what is not proper to be intimated;"[14] in particular circles Masonry would become, as we know it very frequently did, a by-word and a reproach. We will examine how far the Masonry of that day deserved such a stigma.

The lodge was designated as " a place where Masons meet to work." Hence the assembly or duly organized body of Masons is called a lodge; just as the word church is expressive both of the congregation and of the place of worship."[15] The first lodge lesson, therefore, which was taught applied to " God and religion," that the Brethren might never for a moment forget that the masonic society did not tolerate atheism or infidelity, but expected that its members, as Christians, would comply with the usages of the Christian church, as established in this country.[16] But no disquisitions were allowed to be introduced respecting peculiar opinions or forms of worship; because Freemasonry, being a cosmopolitical order, and including Jews and Mahometans as well as Christians, the Brethren were charged " to adhere to that religion in which all men agree, leaving each Brother to his own particular opinions."

[14] Anderson's Const. p. 148, Ed. 1738.
[15] Anderson's Const. p. 144, Ed. 1738.
[16] " In ancient times the Christian Masons were charged to comply with the Christian usages of each country where they travelled or worked." (Ancient Charge i., approved by Grand Lodge in 1722.)

The term G. A. O. T. U. is used amongst Masons for this great and glorious Being, designated by the letter G., that it may be applied by every Brother to the object of his adoration; for none can be admitted into the order of Freemasonry who do not acknowledge, as their sole trust and stay, one supreme Deity, the Creator of heaven and earth. The Jew and the Mahometan, therefore, apply T. G. A. O. T. U. to God the Creator, as worshipped in their respective systems of religion; but the English Masons of the last century, lest any mistake should arise amongst the Brethren on this important point, explained the title to mean " Him that was taken up to the topmost pinnacle of the temple,"[17] or Jesus Christ, the divine author of the Christian religion, in conformity with the doctrine of St. Paul, and other apostles of Christianity.[18]

After inculcating that it is the business of a Mason to perform punctually his duty to God, " never mentioning His name but with the reverential awe which becomes a creature to bear to his Creator, and to look upon him always as the summum bonum which we came into the world to enjoy;"[19] the Brethren were taught their duty to their neighbour and themselves; and then it was impressed upon them that " a Mason is a peaceable subject, and never to be concerned in plots against the state, nor disrespectful to the inferior magistrates."[20] But these recommendations were not to be considered as an excuse for the introduction of political disquisitions, which were absolutely prohibited. Thus the old Gothic constitutions provided that " no quarrels about nations, families, religions, or politics, must be brought within the door of the lodge; for, as Masons we are of the oldest Catholic religion, and of all nations upon the square, level and plumb; and like our predecessors, in all ages, we are resolved against political disputes, as contrary to the peace and welfare of the lodge."[21] And in the method of opening the lodge, as used at that period, it was distinctly proclaimed that " all religious

[17] The ancient Lectures.
[18] 1 Cor. viii. 6. Ephes. iii. 9. Col. i. 16. Heb. i. 10. 2 Pet. iii. 5 See also Prov. viii. 12 to 26. John i. 3.
[19] From a Charge used before 1730.
[20] Ancient Charges, ii. [22] Ancient Charges, vi.

and political disputes were forbidden under a heavy penalty." It would be well if this form were restored.

A candidate for initiation was required to be "free-born, or no bondman, of mature age, and of good report, hale and sound, not deformed or dismembered at the time of his making. But no woman, no eunuch; the son of honest parents, a perfect youth, *without maim or defect in his body*, and capable of learning the mysteries of the art."[22]   And it was further provided by the then existing laws, that no one should be admitted under the age of twenty-five years,[23] except he be a Lewis;[24] nor without the unanimous consent of all the members of that lodge then present when the candidate is proposed and when their consent is formally asked by the Master.[25] In those times the balloting box was unknown, for the decision was expected to be unanimous. It was provided by the primitive regulations of the Grand Lodge, in 1717, that the Brethren should give their consent "in their own prudent way, either virtually or in form, but with unanimity. Nor is this inherent privi-

---

[22] Ancient Charges, iii. iv.

[23] By the laws of Prussia, says the author of the Freemasons' Lexicon, no native of that country can be initiated under twenty-five years of age, even at the present day; and the lodges are allowed to make no exceptions to this rule, except to travellers from foreign countries. The lodges in other nations, which are held under warrants from the three Prussian Grand Lodges, are not bound by this law; but should a young Prussian be initiated abroad, and return to his native country before he has attained his twenty-fith year, he is not permitted to visit a lodge until that age is fully completed.

[24] The masonic explanation of this term is equally simple and pleasing. It was given to the son of a Master Mason, and placed amongst our emblems about the middle of the last century. In operative architecture it is an instrument used to support heavy stones which are to be raised to the highest parts of a building. In like manner, when a Master Mason passes into the vale of years, and becomes incapable of active exertion, he is supported, succoured, and nourished by his son, the Lewis, who is able and willing to bear, in his father's stead, the burden and heat of the day.

[25] Old regulations, Article 6. On the Continent the candidate underwent many strict examinations, which are dispensed with in this country. Ces epreuves seront toujours terminées par celles de *l'eau*, du *feu*, du *calice amer*, &c.; accompagnées d'explications courtes et lumineuses qui démontrent aux Recipiend ∴ que nous ne faisons rien que de conforme aux cérémonies de tous les peuples, &c., &c., vous concluerez de là qu'un homme sans instruction, sans capacité, et sans bonnes qualités, ne sera point reçu Mac.∴

lege subject to a dispensation; because the members of a particular lodge are the best judges of it ; and because if a turbulent member should be imposed on them, it might spoil the harmony or hinder the freedom of their communication, or even break and disperse the lodge, which ought to be avoided by all true and faithful Brothers."

On this subject Noorthouck has some judicious remarks, which I subjoin, in illustration of this important subject. "There is no violation of truth in affirming that, in London especially (A. D. 1784), propositions for initiation into Masonry are often too easily, if not too eagerly received on the bare general recommendation of the proposer, and payment of the customary fees. But if character and circumstances were cautiously weighed in the qualification of candidates, though the society might not be quite so numerous, the members of it would in proportion be more respectable, both as men and as Masons. Charity is a leading feature in the masonic character; we deem ourselves bound to assist a distressed brother to the utmost of our power; but surely this humane obligation does not extend to receiving men amongst us whose imprudence and precarious circumstances obviously tend to reduce them to be objects of charity. Nothing is more common than for giddy young men, just entering into life, to join the society with the mere sinister view of extending their connections. Such men dissipate their time, money, and attention, in running about from one lodge to another, where they rather aim to distinguish themselves in the licentious character of jolly companions, than in the more discreet one of steady good Masons; and, finally, close their masonic career by loading the table in the committee-room with petitions for charity. The number of these applications reduces our benefactions to such scanty portions, that instead of being of effectual service in extricating men from the occasional difficulties of life, they seldom exceed instant supply of pressing necessities, without reaching the cause of those necessities; whereas were the brethren more select, fewer distresses would come before them, those which did come would be deserving of relief, and might obtain it with a liberal hand.

"Once more; the fraternity of Masons being every-

where distinguished by the kind reception and friendly
assistance of strange brethren on their journeys, or on
their arrival to settle among them, gives rise to another
abuse, teeming with evil effects. A man on the point
of removing to a distant country, recollects that the certificate of being a Mason will be a convenient general
letter of recommendation; he accordingly gets himself
proposed, through a second, third, or fourth hand, and
must be hurried through all the degrees in one evening,
because he is to set off early in the morning. Thus, by
trusting to a vague recommendation, a lodge prostitutes
the institution for a paltry fee; vests an utter stranger
with a character he knows nothing of, and furnishes him
with a credential, empowering him, should he be basely
disposed, to abuse the generous confidence of the brethren wherever he goes, to the injury of worthy men
who may afterwards travel the same road. Such hasty
compliances with interested views, ought not, therefore,
to be heedlessly countenanced."[26]

The candidate, at his initiation, was expected " de-
cently to clothe the lodge," which appears to have included not only new aprons and gloves, but also the
necessary and usual refreshment.[27] The proper clothing
of the brethren at that period was a plain white apron
and gloves,[28] and the jewels were suspended from white

---

[26] Const. 1784, p. 393.

[27] In an old Minute Book, belonging to the Witham Lodge at Lincoln,
we find, under date 2d of January, 1732, a minute of this custom. " It
was proposed by our R. W. Master, that Sir Christopher Hales, Bart., be
voted a member of this society, who, being well recommended, the same
was agreed to, on Bro. Thomas Becke undertaking to pay the usual sum
of five guineas for and on behalf of our said Brother elect. And in regard that our R. W. M. was going to London, in a few days, it was
agreed that William Carter, Esq., together with the said Sir Christopher
Hales, should be initiated the same evening ; which was done accordingly
with due solemnity, when our R. W. M. gave an elegant charge : and in
respect to our new Brother it was further agreed to clothe and entertain
the lodge. Paid for gloves and aprons, 2l. 17s.; expended 2l. 3s. 1d."

[28] The Masons on the Continent of Europe had a custom to give the
candidate, at his initiation, a pair of lady's gloves, with the command to
present them to his wife, or to any lady whom he may be desirous of
espousing. The gloves are white, not only to show the purity of our
respect and love for the female sex, but to serve also as an inducement
to the wife or betrothed of a Freemason to act with circumspection in
her journey through life. It is considered that these initiation gloves are
an apt and important present for a young man to make to his bride on the

ribbons. The officers of the Grand Lodge did not deviate from this primitive practice till the year 1731, when it was considered decorous for the Grand Officers to be distinguished by some token from which their dignity might be easily recognized. It appears, also, that some of the brethren had introduced decorations that were unsanctioned by the laws, and, therefore, it was ordered by the Grand Lodge, March 17, 1731, that, "to cure some irregularities, none but the Grand Master, his Deputy and Wardens (who are the only Grand Officers), shall wear their jewels in gold pendant to blue ribbons about their necks, and white leather aprons with blue silk; which sort of aprons may be also worn by former Grand Officers. Masters and Wardens of particular lodges may line their white leather aprons with white silk, and may hang their jewel to white ribbons about their necks."[29] From the above regulation of the Grand Lodge, probably originated the name of Blue, as applied to symbolical Masonry. Blue is the colour of truth or fidelity; and it is a remarkable fact that no brother has ever doubted the genuineness or antiquity of the three blue degrees; while the supplementary degrees are most of them of modern construction. This colour is justly prized amongst Freemasons; for the more they are clothed in the mantle of truth, the greater will be their progress in real knowledge. Azure and gold are ornaments of the greatest value. The unchangeable heavens are blue or azure, and their golden ornaments are the sun, the moon, and the stars.[30]

The above clothing continued to be used by the constitutional Masons till the beginning of the present century; and the first lodge over which the writer of this Essay presided, in 1810, had its jewels suspended from white ribbons, and the Brethren were clothed in undecorated aprons. The section called *ancient* Masons departed from this primitive custom earlier, and introduced blue ribbons with chains of silver, and aprons decorated with masonic devices painted on the leather, and blue edgings

---

wedding day, and they ought to be prized by her as a most valuable ornament.
[29] Minutes of Grand Lodge, 17th March, 1731.
[30] Freemasons' Lexicon—Blau.

and fringes, before the conclusion of the last century.[31]
After the Union, in 1813, the clothing, insignia, and
decorations, which are now used, were enjoined by authority, for the purpose of " establishing perfect uniformity throughout the whole craft."

The labour of the Lodge at that period may be somewhat difficult to describe. It could not be exclusively
confined to a repetition of the masonic catechism, because that was too brief and technical to be permanently
interesting; for the questions appertaining to the Master's
part were only seven in number. A reverend Brother of
the last century says, that the labour of Masonry comprehended the whole circle of arts and sciences. He adds
that " Freemasonry has been the dépôt of learning in all
former ages, and a focus combining every ray of genius
in all climes of the earth. In foreign countries a lodge
is styled an academy, and Masonry is considered as
synonymous to Geometry, the science relating to the
measurement of the earth, and emphatically referring to
its creation; a liberal, or Freemason, signifying a friend
and admirer, or a professor of the liberal sciences."

The Ahiman Rezon says, that masonic labour consisted
in the study of geometry; but an ancient MS., formerly
in the Bodleian library at Oxford, the original of which
is said to be in the handwriting of King Henry VI., extends these studies to " agriculture, architecture, astronomy, geometry, numbers, music, poetry, chemistry,
government, and religion." In another place Masonry
is defined to be " the skylle of nature, the understondynge
of the myghte that ys hereynne, and its sondrye werck-
ynges; sonderlyche, the skylle of rectenyngs, of waightes
and metynges, and the treu manere of façonnynge all

<hr>

[31] I once visited an *ancient* lodge, and found the officers and brethren
clothed in aprons variously diversified, according to the taste of the wearer,
and consequently there was no uniformity—there were not two alike;
although they had a law, which passed their Grand Lodge in 1772,
stating that " it having been represented to the Grand Lodge, that several
brethren had lately appeared in public with gold lace and fringe, together with many devices on their aprons, &c., which was thought
inconsistent with the dignity, propriety, and ancient custom of the craft
—It was Resolved and Ordered, that for the future no Brethren, Grand
Officers excepted, shall appear with gold lace, gold fringe, gold em-
broidery, or anything resembling gold, on their masonic clothing or
ornaments." (Minutes of the Athol Grand Lodge, September 2, 1772.)

thynges for manne's use, headlye, dwelyngs and buyld-
yngs of alle kindes, and al odher thynges that make gude
to manne."[32] A masonic document of still greater antiquity says, that "a loge of Masons taught all the seven
liberal sciences, as joined under geometry, which teacheth met and measure, ponderation and weight of every
thing in and upon the face of the whole earth; for you
know every craftsman works by measure; he or she that
buyeth or selleth, it is by weight and measure; husband-
men, navigators, and painters, all of them use geometry;
for whether, grammar, rhetoric, logic, or any other of the
said sciences, can subsist without geometry, ergo, most
worthy, laudable, and honourable."[33]

Some or all of the above, it is probable, together with
the means of carrying into effect the charitable designs
of the society, constituted the ordinary labour of the
lodges of that period. It was an original law of Masonry, that each particular lodge may dispose of its own
charity for poor Brothers, according to its own by-laws.
But at the Grand Lodge, 21st November, 1724, Brother
Francis Scot, Earl of Dalkeith, afterwards the Duke of
Buccleugh, the Past Grand Master, proposed that, in
order to promote the charitable disposition of Freemasons, and to render it more extensively beneficial to the
society, each lodge may make a certain collection, according to ability, to be put into a joint stock, lodged in the
hands of a treasurer at every quarterly communication,
for the relief of distressed Brethren that shall be recommended by the contributing lodges to the Grand Officers
from time to time. This motion being unanimously
agreed to, formed the germ of our present glorious Fund
of Benevolence.

Such was masonic labour down to the close of the
century, when the authorized lectures, having been considerably extended, a series of legitimate pursuits were
instituted, which might profitably occupy the attention
of scientific Brethren for an indefinite length of time.
In these lectures the philosophy of Masonry began to
be exemplified, and the world became apprized of the
fact in the published works of Calcott and Hutchinson,
each of whom had been the Master of his Lodge, and

[32] MS. temp. Henry VI.   [33] Harl. MS. B.M. vol. 1924.

having delivered from the chair a series of moral lectures
on the chief references of the Order, afterwards printed
them for the edification of the craft; and of Preston,
who illustrated the ceremonies, and extended the history
of the Order down to his own times. These writings
contributed in a great degree to awaken the sympathies
of the public, and to direct opinion into a pure and consistent channel of enquiry.

The symbols of Masonry formed a striking feature in
the system, as it was practised in the eighteenth century. I have, however, no intention of entering on their
explanation here, because I have heretofore treated at
large on the subject.[34] Swift and others attempted to
turn the custom of symbolization into ridicule. Speaking of wisdom in his Tale of a Tub, he says, " the Gru-
bæan sages have always chosen to convey their precepts
and their arts shut up within the vehicles of types and
symbols: which, having been perhaps more careful and
curious in adorning than was altogether necessary, it has
fared with these vehicles after the usual fate of coaches,
over-finely painted and gilt, that the transitory gazers
have so dazzled their eyes, and filled their imaginations
with the outward lustres, as neither to regard or consider
the person or the parts of the owner within. A misfortune we undergo with somewhat less reluctance because
it has been common to us with Pythagoras, Æsop, Socra-
tes, and other of our predecessors. However, that neither
the world nor ourselves may any longer suffer by such
misunderstandings, I have been prevailed on, after much
importunity from my friends, to travel in a complete and
laborious dissertation upon the prime productions of our
society ; which, besides their beautiful externals for the
gratification of superficial readers, have darkly and deeply
couched under them the most finished and refined systems of all sciences and arts ; as I do not doubt to lay
open by untwisting or unwinding, and either to draw
up by exaltation, or display by incision."

This was a sly inuendo against the usages of Freemasonry in that day ; for the illustration of architectural
symbols had been revised and extended in the early days
of the Grand Mastership of Sir C. Wren, and had, doubt-

[34] See the Signs and Symbols, and other of my works on Masonry.

less, excited public attention when this philippic was written. In the subsequent part of his life he was more personal and severe.[35] The excellence, however, of the symbolical system used by our Brethren at the above period, was dilated on by masonic writers with pride, and appealed to as a triumphant illustration of its excellence. This drew out a host of imitators amongst the members of other societies; and even the great moralist, Dr. Johnson, the literary leviathan of the eighteenth century, did not disdain to profit by the example thus afforded him; and in one of his most popular papers he has adopted the symbolical style of Freemasonry; and on this model has given a series of hints for conversation, typified in the ingredients of a bowl of punch.[36]

Of the equality amongst Masons much might be said. The old lectures taught that " the Brethren are all equal by their creation, but much more so by the strength of their obligation."[37] The former part of this illustration evidently refers to man as an animal, without reference to his mind; because, in that respect, we are *not* equal by our creation; for while some are formed with the brightest mental qualifications, others are rude and sensual, and some idiotic and without an idea. But, this diversity is in some measure rectified by the O B, because the old constitutions, provided that none should be initiated who had any defect in body or mind, or who were incapable of learning the mysteries of the craft.[3] And

---

[35] See Masonic Institutes, p. 9.   [36] Idler, No. 34.

[37] The following illustration is sometimes delivered in the E. A. P. lecture. " A king, in the lodge, is reminded that, although a crown may adorn the head, or a sceptre the hand, the blood in his veins is derived from the common parent of mankind, and is no better than that of his meanest subject. The statesman, the senator, and the artist, are there taught that, equally with others, they are exposed by nature to infirmity and disease, and that an unforeseen misfortune, or a disordered frame, may impair their faculties, and reduce them to a level with the meanest of their species. This consideration is a check to pride, and incites courtesy of behaviour. Men of inferior talents, who are not placed by fortune in such exalted stations, are instructed to regard their superiors with respect, when they behold them voluntarily divested of the external trappings of worldly grandeur, and condescending, in the badge of innocence and bond of friendship, to trace wisdom and to follow virtue, assisted by those who are of a rank beneath them. Virtue is true nobility; wisdom is the channel by which virtue is directed and conveyed ; wisdom and virtue alone mark distinction amongst Masons."

[38] It is provided by the present laws of Masonry, that no person shall

18   INTRODUCTORY ESSAY.

Masons are not equal in rank even in the lodge, because
some rule and govern while others submit and obey.[29]
And, therefore, it was declared in the Gothic charges, in
use during the last century, that "though all Brothers
and fellows are upon the level, yet Masonry divests no
man of the honour due to him before he was made a
Mason, or that shall become his due afterwards; nay,
rather, it adds to his respect, teaching us to give honour
to whom it is due, especially to a noble or eminent Brother, whom we should distinguish from all of his rank
and station, and serve him readily, according to our
ability."

In what, then, does the equality of Masons consist? It
consists in the capacity of doing good to each other, and
to our fellow-creatures in general; of being equally zeal-

---

be received as a candidate for initiation, except he be "a free man and
his own master; and at the time of his initiation, be known to be in
reputable circumstances. He should be a lover of the liberal arts and
sciences, and have made some progress in one or other of them." (Const.
Of proposing members, s. 4.)   The following censure of the Grand Lodge
on this point ought to be known; for obvious reasons the name of the
offending lodge is omitted. "It being remarked in the Grand Lodge that
some of the brethren of the lodge No. —, were *unable to write*, inasmuch
as their *marks* only were affixed against their names, and amongst them
was the Junior Warden.   As the above law declares such individuals
ineligible for initiation, the Grand Master gave notice that he shall feel it
a duty he owes to the craft to bring under the cognizance of the Grand
Lodge, the conduct of any lodge which shall, in future, violate this
wholesome and necessary law; a breach of which, as it is declared in the
preamble to the regulations for proposing members, shall subject the
offending lodge to erasure.   And the Grand Master will require his
Provincial Grand Masters to warn the lodges under their respective
superintendence, of this His Royal Highness's determination; and to
report to him any instance which shall come to their knowledge of a
disregard of the law in this respect." (Quarterly Com. 26th September,
1826.)
   [30] And this is the true principle on which human society hinges.   Dr.
Johnson, speaking of a lady who promulgated the doctrine of reducing
all classes to the same level, used to relate the following anecdote. "One
day, when I was at her house, I put on a very grave countenance, and said
to her, Madam, I am now become a convert to your way of thinking.
I am convinced that all mankind are upon an equal footing; and to give
you an unquestionable proof that I am in earnest, here is a very sensible,
civil, well-behaved fellow-citizen—your footman; I desire that he may
be allowed to sit down and dine with us. I thus, sir, showed her the
absurdity of the levelling doctrine. She has never liked me since. Sir,
your levellers wish to level *down* as far as themselves, but they cannot
bear levelling *up* to themselves. They would all have some people under
them; why not, then, have some people above them?"

ous in the promotion of brotherly love in the lodge, of
relief out of the lodge, and of truth always and everywhere. Such an equality is as honourable to the Order
as it is beneficial to its members. When a whole society,
extended over the entire universe, are united in the great
design of promoting the benefit of their fellow-creatures,
each individual exerting himself with equal zeal, according to his ability, they can scarcely fail of receiving the
unqualified approbation of mankind. This, then, is the
object of Freemasonry; and this is the equality of which
they have just reason to be proud; because, while the
humble Brother makes no attempt to derogate from the
temporal rank of his associates, he is still capable of
rising to an equality with them in the practice of virtue.

I have been thus particular in frankly displaying the
customs and usages of Freemasonry, for the purpose of
showing the utter unreasonableness of those who have
considered the Order to be a legitimate object of syste-
matic persecution; and the following pages will show
that, in all ages, men, high in authority, have been found
who have affected to distrust its professions, as an apology for the denunciation of its members and the prohibition of its practice. It is probable, however, that its
enemies have been actuated by envy, and the true reason
of their opposition has been a determination that no
secrets but their own should be tolerated. This has
been peculiarly the case in Spain, Portugal, and Italy;
and, in more modern times, in India, Malta, and—hinc
illæ lachrymæ!—our own dear sister island.

In Spain, the Pope, so early as 1737, fulminated a
furious decree against the Order; in which confiscation
and death were denounced against all Freemasons. A
few years later King Philip V. sentenced several Masons
to the galleys for life, and some he punished with torture in the prisons of the Inquisition, and death by burning. In Portugal Freemasonry has also been scourged
by religious intolerance; and the prisons of the Inquisition re-echoed with the groans of those worthy men who
were guilty of no crime but the practice of brotherly
love. Italy was unfavourable to the spread of the liberal
arts practised in connection with Freemasonry. In 1751
it was prohibited at Naples by Charles III. of Spain;
and members of the craft were subjected to every kind

2

of persecution through the intolerance of a pontifical church. The civil power was always at hand, ready to give effect to the fulminations of the priests, which was an unfortunate coalition for the unhappy Mason who was subjected to their authority. Venice had a lodge of Masons once, but it was abolished by the transportation of its members.

The modern persecutions of Freemasonry, to which I have ventured to devote a chapter in this volume, are still less excusable ; because, in the first place, the general spread of education and the enlightenment of the mind in our own more happy times ought to have extinguished all jealousy and introduced a more liberal feeling than could be found at the beginning and middle of the last century ; added to which the science is better known, and its true principles more universally disseminated. The day is past for any great object to be accomplished by means of persecution ; and those who, at this distinguished era, still persist in the face of a long experience of the utter hopelessness of the task, in their endeavours to extinguish Freemasonry by coercion, will find themselves in the condition so well expressed by Dr. Anderson, in the old Sword Bearer's song :

> "To all who Masonry despise,
>   This counsel I bestow ;
> Don't ridicule, if you are wise,
>   A secret you don't know.
> *Yourselves you banter, but not it ;*
> *You show your spleen, but not your wit.*"

CHAPTER I.

A DETECTION OF DR. PLOT'S ACCOUNT OF THE FREE-MASONS.

"A detractor is one of a more cunning and active envy, wherewith he gnaws not foolishly himself, but throws it abroad, and would have it blister others. He is commonly some weak pated fellow, and worse minded; yet is strangely ambitious to match others, not by mounting their worth, but bringing them down with his tongue to his own poorness. He is, indeed, like the red dragon that pursued the woman; for when he cannot overreach another, he opens his mouth and throws a flood after to drown him. You cannot anger him worse than to do well; and he hates you more bitterly for this, than if you had cheated him of his patrimony."—BISHOP EARLE.

WHAT could induce the sagacious Doctor to step so far out of his way, or to meddle with a matter so foreign to the purpose of a natural historian, may, at this distance of time, be a little difficult to determine;[1] but most certain it is, his rude and insipid conjectures and

---

[1] It is highly probable that the learned Doctor had been led away by a publication, entitled "the Paradoxical Discourses of Fr. Mercur. von Helmont, concerning the Macrocosm and Microcosm of the greater and lesser World, and their union," which made its appearance while he was writing his book; and having found Freemasonry, as he says, very prevalent in Staffordshire, he took this publication for his guide, and repeating the arguments which he found there, he augmented their force by some vague lucubrations of his own. The uninitiated world entertained an opinion that the sublime productions of the ancient operative Masons had been effected by the agency of the devil, as tradition pronounced the temple of Solomon to be built by genii; and therefore they affected to believe the tale which Euclid so well ridiculed in his letter to Dr. Anderson (A. D. 1738,) that "the Freemasons, in their lodges, raised the devil in a circle, and when they had done with him, laid him again with a noise or a hush, as they pleased." Dr. Plot, hearing these, and other wild and improbable stories, and being very credulous, believed them, and thought, most probably, that he should be rendering a service to science by denouncing the Order, and endeavoring to refute its claims to public credence.

misrepresentations of the Freemasons, to whose foundation and history he was an absolute stranger, are not
more false and groundless, than his conduct in that affair
was base, insidious, and unworthy of any writer, who
had the least regard for truth ; and, besides, it was
ungrateful, because the bread he eat was furnished him
by Mr. Ashmole, the greatest Mason of his day,[2] and who
could, had the good Doctor been in the least inclined to
receive it, have given him ample satisfaction, which will
set this unbiassed history in a point of view, very little
to the credit of the supple, and, as it will be found, time-
serving Dr. Plot.[3]   A small portion of gratitude for all
the good things he had received at the hands of his master, should have prompted him to have cleared up, as far
as he was able, the history of Alban, Amphibalus, and
Prince Edwin, all enveloped with great obscurities in
the histories of Britain, though clear and evident enough
in the annals and traditions of Masonry ; it may be presumed, he would have gained much more reputation and
honour than he could ever hope to reap by these unjustifiable censures ; either of which would have found him
sufficient employment, and prevented his attempts to
degrade a society, of whose story his own account marks
him confessedly ignorant.   As this society has been so
very ancient as to rise beyond the reach of records, there

[2] This celebrated philosopher, who founded the museum at Oxford, of
which Dr. Plot was at this time the keeper, was initiated at Warrington,
in Lancashire, 16th October, 1646.   The writer of his life says, this was
"a favour esteemed so singular by the members, that kings themselves
have not disdained to enter themselves of this society.   From these
derived the Adopted Masons, Accepted Masons, or Freemasons, who are
known to one another all over the world by certain signals and watchwords known to them alone."   In Bro. Ashmole's Diary are several notes
of the meetings of lodges where he was present.
[3] The evidence of Dr. Plot is extremely valuable, because it proves
beyond dispute, that the lodges of Masons were numerous in Staffordshire,
and the ceremonies of initiation in full operation, during the seventeenth
century; which completely refutes the confident assertion of De Quincey,
in the London Magazine, where he says, "I affirm as a fact, established
upon historical research, that before the beginning of the seventeenth century, no traces are to be met with of the Masonic order.   And I challenge
any antiquarian to contradict me."   However dogmatical this challenge
may appear, it is utterly disproved and refuted by the above account of
the Freemasons by Dr. Plot; and thus the tirade of this learned antiquary
becomes subservient to prove the truth of that Order, which he took such
pains to destroy.

need not be much wonder made, that a mixture of fable
is found in its early history, about the time of their first
establishment in this island ;[4] as the same defect is avowedly confessed by all historians concerning the ancient
foundations in our own and other nations. I subjoin the
passage entire :

"They have a custom in Staffordshire (says Dr. Plot)
of admitting men into the society of Freemasons, that in
the Morelands of this country seems to be of greater
request than anywhere else, though I find the custom
spread more or less all over the nation ; for here I found
persons of the most eminent quality, that did not disdain
to be of this fellowship ; nor, indeed, need they, were it
of that antiquity and honour, that is pretended in a
large parchment volume they have amongst them : containing the history and rules of the craft of Masonry,
which is there deduced not only from sacred writ, but
profane story; particularly that it was brought into
England by St. Amphibalus, and first communicated to
St. Alban, who set down the charges of Masonry, and
was made pay-master and governor of the king's works,
and gave them charges and manners as St. Amphibalus
had taught him : which were after confirmed by King
Athelstan, whose youngest son Edwyn loved well
Masonry, took upon him the charges, and learned the
manners, and obtained for them of his father a free charter. Whereupon he caused them to assemble at York,
and to bring all the old books of their craft, and out of
them ordained such charges and manners as they then
thought fit : which charges in the said scrole, or parchment volume, are in part declared ; and thus was the

[4] In Rees's Encyclopædia we have the following account :—" Some
have traced the origin of Masonry to the year 674, when the public
buildings in the Gothic style were erected by men in companies, who
called themslves Free, because they were at liberty to work in any part
of the kingdom. Others have derived the institution of Freemasons from
a combination among the Masons, not to work without an advance of
wages, when they were summoned from several counties, by writs of
Edward III., directed to the sheriffs, to assist in rebuilding and enlarging
the castle, together with the church and chapel of St. George, at Windsor. Accordingly, it is said that the Masons agreed on certain signs and
tokens, by which they might know one another, and assist one another
against being impressed, and not to work unless free, and on their own
terms."

craft of Masonry grounded and confirmed in England.
It is also there declared, that these charges and manners
were after perused and approved by King Henry VI. and
his council, both as to Masters and fellows of this right
worshipful craft.[5]

" Into which society, when they are admitted, they
call a meeting (or lodge, as they term it in some places),
which must consist at least of five or six of the ancients
—of the Order, whom the candidates present with gloves,[6]
and so likewise to their wives, and entertain with a
collation, according to the custom of the place: this
ended, they proceed to the admission of them, which
chiefly consists in the communication of certain secret
signs, whereby they are known to one another all over
the nation, by which means they have maintenance
whither ever they travel; for if any man appear, though
altogether unknown, that can show any of these signs to
a fellow of the society, whom they otherwise call an
Accepted Mason, he is obliged presently to come to him,
from what company or place soever he be in: nay,
though from the top of a steeple, what hazard or inconvenience soever he run, to know his pleasure, and assist
him; viz., if he want work, he is bound to find him

[5] Mr. Halliwell says, " in the Gentleman's Magazine for 1753, there is
a reprint of a pamphlet, stated to have been published at Frankfort in
the year 1748, in an octavo volume of twelve pages. It is entitled, ' Cer-
tayne Questions, with answeres to the same, concerning the Mystery of
Maçonrye, wryttene by the bande of Kynge Henrye the Sixthe of this
name, and faithfully copied by me, Johan Leylande, Antiquarius, by the
command of his Highnesse,' (probably Henry VIII). It is singular that
the circumstances attending its publication should have led no one to
suspect its authenticity. I was at the pains of making a long search in
the Bodleian Library, in the hopes of finding the original, but without
success. In fact, there can be little doubt, that this celebrated and well
known document is a forgery." (Early Hist. of Freemasonry, p. 39.)
These observations refer, it is presumed, to the " Scrole or parchment
volume," above mentioned. Now, Dr. Plot published his History of
Staffordshire in 1686, ten years before Mr. Locke's Letter was written,
in which he copiously explains the document, and sixty years before it
was printed at Frankfort; and, therefore, being in existence in the seventeenth century, it could not be a forgery of the eighteenth. I have recorded my opinion of the celebrated MS. in the Freemasons' Quarterly
Review for 1840, p. 10, and therefore must refer the reader to that
volume for further testimony, which it will be unnecessary to repeat in
this place.
[6] This custom has been laid aside in our modern lodges, but is still used
on the Continent of Europe.

some; or if he cannot do that, to give him money, or
otherwise support him till work can be had, which is
one of their articles;[7] and it is another, that they advise
the masters they work for, according to the best of their
skill, acquainting them with the goodness or badness of
their materials; and if they be any way out in the contrivance of the buildings, modestly to rectify them in it,
that Masonry be not dishonoured; and many such like
that are commonly known; but some others they have
(to which they are sworn, after their fashion) that none
know but themselves, which I have reason to suspect
are much worse than these, perhaps as bad as this
history of the craft itself; than which there is nothing I
ever met with more false or incoherent.[8]

"For not to mention that St. Amphibalus, by judicious
persons, is thought rather to be the cloak than master
of St. Alban; or how unlikely it is that St. Alban himself in such a barbarous age, and in times of persecution,
should be supervisor of any works; it is plain that King
Athelstan was never married, or ever had so much as any
natural issue (unless we give way to the fabulous history
of Guy Earl of Warwick, whose eldest son, Reynburn, is
said, indeed, to have been married to Leoneat, the supposed daughter of Athelstan, which will not serve the
turn neither), much less ever had he a lawful son Edwyn,
of whom I find not the least umbrage in history. He
had, indeed, a brother of that name, of whom he was so
jealous, though very young when he came to the crown,
that he sent him to sea in a pinnace, without tackle or
oar, only in company with a page, that his death might
be imputed to the waves, and not to him; whence the
young prince, not able to master his passions, cast himself headlong into the sea, and there died. Who how

[7] Here we have an excellent description of the usages and charges
practised by our brethren in the seventeenth century; from which we
may learn that the Masonry of that period varied very little in the ceremonial from the customs still prevalent amongst ourselves; and this will
be a standing proof of the unchangeable nature of the Order.

[8] How the erudite Doctor could make up his mind to pass this sweeping censure on the fraternity, after having just given them credit for some
of the best feelings of humanity and religion, I am at a loss to conjecture.
He must have been under some more evil influence than appears on the
surface, or he could not have praised and condemned the Order in the
same sentence.

unlikely to learn their manners ; to get them a charter ;
or call them together at York, let the reader judge.

" Yet more improbable it is still, that Henry VI. and
his council, should ever peruse or approve their charges
and manners, and so confirm these right worshipful
Masters and fellows, as they are called in the scrole ; for
in the third year of his reign, when he could not be four
years old, I find an Act of Parliament quite abolishing
this society : it being therein ordained, that no congregations and confederacies should be made by Masons, in
their general chapters and assemblies, whereby the good
course and effect of the statutes of labourers were violated and broken in subversion of law ; and that those
who caused such chapters or congregations to be holden,
should be adjudged felons ; and those Masons that came
to them should be punished by imprisonment, and make
fine and ransom, at the king's will. So very much out
was the compiler of this history of the craft of Masonry,
and so little skill had he in our chronicles and laws.
Which statute, though repealed by a subsequent act in
the fifth of Elizabeth, whereby servants and labourers
are compelled to serve, and their wages limited ; and all
masters made punished for giving more wages than what
is taxed by the justices, and the servants if they take
it, &c. ; yet this act too being but little observed, it is
still to be feared these chapters of Freemasons do as
much mischief as before, which, if one may estimate by
the penalty, was anciently so great, that perhaps it
might be useful to examine them now." (Natural History
of Staffordshire, c. viii. pp. 316, 317, 318.)

St. Alban, the first person honoured with the Doctor's
candid suggestions, is famous for being the first Christian
who suffered martyrdom in this island ; and also for being
the first Master-general, Surveyor or Grand Master of
Masons, as is set forth in an ancient writing, called "the
Ghost of Masonry :" he was born at Verulam, of pagan
parents : in his youth he took a journey to Rome, in
company with Amphibalus, of the city of Caer-Leon,
supposed by many to be by birth a Roman ; and there
served for seven years in the army of the Emperor Dio
clesian.[9] Leland tells us, that at the time St. Alban

---

[9] Dallaway, in his historical account of Master and Freemasons, says—

flourished, learning and the polite arts had been lately introduced by the Romans into Britain, which was now become a province of the empire; and that the youth of quality and distinction used to travel to Rome for improvement in knowledge and the sciences. Being returned home, he lived highly honoured in the town of Verulam, where, through the example and instructions of his fellow traveller Amphibalus, he became a thorough convert to the Christian religion; in the tenth and last general persecution of the Christians, in the year 303,[10] he was beheaded for the same, a favour intended him on account of his noble birth, at Holmhurst, since called Derswald, where now the town of St. Alban stands;[11] to the lasting honour of whose name and merits King Offa, in after-times, founded a most magnificent monastery.[12]

" The first notice that occurs of an associated body of artificers, Romans, who had established themselves in Britain, is a votive inscription, in which the College of Masons dedicate a temple to Neptune and Minerva, and the safety of the family of Claudius Cæsar. It was discovered at Chichester in 1725, in a fragmented state, and, having been pieced together, is now preserved at Goodwood, near that city, the seat of the Duke of Richmond. Pliny, the author of the well known Epistles, when proconsul of Asia Minor, in one which he addressed to the Emperor Trajan, informs him of a most destructive fire at Nicomedia, and requests him to establish a COLLEGIUM FABRORUM for the rebuilding of the city. The emperor refuses, and alleges as a reason—' sed meminerimus provinciam istam et præcipue eas civitates, ab ejusmodi factionibus esse vexatas.' The jealousy entertained by all arbitrary governments against confraternities, whose consultations are held under the seal of impenetrable secrecy, or the penalty annexed to the breach of it, was early displayed by Trajan, who rejects the proposition, under the apprehension of perpetual danger."

[10] This is the correct date, although Alford says (Annal. Eccl. A. D 286)—" The old writer of St. Alban's life pitches upon A. D. 286 for this persecution; and a MS. copy of Bede, which he had met with, agrees with that time." But he urges further, that after the rebellion of Carausius, when Constantius was made Cæsar, the provinces beyond the Alps were committed to him, and that was A. D. 292; and if there were no persecution under Constantius, it must have been before he was Cæsar.

[11] While some workmen were repairing the abbey of St. Albans, in the middle of the thirteenth century, they found the remains of some sheets of lead, on which was the following inscription : " In hoc mausoleo inventum est venerabile corpus Sancti Albani, proto martyris Anglorum."

[12] Offa, the son of Sighere, was a comely person in his youth, and celebrated for his mental acquirements. He reigned eight years; and at length, out of a fondness for a religious life, he forsook his throne, and became a monk. After which his queen took the vows in the abbey of Kineburg, and lived a secluded life.

2*

The Emperor Carausius (under whom Alban bore great
sway, and was the steward of his household, and overseer
or surveyor of his works) governed the empire of Britain
with an upright and unstained reputation;[13] and, above
all, was a very great encourager of learning and learned
men, and improved the country in civil arts; was a man
of real merit, and intended to have established an empire
in Britain; for which end he had made a great collection
of workmen, and other artificers, from all parts. The
people enjoyed perfect peace and tranquillity under him
for several years, is manifest from all our historians.[14]
His builders, and other artificers, were employed by him
in very large bodies, is evident from different writers; but
in particular from the oration of Eumenius, the panegy-
rist, setting forth what great numbers of Masons had then
left the island—" Even your city of Autun," says he,
most devoted to your service, and in whose name I am
especially to congratulate you, has been well stored with
artificers (architects and Masons) since your victory over
the Britons, whose provinces abounded with them;[15] and

[13] Some say that Carausius was an Irishman of humble birth, and
advanced himself to royalty by his desperate valour and daring acts.
Being invested by Maximian with the imperial robe, he governed the
kingdom with an uncorrupt and unstained reputation, and was at length
treacherously slain by Alectus, who succeeded him in the government.
Stukeley makes Carausius a native of St. Davids; but from the three expressions of Eutropius, Amelius Victor, and Eumenius—" Vilissime
natus," " Bataviæ alumnus," and " Menapiæ civis," it should appear that
the place of his birth is very doubtful.
[14] Guthrie's Hist. Eng. v. 1, p. 58.
[15] The following apocryphal account of the origin of Masonry in
Britain, is given by the author of " Multa Paucis for the Lovers of
Secrets," published about the year 1763.—" A. M. 2974, Ebrank, king
of the Trojan race, is accounted the first British architect, and historians
ascribe to him the building of the cities of York and Edinburgh. Bladud,
who flourished A. M. 3100, was educated at Athens, and became a great
mathematician and architect; and upon his return brought with him four
great philosophers, whom he placed at Stamford, making that town a
sort of university; and built the city of Bath. In A. D. 42, Claudius
sent Aulus Plautius into Britain, and ordered Ostorius Scopula, with
other Roman architects, to build many forts and castles. Afterwards
Vespasian sent Julius Agricola, who conquered as far as the isthmus
between the firths of Clyde and Forth, and fortified the same against
the Picts. Adrian fenced the Roman province in Britain with ram-
parts, extending from Tynemouth haven to Solway firth; A. D. 131 Lud,
the first Christian king of Britain, built many churches and religious
houses. In the following century Gordian sent many architects over.

now, by their workmanship, the same city of Autun rises in splendour, by the rebuilding of their ancient houses, erecting public works, and the instauration of temples; so that the ancient name of a Roman brotherhood, which they long since enjoyed, is again restored, by having your imperial majesty for their second founder." From hence it is beyond all doubt, that the reduction of Britain occasioned many excellent artificers to go over to the Continent, who had been entertained by Carausius,[16] and had so greatly contributed to the beauty, convenience, and magnificence of the island, that Constantius Chlorus chose to make it the seat of his empire.[17]

The story of Alban's martyrdom is briefly related by Gildas; but more circumstantially and at large by venerable Bede, who says, that he being yet a pagan (or not publicly known for a Christian) entertained the before-mentioned Amphibalus in his house. The Roman governor being informed that he harboured a Christian, sent a party of soldiers to apprehend him; but Alban putting on the habit of his guest, presented himself to the officers in his stead, and was carried before the magistrate, where he conducted himself with a noble and gallant freedom, which immediately brought on him the punishment already related. The garment of Amphibalus, which Alban upon this occasion put on, is called by Bede, and in ancient writers, caracalla, which is rendered by the Saxon interpreter of Bede, a monkish habit. This caracalla was a kind of cloak with a cowl, most

who constituted themselves into lodges, and instructed the craftsmen in the true principles of Masonry; and a few years later Carausius was made emperor of the British isles, and being a great lover of art and science, appointed Albanus Grand Master of Masons, who employed the_. fraternity in building the palace at Verulam, or St. Albans."

[16] As a great number of medals of Carausius are still preserved, he became a favourite object of antiquarian curiosity, and every circumstance of his life and actions has been investigated with great accuracy and attention. Dr. Stukeley has devoted a large volume to the subject.

[17] This prince is described as being valiant and wise, and a strict friend to the Christians. He rejected the Polytheism of the heathen, and acknowledged one only God, the Creator and Governor of the world. To try the temper of his nobles, he proclaimed a sacrifice to the gods, to which they all cheerfully came, out of compliment to the sovereign; but their compliance was an unfortunate policy, for he dismissed them with this rebuke—that he who is disloyal to his God, can never be faithful to his prince.

resembling the ephod or sacerdotal vestment of the
Jewish priests. Thomas Walsingham relates, that this
garment was preserved in a large chest in the church of
Ely, which was opened in the reign of Edward II., A. D.
1314. This historian says farther, that it was the same
that Alban received from his master Amphibalus, and the
same in which he suffered death. Thomas Rudburn,
who, after relating what Walsingham had done before
him, and both of at least equal authority with Dr. Plot,
goes farther, and says, there was found with the garment
an ancient writing in these words:—" This is the caracalla
of St Amphibalus the monk, and preceptor of St. Alban ;
in which that proto-martyr of England suffered death,
under the cruel persecution of Dioclesian against the
Christians."[18]

It is confessed that the martyrdom of Amphibalus is
not mentioned by Gildas, Bede, or in any of the ancient
martyrologies ; but Matthew Paris, and many other
historians, vouch the matter of fact, and refer to a book
of great antiquity in the monastery of St. Alban. As to
the name Amphibalus, upon which Dr. Plot endeavours
to play, it must be owned that the learned Primate
Usher is of opinion, that it was not the real name of St.
Alban's instructor, but more properly belonged to the
caracalla before-mentioned, as αμφιβαλλειν signifies in the
Greek language the same as induere or accingere, sc.
vestem, a garment.[19] Had Dr. Plot been as modest in
his judgment as the learned archbishop, he had not stept
so far over truth, to assert that many learned and judicious were of opinion, that Amphibalus was rather the
cloak than master of St. Alban, when no author of any
name or credit had mentioned this surmise, save Archbishop Usher, and he only as a probable suggestion, and
not what he had any true grounds to believe. It is

[18] Historians, speaking of the effects of this persecution in Britain, say
that Christian churches were everywhere demolished, the sacred books
of the Christians burned, and every possible means used to root out the
very name of Christianity. Amongst the martyrs on this occasion we
find Alban of Verulam, who was beheaded at Holmhurst ; Amphibalus,
his friend ; Julius and Aaron of Caerleon; and in Lichfield so many, that
the place became another Golgotha, and was named from the field of
dead bodies, which is still emblazoned on the city seal.
[19] Usserii Brit. Eccles. Antiq. p. 77.

remarkable that not only the Cathedral church of Winchester,[20] in the days of Constantine, but many other churches were dedicated to St. Amphibalus, the master of St. Alban; many authors, of the greatest credit and authority, speak of him with reverence and honour, and especially Johannes Caius,[21] who informs us that he was born at Caer-Leon, in which he is supported by several authors; and also that he was rector of the University of Cambridge. It was never alleged among the Masons, or in any of their histories of the craft, that Amphibalus, though owned a worthy brother, was the instructor of St. Alban in any other respect than in those moral and divine subjects, which brought about the conversion of the latter to the Christian faith; so that the discerning doctor, in all probability, thought that Alban could not want an instructor, except in the art of building;[22] and how likely that was, in those ignorant and barbarous times, those times of gross darkness, as his love for truth calls the day (very fitting expressions to salve his own ignorance and vanity), when people were so much deluded as to be converted to the faith of Christ, by thousands and tens of thousands; must be submitted to the judgment of the unprejudiced reader, with this farther remark, that Dr. Plot happens, in his charitable opinion, to stand alone, not having one historian, great or small, credible or fabulous, to prop his flimsy conjectures with.

Having done with the history of St. Alban and Amphibalus, the Doctor proceeds to the story of Prince Edwin, the brother of King Athelstan.[23] In this he deals as ingenuously as in the former. The only blemish that the historians find in the whole reign of Athelstan, is the supposed murder,[24] or putting wrongfully to death his

[20] Tanner's Notitia Monast. folio, p. 152.
[21] Hist. Cantab. L. i. pp. 24, 25.
[22] Alban had learned the art of building in Rome, and needed no further instruction; for he had been received into the Collegia Fabrorum, and brought the art into this country, which was called Opus Romanum, and consisted of the round or semicircular arch, commonly called Saxon.
[23] Athelstan was an expert Master of Masons, and brought the science of architecture to some perfection. He built the walls and towers of Exeter with *squared* stones, which were little used before his time.
[24] The title of this monarch is said to have been attested by the decision of heaven. One of his nobles, accused of having disputed his right to the crown, offered to prove his innocence by a solemn oath in the presence

brother, Prince Edwin, which is in itself so improbable, and, all things considered, so slenderly attested, that it does not deserve a place among good historians.

The excellent writer of the life of King Athelstan,[25] has given so clear and so perfect a view of this event, that the reader cannot receive greater satisfaction than in that author's own words.

The business of Edwin's death is a point the most obscure in the story of this king; and, to say the truth, not even one of our best historians hath written clearly, or with due attention, concerning it. The fact, as commonly received, is this :—the king suspecting his younger brother Edwin of designing to deprive him of his crown, caused him, notwithstanding his protestations of innocency, to be put on board a leaky ship, with his armour-bearer and page. The young prince, unable to bear the severity of the weather, and want of food, desperately drowned himself; some time after, the king's cup-bearer, who had been the chief cause of this act of cruelty, happened, as he was serving the king at table, to trip with one foot, but recovering himself with the other, "see," said he pleasantly, "how brothers afford each other help;" which striking the king with the remembrance of what himself had done, in taking off Edwin, who might have helped him in his wars, he caused that business to be more thoroughly examined, and finding his brother had been falsely accused, caused his cup-bearer to be put to a cruel death, endured himself seven years' sharp penance, and built the two monasteries of Middleton and Michelness, to atone for this base and bloody fact.[26] Dr. Howell, speaking of this story, treats it as if very indifferently founded, and, on that account, unworthy of credit.[27] Abbot Brompton tells the story at large,[28] and after him most of the later writers, as usual, that is, with an addition of various circumstances;

of the pope ; a test which, in those times, was deemed of such supreme efficacy, that falsehood was always punished by a judicial dispensation from above. Athelstan accepted the appeal. The oath was administered, and the perjured thane was seized with sudden convulsions, which put an end to his life.

[25] Biog. Brit. vol. i. p. 63.
[26] Speed's Chronicle, book vii. chap. 38.
[27] Gen. Hist. p. 4. c. 2, sec. 10.   [28] Chron. p. 838.

so that it cannot be said this story is without foundation. Buchanan hath improved it very happily; thus it runs in his writings :—" They, that is, the English writers, make this Athelstan guilty of parricide, in killing his father and his two brothers, Edred and Edwin, whose right it was to succeed their father in his kingdom. Fame increases the suspicion, that Edward was violently put to death, because it attributes to him the title of martyr."[29] Buchanan cites no authority whatsoever for this, because, indeed, there could be no authority cited. Whatever he did by Edwin, most certainly Athelstan did not murder Edred, since he not only survived, but succeeded him in the kingdom. As for the murder of his father, that is the pure effect of Buchanan's ignorance ; he mistook Edward the Elder, who was really the father of Athelstan, for Edward the Martyr, who began his reign in 975, that is, five-and-thirty years after Athelstan was in his grave. Such is the accuracy, such the integrity, of this writer. In like manner Rapin gives us this story, without the least mark of doubt or hesitation ;[30] and yet, we presume, there are some strong reasons against the credit of this whole story, and still stronger against that part of it which alleges Edwin to have been unjustly put to death. Simeon of Durham and the Saxon Chronicle say no more than that Edwin was drowned by his brother's command, in the year 933.[31] Brompton places it in the first, or at farthest in the second year of his reign ; and he tells us the story of the rotten ship, and of his punishing the cup-bearer.[32] William of Malmsbury, who is very circumstantial, says he only tells us what he heard ;[33] but Matthew, the flower-gatherer,[34] stamps the whole down as an indubitable truth. Yet these discordant dates are not to be accounted for. If he was drowned in the second, he could not be alive in the tenth year of the king; the first is the more probable date, because about that time there certainly was a conspiracy against King Athelstan, in order to dethrone him, and put out his eyes ; yet he

[29] Hist. Scot. lib. vi. R. 75.
[30] Histoire d'Angleterre, tom. i. p. 336.
[31] Simeon Dunelm, p. 154 ; Chron. Saxon, p. 111.
[32] Chronicon. p. 828.   [33] De Gest. R. A. lib. ii.
[34] Matth. Florileg.

did not put the author of it to death.[35] It is likely, then,
that he should order his brother to be thrown into the
sea upon bare suspicion? But the reader must remember,
that we cite the same historians, who have told us this
story, to prove that Athelstan was unanimously acknowledged king,[36] his brethren being too young to govern;
one would think, then, they could not be old enough to
conspire. If we take the second date, the whole story is
destroyed; the king could not do seven years' penance,
for he did not live so long; and as for the tale of the
cup-bearer, and his stumbling at the king's table, the
same story is told of Earl Godwin, who murdered the
brother of Edward the Confessor. Lastly, nothing is
clearer from history, than that Athelstan was remarkably
kind to his brethren and sisters, for whose sakes he lived
single; and, therefore, one would think his brother had
less temptation to conspire against him.[37]

How likely is Dr. Plot's whole story of the Pinnace
and the Page, compared with the foregoing? For the
probability of Edwin's calling the Masons together at
York,[38] or getting them a charter, it need but be remem-

[35] Malms. l. ii. c. 6; Spel. Conc. p. 407.
[36] Athelstan is styled by Alured of Beverley—" Primus Monarcha
Anglorum." And he is right. Egbert laid claim to this honourable
title, but without just grounds; for he did not incorporate with his own
kingdom those of Northumbria and East Anglia; and it is even doubtful
whether he had the undisputed supremacy of Mercia. And Alfred, highly
as his virtues and talents exalted him in the estimation of mankind, was
not the monarch of all England, although in his fluctuating reign the
glory of the Anglo Saxon dynasty began to shine with unveiled effulgence;
because he only silenced, but did not destroy the Danish power in England.
It was reserved for Athelstan to unite the whole kingdom under one head,
by the annihilation of the Danish sovereignty, and thus became fairly
entitled to the distinction of its first monarch.
[37] He was succeeded by two of his brothers: first by Edmund, who was
murdered by Leolf, and then by Edred. Athelstan passed a law for the
encouragement of commerce, which displays in a striking manner the
superiority of his ideas. He decreed that a merchant who had made
three long and successful voyages to sea on his own account, should be
admitted to the rank of a thane or gentleman.
[38] The following account, taken from a MS. in the possession of Elias
Ashmole, gives a lucid explanation of the revival of Masonry at this
period. It states, "that, though the ancient records of the brotherhood
in England were, many of them, destroyed, or lost in the wars of the
Saxons and Danes, yet King Athelstan, the grandson of Alfred the Great,
almighty architect, the first anointed King of England, and who translated the Holy Bible into the Saxon tongue, when he had brought the

bered that Athelstan kept his court for some time in that city ; received there several embassies from foreign princes, and presents of various kinds, both rich and costly, from different parts of the world ; and, in short, was loved, honoured, and admired, by all the princes in Europe, who sought his friendship, and courted his alliance. To all his brothers and sisters he was remarkably kind, indeed a father to them ; and, from that his fatherly care, Prince Edwin has been by many ancient Masons called the son of Athelstan ; a thing not uncommon in many instances for ages since that.[39] Moreover, the activity and princely conduct of Edwin rendered him

land into rest and peace, built many great works, and encouraged many Masons from France, who were appointed overseers thereof, and brought with them the charges and regulations of the lodges, preserved since the Roman times; who also prevailed with the king to improve the constitution of the English lodges according to the foreign model, and to increase the wages of working masons. That the said king's brother, Prince Edwin, being taught Masonry, and taking upon him the charges of a Master Mason, for the love he had to the said craft, and the honourable principles whereon it is founded, purchased a free charter of his father for the Masons to have a correction amongst themselves, as it was anciently expressed, or a freedom and power to regulate themselves, to amend what might happen amiss within the craft, and to hold a yearly communication and general assembly. That, accordingly, Prince Edwin summoned all the Masons in the realm to meet him in a congregation at York, in June, A.D. 926, who came and composed a general or Grand Lodge, of which he was Grand Master. And, having brought with them all the old writings and records of the craft extant, some in Greek, some in Latin, some in French and other languages, from the contents thereof that assembly framed the constitutions and charges of an English lodge ; made a law to preserve and observe the same in all time coming, and ordained good pay for the working masons."

[39] Dr. Plot's patron, Ashmole, gives the following account of Masonry in these early times :—" St. Alban, the proto-martyr, established Masonry here ; and from his time it flourished more or less, according as the world went, down to the days of King Athelstan, who, for the sake of his brother Edwin, granted the Masons a charter. Under our Norman princes they frequently received extraordinary marks of royal favour. There is no doubt to be made that the skill of Masons, which was always transcendantly great, even in the most barbarous times, their wonderful kindness and attachment to each other, how different soever in condition ; and their inviolable fidelity in keeping religiously their secret, must expose them, in ignorant, troublesome, and superstitious times, to a vast variety of adventures, according to the different fate of parties, and other alterations in government. By the way, it may be noted that the Masons were always loyal, which exposed them to great severities when power wore the trappings of justice ; and those who committed treason punished true men as traitors."

the fittest person to be Grand Master of the Masons, who at that time were employed in very great numbers in repairing and building churches and other edifices, not only in the city of York, but at Beverly,[40] and other places, which had but lately been overthrown and levelled with the ground, by the Danes and other invaders, till Athelstan became Master of all, who supported and propagated the royal art in perfect peace and security.[41]

To follow the doctor in his good will for the ancient fraternity, the reader must know, that in the infancy of King Henry VI., an act of parliament was passed to prevent the assemblies of Masons.[42] The reasons for this

[40] The charter of Athelstan to the church at Beverly, ran as follows:—

> Yat wi.en al yrt ever been
> Yat yis charter heren and seen
> Yat I the king Athelstan
> Has yaten and given to St. John
> Of Beverlike ont sai I you
> Tol and Theam yat wit ye now
> Sok and sake over al yat land
> Yat is given into his hand
> On ever ilke king's dai
> Be it all free ynu and ay, &c.

[41] The ancient Masonic MS. of the tenth century, which has been published by Mr. Halliwell, thus notices Athelstan's connection with Freemasonry:—

> Thys craft com ynto England as y you say,
> Yn tyme of good kynge Adelstonees day;
> He made tho bothe halle and eke bowre,
> And hye templus of great honowre,
> To sportyn hym yn bothe day and nyght,
> An to worschepe hys God with alle hys myght.
> Thys goode lorde loved thys ful wel
> And proposud to strenthyn hyt every del;
> For dyvers defawtys that yn the craft he fonde,
> He sende aboute ynto the londe
> After alle the masonees of the crafte,
> To come to hym ful evene stragfte.

This was the origin of the Grand Lodge in England.

[42] I subjoin a copy of this act, which was passed in the third year of his reign, and the fourth of his age:—" Masons shall not confederate in chapters or congregations. Whereas by the yearly congregations and confederacies made by the Masons in their general assemblies, the good course and effect of the statutes of labourers be openly violated and broken, in subversion of the law, and to the great damage of all the commons. Our sovereign lord the king, willing in this case to provide a remedy by the advice and consent aforesaid, and at the special request of the commons, hath ordained and established that such chapters and congregations shall not be hereafter holden ; and, if any such be made, they that cause such chapters and congregations to be holden, and thereof convicted, it shall be adjudged felony; and that the other Masons who come to such chapters and congregations, be punished by prisonment of their bodies, and make fine and ransom at the king's will."

severe treatment are very obvious. In the absence of the Duke of Bedford, Regent of France, all the regal power was vested in Humphrey, Duke of Gloucester, his brother, protector of the kingdom, and in Henry Beaufort, Bishop of Winchester, his uncle, guardian to the king; who, being invested with power, began to show his pride and haughtiness betimes, and to support him therein, he wanted not for followers and agents enough. In the parliament held at Westminster, the 17th of November, 1423, to answer a particular end, it was ordained and enacted, that if any person, committed for grand or petty treason, should wilfully break prison and escape from the same, it should be deemed petty-treason, and his goods forfeited.[43]

On the last of April, 1425, the parliament met at Westminster, the servants and followers of the peers and members of parliament coming thither armed with clubs and staves, which occasioned it to be nick-named " the bat parliament." Among other laws, an act passed to abolish the society of Masons,[44] or at least to prevent the holding their yearly congregations, or indeed any of their assemblies.[45] As it must be owned that their meetings

[43] About this time one William King, of Womulton, in Yorkshire, servant to Sir Robert Scott, Lieutenant of the Tower, pretended that he was offered by Sir John Mortimer, then a prisoner in the Tower, and cousin to the lately deceased Edward Mortimer, Earl of March, the nearest in blood to the English crown, ten pounds to buy him clothes, forty pounds a year, and to be made an earl; that Mortimer would raise forty thousand men, and would strike off the heads of the rich Bishop of Winchester, Gloucester, and others; all which the fellow undertook to prove by his own bodily oath. Soon after this, they let Mortimer walk to the Tower-wharf, and then ran after and seized him for breaking prison; whereupon he was deemed convict, was drawn to Tyburn, there hanged, and afterwards beheaded. From whose death there arose no small slauder, murmurings, and discontent amongst the people, which threatened those in power with fatal consequences, as they were observed to spread, not only in public, but in private meetings and secret assemblies. The animosity between the uncle and nephew became every day more formidable than other.

[44] Statutes of the realm, vol. ii. p. 227. Rym. Fœd. vol. v. p. 670.

[45] Dr. Anderson, in the first edition of the Book of Constitutions, makes the following observations on this act :—" This act was made in ignorant times, when true learning was a crime, and geometry condemned for conjuration; but it cannot derogate from the honour of the ancient fraternity, who, to be sure, would never encourage any such confederacy of their working Brethren. By tradition it is believed that the parliament were then too much influenced by the illiterate clergy, who were not Ac-

were very secret, none can wonder that those secret
assemblies gave intolerable displeasure to the arrogant
ambitious priest, who no doubt thought himself ill-used
by any person daring to do what he was not to know.[46]
However, none of them were seized in their lodges, or
any attempt made to do it, the cunning prelate's attention being diverted another way ;[47] for on the morrow of
Simon and Jude's day, when the Mayor of London had
been to Westminster to take his charge, when at dinner,
he was sent for in all haste by the Duke of Gloucester ;
and when come into his presence, he gave him commandment to see the city securely watched the night
following. At nine of the clock the next morning, the
Bishop of Winchester, then called the English Pope,
with his servants and followers, would have entered the
city by the bridge, but were kept back by force ; whereupon the haughty and imperious bishop, being enraged,
gathered a great number of archers, and other men at
arms, and assaulted the gate with shot, and other means
of war ; so that the citizens directly shut their shops,

---

cepted Masons, nor understood architecture, as the clergy of some former
ages, and were generally thought unworthy of this brotherhood. Thinking they had an indefeasible right to know all secrets, by virtue of auricu-
lar confession, and the Masons never confessing anything thereof, the said
clergy were highly offended ; and, at first, suspecting them of wickedness,
represented them as dangerous to the state during the minority, and soon
influenced the parliament to lay hold of such supposed arguments of the
Working Masons, for making an act that might seem to reflect dishonour
upon even the whole fraternity, in whose favour several acts had been
before and after that period made."

[46] They held these secret meetings in the crypts of the cathedrals, which
were principally intended for this very purpose, as a transcript of the sacred valley; although modern writers have attributed to them a very different use. They tell us, but without any authority, that they were used
for the celebration of masses for the dead ; and are *always excavated immediately under the choir*, as the most holy part of the edifice. The fact
— is, they were constructed for the secret assemblies of the Freemasons, who
were the architects and designers of those noble edifices.

[47] Dallaway thinks that the penalties were evaded by the proviso which
the Master Masons insisted upon making in all great contracts, that the
conditions annexed to undue performance should be distinctly specified.
"That these two compulsory acts having lain totally dormant, is a mere
assumption. The fixed wages, however, were considerably higher than
those of any other mechanics ; and if we estimate them by the relative
value of money to what it now bears, sufficiently liberal. Even as late
as Charles the Second's time, the magistrates set an assize for them as
for other artisans." (History of Master and Freemasons, p. 427.)

and went to the bridge in great numbers, so that great
bloodshed would have followed, had not the wisdom of
the mayor and aldermen stayed them in time. The
Archbishop of Canterbury, with Peter, Duke of Co-
nimbria, eldest son of the King of Portugal, and
others, took great pains to bring the uncle and nephew
to agreement; they rode eight, some say ten, times
between them, before they could in anywise succeed, or
bring them to any conformity; and at last they agreed
to stand to the award of the *Duke of Bedford, whereupon the city was in more quiet at present.[48] The
bishop lost no time in making a-bad cause look as glossy
as possible, and wrote the Duke of Bedford the following letter :—

" Right high and mighty prince, and my right noble
and after one, leiuest lord. I recommend me unto your
grace with all my heart. And as you desire the welfare
of the king our sovereign lord, and of his realms of England and France, your own weal with all yours, haste
you hither: for by my troth, if you tarry long, we shall
put this land in jeapourdy with a field; such a brother
ye have here, God make him a good man. For your
wisdom well knoweth that the profit of France standeth
in the welfare of England, &c. The blessed Trinity
keep you. Written in great haste at London, on Allhal-
lowen Even, the 31st of October, 1425,
    " By your servant to my live's end,
            " HENRY WINCHESTER."

This tremendous letter made the Duke of Bedford
hasten the affairs of France; and he returned to London
the 10th of January, 1425-6; on the 21st of February,
he held a great council at St. Albans, adjourned it to
Northampton the 15th of March, and on the 25th of
June to Leicester. Bats and staves were again in use,
but those being prohibited, the followers of the members
of parliament came with stones slung and plummets of
lead.[49] Here the long wished for peace between the

[48] Wolfe's Chron.
[49] Dallaway entertains some doubts about the above act against the
Masons, which are thus stated :—" When it is said that the act of Henry
VI. was passed at the instigation of Cardinal Beaufort, and that the
Bishops Wykeham, Waynflete, and Chichelcy, were Grand Masters, I
must be allowed to prefer evidence to conjecture, but none has been ad-

Duke of Gloucester and the Bishop of Winchester, to appearance was accomplished. Gloucester exhibited six articles against the bishop, one of which was this : " VI. That the Bishop of Winchester had, in his letter to the Duke of Bedford, plainly declared his malicious purpose of assembling the people, and stirring up a rebellion in the nation, contrary to the king's peace."[50] The bishop's answer to this accusation was, " That he never had any intention to disturb the peace of the nation, or raise any rebellion ; but sent to the Duke of Bedford to come over in haste, to settle all things that were prejudicial to the peace ; and though he had indeed written in the letter, 'That if he tarried, we should put the land in adventure by a field, such a brother ye have here,' he did not mean it of any design of his own, but concerning the seditious assemblies of masons, carpenters, tylers, and plaisterers,[51] who, being distasted by the last act of parliament against excessive wages of those trades, had given out many seditious speeches and menaces against the great men, which tended much to rebellion ; and yet

duced. It admits of a doubt whether it were then considered as authorized by ecclesiastical constitutions, that its most eminent members could have presided as Grand Masters, and have been associated with the mysterious brotherhood ; or that they could have been so without the prescribed initiation. If authentic documents were ever in the archives of the fraternity, a modern enquirer would seek for them in vain. But if the mysteries of the Brotherhood are considered to be sacred, why is their true history concealed ?" (Dallaway, ut supra., p. 428.) I answer, the history has never been concealed ; and as to the former objection, we have a right to conclude from analogy, that not only was their admission lawful, but that they had been regularly initiated.

[50] It is a singular fact, that during the commotions between the houses of York and Lancaster, and their adherents, so prejudicial to the progress of the arts of civilization, architecture in England flourished in a great degree. The superior ecclesiastics were confined to their cloisters, as few of them had taken an active part in the dispute ; and some of the fairest structures which remain, arose in consequence of wealth accumulated by instigating the noble and affluent to contribute to the general emulation of splendid churches, built under their own inspection.

[51] The following is a proof of the estimation and rank which a Master Mason held in society in the fifteenth century. The Abbot of St. Edmundsbury, in the year 1439, contracted with John Wood, a Master Mason, for the repairs and restoration of the great bell tower, " in all manere of thynges that longe to Freemasounry ; and to have borde for himselfe *as a gentilman*, and his servant as a yeoman, and thereto two robys, one for himselfe after a gentilmanys livery. Wages of masons, 3s. a man weekly in winter, and 3s. 4d. in summer." (Archæol. vol. xxiii. p. 331.)

the Duke of Gloucester did not use his endeavour, as he
ought to have done in his place, to suppress such unlawful assemblies,[52] so that he feared the king and his good
subjects must have made a field to withstand them ; to
prevent which, he chiefly desired the Duke of Bedford to
come over." The falsehood of this charge of the
bishop's against the Masons is so self-evident, that it
would be injuring the candid reader to suggest it in the
least doubtful, except any can imagine that the lord
mayor, aldermen, and commons of London, were the
Masons that he had decreed for destruction. As he had
begun, so he never abated of his malice against the
Duke of Gloucester till he had accomplished his ruin ;
but being too sensible his actions were not to be justified by the laws of the land, he prevailed with the king,
through the intercession of the parliament, whom his
riches had made his tools, to grant him letters of pardon
for all offences by him committed, contrary to the statute of provisors, and other acts of præmunire.[53] Five
years after this, he procured another pardon, under the
great seal, for all sorts of crimes whatever, from the
creation of the world to the 26th of July, 1437.

Notwithstanding all the cardinal's precautions, the
Duke of Gloucester, in 1442, drew up articles of im-

[52] The Masons, however, continued to hold their meetings unmolested,
and a record of the period says :—" The company of Masons, being otherwise termed Freemasons, of ancient standing, and good reckoning, by
means of affable and kind meetings, diverse times, and as a loving Brotherhood use to do, did frequent this mutual assembly in the time of King
Henry the Sixth, in the twelfth year of his most gracious reign ; when
Henry was thirteen years of age, A. D. 1434." And the said record describing a coat of arms, much the same with that of the London Company
of Freemasons, it is generally believed that the said company is descended
of the ancient fraternity : and that in former times no man was made free
of that company until he was installed in some lodge of Free and Accepted
Masons, as a necessary qualification. So that before the troubles of this
unfortunate king, the Masons were everywhere in great esteem, and
much employed ; for the above record says further :—" That the charges
and corrections of the Freemasons have been seen and perused by our
late sovereign King Henry the Sixth, and by the lords of his most honourable council, who have allowed them, and declared that they be right,
good, and reasonable to be holden, as they have been drawn out and
collected from the records of ancient times," &c.
[53] Horace said that in his time
Jura inventa metu injusti fateare necesse est,
Tempora si fastosque velis evolvere mundi.

peachment against him, and presented them with his
own hands to the king, desiring that judgment might
pass upon him according to his crimes. The king referred the matter to his council; but they being most ecclesiastical persons, favoured the cardinal; so that, grown
weary with their delays and underhand dealings, he
dropped the prosecution, and the cardinal escaped.

The wickedness of his life, and his mean, base, and
unmanly behaviour in the article of death, will ever be
a bar against any vindication of him for the good he did,
or the money he left behind him. When dying, he uttered these mean expressions: " Why should I die, that have
so much wealth ? If the whole kingdom would save my
life, I am able by my policy to get it, or by my money
to buy it. Will not death be bribed, nor money do anything !" The inimitable Shakspeare, after giving a most
horrible picture of despair and a tortured conscience, in
the person of the cardinal, introduces King Henry to
him with these sharp and killing words :—

> Lord Cardinal, if thou think'st on heaven's bliss,
> Lift up thy hand, make signal of that hope.
> (He dies and makes no sign.)   (Hen. VI., Act III.)

Sovereign authority being vested in the Duke of
Gloucester, as Protector of the Realm, the execution of
the laws, and all that related to the civil magistrate
centred in him.   Had it not been so, the Masons had
certainly been most severely punished, as a load of infamy,[54] and holding unlawful assemblies, had been charged
upon them, and a law made against them by the Bishop
of Winchester and his creatures ; which, however, they
never could get executed, as the protector well knew

[54] The Masons of this period were men of very superior talent ; as
witness, amongst many other superb edifices, the construction of King's
College Chapel at Cambridge, of which Sir Christopher Wren is reported
to have said that it was beyond his comprehension ; but that if any person would describe to him where the first stone should be placed, he
would then be enabled to effect it. The merit of being the designer of
this superb edifice seems to be assignable to Nicholas Klaus, Bishop of
Lichfield, who had been entrusted with the chief management of the
works. Hearne, however, tells us that he was assisted by his father, who
was a Flemish architect. The three Master Masons who constructed it
were, John Woolrich, John Wastell, and Henry Semerk. The latter is
styled " oon of the Wardens of the kynge's works at the College Royal
at Cambridge." (Britton. Arch. Antiq., vol. i., p. 12.)

them not to be blameable, nor in any respect aggressors, except in holding their assemblies in the same secret manner they had done in all ages, without meddling with any affairs of civil policy. As the Masons were under the lash of an act of parliament,[55] then recent in the mind of every one, the bishop very kindly transferred the charge of rebellion, sedition, and treason, upon them, though it is most apparent that himself and his followers were the first to disturb, as well as to break the public peace, and kindle the flames of civil discord, and whom no reasonable concessions could satisfy; his ambition being to surmount all others, both in honour and dignity, howsoever unworthily accomplished.

The renowned Protector Humphry, Duke of Gloucester, our most worthy and princely Brother, made King Henry a Mason in the year 1441,[56] or, as some think, 1442; and many lords of the court followed his example;[57] for at that time he was greatly beloved of the

[55] The severe edict passed against the society at this time, and the discouragement given to the Masons by the Bishop of Winchester and his party, induced Henry VI., in his riper years, to make a strict scrutiny into the nature of the masonic institution; which was attended with the happy circumstance of gaining his favour and his patronage. Had not the civil commotions in the kingdom during his reign attracted the notice of government, this act would probably have been repealed through the intercession of the Duke of Gloucester, whose attachment to the fraternity was conspicuous.

[56] The following letter, from the celebrated and learned John Locke to the Earl of Pembroke, will throw some light upon this subject:—

May 6, 1696.

"My Lord—I have at length, by the help of Mr. Collins, procured a copy of that MS. in the Bodleian Library which you were so curious to see; and in obedience to your lordship's commands, I herewith send it to you. Most of the notes annexed to it, are what I made yesterday for the reading of my Lady Masham, who is become so fond of Masonry, as to say that she now more than ever wishes herself a man, that she might be capable of admission into the fraternity. The MS. of which this a copy, appears to be about one hundred and sixty years old; yet (as your lordship will observe by the title) it is itself a copy of one yet more ancient by about one hundred years; for the original is said to have been the hand-writing of King Henry VI. Where that prince had it is at present an uncertainty; but it seems to me to be an examination (taken perhaps before the king) of some one of the Brotherhood of Masons, among whom he entered himself, as it it said, when he came out of his minority, and thenceforth put a stop to a persecution that had been raised against them."

[57] It was ordained during this reign, as appears by an ancient masonic MS., that kings and other male sovereigns are Grand Masters during life.

3

king, which increased the Cardinal of Winchester's inveteracy so much, that it was resolved to take away his
life. He accordingly felt the first fatal blow of the destroying angel, sent to punish England and extirpate her
nobility.

The duke had always been a brave opposer of all
things detrimental to the public good ; and, indeed, the
only man who, by his prudence, as well as the authority
of his birth and place, had hindered an absolute sovereign power from being vested in the king's person ;
which instance alone enabled Winchester to gain over
many who, on that account only, were wrought upon to
concur in his ruin ; though thereby they threw open the
flood-gates that overwhelmed them all in a deluge of
blood. His duchess had been convicted of sorcery and
witchcraft, and afterwards charged with treason. She
was put to public penance in London for three days,
with extraordinary shame to her person, and then imprisoned for life.[58] The protector, being provoked with
such repeated insults offered to his wife, made a noble
and stout resistance to their most abominable and shameless proceedings, which directly brought on his own destruction ; for on the second day of the sessions of par-

and appoint a deputy, or approve of his election, to preside over the fraternity, with the title and honours of Grand Master ; but if the sovereign
is a female, or not a Brother ; or a minor under a regent who is not a
Brother ; or if the male sovereign, or the regent, though a Brother, is negligent of the craft, then the old grand officers may assemble the Grand
Lodge in *due* form to elect a Grand Master, but not during life, only he
may be annually re-chosen while he and they think fit.

[58] This was a most shameful transaction. It was pretended, says Hume,
that there was found in her possession a waxen figure of the king, which
she and her associates, Sir Roger Bolingbroke, a priest, and one Margery
Jordan, of Eye, melted in a magical manner before a slow fire, with an
intention of making Henry's force and vigour waste away by like insensible degrees. The accusation was well calculated to affect the weak and
credulous mind of the king, and to gain belief in a ignorant age ; and the
duchess was brought to trial with her confederates. The nature of this
crime, so opposite to all common sense, seems always to exempt the
accusers from observing the rules of common sense in their evidence.
The prisoners were pronounced guilty ; the duchess was condemned to do
public penance, and to suffer perpetual imprisonment, but the others were
executed. But as these violent proceedings were ascribed solely to the
malice of the duke's enemies, the people, contrary to their usual practice
in such marvellous trials, acquitted the unhappy sufferers, and increased
their esteem and affection towards a prince who was thus exposed, without protection, to those mortal injuries.

liament, held at St. Edmundsbury, 1447, he was arrested for high treason, and the next day basely and shamefully murdered. Five of his servants being condemned to be hanged, drawn and quartered, the Marquis of Suffolk, through a mean and pitiful affectation of popularity, brought them pardons, and saved their lives, after they had been hanged, cut down alive, stripped naked, and marked with a knife to be quartered. By a pardon granted to one of his servants, may be seen the pretence made use of for committing the murder ; that he was one of the many traitors who came with the Duke of Gloucester to destroy the king and parliament, and set his wife Eleanor at liberty.[59]

So fell this great prince, doubly murdered in his person and reputation. His death was universally lamented by the whole kingdom, from whom he had long obtained, and well deserved, the surname of " Good ;" for he was a lover of his country, a friend to good men, the saviour of the Masons, a protector of the learned, himself one, and so great an encourager of them, that he built the Divinity Schools at Oxford, and a public library there— works worthy of everlasting memorial.[60] His opinions

[59] The true reason why the Masons were objects of jealousy to the party then in power was, because their superior talents caused them to be suspected, like the unfortunate duchess, of sorcery and witchcraft ; which was rendered more probable by the practice of secresy. And this is not to be wondered at in such a dark age, when the genuine principles of science were little understood, except by the Freemasons. " Gothic architecture," says Bardwell, (Temples, p. 3, n.) " has always the charm of mystery ; it does not exhibit itself naked and bare like a Greek temple perched on a rock ; but it appeals to the imagination, veiled itself with walls, and screens, and towers ; inducing fancy to supply the deficiencies of the material science. It delights in bold, striking, and picturesque irregularities, and always appears larger than its actual dimensions ; the mouldings, the pillars, and the arches, always create receding shadows, and, to the eye, the idea of *space* arises from the succession of shadows and multitudinous parts of unequal dimensions, just as the conception of *time* results from the conception of *ideas*."

[60] This prince is said to have received a better education than was usual in his age, to have founded one of the first public libraries in England, and to have been a great patron of learned men. Among other advantages which he reaped from this turn of mind, it tended much to cure him of credulity ; of which the following instance is given by Sir Thomas More. There was a man who pretended that, though he was born blind, he had recovered his sight by a miracle. The prince questioned the man closely, and amongst other things, asked him the colours of several cloaks worn by persons of his retinue. The man told them very readily. " You

in policy do him no less honour; his judgment and views
concerning the French dominions were always thwarted
and rendered abortive by the Bishop of Winchester and
his faction, who would hear of nothing but peace, though
on the most unworthy and abject terms, which ended in
the loss of the whole kingdom of France; to which the
heroic and gallant duke, nicely insisting on the honour,
majesty, and glory of the English name, was a professed
enemy. His infernal persecutor, the hypocritical bishop,
lived but two months after him; and then went down
to his place with all the daggers of divine vengeance
sticking in his heart, as has already been related. The
memory of the wicked shall rot, but the unjustly persecuted shall be had in sweet and everlasting remembrance.

It has been already said that King Henry was made a
Mason;[61] and by what follows, it will be found that he
was very intent upon a thorough knowledge of the royal
art; and how doubtful soever this event might appear
to Dr. Plot, it is supported with such undeniable testimonies as will effectually overthrow all his impossibilities.
No doubt but every reader will feel some satisfaction in
looking over this antique relation,[62] though none more so
than the true and faithful Brother, in observing the glimmering conjectures of an unenlightened person, upon the
fundamental principles, history, and traditions of the
royal art, though a philosopher of as great merit and
penetration as this nation ever produced.[63]

are a knave," said the prince; "for if you had been born blind. you
could not distinguish colours;" and immediately ordered him to be set in
the stocks as an impostor.

[61] One of the first acts of the ill-fated Henry VI., after he had taken
the government into his own hands, was the foundation of two magnificent
colleges at Cambridge and Eton. His chief counsellor, with whom these
plans were consulted, was William of Wayuflete, Grand Master of Masons; and he charged the Duchy of Lancaster with a payment of 2000l.
a year for twenty years, towards their erection.

[62] The contents of the MS. are purposely omitted, because they are
already familiar to every Brother who cares anything about the institution; having been published in the Gentleman's Magazine, the Ahiman
Rezon, and by Hutchinson, Preston, and many other masonic writers; and
its authenticity is attested in the Life of Leland.

[63] The philosopher here referred to is the celebrated John Locke, whose
letter to the Earl of Pembroke we have just seen, and whose annotations
on this ancient document have been the delight of every Mason who has

From all that has been said, it will appear beyond doubt that Dr. Plot's charge against the Masons was principally of his own invention, as everything that he has advanced, touching the falsehood or incoherency of their history, either has not the least probability of truth, and which he must with design have misrepresented, or what he could not by any means perfectly know to be true; and if every part of his history is no better founded than this, a greater imposition was never offered to mankind under so sanctified and sleek a garb.[64] He either wanted the ability, or was too indolent to make a nice scrutiny into the history of his own country; for what he offers at, seems rather to be what he wished than what could be proved from facts.[65] The barbarous age, that his ignorance calls the time of St. Alban, was, in every respect, the reverse. The great probability, nay, certainty, of his being a surveyor over works when thousands of workmen were employed, and he the most capable of the service, is obvious. The story of the cloak and tutor, though the doctor and his judicious persons might think St. Cloak and St. Amphibalus to be the very same; yet here the current runs strongly against them, what affinity soever they might suggest to be between the one and the other. Indeed, none other than some of Dr. Plot's barbarians could possibly have dedicated a cathedral-church to a cloak, within a few years of the death of St. Alban's tutor, when there must have been great numbers of Christians alive who personally knew him.

had the good fortune to peruse them; and though he was not at that time a member of the fraternity, he seems to have taken a very correct view of the system; and there can be no doubt that after his initiation he would find his views confirmed.

[64] These remarks are rather too severe. The doctor neither wanted talents nor industry. His besetting fault was credulity. He believed everything that was told him, without examining the credibility of his authority; and hence he fell into all the absurd errors which deform his book.

[65] The age was not barbarous, because the chief persons in Britain sent their sons to Rome for education. Besides, the Druids, who swayed the destinies of the people, were learned and polite. They taught the liberal sciences, and particularly astronomy; for at the irruption of Cesar, they had divided the heavens into constellations, and were conversant with the laws and motions of the planets. Their botanical knowledge was extensive, and they are said to have been the best anatomists at that time existing in the world. The poetry of the bards has been the subject of high commendation.

The history of Prince Edwin is sufficiently cleared up
to show the doctor a mean follower of the legendary
writers, and to have carefully gleaned up every little
circumstance that his malice could furnish him with
against the Masons, who, it seems, merited his highest
displeasure. Whether the Masons were concerned in
any seditious practices, or Henry VI. and his council
should see and procure, or approve the charges and manners, or himself and many nobles of his court should have
been made Masons, must rest upon what has already
been offered ; and as the doctor thinks the last event the
most improbable circumstance of all, the Masons will
readily give up all the doctor's conjectures for indubitable
truths upon the proof of this being false.

The doctor did not intend to leave the Masons to enjoy
their falsehoods quietly, or to leave them in the midst of
their errors, but to bring them to open shame and punishment; not for their fabulous history, but for their
wicked and secret practices. "For," says he, "it is still
to be feared these chapters of Freemasons do as much
mischief as before, which, if one may estimate by the
penalty, was anciently so great, that perhaps it might be
useful to examine them now."[66]   Such was this Christian
doctor's candour and charity, such his detestation of persecution; but it must be remembered that he wrote at a
time when it was fashionable to decry anything that
looked like a secret assembly, lest matters disagreeable to
some might there be canvassed—when their liberty and
religion were both openly attacked by the government,
and the doctor more a man of mode than to cut his coat
contrary to the court fashion.[67]   All the doctor's laboured

[66] But even Robison admits the benevolent character of the society at
the very period when Dr. Plot wrote. He says that "Masons being frequently led by their employment far from hence, and from their friends,
might be greatly benefited by such an institution, which gave them
introduction and citizenship wherever they went, and a right to share in
the charitable contributions of Brethren who were strangers to them.
Universal benevolence was the great aim of the Order." (Proofs, p. 24.)

[67] Dr. Plot composed his work during the attempt of Monmouth to
obtain the crown, and while Kirke and Jefferies were executing their
blood-thirsty commissions to curry favour with the arbitrary court of
James. Nothing could satiate the spirit of rigour which possessed the
administration. Even those who were pardoned were subjected to such
heavy fines as reduced them to beggary ; and when they were no longer
capable of paying, they were scourged and imprisoned. It is surprising,

objections to the Masons being obviated, and shown to be false and groundless, it may be inferred that no persons, however eminent in quality, needed to disdain the fellowship of Masons, on account of its high antiquity and honour. As Staffordshire did then, so it does now, furnish us with some of as great names as ever graced the annals of Masonry.[68]

It will, perhaps, be deemed uncharitable to surmise that any of those eminent and great persons, that Dr. Plot says were Masons, encouraged him in his work. Yet it too clearly appears that either they did not, or that he rewarded them in the same grateful manner as he had done his master, Ashmole.[69] Those whom he has mentioned as the promoters of his undertaking, without any disrespect to their names be it said, he has so shamefully flattered, and laid his daubing on so thickly, that nothing but his own words can influence the reader to think that a man of such esteem among the learned, and who passed for a man of real learning himself, could be capable of it. He calls them " ingenious and every way accomplished; the severely inquisitive and worshipful; my truly noble patron, the right worshipful; the virtuous and most accomplished lady; the most hopeful and inquisitive young gentleman, and his virtuous sister, Mrs. Anne; the fair lady of Lyswys;" and, to crown the whole, says of a lady, that she had "a most exquisite sagacity and perspicacious insight into the most hidden recesses of nature." Yet it were well had this adulating faculty been the only fault of the doctor, for he appears to be

however, that the learned doctor should have attributed state plots to Masons, because many of the adherents of James were Brethren of the Order, although the king himself does not appear to have frequented the lodges, nor is there any evidence to prove that he was a Mason; but in his reign Sir Christopher Wren was the Grand Master, and Brothers Gabriel Cibber, and Edward Strong, the Grand Wardens.

[68] This observation is as true at the present day as it was at the time when the above reply was written; and the Editor has many personal friends amongst them, with whom he considers it a happiness to be acquainted.

[69] Ashmole himself appointed Dr. Plot first keeper of his museum; and about the same time the vice-chancellor nominated him first professor of chemistry in the university of Oxford. He was secretary to the Earl Marshal; registrar of the court of honour, and historiographer to King James II. This may have been the true cause of his servility, although he evidently overshot his mark by abusing the Freemasons.

the greatest believer, where the matter he handles is
beyond all credibility. He relates with firm alliance the
most astonishing stories; and none with greater bitterness than those of witches and wizards, against whom he
shows as much, if not more gall than against the Masons.[70] The good wives and colliers in Staffordshire
were his principal informers. He talks with great faith
of the music of a pack of hounds in the air; a heavenly
concert; the raining not only of rats, mice, and frogs,
but of wool, iron, tiles, bricks, and great stones;[71] with
innumerable other unaccountable, unnatural, and in-
credible relations, picked out of various authors, and of
various countries, to buttress up what he met with of
the same kind in Staffordshire. The history of the
whistlers, and in particular of William Creswell, the
whistler of Rugely, apprentice to Anthony Bannister;
the story of Mary Woodward, of Hardwick; of the black
meere of Morridge, told him with admiration by every-
body at Leek; John Duncalf and his Bible; and Captain
Basil Wood, are verily most marvellous relations, and
savour so strongly of truth, that it will be quite needless
to entertain the reader with them, and especially as they
have been transplanted by the ingenious Mr. Robert
Burton, in those extraordinary books called Wonderful
Events, the History of Witches, and the Kingdom of
Darkness.[72]   .

[70] It is rather surprising that he did not blend the two charges together, for it was the cant of the day. Thus a writer against Masonry
says that "it was much connected with the schisms in the Christian
church; that the Jesuits had several times interfered in it; and that
most of the exceptionable innovations and dissensions had arisen about
the time that the order of Loyola was suppressed; so that it should seem
that these intriguing brethren had attempted to maintain their influence
by the help of Freemasonry. It was much disturbed by the mystical
whims of Behmen and Swedenborg—by the fanatical and knavish doctrines of the modern Rosicrucians—by magicians—magnetisers—exor-
cists." (Robison, Proofs, p. 6.)
[71] Nat. Hist. Staff. pp. 14, 20, 22, 24.
[72] However, Dashfield, the astonishing collier of Wednesbury, must
not so be passed over. The doctor says he was told "that this same
collier being searching for coal in some old hollows, and wanting air,
repaired to an old shaft that had been filled up some years before, where
loosening some earth at the bottom, in hopes it would crack to the top,
and give him air, it so suddenly coped down upon him, that being
environed on all sides with it, he could not return, insomuch that the
people concluded him smothered; but while they were debating how to

A position of the doctor's concerning water-spouts, is thus advanced:—" In these spouts, together with the water, the fish many times, in the sea thereabouts, are lifted up, which sometimes being carried by the winds over land before their fall, has often occasioned the wonderful raining of fish, as it did whitings at Stansted, in the parish of Wrotham, in Kent, in 1666, and herrings in the south of Scotland, in 1684, as his most sacred Majesty King James II. most judiciously determined the problem there."[73] How this problem was determined is not discernible, without the water-spout does it; but as a respectable person is here drawn in to vouch for the doctor, it can give no offence to say, that there never have been any whiting or herring rains since. For the person last mentioned it was that the doctor wrote, and seems to have no opinions but what were reflected from the crown. He turns tail of all his Staffordshire supporters, by telling the public " that he appeals only to the royal judgment, and, therefore, shall little value what other men think, but cheerfully acquiesce in his majesty's decision.[74]

Finally, be it far from a Mason to detract from any man's real worth, or endeavour to blemish what is praiseworthy and meritorious in any man's conduct or writings, though some parts may be dappled with falsehood or error; and, therefore, with allowing all due praise to his literary acquisitions, in which it must be confessed he took great pains, yet it is most certain a man of less judgment, and more credulity, never lived than Dr. Plot.

get him out, he, by the help of his maundrill, by degrees so wrought away the earth over head, and getting it under his feet, so raised himself higher and higher, that at length he came out above ground safe and sound, having worked thus upwards at least twenty-seven feet in an hour's time; which even the people thereabouts, who understand these works, look upon to this day as so strange a performance, that the man (now living) is still called Witch Dashfield." (Nat. Hist. Staff. pp. 284, 288, 291, 304, 305, 306, 329.

[73] Nat. Hist. Staff. pp. 249, 250
[74] Dedication to King James.

3*

CHAPTER II.

AN APOLOGY FOR THE FREE AND ACCEPTED MASONS.

OCCASIONED BY THEIR PERSECUTIONS IN THE CANTON OF BERNE, WITH THE PRESENT STATE OF MASONRY IN GERMANY, ITALY, FRANCE, FLANDERS, AND HOLLAND.[1]

"——————— Then the witch
Began a magic song,
One long low tone, through teeth half closed,
Through lips slow moving, muttered slow;
One long continued breath,
Till to her eyes a darker yellowness
Was driven, and fuller swoln the prominent veins
On her loose throat grew black.
Then looking upward, thrice she breathed
Into the face of heaven;
The baneful breath infected heaven;
A mildewing fog it spread
Darker and darker; so the evening sun
Poured his unentering glory on the mist,
And it was night below."   SOUTHEY.

THE Free and Accepted Masons, so famous in our times, are a society of men of all ages, conditions, religions, and countries, who have ever been such lovers

---

[1] The following papal decree was issued against this pamphlet by the Apostolical Chamber at Rome in 1739 :—" The 18th day of Feb. 1739. The sacred congregation of the most eminent, and most reverend cardinals of the holy Roman See, and inquisitor-general in the Christian republic against heretical pravity, held in the convent of St. Mary Supra Minervam, thoroughly weighing that a certain book, written in French, small in its size, but most wicked in regard to its bad subject, entitled 'The History of, and an Apology for the Society of Freemasons, by J. G. D. M. F. M., printed at Dublin for Patrick Odoroko, 1739,' has been published to the great scandal of all the faithful in Christ, in which book there is an apology for the society of Freemasons, already justly condemned by the Holy See; after a mature examination thereof, a censure, and that published by our most holy lord, Pope Clement XII., together with the suffrages of the most eminent and most reverend lords, the car-

of virtue, as always to seek and never betray it; and yet
happier in seeing those amiable ends constantly practised
by all that are true and faithful. From hence it is, that
they are united by the most indissoluble ties of brotherly
affection, and instructed with unanimity to aspire after
that which makes their lives happy, by uniting the profit
and the good of mankind.[2] However resplendent this

dinals, by the command of his holiness, condemns and prohibits, by the
present decree, the said book, as containing propositions and wicked
principles.

"Wherefore, that so hurtful and wicked a work may be abolished, as
much as possibly it can. or at least that it may not continue without a
perpetual note of infamy, the same sacred congregation, by command as
above, has ordered that the said work shall be burnt publicly by the
minister of justice in the street of St. Mary Supra Minervam, on the 25th
of the current month, at the same time the congregation shall be held in
the convent of the same St. Mary.

"Moreover, this same sacred congregation, by the command of his
holiness, positively forbids and prohibits all the faithful in Christ, that
no one dare by any means, and under any pretence whatsoever, copy,
print, or cause to be copied or printed, or retain or presume to read the
said book in any language and version now published, or (which God
forbid) may be published hereafter, and now condemned by this decree,
under the pain of excommunication, to be incurred *ipso facto* by those
that shall offend therein; but that they shall presently and effectually
deliver it up to the ordinaries of such places, or to the inquisitors of
heretical pravity, who shall burn it, or cause it to be burnt, without
delay.

"Twenty-fifth of February, 1739.
            "Paul Antinus Capellorius, notary-public of the Holy
              Roman and Universal Inquisition.
                "The place + of the seal.

"Upon the 25th of February, 1739, the above-cited decree was fixed
and published at the gates of the church of the Prince of the Apostles,
at the palace of the holy office, and at the other customary places within
the city, by me, Peter Romolatius, officer of the Holy Inquisition."

[2] Thus a writer of the last century concludes his book in the following
words:—'Throughout this golden æra of the fraternity, the royal art
has been carefully and diligently propagated, the noblest evidences of
true old architecture everywhere abounding, and perhaps never appeared
to greater advantage since the Augustan age; as these nations, in their
high taste for building and culture of the sciences, far exceed the rest of
Europe; so that the absolute and complete restoration of everything
ancient, noble, great, and elegant in architecture, has been by fate
reserved to be completed in these happy islands; and that whilst any
of those goodly structures continue to resist the ruins of time, the fame
and glory of the most ancient fraternity in the world will be honoured
and esteemed by all that love true knowledge; and joining the operative
and moral architect, together with the constant practice of the most
extensive humanity, benevolence, and charity, seem to promise a continuation till the final consummation of all things."

picture of the fraternity may appear at first view, the colouring yet very much falls short of the original; and more so, as these qualifications have exposed them to many unjust and cruel persecutions,[3] under various pretences, very false in themselves, as the reasons of such vexatious troubles proceeded from imaginary and groundless stories propagated among the vulgar.[4] It is the right of the unjustly-persecuted to complain, and to wish for redress. It is a token of real goodness and virtue to bear the scourge of ignorant and mistaken zealots with such becoming fortitude and patience, as will at length prevail. By thus magnanimously bearing undeserved reproach, they are sure at least of the hearty good wishes of all that are true and faithful throughout the world.

The States-general of the United Provinces were the first among the powers of Europe who took notice of the Freemasons; for, finding that they held their chapters or congregations in almost every town under their government, they began to be exceedingly alarmed, as it was judged impossible that architecture could be the only motive for holding such assemblies.[5] Under this per-

[3] Men of sense and discrimination usually endeavour to induce others to embrace their opinions by persuasion—bigots by persecution. Christ established his gospel by mildness—Mahomet by the sword. The persecutions of the early popes were carried on by the agency of ignorant zealots. Pope Innocent III. perceived in the Dominican and Franciscan friars all the qualities necessary for carrying on his persecuting schemes. They appear to have been descended from the dregs of the people; they were severe and inflexible, and entirely devoted to the interests of the court at Rome. The pope having secured their services, sought for every opportunity to increase their authority; and at length the inquisition was established, where they were to sit and hear, and pronounce sentence against reputed heretics, as judges delegated by him, and representing his person.

[4] These stories were propagated by means of a swarm of pamphlets, with which its enemies thought to destroy the existence of Freemasonry, as the locusts did the fruits of the land of Egypt. (See Masonic Institutes, p. 17.) These pamphlets were generally treated by the fraternity with perfect indifference, and even made by them the subjects of ridicule. Two of them were satirized in the secretary's song; and when they were thus brought prominently under the notice of the lodge, they proved a fund of amusement to the Brethren present.

[5] The first of a series of regular meetings took place at the Hague, in 1734, under the direction of Bro. de la Chapelle; but in the third year of their establishment, proclamations were issued against them, which were followed by the order of the Emperor Charles VI., in 1738, prohibiting

suasion the States published an edict, in the year 1735, in which they ordained that, though they had not discovered anything in the behaviour or practices of the fraternity, contrary to the peace of the Republic, or to the duty of good subjects, they were resolved, nevertheless, to prevent any bad consequences that might ensue, that the congregations, assemblies, or lodges of the Freemasons should be entirely abolished.[6] Far from blaming the conduct of these wise republicans, it will be found to accord with the policy of their government, ever remarkably suspicious of all new or secret assemblies;[7] be-

the continuance of masonic assemblies in his Netherland dominions, or any part of Flanders. Despite these edicts, the lodge at the Hague continued its work, and adopted, in the year 1749, the title of Mother Lodge; diffusing in all directions its kindness, and rendering assistance to all that required it. In 1759, the Baron Charles von Boetzelaer was elected Grand Master; and he entered so actively on its duties, that to his interference and management the prosperity of Masonry in Holland may be ascribed. It survived the persecution there, and is at present in a flourishing state. (Freemasons' Quarterly Review, 1844, p. 158.)

[6] Let us see what the London Masons were about at the time when this sweeping ordinance was decreed. In turning to the history of Masonry, we find Thomas Thynne, Lord Viscount Weymouth, the Grand Master; John Ward, Esq., Deputy Grand Master; Sir E. Mansell, Bart., and Martin Clare, A. M., F. R. S., the Grand Wardens. The Grand Master elect, on April 17, 1735, was attended at his house, in Grosvenor-square, by Grand Master Crauford and his officers, by the Dukes of Richmond and Athol, the Marquis of Beaumont, the Earls of Winchelsea, Wemys, Loudon, and Balcarras, the Lord Vere Bertie and Lord Cathcart, with many other eminent and worthy Brethren, clothed proper, and with a band of music proceeded through the city with great state and solemnity to Mercer's Hall, where good old customs were strictly observed. In the several communications, Deputy Grand Master Ward, being in the chair, made a most excellent speech, recommending temper, decency, and good decorum to the whole assembly; moved that a law might be made to enforce the same; and then proposed a regulation of ten rules for the good government of the communications, which passed unanimously. It not suiting the Grand Master to attend, the Deputy Grand Master performed all to the lasting honour, safety, and well-being of the craft.

[7] Notwithstanding the above ordinance, a lodge composed of several respectable gentlemen continued to meet at a private house in Amsterdam. The magistrates getting intelligence of it, ordered the whole lodge to be arrested; when the Master and Wardens declared, that although they were incapable of satisfying the magistrates respecting their particular secrets or ceremonies, yet if any of the magistrates chose to be initiated, they would then be satisfied that Masonry contained nothing but what was good and commendable. The magistrates accepted the offer and ordered the town clerk to be initiated, which was accordingly done; and he made such a favourable report of the proceedings in the

sides, at that time, they knew no better, for they had not
a clear and distinct knowledge of the harmless nature,
and of the end and design, of the fraternity; which, as
the time this happened, were holding their lodges under
the sanction of the Grand Master of England and were
rapidly spreading all over Europe, under the same great
authority,[8] which procured them peace and an honourable reception, where otherwise they should not have
found it. The States-general having since experienced
the good behaviour of the fraternity,[9] and acquainted
themselves with the charges, laws, and essential usages
of that illustrious body, do not only permit any of their
subjects to become of the craft, but also countenance,
encourage, and protect the lodges in the cities and towns
of the Republic.[10]

France, in the year 1737, followed the example of
Holland; though many of the greatest personages in

lodge, that all the magistrates became Masons, and established a new
lodge for their own particular use.

[8] There was an authorized compact between the Right Honourable
Lord Petre, Grand Master of England, and his Serene Highness the
Prince of Hesse Darmstadt, Grand Master of Germany, in which the
Grand Lodge in London confirmed the power and authority of his
Serene Highness in Germany ; and the latter agreed not to constitute
any new lodges, or grant any masonic power or authority, except within
the empire of Germany. And the two contracting Grand Lodges mutually agreed to use their best endeavours to destroy all schisms and
innovations in Masonry, and more especially that sect of Masons who
call themselves the Strict Observance, whose principles are pronounced
in their compact to be inconsistent with true Masonry.

[9] The first lodge at Amsterdam was opened by the grand officers from
the Hague, and consisted of the first men in the country ; but it was interdicted, as we have just seen, and the result was creditable to the
Order. From that period all prohibitory proclamations were withdrawn,
and the Order became protected by the laws, excepting in the provinces
under the sway of the Emperor Charles VI.

[10] The progress of Masonry in Holland is thus given in the foreign
periodical called Latomia : " The only original, traceable, and regular
lodge at the beginning of the seventeenth century, is the Mons lodge of
Perfect Union, under the warrant of the Duke of Montague ; from that
nucleus it gradually increased, but principally in the south. In 1731 the
Grand Duke of Tuscany was introduced into Freemasonry by the English
ambassador, Lord Chesterfield : but the lodge, with one exception, consisted of Englishmen. It appears that Bro. Vincent de la Chapelle held
a lodge under the title of ' the Reunion of the Grand Masters of the
Provinces, and the resort of the generality ;' from which time may be
dated the commencement of the persecution by the clergy and populace,
who supposed it to have a political tendency."

that kingdom had defended the lodges of Masons, and interested the court in their behalf, yet they were decreed to the same fate as in the United Provinces, by reason that under the pretence of the inviolable secrets of their Order, they might cover some dangerous design, which might in the end be to the disadvantage, not only of religion, but of the kingdom's peace.[11] But these days have been. At this time there are none so scrupulous, in regard to Masonry, as they were some years ago. It is known that the Prince of Conti, that illustrious hero, glories in having been made a Mason ; and that he sometimes lays aside his warlike habiliments, to wear the honest and humble apron, and work with surprising diligence and assiduity in carrying on the grand design.

The persecutions the Freemasons have undergone at Vienna might have passed unnoticed, as it was occasioned by the jealousy of some ladies belonging to the court, who having endeavoured, by various artful and crafty devices, to get some of their tools and agents into many of the lodges, though without any effect, they then attempted to inflame the mind of the empress-queen against the fraternity, and carried it so far with that princess, as to get an order for surprising them in all their lodges, to revenge themselves, in as open a manner as possible, for some affronts they imagined had been given them by the fraternity. But the success of their undertakings did not by any means answer the intentions of their diligence and industry ; for no less a person than his imperial majesty, the first Mason in Europe, instantly put a stop to all their proceedings, and declared himself ready to answer for their conduct,[12]

[11] At this period the Continent of Europe was over-run with infidelity. The court, the church, and every other class of society swarmed with Free-thinkers—and the tendency of some of the interpolated degrees, viz., the Elus, the Chevalier du Soleil, &c., gave rise to an opinion that Masonry was a system of infidelity. Hence, probably, arose the persecutions to which Freemasonry was exposed. In France Masonry was abolished in 1737, under the pretence that the inviolable secrets of the lodges might cover some dreadful design hostile to religion, and dangerous to the kingdom. These suspicions, however, were speedily removed, and the Order was restored to its former prosperity and splendour.

[12] That enlightened monarch, Joseph II., allowed the Freemasons every indulgence and privilege, restricting the number of lodges to three in large towns, but giving plain instructions to all departments in the state

and to redress any plea that could be alleged against them ;[13] but that the ladies or their abettors must find some better foundation for complaint, before he should enter into the merits of the cause, as what had already appeared was only falsehood and misrepresentation.

The court of Rome, instigated by the impositions of evil-minded persons, poured out its bulls and decrees against the Masons,[14] whereby they were condemned in a more severe and tyrannical manner—the peculiar characteristic of the inquisition—than they had ever yet undergone in any nation, and that without the least foundation for such proceedings, his holiness being utterly ignorant of what was so zealously to be interdicted. The words of the said bull, with the edict and decree

to assist and support the Freemasons. Affairs were altered, however, by his successors. The meetings were prohibited, and Francis II. requested all the German princes to do the same. The ambassadors of Hanover, Brunswick, and Prussia protested against it, saying that the emperor might do as he pleased in his own country, but beyond that he had no right to legislate. Austria complied with his requests; and every man officially employed was sworn that he was not, and never would become a member of the secret societies of Freemasons, Rosicrucians, Illuminati, or whatever other name they might bear. (Freemasons' Quarterly Review, 1844, p. 162.)

[13] The prayer of this excellent monarch on the present occasion is worthy of perusal, and may be found in the Freemasons' Quarterly Review, 1843, p. 472. It was taken from an old German work, and will well repay a perusal. In it he says, addressing the Deity—" I will try to be like thee, as far as human efforts can approach infinite perfection. I will be as indulgent, as thou art, to all men whose tenets differ from mine, and all unnatural compulsion, in point of conscience, shall be banished from my kingdom!"

[14] The republication of this tract will be extremely useful at the present period, when the absurd denunciations against Freemasonry have been repeated from authority. I subjoin an episcopal denunciation, extracted from the " Monita et Statuta," promulgated by the English vicars apostolic.—" We enjoin that the Catholics be warned against entering into the society of them who are vulgarly called Freemasons." This document was signed on the 4th May, 1838, by the bishops of Siga, of Cambysopolis, of Trachis, and of Olena. This was not enough for the latter, who, in April, 1842, promulgated an additional injunction, to be observed in the London district, declaring that " a confessor cannot lawfully or validly grant sacramental absolution to men belonging to the society of Freemasons, unless they absolutely, positively, and for ever, abandoned the aforesaid condemned society. This rule must be implicitly followed, where the penitent is avowedly associated with a body of Freemasons, or where, in confession, he declares himself to be a Freemason."

which followed, will best depicture the impure fountain they sprang from.[15]

"*The Condemnation of the Society of Conventicles De Liberi Muratori, or of the Freemasons, under the penalty of ipso facto Excommunication, the Absolution from which is reserved to the Pope alone, except at the point of Death.*

"CLEMENT BISHOP, SERVANT OF THE SERVANTS OF GOD, TO ALL THE FAITHFUL OF CHRIST, HEALTH AND APOSTOLICAL BENEDICTION.

" Placed (unworthy as we are), by the disposal of the divine clemency, in the eminent watch-tower of the apostleship, we are ever solicitously intent, agreeable to trust of the pastoral providence reposed in us, by obstructing the passages of error and vice, to preserve more especially the integrity of orthodox religion, and to repel, in these difficult times, all danger of trouble from the whole Catholic world.

" It has come to our knowledge, even from public

---

[15] " These bulls against Freemasonry," says Bro. O'Ryan, " are no more the law of the church of Rome, than the lunatic manifesto of Carnana of Malta is the production of the mind of either a scholar or a Christian. It should, however, be borne in mind, that Leo XII. used very strong measures to uproot a society, well known by the name of the Carbonari, whom many, most erroneously, confound with Freemasons, with whom they have nothing in common, save secrecy. The one is a society admitting its objects to be those of violence and blood, assuming as its war-cry, ' Revenge for the land crushed by the wolf,' and binding its members on admission to hatred to tyrants. The other enjoins obedience to law, human and divine, and inculcates charity. The one is confined to a particular locality, the other extends to every region of the civilized world ; the former aims at the infliction of vengeance on men for their evil actions, the latter seeks to unite the whole human family in a sublime and sacred bond of brotherhood, and endeavours not to encourage strife, but to promote benevolence. The Carbonari throughout Italy were visited by law with the punishment of death, at so late a period as 1821, while on the passing of an act to suppress secret societies in this country, the British parliament especially excepts Freemasons ; affording thereby a proof that their character as citizens, and their loyalty as subjects, are unquestioned. Now may it not be very probable, that this often-quoted bull is directed against the Carbonari, not the Freemasons? Admitting it, however, to be against the latter, it is but the opinion of one man, which cannot, contrary to the evidence of our senses, and the approval of our consciences, persuade us that that is criminal which we know full well to be righteous." (Intolerance, p. 53.)

report, that certain societies, companies, meetings, assemblies, clubs, or conventicles, commonly called De Liberi Muratori, or Freemasons, or by whatsoever other name the same in different languages are distinguished, spread far and wide, and are every day increasing ; in which persons, of whatever religion or sect, contented with a kind of an affected show of natural honesty, confederate together in a close and inscrutable bond, according to laws and orders agreed upon between them ; which likewise, with private ceremonies, they enjoin and bind themselves, as well by strict oath taken on the Bible, as by the imprecation of heavy punishments, to preserve with inviolable secrecy.

" We, therefore, revolving in our mind the great mischiefs which generally accrue from this kind of societies or conventicles, not only to the temporal tranquillity of the state, but to the spiritual health of souls ; and that, therefore, they are neither consistent with civil nor canonical sanctions ; since we are taught by the Divine Word to watch, like a faithful servant, night and day lest this sort of men break as thieves into the house, and, like foxes, endeavour to root up the vineyard ; lest they should pervert the hearts of the simple, and privily shoot at the innocent ; that we might stop up the broad way, which from thence would be laid open for the perpetration of their wickedness with impunity, and for other just and reasonable causes to us known, have by the advice of some of our venerable brethren of the Roman church, the cardinals, and of our own mere motion, and from our certain knowledge and mature deliberation, by the plentitude of the apostolical power, appointed and decreed to be condemned, and prohibited, and by this our present ever-valid constitution, we do condemn and prohibit the same societies, companies, meetings, assemblies, clubs, or conventicles, De Liberi Muratori, or Freemasons, or by whatever other name they are distinguished.

" Wherefore all and singular the faithful in Christ, of whatever state, degree, condition, order, dignity, and pre-eminence, whether laity or clergy, as well seculars as regulars, worthy all of express mention and enumeration, we strictly, and in virtue of holy obedience, command that no one, under any pretext or colour, dare or presume the aforesaid societies, De Liberi Muratori, or Freemasons, or by whatever other manner distinguished, to enter into, promote, favour, admit, or conceal in his or their houses, or elsewhere, or be admitted members of, or be present with the same, or be anywise aiding and assisting towards their meeting in any place ; or to administer anything to them, or in any manner publicly or privately, directly or indirectly, by themselves or others, afford them counsel, help, or favour ; or advise, induce, provoke, or persuade others to be admitted into, joined, or be present with this kind of societies, or in any manner aid and promote them ; but that they ought by all means to abstain from the said societies, companies, meetings, assemblies, clubs or conventicles, under the penalty of all that act contrary thereto, incurring excommunication *ipso facto*, without any other declaration ; from which no one can obtain the benefit of absolution from any other but us, or the Roman pontiff for the time being, except at the point of death.[16]

" We will moreover and command, that as well bishops and superior prelates, and other ordinaries of particular places, as the inquisitors of heretical pravity universally deputed, of what state, degree, condition, order, dignity, or pre-eminence soever, proceed and inquire, and restrain and coerce the same, as vehemently suspected of heresy, with condign punishment ; for to them, and each of them we hereby give and impart free power of proceeding, inquiring against, and of coercing and restraining with condign punishments, the same transgressors, and of calling in, if it shall be necessary, the help of the secular arm ; and we will that printed copies of these presents, signed by some notary public, and confirmed by the seal of some person of ecclesiastical dignity, shall be of the same authority as original let-

[16] Thus it appears that, except in danger of death, a confessor has not the power to absolve a penitent who is a Freemason without special permission from the pope. A confessor can absolve a penitent guilty of usury, adultery, murder, or any other crime, however heinous, provided he be contrite ; but if guilty of a breach of discipline by becoming a Freemason, from Rome only can absolution come ; the inference deducible therefrom being, that a breach of human discipline is an offence more aggravating than an actual violation of the commands of the Decalogue; and to disobey your fellow-man, is more criminal than to trample on the laws of the Deity !" (O'Ryan ut supra, p. 52.)

ters would be, if they were shown and exhibited. Let no one, therefore, infringe, or by rash attempt contradict this page of our declaration, damnation, command, prohibition, and interdict ; but if any one shall presume to attempt this, let him know that he will incur the indignation of Almighty God, and of the blessed apostles Peter and Paul.

"Dated from Rome at St. Mary's the Greater, in the year of the incarnation of our Lord 1738, the fourth of the calends of May (28th of April, N. S.) in the 8th of our pontificate.

A. CARD, Vice-Datary.

C. AMATUS, Vice-Secretary.

VISA DE CURIA N. ANTONELLUS.

The place + of the leaden seal.

I. B. EUGENIUS.

Registered in the Secretary of the Briefs Office, &c.

"In the above-mentioned day, month and year, the said condemnation was fixed up and published at the gates of the palace of the Sacred Office of the Prince of the Apostles, and in other usual and accustomed places of the city, by me, Peter Romolatius, Cursitor of the Most Holy Inquisition."

"EDICT.—*Joseph Cardinal Firrao, of the Title of St. Thomas in Parione, and of the Sacred Roman College Cardinal Priest.*

"Whereas, the holiness of our sovereign lord, Pope Clement XII. happily reigning, in his bull of the 28th of April last, beginning *In eminenti*, condemned, under pain of excommunication, reserved to himself, certain companies, societies, and meetings, under the title of Freemasons, more proper to be called conventicles, which, under the pretext of civil society, admit men of any sect and religion, with a strict tie of secrecy, confirmed by oath on the sacred Bible, as to all that is transacted or done in the said meetings and conventicles ; and whereas such societies, meetings, and conventicles, are not only suspected of occult heresy,[17] but even dangerous to public

----

[17] The above refers to the practice of the Rosicrucians, who had been admitted into the Order, and had succeeded in engrafting many of their conceits upon it ; taken from the elaborate cabalistical work of Studion,

peace, and the safety of the ecclesiastical state, since if they did not contain matters contrary to orthodox faith, to the state, and to the peace of the commonwealth, so many and strict ties of secrecy would not be required, as it is wisely taken notice of in the aforesaid bull; and it being the will of the holiness of our said lord, that such societies, meetings and conventicles totally cease and be dissolved, and that they who are not constrained by the fear of censures, be curbed at least by temporal punishments.

" Therefore, it is the express order of his holiness, by this edict to prohibit all persons, of any sex, state, or condition soever, whether ecclesiastical, secular, or regular, of whatever institute, degree, or dignity, though ordinarily or extraordinarily privileged, even such as require special and express mention to be made of them, comprehending the four legations of Bologna, Ferrara, Romagna Urbino, and the city and dukedom of Benevento; and it is hereby forbidden that any do presume to meet, assemble, or associate in any place under the said societies, or assemblies of Freemasons, or under any other title or cloak whatsoever, or even be present at such meetings and assemblies, under pain of death and confiscation of their effects, to be irremissibly incurred without hopes of grace.

" It is likewise prohibited, as above, to any person soever to seek or tempt any one to associate with any such societies, meetings, or assemblies, or to advise, aid, or abet to the like purpose the said meetings or assemblies, under the penalties abovesaid; and they who shall furnish or provide a house, or any other place, for such meetings or conventicles to be held, though under pretext of loan, hire, or any other contract soever, are hereby condemned, over and above the aforesaid penalties, to have the house, or houses, or other places where such meetings and conventicles shall be held, utterly erased and demolished; and it is his holiness's will, that to incur the abovesaid penalty of demolition, any human conjectures, hints, or presumptions, may, and shall suffice for a presumption

called " Naometria, or Temple Measuring; or, the Temple opened by the Key of David. Auctore Simone Studione inter Scorpiones. Anno 1604."

of knowledge in the landlords of such houses and places, without admission of any excuse soever.

" And because it is the express will of our said lord, that such meetings, societies, and conventicles do cease, as pernicious, and suspect of heresy and sedition, be utterly dissolved ; his holiness does hereby strictly order, that any persons, as above, who shall have notice for the future of the holding of the said meetings, assemblies, and conventicles, or who shall be solicited to associate with the same, or are in any manner accomplices or partakers with them, be obliged, under the fine of a thousand crowns in gold, besides other grievous corporal punishments—the gallies not to be excepted—to be inflicted at pleasure, to denounce them to his eminence, or to the chief magistrate of the ordinary tribunal of the cities. or other places in which the offence shall be committed, contrary to this edict ; with promise and assurance to such denouncers or informers, that they shall be kept inviolably secret and safe, and shall farther obtain grace and immunity, notwithstanding any penalty they themselves may or shall have incurred.

" And that no one may excuse himself from the obligation of informing under the borrowed pretext of natural secret, or the most sacred oath, or other stricter tie, by order of his said holiness, notice is hereby given to all, that such obligation of natural secret, or any sort of oath in criminal matters, and already condemned under pain of excommunication, as above, neither holds nor binds in any manner, being null, made void, and of no force, &c.

" It is our will that the present edict, when affixed in the usual places in Rome, do oblige and bind Rome and its district, and from the term of twenty days after, the whole ecclesiastical state, comprehending even the legations and cities of Bologna, Ferrara, and Benevento, in the same manner as if they had been personally notified to each of them. Given in Rome this 14th day of January, 1739.

JOSEPH, Cardinal Firrao.
JEROME DE BARDI, Secretary.

Rome, in the printing-office of the Reverend
       Apostolic Chamber. 1739."

Notwithstanding these abominable infractions upon human liberty, and being thus oppressed in the ecclesiastical state,[18] the fraternity found a safe refuge from time to time in many parts of Italy, who being better enlightened than those of Rome,[19] did not by any means oppose the spreading and propagating an art, founded on the most exalted maxims of sound morality, and which could not but tend to the greatest advantage of every kingdom.[20] The malicious reflections and invectives raised and spread against the Masons all over Europe, and with which they have been without mercy bespattered, and which would fill a volume, must be passed over in silence, to treat of matters that are of much greater consequence and nearer concern to the fraternity. At a time when they enjoyed peace and tranquillity in Switzerland to the utmost of their wishes, all at once a cloud arose in a certain quarter that threatened a heavy storm; nor less it was than to root out and extirpate the hitherto unshaken and im-

[18] The Roman Catholics were not generally satisfied of the policy, or even the justice of these arbitrary edicts. Dr. Doyle said, in his evidence before the House of Commons—"I should be satisfied that a sentence was just and lawful, before I would make myself an instrument in executing it; for they are guilty of death, says the Apostle, not only those who do evil, but those who consent to the doing of it; and if I become the pope's agent in pronouncing sentence of excommunication against a Christian not guilty of a crime, in my opinion, deserving it, I should be an accomplice in the pope's injustice."

[19] In the archives of the Grand Lodge of Scotland, is deposited an old parchment-bound minute book, with the following explanatory memorandum respecting the lodge at Rome in 1735. "Pope Clement XII. having published a most severe edict against Freemasonry, the last lodge held at Rome was on the 20th August, 1737, when the late Earl of Wintown was Master. The officer of the lodge, who was a servant of Dr. James Irvin, was sent, as a terror to others, prisoner to the Inquisition, but was soon released." See the whole account in the Freemasons' Quarterly Review, 1842, p. 393, where the transactions of this lodge are recorded.

[20] In Spain, however, these edicts excited a severe persecution of the fraternity. In 1742, the Inquisition of that country imprisoned Bro. Alexander James Mouton, a French Artist, and John Coustos, a native of Berne, in Switzerland, for being Freemasons; the father of the latter came into England in 1716, and was naturalized. The crimes brought against them by that horrid Inquisition were, that they had infringed the pope's orders, by their belonging to the sect of Freemasons; which sect was a horrid compound of sacrilege, unnatural, and other abominable crimes; of which the inviolable secresy observed therein, and the exclusion of women, were but too manifest indications; a circumstance that gave the highest offence to the whole kingdom. See Chap. IV. of the present volume.

moveable foundations of Masonry, and at once to over
throw the superb structure that .had been erecting for
many ages.[21]   This must be farther, and more at large,
explained for the benefit of those who are not already
acquainted with the facts.   None can be ignorant that,
after the example of France and Holland, the Swiss cantons received the Masons amongst them, and afforded
them treatment equal to their merit.[22]   The eagerness
with which all ranks of people applied themselves to
what might aggrandize that illustrious body, has served
as a pattern for all other nations in Europe. who value
themselves for their brightness of understanding, or love
for the liberal arts.   What fatal destiny, what fanatical
fury, could transport the magistrates of Berne to become
the enemies of Masonry—the enemies of a society who
had never done them wrong, or impeached of one unworthy deed ?   Is it then that innocence, capable everywhere of curbing the fiercest and most malignant dispositions, can make no impression upon the callous hearts
of those sage republicans?   No; the cruel prejudices
with which they armed themselves against the noble
craft, has caused them to publish an ordonnance for their
abolition, containing assertions as unjust as ill-founded
against the society of Freemasons, "who had slyly and
artfully crept into that country."   On reading this, who
could restrain the fervency and zeal with which he must
be inflamed for the honour and glory of this ancient and
venerable society?   This it was that led the writer of
this little Essay to make all possible efforts for their defence, by imparting to the public some reflections by way
of apology for the Masons, upon their being so violently
attacked by the magistrates of Berne.   But that the

[21] The first lodge in Switzerland was founded at Geneva, in 1737; the
second in Lausanne, by a warrant from the Duke of Montague, in 1739.
which was subsequently made the Grand Lodge. Accession to Freemasonry was forbidden ; but no particular regard was paid to the decree at
present ; but it operated as a clog upon the craft, and prevented, to a
certain extent, the dissemination of its principles.
[22] And this might, as it should appear, be done safely when the King
of Prussia was the avowed protector of the Masons of Germany, and the
reigning Duke of Brunswick their Grand Master ; the Princes of Lunen-
burg, Hesse Cassel, &c., Prov. Grand Masters in Denmark, Hamburgh,
&c.; and H. R. H. Joseph, Duke of Courland, protector of the Masons
there.

several articles of this ordonnance may by the reader be
better examined one by one, and by which he will be the
better enabled to judge the force of the reasons made use
of against it, made it necessary to insert the said ordonnance here at length, not deviating in the least from the
original.   It is set forth in these words :—

We the advoyer, the little and great council of the
city and republic of Berne, make known to all men by
these presents :   Having learnt that a certain society,
called Freemasons, spreads itself every day more and
more into all the cities and towns under our government,
and that the persons who have joined the said society
are received under various solemn engagements, and even
by oath.   Wherefore, having seriously reflected upon
the consequences thereof, and considered that such meetings and associations are directly contrary to the fundamental laws and constitutions of our country, and in
particular to the protection required on our part to dis-
countenance any assemblies under our government,
without our knowledge and express permission ; moreover it has appeared to us, that if an effectual remedy
was not immediately taken, the consequence of that
neglect might be dangerous to the state.   For these reasons, and through our paternal affection as much for the
public good as the private advantage of all our citizens
and subjects, we have found it absolutely necessary to
dissolve and totally abolish the said society, which we
do by these presents ; and henceforth for ever we forbid,
annul, and abolish it in all our territories and districts,
to all persons that now are, or shall hereafter come into
our dominions: and we do in the first place ordain and
decree, that all those, our citizens and subjects, who are
actually known to be Freemasons, shall be obliged immediately to abjure, by oath, the engagements they have
taken in the said society, before the bailiff or officer of
the district where they live, without delay.   And as to
our citizens and subjects who actually are. Freemasons,
and not publicly known to be such, and who, nevertheless, at present reside in our dominions, or may hereafter
come under our obedience, our sovereign will and pleasure is, that those who shall be found in our dominions
shall be bound to renounce their obligation in the space
4

of one month from the date hereof; and those who are
absent must submit to the same terms, to be reckoned
from the day of their return, not only to accuse themselves, but to abjure and renounce their engagements,
those who present themselves in our capital city, to the
reigning Advoyer, and in other cities, and in the country, to the bailiff of the place; and from them they shall
receive assurance of safety to their persons, if they abjure
and renounce their obligations without delay, in the same
form as all other Masons are obliged to do.

Upon failure in any part hereof, they shall all undergo
the punishment hereafter declared. But to the end that
no person shall dare, for the time to come, to entice,
tempt, solicit, or be so enticed, tempted, or solicited, to
engage him, or themselves, into this same society of
Freemasons, we have thought fit to ordain and decree as
follows :

That all those Masons who shall hold their assemblies
in our dominions, or who shall entice, tempt, or solicit
others into their associations, as well as all our citizens
and subjects in our dominions, and elsewhere, as also
those who have been set at liberty, shall for the future
frequent such assemblies, they shall all and every of
them be subjected to the fine of one hundred crowns,
without remission ; and likewise be deprived of whatever place, trust, benefit, or employment, he shall now
hold ; and if they have no present employment or office,
shall be rendered incapable of holding any such for the
time to come.

And touching the place or lodge where this kind of
assemblies are held for the future, the person or persons
who shall let or furnish them with a house, room, or
place, for the holding of such lodge, shall be subjected
to the same fine of one hundred crowns; one-third of
which to the informer, one-third to the bailiff of the
place, and one-third to the hospitals, or fund of the poor,
where such assembly shall be held. Let it be well understood that all offenders who shall leave our dominions,
in order to satisfy the payment of the said fine, shall be
banished from our dominions for ever, or till they shall
have paid the said fine, and shall not return again till
they have paid it, upon pain of death. We moreover
reserve, at pleasure, to punish with more or less rigour,

according to the case of the person so rendering himself up to our sovereign pleasure, or those who, notwithstanding their abjuration, shall have again entered into the society, or frequent any of their assemblies.

We do finally ordain and command, that all our bailiffs and ministers of justice do cause these presents to be published in all churches, and to be fixed up in the accustomed places, and see that these, our commands, are strictly and faithfully executed.

Given in our great council the 3rd of March, 1745.

It is not intended to assert that princes have not the right to forbid their subjects from entering into any society or community, but really to show the contrary by unexceptionable arguments. All sovereigns have the authority to determine the actions of their subjects, provided they are by a necessity, as well natural as moral, or by the fundamental laws of the place, capable of an obvious determination. The exercise of Masonry, then, comes not under the number of those determinable actions, which, by necessity or fundamental laws, are exempted from the sovereign authority. Princes may act as they think fit with respect to the exercise of Masonry; yet let it be well noticed, that what is here asserted will oftener accord with the absolute power of a sovereign than with the common and natural rights of mankind and strict justice, which are frequently of a direct contrary tendency. The ordonnance of the Canton of Berne is not to be attacked on the side of sovereign power, but in the unjust motives, suppositions, and groundless imputations, that occasioned the over-hasty magistrates to accomplish the extirpation of the fraternity. This event has, however, answered one salutary end of clearing up the integrity of the Masons, and setting their innocence and sufferings, their noble and unexceptionable demeanour, and other their admirable deeds, in a proper point of view; which shining merits, it should have been thought, might have produced the highest praise, instead of unworthy and unjustifiable reproach.[23] The ordonnance sets forth " that if an effec-

---

[23] A writer in the Freemasons' Quarterly Review, (Sit Lux) under date 1845, very truly says: " In the present day we are looked upon with a

tual remedy was not immediately taken, the consequence
of that neglect might be dangerous to the state." Is it
possible that the clear-sighted republicans of Berne could
discover such gross ignorance, and afford their countenance and attention to the mean and base surmises everywhere industriously propagated and served up to the
higher powers against the Masons? What dangerous
consequence could ensue if they were not afraid of the
fraternity's stirring up sedition and rebellion against the
government? The supposition is worthy the supposers.
The abolishing of supreme power, let it be exercised by
whomsoever it will—by kings, or by particular persons,
lords or magistrates, invested with sovereign power,
could tend to no other end than subverting all order in
civil society, create confusion, and involve the country
in destruction. The state or government, say the enemies of Masonry, ought to examine narrowly into and
abolish the fraternity, because it spreads all over the
world, and its members are united by obligations, so
much the more strong and durable, as they are the less
exposed to open day and vulgar eyes; a word can call
them together; wound one, and you maim the whole
body; one common interest unites them all as Brethren.
Their mysteries must then cover some scheme for a revolution, which must be prevented. As they profess an
indiscriminate obedience to their Grand Master and his
officers,[24] all the world is threatened with being reduced

considerable degree of shyness by the Romish church, and indeed are
openly denounced by some of their clergy as an unchristian body; while
in old times the fraternity was chiefly composed of Roman Catholics;
and it is to them we are indebted for those specimens of ancient architecture now remaining, the principle of which style of building was confined
to themselves, and in my opinion formed one of the great secrets preserved
among Masons, and the knowledge of which Sir C. Wren acknowledged
to have been lost even in his day. That peculiar style of ecclesiastical
architecture, the knowledge of which was formerly confined to our ancient
Brethren, contained a secret reference to the doctrine of the cross, and
the mystery of the Trinity; and yet, strange to say, we, who as an Order
are descended from those ancient Brethren. are now denounced as anti-
christian; and our system as unholy, though we contend that it is founded
on the purest principles of piety and virtue." There is a great deal of
truth in these observations; and they are fully exemplified in the "Apology for the Freemasons," published by Bro. Spencer in 1846.
  [24] MAGISTER was the original term universally applied to an architect,
and which, in distinction to his small band of associated Masons, was
continued to the latest period. Thus, Alexander de Berneval was Maitre

to slavery and bondage by them, if they are not immediately extirpated without distinction. Every one will readily perceive the folly and impertinence of these frivolous and pitiful suggestions, as it requires but a small portion of common sense to discern both their malice and ignorance.[25]

If the conduct of the fraternity be examined in every place where they have yet been established, it is utterly impossible to suppose Masonry so pernicious or so destructive in its designs and tendency; and to have nothing in view but the subversion of the civil power, which they are ready to own comes directly from Almighty God.[26] How can it be thought credible that

des œuvres de Maçonrie, at the cathedral at Rouen. *Depositor operum*, literally, he who lays a foundation or gives a plan. The generic word was Cæmentarius, which, or Magister lapidum, was used by the earliest Italian writers upon architecture. In the epitaph of the Master Mason of the abbey of Caen, in Normandy, he is styled "*Gulielmus jacet Petrarum summus in arte;*" and in St. Michael's Church, at St. Albans—"T. Wolvey, *Latomus summus in arte,*" &c. Latomus or Lithotomus is, literally, Stonehewer *(Lapicida)*, and differs in some degree from Cæmentarius; the first-mentioned is a rough Mason or E. A. P., the other squared and polished the blocks of stone or ashlars, being the Fellow-crafts.

[25] This, however, has been the uniform course adopted by bigots and tyrants. The mysteries of Freemasonry were the object of suspicion. It was this which induced Trajan to reject the advice of Pliny, when he recommended colleges or lodges of Masons to be formed for rebuilding the city of Nicodemia, which had been burnt down. Pliny says, (Epist. xlii.)—"Tu Domine despice, an instituendum putes, Collegium Fabrorum, duntaxat hominum cl.; ego attendam ne quis nisi Faber recipiatur, neve jure concesso, in aliud utatur. Nec erit difficile custodire tam paucos." The emperor refuses for this extraordinary reason—"Sed meminerimus provinciam istam et præcipue eas civitates, ab *ejusmodi factionibus esse vexatas.*"

[26] Nothing can show the absurd pretences which were resorted to for persecution more than the following anecdote, taken from the Freemasons' Lexicon :—"Aix-la-Chapelle is remarkable for a persecution of the Freemasons in 1779. A Dominican monk, named Ludwig Greinemaun, a lecturer on theology, endeavoured to prove, by a course of sermons preached during Lent, that the Jews who crucified our Saviour were Freemasons; that Pilate and Herod were the Wardens of a Masons' Lodge; that Judas, before he betrayed his Master, was initiated in the Synagogue; and that when he returned the thirty pieces of silver, he did no more than pay the fees for initiation into the Order. The magistrates, to quiet the commotion raised among the people by these discourses, published a decree, which provided that " if any one shall offer a refuge in his house to the Freemasons, or allow them to assemble there, he shall be punished for the first offence with a fine of one hundred florins; for the second offence, two hundred florins; and for the third offence, with perpetual banishment from the city and its territories."

they should admit not only magistrates, but noblemen, great princes, and even crowned heads, to the mysteries of an Order, the end of which was only to subvert and destroy their power? Can such a thought as this enter into the mind of a man endowed with one grain of common sense? It is not to be found in the earliest histories from the first establishment of Masonry to this day, that they ever bore a part in the intrigues and troubles that have been the forerunners of most cruel revolutions in many kingdoms and states of the world.[27] Even in England, a kingdom of all others the most subject to these convulsions, the fraternity always appeared with the greatest lustre and glory; yet such was the decorum they observed there, that none can discern the least shadow or pretence that might cause them to be suspected of what is called in that renowned island, " party faction," a thing directly contrary to the preservation and continuance of that sacred tie which unites them all upon their becoming Brethren. From the same motives it is that they are enjoined in all their assemblies on no account to speak of political affairs,[28] not only that no umbrage may be given to the civil powers, but that no dissensions of that kind may arise in the lodges, which

[27] The earliest charge to a newly-initiated Brother which I have met with, contains the following extract on the above subject. It was used before 1730; and is valuable on account of its antiquity, and because it shows the ancient creed of a Mason respecting his conduct as a member of civil society:—" Brethren, you are now admitted, by the unanimous consent of our lodge, a fellow of our most ancient and honourable society; ancient, as having subsisted from times immemorial; and honourable, as tending in every particular to render a man so, that will be but conformable to its glorious precepts. The greatest monarchs in all ages, as well of Asia and Africa as of Europe, have been encouragers of the royal art; and many of them have presided as Grand Masters over the Masons in their respective territories, not thinking it any lessening to their imperial dignities to level themselves with their Brethren in Masonry, and to act as they did."

[28] The very foundation principle of Masonry is the exclusion of religion and politics; because the lodges ought to admit men of all religious and political opinions. To exclude them would be a species of intolerance as bad as that which prompted the papal persecutions of the Order. It is equally inconsistent with the tenets of our profession, and at variance with the ancient landmarks of the Order, which all unite to conciliate true friendship amongst the members of the masonic family, and to embrace men of every country, sect, and opinion, who have been initiated into its mysteries.

have sown the seeds of discord and hatred among the most intimate friends. Against this, the oath they take is so sacred, that it is held as the most heinous crime to violate it. Who can suspect the Masons of engaging in plots which rarely have ended but by bringing the most flourishing kingdoms to the brink of destruction? Surely neither the religion nor policy of a state or kingdom had so often been shaken, or such seas of blood been spilt, if those who govern had been Masons, or at least had put in practice what they account as a crime. Far from degrading the authority of sovereigns, the Masons always have been, and ever will be, faithful, steady, and zealous defenders of it.[29]

From what has been said, it must appear plainly to all that will throw aside partiality and imaginary prejudices, that the grave magistrates of Berne have been the most mistaken of any people in the world in the pretensions of their ordonnance, to think that any dangerous consequences could accrue to them from the assemblies of the Masons—a society which has no other intentions than to promote peace, love, union, and harmony among all men;[30] and who might have flattered themselves, not only with being cordially received, but protected in every state, as they propagated nothing but what would make every one happy who is willing to be so. Another article of the ordonnance runs thus : " All those who are actually known for Freemasons, shall be obliged to abjure by oath the engagements they have taken in the said society." This matter must be closely examined, to see if the gentlemen of Berne had a right to push their ill-will to this great extremity, and to oblige their

[29] Smith's " Use and Abuse of Freemasonry" was dedicated to the King of Prussia, where we find him saying—" As the author had the honour to learn the first rudiments of war in your majesty's service, during seven instructive campaigns, and is connected with some of the most ancient and noble families in the Prussian dominions. is thereby induced to offer this work as a tribute of his unfeigned duty and respect to the greatest of kings, to the most valiant of heroes, the greatest philosopher, poet, and politician the world ever beheld."

[30] Masonry expands itself, says a celebrated writer of the last century, over the whole universe ; and as " it shines refulgent by the splendour of its buildings, and the excellence of its work, let Masons also shine as lights of the world by their virtue, their benevolence, their charity. As the walls of a lodge circumscribe the social band, let friendship unite our hearts by every virtuous tie; so that our Order may be for ever established in truth and righteousness."

subjects to take this unheard-of step, and accuse themselves, which will appear the more violent from the considerations that follow.

The reception or initiation of a new brother is, by an express agreement, made between the Master of the lodge and the person who requests to be admitted. By this agreement or compact, not only the lodge of which he is Master, but also the whole Order of Freemasons, acquire a well-grounded right, which obliges this new-made Brother to an exact and faithful observance of the laws of the fraternity, and to set his hand thereto ; and also not to commit any action that may ever so remotely tend to the discredit or disgrace of the fraternity in general. This no prince or magistrate would ever have known, and therefore could not have deprived them of; but that the exercise of Masonry not being before interdicted, enjoying, not only in Berne, but in other parts of Switzerland, perfect liberty and freedom, rendered it of no moment to make public. The subjects, in becoming Masons, have not done anything contrary to the laws of the country under which they live, and, of course, cannot, with the least appearance of justice, be taxed or punished at all, not having committed any crime. But to force a Mason to abjure by oath the solemn and harmless engagements he has entered into by his own free choice, and without solicitation, would be the most shameful breach of human liberty, the severest infliction, and greatest disgrace that ever befel a Mason. No, death itself would be more welcome to him than to be necessitated to commit so base and foul an action. And surely it may be inferred that the magistrates of Berne can never be so cruel as to attempt putting this infernal article into execution, it not being more contradictory to natural justice than to the sacred observance and only tie among men—an oath.

It may be deemed superfluous to say that a voluntary renunciation is the most ridiculous thing that could be required of a Mason. It is nevertheless set forth that they are not only to accuse themselves, but in consequence of that accusal or renunciation, they must abjure their engagements without delay.[31] A voluntary renun-

[31] Plutarch relates that during the persecutions of the Pythagorean Order, when the members were banished, a few secretly assembled in a

ciation is acknowledging they have done wrong, or that they have offended against some laws of the country. Therefore, in order to induce the Masons to confess that they are in the wrong, the Canton of Berne must prove the rectitude of their proceedings from laws of more ancient date than their said gracious ordonnance, which they never will be able to do.

" But to the end that no person should dare to enter into the society of Freemasons, we ordain," &c.

That is to say, the magistrates of Berne having been so grievously misinformed of the real end and designs of the fraternity, not to know what was most for their welfare ; because by their ordonnance they have destroyed the endeavours which only tended to make their subjects happy. Jealousy and envy have taken absolute possession of the hearts of these republicans, and carry with them a most cruel characteristic, because they sacrificed an advantage worthy of being envied, and which many other provinces received with open arms. They have strove hard that the happy effects attending their subjects should be enjoyed by strangers. Instead of repining at their conduct, the fraternity, without regret, left this savage and scabby country—the frightful mountains, and dreadful precipices—to procure to themselves a more delightful and pleasant retreat, where they may enjoy the delights of Masonry, true peace, and the good things of this life, without discontent or persecution.[32]

It is grievous to be obliged to make these gentle and condescending reflections ; but they are our enemies, have put the sword into our hands, and the law of nature directs every man to defend himself, when he is unjustly

house at Metapontum, when the inhabitants, in their bigotted fury, set fire to the house, and destroyed them all except two, who, being young and active, escaped through the fire. One of them fled to the Lucanians, where he collected a strong party ; they vanquished their persecutors, and re-established their society.

[32] It does not appear that they were absolutely safe even in other parts of the world ; for Major Françoise d'Alincourt, in 1767, a French gentleman, and Don Oyres de Ornellas Praçao, a Portuguese nobleman, were sent to prison by the governor of the island of Madeira for being Freemasons. They were sent to Lisbon as prisoners, and confined in a common goal for fourteen months ; where they would absolutely have perished, had not the brethren at Lisbon generously supported them, and by their intercession with Don Martinio de Mello they were at last released.

4*

attacked. The liberty we profess and avow makes us look upon the assults of these miscreants with contempt; all the revenge we seek, for the injurious reflections they cast upon us, is to demean ourselves everywhere, so as to gain the esteem of all who choose to be guided by sound reason. There really is very little in the pompous ordonnance worthy of notice, but what vanishes in smoke, unless the swaggering title seems to tell you the contrary. Should it not seem to be a work of more than ordinary wisdom against the Masons, since the magistrates of Berne were so good as to let the world know they had condemned what they never either saw or knew, that is to say, a true description of Masonry, and a picture of a real Mason ?[33] They must then be indulged; it is to be hoped they will not be offended at having the portrait of a Mason drawn for them, to convince them, if possible, of the error into which they have unfortunately plunged themselves. But, having in the beginning of these reflections given a distant view of Masonry, we shall here trace out its effects upon the conduct of human life. It always affords inward peace, but a peace not in the least tending to a careless inactivity; it is productive of the best actions, preserving such an evenness and tranquillity, under all discouraging events, as places them far above the little trifling incidents that affect the human race in their pursuits after happiness. They know that bitterness and remorse of conscience ever attend the doing wrong, and are the greatest reproach to the probity they have ever maintained, and, therefore, endeavour to enlarge the good conduct they so rigidly impose, to avoid reproach from their enemies, and to show that the practice of real goodness is the only thing that can make a good and true Mason. They are taught to hope mo-

---

[33] Masonry now flourishes among the Protestants of this country, and it has a Grand Lodge called "The National Lodge of Switzerland," which has issued a book of ceremonies, drawn up in the true spirit of Masonry, although containing some errors. It is called "The Helvetian Ceremonies of Masons, said to come from Egypt." And it commences thus :—" Master Masons will know that in this ritual there are none of our mysteries ; the book is intended to assist Masters of lodges in solemn days and great ceremonies of Freemasonry ; as also to instruct them in some things of importance for the external dignity of the craft. On the 2nd of June, 1847, a representative of the Grand Lodge of Switzerland was formally introduced to the Grand Lodge of England

derately, to suffer patiently, to take pleasure in what
they enjoy, to hope for little, and that little to be need-
ful. Their duty is their good-will to mankind; and they
live not so much for themselves as for others; their es-
chewing evil and doing good exalts their understandings,
renders pleasure more pleasurable, and makes them more
happy in happiness, and less miserable in trouble.[34] In a
word, if truly noble institutions, backed with all the
force and strength of reason and refined taste, if that
which is solidly happy, and truly virtuous, deserves any
praise, they have a just claim to it, in spite of the dirty
efforts of those mean and wicked persons, the fautors of
falsehood, who are eternally exclaiming against the vices,
the passions, and imperfections of men, and are the first
to commit what they condemn, though under the covering of puritanical sanctity.

Masonry is the daughter of heaven; and happy are
those who embrace her! By it, youth is passed over
without agitation, the middle age without anxiety, and
old age without remorse. Masonry teaches the way to
content—a thing almost unknown to the greatest part of
mankind. In short, its ultimate result is to enjoy in
security the things that are; to reject all meddlers in state
affairs or religion, or of a trifling nature; to embrace
those of real moment, and worthy tendency, with fervency and zeal unfeigned, as sure of being unchangeable,
as ending in happiness. They are rich without riches,
intrinsically possessing all desirable good; and, in short,
have the less to wish for, by the enjoyment of what they
have. Liberty, peace, and tranquillity are the only
objects worth their efforts, trouble, and diligence. Un-
discerning mortals think to procure these by heaping up
riches; and riches are the only obstacles against what
they, with so much diligence and industry, desire to attain.
What is more common than to see men argue less reasonably, when they pretend to have most reason? Is it reasonable to be exclaiming at all times, and in all places,
against the fickleness and instability of fortune, making

[34] Shakespeare well described the influence of Masonry on the human
heart, when he put into the mouth of Hamlet these noble ideas :—" What
a piece of work is man! how noble in reason! how infinite in faculty!
in form and moving how express and admirable! in action how like an
angel! in apprehension how like a god!"

idle and impertinent reflections on past events, and either
give themselves up to continual murmuring for the present, or to the most frightful apprehensions for the time
to come? The reasonable man, it may be said the good
Mason, is contented in his situation, finds his temper
sweetened, and his manners refined, happy in the time
present, and thinks of the time to come without any
dread of it; he knows so well how to enjoy it, as not to
be led away with empty and vague pursuits; instead of
troubling the public with his thoughts and reflections,
he only studies to accomplish the desirable end of public
utility, by privately inculcating every necessary duty.
He chooses a way of life suited to his fortune, makes
choice of friends conformable to his own character; and
by acting thus, he gives no mean proof of his wisdom
and taste of true virtue, so much talked of, and so seldom
found among those mean and gloomy souls, who think
that the greatest piety consists in making scruples of all
kinds, in having the holy leer and hypocritical cant of a
strait-laced Christian, who, not having discernment enough
to see anything as it should be, would represent Almighty
God like themselves, for ever with the brand of destruction in his hand.[35]

The Masons detest this infernal spirit, wishing nothing
but peace and union to all mankind, which, together
with the rectitude of their lives, enables them to hope
for all the peace and rest that is to come. Strict among
themselves, not judging the faults of others, regular and
attentive to all necessary duties, modest in prosperity,
calm in adversity, always as ready to be taught as to

---

[35] Capt. Smith, who wrote in 1783, says:—"This general diffusion of
masonic knowledge is one effect of that happy constitution of government,
which, towards the close of the last century, was confirmed to us, and
which constitutes the peculiar glory of the nation. In other countries
the great body of the people possess little wealth, have little power, and,
consequently meet with little respect; except among the extensive body of
Freemasons, who are not only a most respectable community, but are universally esteemed in all foreign parts; in Great Britain the people are opu-
lent, have great influence, and claim, of course, a proper share of attention,
except among the society, where very little regard is paid them, owing to
their inferior rank in life and abilities. To their improvement in the
masonic art, therefore, men of letters have lately directed their studies;
as the great body of Masons, no less than the dignified, the learned, or the
wealthy few, have an acknowledged title to be amused and instructed."

teach another, equally incapable of all baseness, ill-grounded complaints, and, above all things, of offending a Brother, speaking well of him, both publicly and privately, doing all things according to the strictest justice. Such is the true Mason! such Masonry, it may be hoped not only in Switzerland, but everywhere upon the face of the earth, where that noble society is entertained![36] O glorious architecture! which never fails amply to recompense all who attach themselves to thee. O delightful society! no greater liberty can be on earth than in thee, nor truer peace and content than under thy banners.[37]

One of the noblest qualifications belonging to Masons, and the innocent cause of all the persecutions and reproaches they have suffered, is secrecy. Certain it is, that in conducting all worldly affairs, secrecy is not only essential, but absolutely necessary. The Italian proverb says—" If you would live well and enjoy peace, you must be deaf and dumb." The chief aim and principle of the famous philosopher Pythagoras was to bridle the tongue. We read that Demosthenes, who was an orator and philosopher of exemplary life and great authority, among his many good qualities was guilty of talking too

[36] This hope has been gloriously fulfilled. In 1803 Masonry was revived in Switzerland. Berne took the lead by opening the Lodge of Hope, under the authority of France; which was subsequently deputed to consecrate lodges at Lausanne, Basle, Solothun, and other places. This induced the formation of the Grand Orient of the National Roman Helvetique, under Grand Master Glayre, who, many years ago, had restored Freemasonry in Poland. In 1811, the Orient of Zurich made its appearance in Basle, but returned very soon after to its original position. Lodges were also opened in 1818, under the English constitutions; and the Duke of Sussex appointed Bro. Von Tavel the Provincial Grand Master.

[37] I have much pleasure in quoting some judicious remarks of a very worthy and intelligent brother, William Tucker, Esq., of Coryton Park, Provincial Grand Master for Dorset, in a speech at Weymouth, August, 1846. He said:—" As the sacrifices of the ancient Jews pointed to that great atonement whereby man became reconciled to God; so the mysteries of Masonry direct the inquiring mind to that period when the sun of righteousness shall arise, and, with healing on His wings, dispel the mists which overshadow the nations of the earth, and the Trinity in unity shall be universally acknowledged and adored. And as the principles of our ancient institution, in the earlier days, prepared the mind for the reception of this great truth; so will the mind now be improved by the moral influence of those principles, and rendered fit for the enjoyment of the full blaze of light, when it shall be revealed in all its majesty and glory."

much, which obliged the Athenians, one day assembled in council, to assign him a pension, not for him to teach philosophy, but to make him hold his tongue, in order that his chattering might not do more mischief, and create more misunderstandings, than the citizens of Athens could ever rectify. Princes, states, and republics ought, then, to esteem it a blessing to have their subjects complete masters over that unruly member, the tongue. In the affairs of council, silence is of the utmost importance. It were to be wished that all ministers of state would practise this excellent virtue. That royal art not only faithfully teaches how to conceal what is properly called a secret, but also to be so discreet in all words and actions, that none shall think it to be so, or they cannot in order thereto walk worthily by the square and compass.[38]

Most of the sovereign princes of Europe, and especially those of England and Germany, have admitted the fraternity under their protection, and do not refuse what in justice they deserve, encouragement and countenance to all who profess it in their kingdoms;[39] several of them

---

[38] A memorable instance of this discretion, even under the most painful circumstances, is recorded in the Freemasons' Quarterly Review, 1839. During the rebellion in Ireland, it will be recollected the Habeas Corpus Act was suspended, and many scenes of violence occurred. One of the means employed to extract information from their prisoners was by flogging. A Freemason of good character was once unfortunately brought before Major Sandes, on the charge of being privy to some misdeeds committed by others; and as nothing could be extracted from him by common examination, he was ordered to be tied up to the halberts. It was in vain that he protested his innocence; and therefore he appealed to the Deity, in a manner known only to the true craftsman, exclaiming :—" is it possible that an innocent man should thus suffer !" The major, who was a Mason, immediately understood him, and said—" Confound you, why did you not tell me *that* before ?" He immediately countermanded the punishment, and a very few minutes' conversation in private satisfied him of his innocence, and procured his release.

[39] Freemasonry had declined in England from the time of the commonwealth ; for it received a great blow and discouragement during the civil wars. And whether these unholy dissensions disunited the ties by which the fraternity were cemented, and thus caused the lodges to disperse ; or whether Cromwell, as has been confidently asserted, used it to promote his own designs, the result was the same. The general Grand Lodge at York never effectually resumed its functions as the head of the Order ; and though the lodges held their meetings during the reigns of Charles II. and the Jameses, yet no quarterly communications were convened from the above period till a Grand Lodge was formed in the metropolis in 1717.

have not disdained to become of the fraternity, and labour jointly with their subjects in erecting the edifice which was so happily begun. This shows itself from the prodigious number of lodges spread all over the world. Not to be confined to those of England and France, which are almost numberless, it will be sufficient here to mention the surprising progress that Masonry has made in Germany.[40] The Germans being naturally teachable, and strongly addicted to perfect themselves in all arts and sciences, it is no wonder then that the fraternity have met with so many zealous advocates amongst them. At Berlin, Masonry is advanced to the highest pitch of splendour and glory,[41] supported by the generous protection, and all necessary aid, from his majesty the King of Prussia.[42] The Masons assemble there four times

A French writer gives the following account of the use which Cromwell is alleged to have made of Masonry. After ascribing its invention to that regicide for the purpose of overturning the altar and the throne, he goes on to say :—"It was to complete the resemblance that Cromwell created the different classes of the society, and attached to each certain secret ceremonies, which were explained to the candidate as he advanced from the lower to the higher degrees, in order to preserve the Order in its purity, and to concentrate within his own influence a crowd of devoted men. The oath which he exacted from every candidate was the wonderful means he made use of, which was constructed according to the degree of knowledge that was attached to each particular step."

[40] In Germany there is no uniform system of Masonry practised at present. The Order, under one form or another, flourishes abundantly; but the rituals vary in different states, and under different Grand Lodges; and a section is now under a cloud with the rest of the masonic world, by reason of its refusal to admit Jewish Masons as visitors in its lodges.

[41] At present there are in Berlin three Grand Lodges; that of the Three Globes, which is the oldest, and is said to have been founded by Frederick the Great. The Royal York Grand Lodge, which was established by Brethren from France; and here the late Duke of York was initiated while on his travels; whence the name, for it was previously called St. John's Lodge l'Amitie aux trois Colombes. And the Native Grand Lodge, founded in 1773, by two Brethren who split off from the Grand Lodge of the Three Globes. They adopted the system of Zinnendorff, and worked also in the higher degrees.

[42] The initiation of this prince is thus noticed by Campbell, in his work entitled, "Frederick the Great and his Times:"—"One day, at table, the conversation turned upon Freemasons, against whom Frederick launched out with great acrimony. The Count of Lippe Buckeburg, himself a member of the fraternity, defended it with such warmth and eloquence, that the prince afterwards privately intimated to the count his wish to join a society which numbered such staunch champions of truth amongst its members. The count accordingly requested some of the Brethren residing at Hamburg and Hanover to meet at Brunswick, for the purpose

every month, and work the lodge alternately in French
and German. The grand entertainment which the Masons gave at Berlin in the year 1743, is a proof to all
Europe of the great regard paid to that venerable body
by the nobility, gentry, and all ranks and degrees of persons. The cities of Hamburg,[43] Leipsic,[44] Dresden, Bres-
lau, Halle, and Vienna, have proved safe asylums for the
illustrious Brotherhood, and in spite of what happened in
the latter, the Order is still supported under the auspi
cious government of his imperial majesty.

His Serene Highness the Margrave of Brandenburg
Bareith, in the year 1741, established a lodge in the
place of his residence; and the inauguration was celebrated with amazing pomp and magnificenc. At Frankfort on the Maine is the great lodge of the Union,[45]
composed of the most noble personages; and at this
time there is one of equal dignity established at Marburg,
in Hesse-Cassel. The fraternity had a lodge constituted
at Brussels in 1743, and called it the Equity; they
caused a medal to be struck, which represented on one

of the initiation. The celebrated Brother Bielefeld was of the number.
When the preparations were fully made, the prince royal arrived, accompanied by Count Wartensleben, a captain in the king's regiment at Pots-
dam. The prince introduced him to us as a candidate, whom he very
warmly recommended, and begged that he might be admitted immediately
after himself. At the same time he desired that he might be treated like
any private individual, and that none of the usual ceremonies might be
altered on his account. Accordingly, he was admitted in the customary
form; and I could not sufficiently admire his fearlessness, his composure,
and his address. When all was over, the prince returned to the ducal
palace, apparently as well pleased with us as we were charmed with him."
[43] The Grand Lodge of Hamburg is one of the most ancient lodges in
Germany, and was formed in 1733 by a warrant obtained in London.
They have, however, changed the English ritual for that of Schræder.
Its independence was acknowledged in 1814, and it has, under its jurisdiction, twenty-five private lodges.
[44] Freemasonry has existed in Leipsic for more than a century. In
fact, it was introduced in 1738 by a French officer, who formed a lodge
called the Three White Eagles. It has gradually progressed ever since;
and, although royal support was never publicly conceded to the fraternity, they were never molested in the practice of their rites. There are
several public charities attached to it.
[45] The Grand Lodge at Frankfort numbers under its jurisdiction the
lodges of Nuremberg, Erlangen, Darmstadt, Worms, Mayence, Offenbach,
and Alzey. It was originally a provincial Grand Lodge under the English constitutions; but it became independent in 1782. It is very much
indebted for its prosperity to the tact and indefatigable exertions of the
celebrated Zinnendorff.

side a heap of rough stones, with this inscription, *Æqua
Lege sortitur Insignes et Imos;* on the other side appeared
Silenus, covered with the skin of a wolf, full of eyes and
ears, and out of a cornucopia, which he held in one hand,
he poured out squares, and other instruments of Masonry. He lays the other hand upon his mouth, with these
words, *Favete linguis;* and a little lower, *Æquitas, Con-
cordia, Virtus,* which are the three great pillars of the
fraternity.[46]

Let any one judge, after such ample proof, whether
the conduct of the magistrates of Berne can be justified;
and whether there is the least appearance of truth in
their suggestions of dangerous consequences to the state;
or whether they had any authority to force the Masons
to abjure their engagements; on the contrary, it bespeaks
the greatest absurdity to force them to renounce the
society. Every man who judges impartially, or without
being prejudiced against the Masons, will, without doubt,
acknowledge the natural picture of a prince, who, on all
occasions, has at heart the happiness of his subjects, and
who has been so far from banishing the Masons his dominions, that he finds himself bound in conscience to
gain their love, and protect them in all things that
depend on him.[47]

[46] Several similar medals were struck about the same time at other
places. At Hamburg, the St. John's lodge struck a medal in 1742, to
commemorate the connexion between Freemasonry and the sciences.
On one side is a Mason leaning against a pillar, with a plumb rule in his
hand, and the inscription, *Labor Silentium Libertas;* on the other side is
a pyramid, ruins of houses, and masonic tools, and inscribed, *Connubia
Scientiarum Honesta.* Another medal was struck at Hamburg, in the
same year, to explain the reason why the Brethren assembled in the
evening, containing the following hieroglyphics:—the sun and moon
appear to be casting their light upon the earth, while the All-seeing eye
of God overlooks the labours of the Brethren. It is inscribed, *Facies
Supremi Eadem.* Several other medals were produced on the continent
at a later period.

[47] In speaking of His Royal Highness the Duke of Sussex, the "Illustrated London News" says—"There is no dignity in which he more
rejoices, or in which many thousands of persons are more proud to do
him honour, than that of Grand Master of the Freemasons of England."
This, then, will form the natural picture of a prince. " The above words
are his purest and best emblazonment of Christian renown; they are in
themselves the symbols of a Brotherhood; the most beautiful in its foundation; the most widely extended in its influence; the most enduring in
its stability; the most binding in its principles of love and charity; the
most thoroughly affectionate in spirit, and pervaded with the warmest

As much has been said of the injustice done the Free-masons, it cannot be greatly out of the way to mention the proceedings of the furious and horrible inquisition in Spain, Portugal, and Italy,[48] which in direct opposition to reason, justice, and humanity, endeavour to extort from Masons the secrets of their art by the most cruel torments, and finally by fire and faggot. O, what in-humanity! Dare they in a Christian country attack the innocent in such a manner as barbarians would look upon with horror! False devotees accustom themselves to infuse into the minds of the credulous multitude a baneful poison against everything that they imagine may affect their reveries, and particularly against the moral virtues, which they only know by theory; from them the fraternity may expect the most dreadful consequences.[49]

impulses of the human heart; of all the speculations of mankind for pro-moting the sympathies of our nature, or adding to the crime-curtailed pittance of man's happiness on earth. More and more do the beauties and virtues of Freemasonry impress themselves upon the world of Breth-ren whom it has gathered within its glorious circle. In all emergencies of difficulty and danger—in war, in plague, in prison—they have softened the asperities of tyranny, and quailed the cruelty of revenge; they have set up BROTHERHOOD as the sign of succour, and made peace smile amidst havoc and bloodshed at the mouth of the cannon, and upon the edge of the sword. More life has been saved by Freemasonry, more assistance rendered to distress and misery, more violent passions conquered, and more malice humbled into shame, than by any other foundation short of the divine one of Christianity itself. To be at the head of so grand, so vast, wide-spread, and philanthropic an institution, in a mighty country like our own, is almost to hold the spring of the fountain from which its beauty and its goodness flow."

[48] Laurie says that—" Notwithstanding these attempts to suppress and exterminate the society, Freemasonry appears to have made a head in several parts of Italy. In the year 1751 another bull was issued, renew-ing the former prohibitions against the meetings of masonic lodges, either at Rome, or in any of the ecclesiastical dominions, and praying the princes and states of the Roman communion to forbid them in their respective territories. At Naples, several Freemasons were seized and imprisoned; but as divers persons of distinction frequented the lodges there, and much murmuring appeared amongst them. his Sicilian majesty order-ed the commissioners, who were appointed to execute the edict, to search thoroughly into the true state of the case. This they accordingly did, and reported that they could find nothing contrary to religion or virtue in the proceedings of the lodges of Freemasons; and that there was no reason for suspecting the members of holding maxims pernicious to the state; whereupon the king ordered all inquiries and prosecutions on the subject to cease."

[49] A most diabolical act of treachery was practised at this period against the Freemasons by the inquisitor of Spain, whose infamous name

Still full of that blind zeal which stirred up the fran-
tic pagans to persecute the primitive Christians, they
think that Masons must be the like victims to their
vengeance. It is from hence that Rome, that tender
mother, who has often used barbarities to her best children, came to extend her favours to the Masons, who
neither love nor fear her threats. She falsely persuades
herself, that in the lodges of the Masons, they not only
act contrary to good manners, but commit the most
enormous crimes :[50] form plots against holy church, and,
in short, that the lodge is the head-quarters of Satan, and
the theatre of atheism.[51] The populace credit these

was Peter Torrubia. This individual, having first made confession, and
received absolution, became a Freemason, for the express purpose of be-
traying it, and of handing to the executioner the unfortunate members,
before he knew what their deserts might be. He was initiated in 1751,
and immediately made himself acquainted with the entire ramifications of
the craft, and names of the subscribers. Being unable to accuse them of
any malpractices, he named for punishment the members of ninety-seven
lodges, without any pretext whatever ; and as he himself was the accuser,
witness, and judge, the whole of them were subjected to torture on the
rack. (See the account in Freemasons' Quarterly Review, 1844, p. 16.)
[50] Even Robison admits the reverse of all this. He says—speaking of
an elegant entertainment which he visited in the female *Loge de la Fidé-
lité*—" Every ceremonial was composed in the highest degree of elegance;
everything conducted with the most delicate respect for our fair sisters,
and the song of brotherly love was chanted in the most refined strain of
sentiment. I do not suppose that the Parisian Freemasonry of forty-five
degrees could have given me more entertainment." (Proofs, p. 3.)
[51] A Roman Catholic Freemason, who wrote to the editor of the
" Nenagh Guardian" in 1844, puts the supposed infallibility of the pope
in a strong point of view, and his words are worth quoting.—" Take
England for example, and open those pages of her history which record
the events that occurred during the reign of John—as vile as miscreant as
ever provoked a nation's malediction. During the reigns of Henry I.,
Stephen, and Henry II., charters conferring various privileges had been
granted, but the enjoyment of which John refused to cede. To enforce a
confirmation of those charters, the barons of England and the Cardinal
Archbishop Langton held a 'monster meeting' at Runnimede, electing
Fitzwalter as their general, and cold steel being always a powerful supported of warm argument, John, whose cowardice was commensurate
with his tyranny, trembling for his own safety, signs the charter, and con-
firms it on his solemn oath, determined to prejure himself on the first
favourable opportunity. He had been previously excommunicated by
Pope Innocent ; but having written a letter of repentance, couched in the
most abjectly submissive and subservient terms, Innocent at once receives
the penitent sinner with open arms. John sends to other countries, hires
battalions of butchers, as well suited for his purpose as the mercenaries
who visited our fathers in '98; the accident of a shipwreck alone saves
England from a scene of carnage, in which ' her tears could not number

well-grounded motives, and look no farther, though it
be trumpeted abroad by the most infernal calumniator.
In the meantime the Mason quietly enjoys the religion
in which he was born; is obliged to be faithful, just, and
true to his country; and the engagements he enters into
do not by any means dispense with the obligations that
he owes to God and his sovereign; but this declaration
will not appease our enemies, they require something
more than being innocent of all the charges alleged
against us.[52]

The secrets of the fraternity, then, being neither contra y to religion, nor the duty of subjects to their prince,
nor, in truth, to any law divine or human ;[53] it must then

---

the dead.' Providence favours Britain, not so the pope—who threatens
the barons for having, without consulting him! presumed to wrest the
charter of their country's liberties from a tyrant's grasp. He absolves
John from his oath—declares the charter null and void—excommunicates
the barons, and suspends Langton for refusing to publish the bull of excommunication. Though centuries have passed by since he descended to
an honoured grave, the memory of Stephen Langton is still cherished in
grateful remembrance, not only by Englishmen, but by the natives of
every country in the universe where patriotism has an admirer, or liberty
a votary ; yet this was a man who, in 1210, was put under ban by an authority which in 1844 is declared infallible by Caruana of Malta, and
John of Tuam. So much for the infallibility of popes ; and in the face
of such startling historic facts, who will dare affirm the bull of Leo XII.
against Freemasonry—an authority before which Roman Catholics are
bound in conscience to bow, his own judgment convincing each Mason
that the censure is unmerited ? As a Roman Catholic, I recognize the
authority of a general council on all matters of faith, and I defy any man
to take the eighteen general councils of the church of Rome, and from
Nice to Trent to point out one passage condemnatory of our Order."

[52] It is strange that in our own times, some of the Protestant clergy
should have adopted these barbarous opinions. The " Freemasons' Quarterly Review" has recorded and perpetuated the fact, that " at the installation of a Provincial Grand Master at Falmouth, in the year 1844, the
Rev. Mr. Blount expressed his opinion that the church had nothing to do
with such matters, that is, with Freemasonry, and that her services ought
not to be mixed up with them. ' Where ignorance is bliss, 'tis folly to
be wise ;' and so Mr. Blount dogmatically pronounces Freemasonry as
undeserving the countenance of the church ; and stated that the refusal
of his pulpit on the occasion referred to, had the bishop's sanction." If
the reader will take the trouble to look over my " Apology for the Freemasons," published in the above year, he will find all Mr. Blount's arguments fully refuted.

[53] When Bro. John Nepomuck von Delling was examined before the
privy council of the Elector of Bavaria, in 1785, on the charge of being
a Freemason, he replied :—" I do not deny having been a member of the
Order of Freemasons ; but I must observe, that I was a member of that

necessarily follow, that the wicked suggestions of those incendiaries, who, under the similitude of a Mason, represent the most horrid monster that ever existed in human shape, are void of all truth. In seeking for the secrets of the fraternity, these men will for ever seek in vain ; they who are curious to know them, and have all the necessary qualifications for it, with a general good character, and being well recommended, have only to become Masons to know all in a proper length of time ; they may depend upon it they will not be refused. They who have endeavoured to compel the Masons by force to reveal the secrets of their art, at first sight, to the profane, would have them act contrary to the essential nature of a secret ; because, when a secret is made known, it is no longer such.[54] The inquisition, every one knows, has too often made the innocent tremble, have found all their gallies, engines, and tortures to be without effect ; they never will meet with a Mason base enough to betray

society at a time when I justly could suppose that his electoral highness would tolerate a lodge in his country, like many other German princess I was assured on my reception that all the principles of the Order contain nothing that is inimical to religion, the state, or the sovereign ; and I do solemnly protest never to have seen or heard, in the Order, anything that is injurious to either ; of which his electoral highness may convince himself, if he will order a vigorous inquiry to be made into the accusations that have been exhibited against the Freemasons from private motives, and with a malicious design against the lodge. His electoral highness having last year declared by proclamation his sentiments relative to all secret societies, I have not hesitated to obey the commands of my sovereign, and to break off all connexion with the Freemasons, conformably to the duties incumbent upon a loyal subject."

[54] Even De Quincey admits this fact, because, he says—"Their main object was a mystery ; and that it might remain such, an oath of secrecy was demanded of every member on his admission. Nothing of this mystery could ever be discovered by a visit from the police ; for when such an event happens, and naturally it has happened many times, the business is at an end—and the lodge, *ipso facto*, dissolved. Besides that, all the acts of the members are symbolic, and unintelligible to all but the initiated. Meantime, no government can complain of this exclusion from the mysteries ; as every governor has it at his own option to make himself fully acquainted with them, by procuring his own adoption into the society. This it is which, in most countries, has gradually reconciled the supreme authorities to the masonic societies, hard as the persecution was which they experienced at first. Princes and prelates made themselves Brothers of the Order as the condition of admission to the mysteries. And, think what they would of these mysteries in other respects, they found nothing in them which could justify any hostility on the part of the state." (Lond. Mag. 1824, p. 9.)

his trust, and to buy his liberty, and even life at the expense of honour and remorse of conscience. No man,
suppose him as wicked as you will, has ever revealed the
secrets of Masonry, or ever will reveal them. They do
no not fear being confuted on this point. Everything
published with regard to the secrets of Masonry are
mere chimeras and ridiculous fancies.[55] The public seek
after words and signs. These ingenious gentlemen gratify that itching curiosity by patching up some quaint
conceits, which may be true for what they know to the
contrary, the better to impose on mistaken credulity;[56]
and, moreover, to answer a much more necessary end of
putting the long-wanted penny into their pockets.[57] All

[55] Major Allyn gives a curious reason for publishing, what he calls, the
Secrets of Masonry.—" We come to lay before the world the claims of
an institution which has been sanctioned by ages, venerated for wisdom,
and exalted for light; but an institution whose benefits have always
been over-rated, and whose continuance is not in the slightest degree
necessary. We meet it with its high requirements, its time-honoured
customs, its swelling titles, and shall show it in its nakedness and simplicity Strip it of its borrowed trappings, and it is a mere nothing—a
toy not now worthy the notice of a child to sport with. If we would
climb the high ascent of human science, and trace the mighty progress
of human genius, in every gigantic effort of mind, in logic, geometry,
mathematics, chemistry, and every other branch of knowledge, we ridicule the idea that Masonry contains the arts and sciences—the strictest
Mason in the whole fraternity is not bold enough to uphold or maintain
the opinion for one moment in sober reality." (Ritual. Introd. viii.)
Poor simpleton! he proceeds to describe his reward, styling himself, by
the way, " a man of high rank and standing!" He got lots of pence, and
lots of pelting, as he richly deserved. He confesses that " he was insulted,
mobbed, sued, imprisoned, abused, and libelled; the house in which he
lectured was more than once torn down; and often the windows and
doors were broken and battered with stones and other missiles; while he
sought, in vain, the protection of that law *which he had not violated!*
But in all this," he adds, " I moved forward, undaunted, in the path of
duty. With a modest deportment, an unstained honour, a veracity unquestioned, a resolution unshaken, a reputation unblemished, I will still
continue to press against the common enemy!" How very virtuous! He
was merely violating a series of obligations, *by his own confession,*
solemnly entered into; and deliberately breaking the laws both of God
and man.
[56] These books are seldom read. Such works were published a few
years ago in America by Morgan and others; and of them a contemporary thus speaks :—" Morgan's book was at first sought after with considerable avidity. Few, however, have had patience to read it through;
and of those few, but a small part are willing to acknowledge it. It has
sunk almost into oblivion, and scarcely affords a subject for conversation."
(Brown's Narrative, p. 72, A. D. 1829.)
[57] I have already offered an opinion on the above subject in the Intro-

the stratagems made use of to entrap the unwary Mason, if any such there be, will for ever be fruitless, because it is as impossible to accomplish it, as to push the moon out of its sphere.

But what is really wonderful, and what will render the glory of the fraternity immortal, is, that all these pretended revealers themselves, do them the justice to give a tolerable clear idea of their manners, their duty to princes, and their remoteness to everything that might create discord among mankind.[58] Though all this had been owned and published by the Masons, yet the revealers found the way of making it be believed. Though innocence is a bitter root, it never fails of producing sweet and delicious fruit. The wrongs which it endures tend to its glory in the end ; the troubles which it undergoes end in joy; the load of injustice produces praise ; and

ductory Essay, prefixed to the first volume of the Golden Remains, to which I have subjoined a detailed list of these catch-penny publications, which I am gratified to find has been received by the fraternity with considerable interest and satisfaction. Barruel labours hard to establish the credibility of this trash. He says, in the course of his argument,— "I might have quoted the testimony of another adept, who writes as follows to the authors of the Endemonia :—' I also can declare that I have been present at the grand mysteries, particularly that in 1785, I was entrusted with the degree of Mage, or Philosopher ; and that the short description given in the Endliches Schicksal, or the last object of Freemasonry, is perfectly exact and well-grounded.' The author of the Endliches Schicksal has only, like myself, copied the text from Biederman. I have no knowledge of the new adept. I see he has signed his letter, desiring the authors of the Endemonia not to make use of his name without an absolute necessity. Besides, I am a Roman Catholic ; and *I might find disagreeable consequences from not having asked to be absolved from my oath, before I published what I promised to keep secret."* (Hist. Jac. vol. iii. p. 259.) Admirable logic! worthy an opponent of our ancient and honourable society.

[58] To do Barruel justice, he was candid enough to admit that, "in treating of Freemasonry, a regard to truth rigorously compels us to begin with an exception that exculpates the greater part of those Brethren who have been initiated, and who would have conceived a just horror for this association, had they been able to foresee that it could ever make them contract obligations which militated against the duties of the religious man and of the true citizen. England, in particular, is full of those upright men who, excellent citizens and of all stations, are proud of being Masons, and who may be distinguished from others by ties, which only appear to unite them more closely in the bonds of charity and fraternal affection. And it is not the fear of offending a nation, in which I have found an asylum, that has suggested this exception." (Hist. Jac. vol. ii. p. 263.)

every means made use of for its destruction, renders the overcoming of all the more triumphant. Supported by patience and hope, and divine justice to plead its cause, all the malice, and all the efforts of wicked and designing men, but tend to raise it so much the higher in glory. As the application is easy, the candid and unprejudiced reader is left to his reflections thereon.

CHAPTER III.

> " While the sun shines with even light
>   Upon masters and knaves, I shall declare
> The law of might according to right.
>   Place the king's seat true and square ;
> Let every measure, for justice sake,
>   Be given in sight of God and man,
> That the plaintive his complaint may make,
>   And the defendant answer—if he can."
>   CEREMONIES OF THE VEHME GERICHT.

THE society of Freemasons, which, notwithstanding
the opposition of human power, civil and ecclesiastic,
has now subsisted for many ages, and always maintained
its inseparable character of secrecy, prudence, and good
manners, stands at this day in such high repute, that an
apology in its behalf is certainly unnecessary.[1]

Public esteem has always been reputed a crime in
the eyes of malevolence, and virtue and goodness have
always been held as declared enemies by hypocritical
sanctity and bigot zeal.   To such impure sources alone
can be attributed a very extraordinary act, lately pro-

---

[1] "When we speak of the moral principles of Freemasonry, we mean
such as emanate from the divine essence and immutable perfections of
God.   Such as impress their own truth, and carry conviction of a just
sense of duty to every enlightened conscience.   Such as are perfectly
adapted to the constitutional endowments of man, as an intellectual
moral, and social being, and especially such as the understanding will at
once perceive to involve his highest and best interests, both as a creature
of time and of immortality.   In this, we are not to be understood as saying,
the masonic code embodies every distinctive principle of moral virtue in
its more expanded form, but only such as may be brought to bear on a
specific object of common interest, and in the best manner subserve the
accomplishment of a special purpose connected with the happiness of all
our species." (Town's Prize Address.)

5

nounced against this venerable society, by the synod of
the Associate Brethren, and published in the Scots' Magazine for August, 1757, of which the following is a
copy:

" Whereas an oath is one of the most solemn acts of
religious worship, which ought to be taken only upon
important and necessary occasions ; and to be sworn in
truth, in judgment, and in righteousness, without any
mixture of sinful, profane, or superstitious devices.

" And whereas the synod had laid before them, in
their meeting at Stirling, on the 17th of March, 1745,
an overture concerning the Mason oath, bearing, that
there were very strong presumptions, that among Masons an oath of secrecy is administered to entrants into
their society, even under a capital penalty, and before
any of those things which they swear to keep secret be
revealed to them ; and that they pretend to take some
of these secrets from the Bible ; beside other things,
which are ground of scruple, in the manner of swearing
the said oath ; and therefore overturing, that the synod
would consider the whole affair, and give directions with
respect to the admission of persons engaged in that oath
to sealing ordinances.

" And whereas the synod, in their meeting at Stirling
on the 26th of September, 1745, remitted the overture
concerning the Mason oath, to the several sessions subordinate to them, for their proceeding therein, as far as
they should find practicable, according to our received
and known principles, and the plain rules of the Lord's
Word, and sound reason.

" And whereas the synod, at their meeting at Edin-
burgn on the 6th of March, 1755, when a particular
cause about the Mason oath was before them, did appoint all the sessions, under their inspection, to require
all persons in their respective congregations, who are
presumed or suspected to have been engaged in that
oath, to make a plain acknowledgment, whether or not
they have ever been so ; and to require that such as
they may find to have been engaged therein, should
give ingenuous answers to what further inquiry the sessions may see cause to make, concerning the tenor and
administration of the said oath to them : and that the

sessions should proceed to the purging of what scandal
they may thus find those persons convicted of, according
to the directions of the above-mentioned act of synod in
September, 1745.

"And whereas the generality of the sessions have,
since the afore-mentioned periods, dealt with several
persons under their inspection about the Mason oath; in
the course of which procedure, by the confessions made
to them, they have found others, beside those of the
Mason craft, to be involved in that oath : and the synod
finding it proper and necessary to give more particular
directions to the several sessions, for having the heinous
profanation of the Lord's name by that oath purged out
of all the congregations under their inspection.

"Therefore the synod did, and hereby do, appoint that
the several sessions subordinate to them, in dealing with
persons about the Mason oath, shall particularly interrogate them—if they have taken that oath, and when and
where they did so?   If they have taken the said oath, or
declared their approbation of it, oftener than once, upon
being admitted to a higher degree in a Mason lodge?   If
that oath was not administered to them, without letting
them know the terms of it, till in the act of administering the same to them?   If it was not an oath binding
them to keep a number of secrets, none of which they
were allowed to know before swearing the oath?   If,
beside a solemn invocation of the Lord's name in that
oath, it did not contain a capital penalty about having
their tongues and hearts taken out in case of breaking
the same?   If the said oath was not administered to
them with several superstitious ceremonies : such as the
stripping them of, or requiring them to deliver up, anything of metal which they had upon them—and making
them kneel upon their right knee bare, holding up their
right arm bare, with their elbow upon the Bible, or with
the Bible laid before them—or having the Bible, as also
the square and compasses, in some particular way applied
to their bodies?   And if, among the secrets which they
were bound by that oath to keep, there was not a passage of scripture read to them, particularly 1 Kings, vii.
21, with or without some explication put upon the same,
for being concealed.

"Moreover, the synod appoint, that the several sessions

shall call before them all persons in their congregations
who are of the Mason craft, and others whom they have
a particular suspicion of, as being involved in the Mason
oath, except such as have been already dealt with, and
have given satisfaction upon that head ; and that, upon
their answering the first of the foregoing questions in the
affirmative, the sessions shall proceed to put the other
interrogatories before appointed : as also, that all persons
of the Mason craft, applying for sealing ordinances, and
likewise others, concerning whom there may be any presumption of their having been involved in the Mason
oath, shall be examined by the ministers if they have
been so ; and upon their acknowledging the same, or
declining to answer whether or not, the ministers shall
refer them to be dealt with by the sessions, before admitting them to these ordinances ; and that all such
persons offering themselves to the sessions for joining in
covenanting work, shall be then examined by the sessions,
as to their concern in the aforesaid oath.

" And the synod further appoint, that when persons
are found to be involved in the Mason oath, according to
their confessions in giving plain and particular answers
to the foregoing questions, and professing their sorrow
for the same; the said scandal shall be purged by a ses-
sional rebuke and admonition—with a strict charge to
abstain from all concern afterwards in administering the
said oath to any, or enticing any into that snare, and
from all practices of amusing people about the pretended
mysteries of their signs and secrets. But that persons
who shall refuse or shift to give plain and particular
answers to the foregoing questions, shall be reputed
under scandal incapable of admission to sealing ordinances, till they answer and give satisfaction, as before
appointed.

" And the synod refer to the several sessions to proceed unto higher censure as they shall see cause, in the
case of persons whom they may find involved in the said
oath with special aggravation, as taking or relapsing into
the same, in opposition to warnings against doing so.

" And the synod appoint, that each of the sessions
under their inspection shall have an extract of this act,
to be inserted in their books, for executing the same
accordingly."

From this act the practices of this holy association appear so agreeable to those of the Roman Catholic church, that they afford a shrewd suspicion, that the principles from which such practices result, are of the same nature, and have the same dangerous tendency, with those professed by the Roman See.[2]

In the year 1738, his holiness at Rome, by the plenitude of the apostolic power, issued a declaration condemnatory of the society of Freemasons;[3] with an absolute prohibition to all the faithful in Christ, to enter into, promote, or favour that society, under no less penalty than an *ipso facto* excommunication; and the help of the secular arm is commanded to enforce the execution of this declaration.[4] By an edict, consequent to this

[2] An attempt has been recently made to revive this persecution. But I am persuaded, with Bro. O'Ryan, himself an intelligent Roman Catholic, that " if the Roman Catholic clergy and the Freemasons of Ireland were brought together, a far greater number of literary men would be found amongst the latter than the former. It is needless to detail the benefits conferred on Society in general by the Masonic Order ; but it effects one good at least, which may be estimated by those outside its pale—it softens down the rancorous feelings of sectarian prejudice and political partisanship. Bound to our Protestant brother Masons by a tie as sanctified as it is sublime, we abhor that narrow-minded bigotry which leads one man to dislike another, solely because he worships the same God at a different altar, whilst the Protestant, reciprocating this feeling, vies with his Catholic brother in a noble rivalship—the rivalship of kindness and philanthropy."

[3] In France, says Bro. Mackey, the bull of Clement met with no congenial spirits to obey it. On the contrary, it was the subject of universal condemnation as arbitrary and unjust, and the parliament of Paris positively refused to enrol it. But in other Catholic countries it was better respected. In Tuscany the persecutions were unremitting. A man, named Crudeli, was arrested at Florence, thrown into the dungeons of the Inquisition, subjected to torture, and finally sentenced to a long imprisonment, on the charge of having furnished an asylum to a masonic lodge. The Grand Lodge of England, on learning the circumstances, obtained his enlargement, and sent him pecuniary assistance. Francis de Lorraine, who had been initiated at the Hague in 1731, soon after ascended the grand ducal throne, and one of the first acts of his reign was to liberate all the Masons who had been incarcerated by the Inquisition, and still further to evince his respect to the Order, he personally assisted in the constitution of several lodges at Florence, and in other cities of his dominions.

[4] In the Romish Church there are two sorts of judges in matters of faith : the first by virtue of the employment with which they have been invested, as the pope and the bishops, who, at their consecration, are supposed to receive from heaven an absolute jurisdiction over heretics ; the second are delegated by the pope, who transfers to them the above

declaration, informations are commanded, under the severest corporal punishment, and encouraged by an assurance from the infallible chair, " that oaths of secrecy in matters already condemned, are thereby rendered void, and lose their obligation."

Let it be recorded in history, to the honour of their holinesses, the Associate Synod in Scotland, that, in the year 1757, they also thundered out their tremendous bull against Freemasons : whereby all their votaries are enjoined to reveal everything which under the sanction of a solemn oath they are obliged to conceal, they are thereafter to abstain from such societies themselves: nor are they to entice others to enter them, under the terrible certification of being reputed under scandal, debarred from sealing ordinances, and subjected to higher censure, as there should appear cause.[5]

The professed reasons which brought the fraternity under the papal displeasure, were, that they confederated persons of all religions and sects, under a show of natural

jurisdiction. These are called Apostolical Inquisitors ; and the employment is of such dignity, that they rank with the bishops, and were exempt from the episcopal power. They have the authority to publish edicts against heretics, to punish them at their pleasure, to excommunicate them or take away their lives.

[5] Laurie gives the following detailed account of this transaction :—" In the year 1745, the Associate Synod, consisting of a few bigotted dissenters, attempted to disturb the peace of the fraternity ; and had they been possessed of half the power of the Church of Rome, or the Council of Berne, their proceedings, prompted by equal fanaticism, would have been marked with the same severity ; but, fortunately for the Order, their power extended only to the spiritual concerns of those delinquents, who were of the same sect as themselves. In the beginning of the year 1745, an overture was laid before the Synod of Stirling, stating that many improper things were performed at the initiation of Masons, and requesting that the synod would consider whether or not the members of that Order were entitled to partake in the ordinances of religion. The synod remitted this overture to all the kirk sessions under their inspection, allowing them to act as they thought proper. In 1755, they ordered that every person who was suspected of being a Freemason should return an explicit answer to any question that might be asked concerning the Mason oath. In the course of these examinations, the kirk session discovered (for they seem hitherto to have been ignorant of it) that men who were not architects were admitted into the Order. On this account the synod, in the year 1757, thought it necessary to adopt stricter measures. They drew up a a list of foolish questions, which they appointed every kirk session to put to those under their charge. These questions related to what they thought were the ceremonies of Freemasonry ; and those who refused to answer them were debarred from religious ordinances." (Hist. p. 132.)

honesty, in a close and inscrutable bond, and under certain ceremonies, which, by an oath taken on the Bible, they obliged them, by the imprecation of heavy punishments, to preserve with inviolable secrecy.[6] These, urged by the seceders as the motive of their proceedings, are, that the Masons administered their oath of secrecy, under a capital penalty, without first declaring what the matters to be concealed are ; and that some of these things are taken from the Bible. And the publishers of the Scots' Magazine very quaintly insinuate another reason, that the whole matters thus communicated under the strictest ties of secrecy, are a bundle of *trifles and inconsistencies*, unworthy of the solemnity of an oath ;[7] this they do by a reference made to a pretended

---

[6] This ordinance is perfectly correct. Masonry is a cosmopolitical institution, and makes no inquiry into the religion of a Brother, provided he shall furnish the lodge which he desires to visit with a certificate of moral worth, according to the regulations of the Grand Lodge, Dec. 27, 1663, that "no person hereafter who shall be accepted a Freemason, shall be admitted into any lodge or assembly, until he has brought a certificate of the time and place of his acceptation, from the lodge that accepted him, unto the Master of that limit or division where such lodge is kept." This regulation has since been reiterated on several occasions, and is a custom prevalent in every country where Freemasonry flourishes.

[7] Trifles and inconsistencies ! Hear the testimony of the wise and good ; and first the Marquis of Hastings. He said, in his reply to an address by the Freemasons of Calcutta, that " the secrecy observed in masonic proceedings, and the rigid scrutiny exercised into the private character of candidates for admission, has excited the curiosity of the higher ranks, and at the same time removed every fear of their discrediting themselves by becoming members of the fraternity. Once initiated, *they received lessons which never could have reached them in any other situation.*" Hear what Bro. Lewis Crombie, Esq., says in his address to the Duke of Richmond :—" In the history of man there are few things more remarkable than that Masonry and civilization, like twin sisters, have gone hand in hand. Dark, dreary, and comfortless were those days when Masonry had not laid her line, or extended her compasses. The great end of Masonry is to promote the happiness of the whole human race. Our creed is—faith, hope, and charity ; our motto—concord, harmony, and peace." And, finally, hear the opinion of our late princely Grand Master, the Duke of Sussex :—" I have endeavoured, all through my masonic career, to bring into Masonry the great fact, that from the highest to the lowest, all should feel convinced that one could not exist without the other. In my career, I have met with many and severe trials —trials to which human nature ought to be exposed, and which, as a Mason, I have been able to bear. When the profane, who do not know our mysteries, are carried away by prejudice, and do not acknowledge the value of our society, let them learn by our conduct, that a good

discovery of the secrets of Masonry, published in their Magazine, 1755, p. 133, and communicated to them, it may be presumed, by the same correspondents.

The great conformity betwixt these two bulls leaves small room to doubt but the last, as well as the first, would have had the sanction of corpora¹ punishments, if God, for the curse of mankind, had strengthened the hands, and seconded the intolerating views of its authors, with secular power.[8] They have not, however, omitted what was within their grasp; but have attempted to erect a dominion over the consciences of mankind, by assuming a power of dispensing with human obligations. This is a privilege which, however envied, the reformed clergy have hitherto left, together with his pretended infallibility, in the possession of their elder brother at Rome;[9] till, in the more enlightened age, these bold asserters of the Christian rights have dared to reclaim and vindicate it as their own; for, should Antichrist enjoy any benefit which the saints are not better entitled to?

This is not the least engine which has been successfully employed to rear up and support the enormous fabric of the Roman hierarchy. The most solemn treaties betwixt princes and states, the allegiance of subjects to their sovereigns,[10] the obligations of private contracts,

Mason is a good moral man." (Speech at the presentation of the Sussex Offering.)

[8] Thus the fiery bigot is supposed to say:—

    "Let the Inquisition rage, fresh cruelties
    Make the dire engines groan with tortured cries;
    Let Campo Flori every day be strew'd
    With the warm ashes of the Lutheran brood;
    Repeat again Bohemian slaughter o'er,
    And Piedmont valleys drown with floating gore;
    Swifter than murdering angels, when they fly
    On errands of avenging destiny.
    Fiercer than storms let loose, with eager haste
    Lay cities, countries, realms, whole nature waste.
    Sack, ravish, burn, destroy, slay, massacre,
    'Till the same grave their lives and names inter."
                     (OLDHAM, sat. iii.)

[9] The papal fulminations have often made the Christian world tremble; but at this period the storms which gathered in the Vatican seldom extended farther than Italy, Spain, and Portugal; at least they found it a very difficult matter to cross the Alps. The thunder of Jupiter Capitolinus, however, thank heaven, though its noise may be imitated, is no longer clothed with its ancient terrors.

[10] As an instance of its unscrupulous conduct in these respects, the inquisition of Castile attempted to prosecute the memory of the Emperor

the marriage vow, and every other the most sacred bond of human society, are dissolved, and fly off at the breath of this dispensing power, like chaff before the wind; and to this, as to their native source, may be ascribed those many wars and devastations, rebellions, massacres, and assassinations, with which every page of the history of the Christian world is defiled. Is it possible that a doctrine attended with such a train of dreadful consequences can have any foundation either in reason or revelation?[11]

The nature of an oath, particularly of a promissory oath,. which this pretended power only respects, comprehends a solemn invocation of the name of God, the Supreme and Omniscient Being, the searcher of the hearts and the trier of the reins of the children of men, not only as an impartial witness[12] of what is promised, but likewise as the judge and certain avenger of perjury, falsehood, and deceit.[13] The performance of the oath

Charles V., and to sentence his will to the flames as heretical, because it was not drawn up after the manner of the Roman Catholics; or, in other words, that no sums of money were bequeathed for saying masses. This gave great offence to the inquisitors, and therefore they sentenced it to the flames. Philip, the son of Charles, who had hitherto beheld with the utmost indifference the conduct of the inquisitors, now roused as from a lethargy, and endeavoured to stop the prosecution, employing the gentlest expedients for fear of the inquisitors. But his son Don Carlos, entertaining the utmost veneration for his grandfather's memory, was highly offended at the insult, and threatened to extirpate the inquisition when he came to the throne for this abominable outrage; to prevent which, the inquisitors determined to sacrifice him to their vengeance; and for this purpose they obtained such an entire ascendancy over the mind of this weak monarch, that he sentenced his son to die; and the only indulgence allowed him was to choose the manner of his death. He had recourse to the hot bath, in which the veins of his arms and legs being opened, he died gradually; and thus fell a martyr to the merciless inquisitors.

[11] The pope, as the head of the universal church, imagines himself possessed of the power of Jesus Christ to open and shut the gates of heaven. He is the person who forgives sins, and by his dispensations makes that lawful which the scripture pronounces unlawful. He draws out of his treasury indulgences to pardon and enliven those who are dead in trespasses and sins. On the payment of certain sums of money he restores those who have been degraded; and pronounces excommunication against heretics, rebels, and transgressors.

[12] Jeremiah xlii. 5.

[13] Oaths are imposed under all systems of religion, and under every political institution. (See the Golden Remains, vol. i. lect. 2; and vol. ii. lect. 3.) I find a similar practice amongst the followers of Mahomet. Lane says, that amongst a people by whom falsehood, in certain cases, is

5*

becomes thereby cognizable by the omniscience of the
divine tribunal;[14] and his justice and omnipotence will
not fail to pour out the phial of his threatened vengeance
upon that execrated head which has dared to invocate
the name of the Lord in vain.[15]

Such are the conclusions of sound reason, warranted
by scripture. Can it, then, be imagined that God has left
it in the power of man to alter these established rules of
his judgments and procedure?[16] Would not this be, as
the poet says, to

"Snatch from his hand the balance and the rod,
Rejudge his justice—be the God of God."—POPE.

There arises likewise from an oath a requisitional right
to the person in whose behalf it is conceived. The thing
promised becomes his property ; of which, so far as the
acquisition does not infringe any anterior obligation, he
cannot be defrauded by any dispensing power, without
manifest injustice, and the exercise of an arbitrary and
despotic authority.

The cause of introducing oaths into civil society affords
another forcible argument against this dispensing power [17]

not only allowed but commended, oaths of different kinds are more or less
binding, and may sometimes be expiated. There are some oaths which
few Moslims would falsely take ; such as saying three times, " by God the
Great," and the oath upon the Koran, " by what this contains of the word
of God." This latter is rendered more binding by placing a sword upon
the sacred volume, and still more so, by the addition of a cake, or a piece
of bread, or a handful of salt.

[14] Jeremiah xxix. 23.

[15] Zechariah v. 4. Juris jurandi contempta religio satis Deum ultorem
habet. (Pand. l. 2, c. de Reb. cred. et Jurejur.)

[16] In Roman Catholic countries, as we learn from the catechism of
Bossuet, when the church imposes any painful and laborious penances
upon sinners, and they undergo them with patience and humility, this is
called a satisfaction ; and when the church shows any regard, either to
the ardent devotion of the penitents, or to other good works which she
prescribes, and remits any part of the punishment due to them, it is called
an indulgence.

[17] The presumed masonic oath constituted the great engine which was
wielded with such effect during the antimasonic persecutions of our Brethren in the United States, a few years ago. The most moderate writer of
the party thus expresses himself:—" Swear not at all, is the command of
Him who spake as never man spake ; and although, in the imperfect condition of human society, a literal compliance with this divine injunction
has been deemed impracticable, yet it is a golden rule, which ought never
to be transgressed when its violation can be avoided. Nay, more, any
society, secret or otherwise, that administers oaths, must be dangerous to

The natural and indispensable obligations to justice and equity, even assisted by the fear of civil punishments, were found insufficient to correct the depravity of the human mind, and prevent a bias to apparent self-interest in the performance of mutual contracts. It was found necessary to assume the aid of religion, and upon the faith of an oath to establish a mutual trust. This arises from a confidence, that he who swears will never violate that promise to which he called God to be his witness, and of the breach whereof he has obtested him to be the judge and avenger.[18] But, if there is anywhere on earth lodged a power of absolving from these obligations, mutual error and diffidence must take place of the happiness and tranquillity expected from civil society, of which the utter subversion must ensue.[19]

However extraordinary this claim may appear, his holiness the pope arrogates it to himself very consistently with his other high attributes. He is the viceroy of God, and, under him, the spiritual lord of the universe. All mankind are his subjects, and every oath, every con-

the well-being of the community, if those oaths can be supposed by any one who takes them to be of higher obligation than the laws, or if they can be so far tortured as to allow of such a construction. That the obligations of the Masonic Order, in some portions of our country, have been thus construed, and thus acted upon, appears so clearly as to render a denial impossible. And this single fact, were it unsupported by any other circumstances, would, in my mind, be sufficient to render it obligatory upon the Masons to relinquish the Order !" (Stone's Letters, p. 65.)

[18] An oath is a solemn appeal to God, as to an All-seeing witness, and an Almighty avenger, if what we say be false. (Heb. vi. 16.) It is an act of religious worship ; whence God requires it to be done in his name (Deut. x. 20) ; and points out the manner in which it ought to be administered, and the duty of the person who swears. (Ps. xv. 4 ; xxiv. 4 ; Jer. iv. 2.) An oath in itself is not unlawful, either as it is a religious act, or as God is called on to witness.

[19] " We believe," says M. Bossuet, " that it was the will of Jesus Christ, that those who have submitted themselves to the authority of the church by baptism, and have afterwards violated the laws of the gospel, shall be subject to the decision of the same church in the tribunal of penance, when she exercises the full power granted her of absolution and remission of sins. The terms of the commission which is given to the ministers of the church to forgive sins, are so general, that it would be presumptuous to confine it to public sins only ; and as when they pronounce absolution in the name of Jesus Christ, they only observe the express terms of that commission ; so the sentence is regarded as passed upon them by Jesus Christ himself."

tract, is with a reversion of its being to him well pleasing.[20]

But upon what consistent bottom their holinesses the brethren of the association found their absolving power, is not so evident. Perhaps, like the Jesuits, those expert casuists, and subtile divines, they will distinguish and re solve it into a declaratory; whereby, from their profound knowledge, they only show that certain oaths, from the particular circumstances that attend them, are unjust or wicked; and the performance of them will not therefore be expected by God; nor is it eligible by man, or obligatory on the conscience.

In this view let us examine their conduct towards the Freemasons; and endeavour to explore on which side the imputation of blasphemy and impiety will fall.

In this conflict the match is very unequal: a Freemason, while he defends the mysteries of the craft, is at every step under the awe and reverence of his oath. He cannot, therefore, exhibit those mysteries to view, or subject them to examination. He must, then, like the lion in the fable, suppose the picture such as it is represented by his antagonists.

Untainted probity frequently meets with strong opposition from villainy supported by fraud. Experience has taught her to oppose prudence to cunning, and secrecy and resolution to the dark designs and dire machinations of her foes. But the depravity or facility of mankind

---

[20] The pope takes place of all Christian princes as the vicar of Jesus Christ here on earth. The emperors in former times went to Rome to receive the imperial diadem from the hands of his holiness, and there solemnly promised and bound themselves to support the church and its supreme head to the utmost of their power. They then took the usual oaths; and after thus securing to the pope his rights and privileges, the petitioning emperor was admitted, and was received by his holiness seated in state upon his throne; before which the emperor gradually approaching, with one knee always upon the ground, kneeled down and kissed his holiness's feet. But before his imperial majesty could be crowned, he was obliged to take another oath to secure the pope's prerogative, and the domains of the church. After the coronation there was a solemn procession, in which his imperial majesty appeared with the crown, sceptre, and globe; but as he went out of the basilica, he was obliged to divest himself of these, in order to hold the pope's stirrup while he mounted his horse, which he led by the bridle for some considerable distance, before he was allowed to resume the insignia of his rank.

soon discovered the difficulty of attaining that degree of secrecy, upon which the success of enterprise must often depend; and, from a confidence of which, resolution and activity result. To remedy this defect, religion opportunely interposes, and affords the sanction of an oath; under the security of which the schemes suggested and maturely planned by judgment are entrusted to prudence and resolution for their execution. Hence, oaths of secrecy have become one of the necessary hinges of government; they have been adopted by every civil state, and every branch of administration requires them.[21] To them must be ascribed the success of the greatest enterprises. Under their influence the noble, generous plan of British liberty was matured into execution, and the purposes of popish tyranny rendered abortive by the revolution; and to them the Freemason owns his grateful acknowledgments, for the unrestrained liberty of defending his craft, and of detecting the damnable principles and black practices of the pretended messengers of Christ, without the dread of a merciless inquisition. The innocence of such oaths cannot, then, be doubted; and their necessity sufficiently sanctifies their use.[22]

But it seems the seceders hold it a crime to exact an oath of secrecy, before the things required to be kept secret be revealed. Can anything be more ridiculous

[21] An oath is accompanied with an invocation of God to witness what we say; and with an imprecation of his vengeance, or a renunciation of his favour, if what we affirm be false, or what we promise be not performed. The laws of all civilized states have required the security of an oath for evidence given in a court of justice; and on other occasions where it may be lawfully administered.

[22] "The Church of Rome," says Laurie (p. 133), "were contented with dispersing the fraternity, and receiving its repentant members into their communion. The council of Berne went no farther than abolishing the society, and compelling the Brethren to renounce their engagements, lest these should be inconsistent with the duties of citizens. But a synod of Scottish dissenters, who cannot imitate, in these points, the Church of Rome, and the Council of Berne, must, forsooth, outstrip them in another. They must compel the Freemasons of their congregation to give them an account of those mysteries and ceremonies which their avarice and fear hinder them from obtaining by regular initiation. And what, pray, becomes of those perjured men from whom such information is obtained? They are promised admission into the ordinances of religion, from whom something worse than a demoniac had been ejected. The criminality, may we not say, the villainy of such proceedings, should be held up to the ridicule and detestation of the public."

than this objection? The purpose of such oaths would thereby be disappointed; for the secret would be communicated without any security or obligation to preserve it—and it would then become optional to grant it or not. Cromwell, that arch politician, when he imagined his secretary's clerk, who was fast asleep, had overheard him deliver some important orders, would not trust to the security of a subsequent oath, and thought that secrecy could be assured only by his immediate death.[23] The common practice of the world refutes the objection, which could only proceed from those whose want of modesty equals that of their honesty.

Mankind is so prone to religion, that it requires only confidence enough for any person, however unqualified, to assume the character of spiritual guides, and they will not fail to obtain votaries. These, from that same tendency, soon yield up their judgment and consciences to the direction of their teachers; and their affections or antipathies, which become no longer their own, are pointed at particular objects, as the zeal or private interest of their priest shall dictate.

One distinguishing characteristic of the associate brethren seems to be, an abhorrence of every oath not devised by themselves,[24] and framed to promote the interest of faction, rebellion, and schism.[25] They have not

[23] A French writer, however, who ascribes the invention of Masonry to Cromwell, confesses that he was perfectly satisfied with the security of an oath. He says—"It was owing to this wise management of Cromwell that Masonry was divided into several degrees. Taking the building of Solomon's temple for his model, nothing escaped him which might aid his purpose. All these different classes, viz., the Entered Apprentice, the Fellowcraft, the Master Mason, &c., were among those whom Solomon employed in the building; and he bound them all with an oath, which in all cases was inviolable; and it was this that accelerated his success, and paved the way for him to mount the throne of England."

[24] Such was the case in the United States with the anti-masonic party during the persecution of Masonry in 1833, as witness the following act against masonic oaths :—"Be it enacted, &c., that if any person, authorized or not authorized by law, shall administer to any person or persons any oath, affirmation or obligation in the nature of an oath, not authorized by law; or if any person shall permit or suffer any such oath, &c., to be administered in their presence, he shall forfeit the sum of one hundred dollars for the first offence, and for the second, shall, in addition to the above penalty, be for ever disqualified from holding any public office."

[25] They have in their synods condemned, as unlawful, the clauses in burgess oaths, with respect to religion and allegiance to the king.

as yet, however, perverted the morals of all their followers ; some of them, notwithstanding all their endeavours, still retain a regard for an oath, as the sacred
and inviolable bond of society. This, they perceived,
was a check to their ambitious views of an unlimited
obedience from their people. It was therefore necessary
to diminish that reverence in hopes that, when their
deluded flock had learned to overleap the fence in one
instance, they would not be scrupulous to do it in any
other. And for this end the nature of an oath of secrecy
is deliberately misrepresented, and rashness and profanity
ascribed to it.[26]

As I am obliged to suppose the secrets of Masonry
such as they are represented by the associate brethren, I
shall follow the order laid down for their interrogatories
in their act.

They object, that the Mason oath is administered by
an invocation of the name of God, attended with certain
rites and ceremonies of a superstitious nature, and under
a capital penalty.[27]

By attending to the nature of an oath, it will appear,
that the obtesting God, as a witness and avenger, necessarily implies an imprecation of his wrath ; which, if the

---

[26] The real object in view was to dissolve the institution, but it failed,
as every similar attempt has done which had the same intention. The
antimasons in the United States bent their whole strength to the work,
without success. The celebrated Hon. Richard Rush, attorney-general
and secretary of state, in an address to the antimasons of Pennsylvania,
held out a most magniloquent boast to this effect :—" We have been told
that Masonry is too strong to be put down ; that such attempts have been
made in European countries, and have failed. Let this animate you but
the more. Already it has been the glory of America to set Europe the
example of conquest over public abuses in many memorable ways. It
may be her further glory to be the first to dispel the solemn folly, and
break the tyrannical fetters, of Masonry. The day that shall witness this
triumph among us, may well deserve to stand next in our celebration to
the Fourth of July."—That day never came ! The fraternity heard the
thunder in silence, and it passed over innocuously.

[27] The Ex-President Adams hinges the existence of Masonry on the
presumed oath. " The whole cause," he says, " between Masonry and
antimasonry, now on trial before the tribunal of public opinion, is con-
centrated in one single act. Let a single lodge resolve that they will
cease to administer that oath, and that lodge is dissolved. Let the whole
Order resolve that this oath shall no longer be administered, and the
Order is dissolved ; for the abolition of that oath necessarily implies the
extinction of all the others."

doctrine of providence is believed, must imply all temporal as well as eternal punishments, it matters not
whether any penalty is expressed; nor does the doing
so in any degree alter the nature of the obligation.[28]

As to the ceremonies pretended to be adhibited to this
oath, they appear to be innocent in themselves; and, if
the Masons use any such, instead of ascribing these to a
superstitious regard, charity would conclude that they
were not without an emphatic and allegorical meaning.

Oaths have almost universally had some rite or ceremony annexed, which, however insignificant in themselves, were originally expressive of something that
tended to increase the awe and respect due to that solemn
act. The casuists agree, that, though the oath is equally
obligatory without them, the perjury is, however, increased by the solemnity.[29]   All nations have adopted
them; the Hebrews, by putting their hand below the
thigh of the person to whom they swore;[30] the pagans,
by taking hold of the altar;[31] and both, protending their
hands to heaven;[32] in which last they have been followed
by all Christian nations; some of whom, particularly
our sister kingdom, when they take an oath, touch or

<hr/>

[28] " Illud videtur esse certum, omne juramentum promissorium, qua-
cunque forma concipiatur, explicatiore vel contractiore, utramque virtu-
aliter continere attestationem, sc. et execrationem. Nam in juramento,
et execratio supponit attestationem, ut quid sibi prius; et attestatio
subinfert execrationem ut suum necessarium consequens." (Saunderson,
de oblig. juram. præl. 1, sect. x.)

[29] An extraordinary kind of oath, as it may appear to us, was used in
Egypt. " As Pharoah liveth " (Gen. xlii. 15), or by the life of Pharoah.
This custom of swearing by the king still continues in the East. Hanway
(Trav. vol. i., p. 313) tells us, that the most sacred oath amongst the
Persians is, " by the king's head;" and in the Travels of the Ambassadors (p. 204), we find the following instance :—" There were but sixty
horses for ninety-four persons. The mehemander swore by the head of
the king (which is the greatest oath among the Persians) that he could
not possibly find any more." And Thevenot says (Trav. pt. ii., p. 97),
" that if they swear by the king's head, their oath is considered of
greater credit, than if they swore by all that is most sacred in heaven
and earth."

[30] Genesis xxvi. 2; xlvii. 29.

[31] " Et ut mos Græcorum est, Jurandi causa, ad aras accederet." (Cic.
pro Balbo.)

[32] Genesis xiv. 22.
    " Suspiciens cœlum, tenditque ad sidera dextram,
    Hæc eadem, Ænea, terram, mare, sidera juro."
                                        (Virg. I. 12, v. 196.)

kiss the holy gospels; and not only so, but every private society, every court of justice have forms of administering oaths peculiar to themselves. Shall not, then, the society of Freemasons be allowed that privilege, without the imputation of superstition and idolatry ?[33]

The matter of the oath comes next under consideration. The Freemasons pretend to take some of their secrets from the Bible; a grievous accusation, truly! "Jack," in the Tale of a Tub, "could work his father's will into any shape he pleased; so that it served him for a night-cap when he went to bed, or an umbrella in rainy weather. He would lap a piece of it about a sore toe; or, when he had fits, burn two inches under his nose; or, if anything lay heavy on his stomach, scrape off and swallow as much of the powder as would lie on a silver penny—they all were infallible remedies." But it seems Knocking Jack of the North[34] will not have all

---

[33] There is a remarkable passage in Prov. xi. 21, thus rendered by our translators—" Though hand join in hand, the wicked shall not go unpunished; but the seed of the righteous shall be delivered;" i. e., though they make many associations, and oaths, and join hands among themselves, yet they shall be punished. But Michaelis proposes another sense of these words, *hand in hand*, my hand in your hand, i. e., as a token of swearing —the wicked shall not go unpunished. How far this sense of the passage is illustrated by the following extract from Bruce (Travels, vol. i., p. 199), the reader will judge :—" I cannot here help accusing myself of what, doubtless, may be well reputed a very great sin. I was so enraged at the traitorous part which Hassan had acted, that at parting I could not help saying to Ibrahim, ' Now, Shekh, I have done everything you have desired, without ever expecting fee or reward; the only thing I now ask you, and it is probably the last, is, that you avenge me upon this Hassan, who is every day in your power.' Upon this, HE GAVE ME HIS HAND, saying, ' He shall not die in his bed, or I shall never see old age.' "— (Taylor's Calmet, in v. Oath.)

[34] John Knox, the Scottish reformer, is here indicated. The passage alluded to is as follows :—" And now the little boys in the streets began to salute him with several names. Sometimes they would call him Jack the Bald ; sometimes, Jack with a Lantern ; sometimes, Dutch Jack ; sometimes, French Hugh ; sometimes, Tom the Beggar ; and sometimes, Knocking Jack of the North." (Tale of a Tub, s. vi.) The character of Knox is thus drawn by Dr. Robertson :—" Zeal, intrepidity, disinterested ness, were virtues that he possessed in an eminent degree. He was acquainted with the learning of the age, and excelled in that species of eloquence which is calculated to rouse and to inflame. His maxims, however, were often too severe, and the impetuosity of his temper excessive. Rigid and uncomplying, he showed no indulgence to the infirmities of others. Regardless of the distinctions of rank and character, he uttered his admonitions with an acrimony and vehemence more apt to irritate

these pearls to be cast before swine, and reserves them
only for his special favourites. What magical virtue
there can be in the sacred passage mentioned in the act,[25]
the world will be at a loss to discover; and the holy
brethren, so well versed in the mysteries, are the most
proper to explain.

But there are other things which are ground of scruple
in the manner of swearing of the said oath. This the
synod have not thought fit to mention ; but their pub-
lisher has supplied the defect, by a reference to a Mason's
confession of the oath, word, and other secrets of his
craft :[26] which, indeed, contains variety of matters insignificant and ridiculous in themselves, and only fit for the
amusement of such persons as the ignorance and incohe-
rence of the author display him to be.[27]

The Freemason does not think himself at all concerned
to defend and support whatever nonsense shall be father-
ed upon the craft by the ignorant and malevolent. The
honour of the fraternity is not in the least tarnished
by it.

The whole narrative, particularly the method of discovering a Mason, the prentice's shirt, and the Monday's
lesson, cannot fail to move laughter, even in gravity
itself.[28] But absurd and ridiculous as the whole of this
matter must appear, a passion of another nature is thereby excited, which respects the discoverer himself; and

than to reclaim ; and this often betrayed him into indecent expressions,
with respect even to the greatest personage in the kingdom."
    [25] 1 Kings, vii. 21.   [26] Vide Scots' Mag. 1755, p. 133.
    [27] The Quakers and Moravians, taking the text in Matt. v. 34 literally,
"swear not at all," refuse their evidence on oath even in a court of justice ; and these scruples arise from a defective method of distinguishing
between the use and abuse of swearing. It is blasphemy to use the name
of God in common conversation ; but it is perfectly lawful to call upon
Him solemnly to witness important truths. If it be lawful to ask Him
for our daily bread, it is equally lawful reverently to invoke him to witness the truth of our assertions, when character, property, and life may
be at stake ; and on other occasions which embrace the permanent welfare of any society or body of men.
    [28] This is of a piece with the magical head mentioned by Barruel, as
being the deity of the Templars, and which is to be found again in the
magic mirror of the cabalistic Masons. They call it the being of beings,
and reverence it under the title of Sum. It represents, in their code, the
great Jehovah ; and, in the opinion of Barruel, is one of the links which
form the chain of connection between Masonry and the Templars. A
most bigotted conclusion, worthy of the credulous Abbé.

that is an honest indignation of the perjury he has committed. For, if this person, scrupulously conscientious as he is represented, was actually under the oath he pretends, however trifling and insignificant the thing itself might be, yet, in the opinion of the most eminent casuists, he was obliged to keep his oath ;[39] the respect due to truth and falsehood being the same in trivial matters as in those of greater importance; otherwise God must be invoked as witness to a lie.[40]

But, if ignorance or imbecility, deluded by hypocritical sanctity, or head-strong zeal, can afford any alleviation (for an absolute acquittance it cannot), the charge must fall with redoubled weight upon those who induced him, and would induce others, over whom this influence extends, to put such an affront upon the honour of God, and to habituate themselves to the practice of insincerity and injustice towards man. Is not this to adopt the practices and opinions of their religious predecessors in hypocrisy, sedition, and rebellion? who held that

> " Oaths were not purpos'd, more than law,
> To keep the good and just in awe ;
> But to confine the bad and sinful,
> Like moral cattle, in a pinfold."—HUDIBRAS.

The natural curiosity of mankind, always eager and impetuous in the pursuit of knowledge, when disappointed of a rational account of things, is apt to rest upon conjecture, and often embraces a cloud in place of the goddess of truth. So has it fared with the secret of Masonry. That society, though venerable for its antiquity, and respectable for its good behaviour, has, through falsehood and misrepresentation, groundlessly awakened the jealousy of states, and the obloquy of malicious

---

[39] The antimasons of America condemned the fraternity for refusing to disclose their secrets, even under a civil oath. Thus Mr. Sprague, one of the legislative committee, put this question, in his examination of a Brother :—" When you enter or leave a lodge or chapter, do you make any sign or motion? If so, to what does it allude? Is it intended to impress upon the mind the penalty of that degree?" " Would you think it," exclaims the antimasonic commentator, " every Mason, though sworn to tell the whole truth, refused plumply to answer this question. Their uniform reply was :—' I do not intend to answer anything in reference to the secrets and ceremonies of Masonry.' "

[40] Saunderson, de obl. jur. præl. iii. sect. 15.

tongues.[41] Their silence and secrecy, as they gave ample room for the most extravagant conjectures, so they likewise afforded an opportunity for the grossest imputations, without fear of a refutation. They have been traduced as atheists and blasphemers, branded as idolaters, and ridiculed as the dupes of nonsense.[42] The hard names liberally bestowed on their secrets by the seceders, partake of all these ;[43] but their proof relates only to the

[41] It is wonderful how far misrepresentation has been carried during the unholy persecutions of Masonry. Even Col. Stone is willing to admit this. He says :—" I have been astonished, since I began this investigation, to find that Elder Barnard has affirmed this misrepresentation. His words are :—' The reader will here learn one reason why those who enter a lodge never come out until they have taken a degree. The candidate is made to promise upon his honour that he will conform to all the ancient established usages and customs of the fraternity ; hence, let him be ever so much opposed to the ceremonies of initiation, or the oath of the degree, he cannot go back ; for he feels bound by his promise. Should he, however, feel constrained to violate his word, the persuasions, and, if necessary, the threats of the Master and Brethren compel him to go forward !' (Barnard's Light, p. 17.) There is not," continues Stone, " so far as I have any knowledge of the usages of Masonry, a single syllable of truth in the passage I have here quoted. Nor do any of my masonic acquaintances hesitate to declare their utter and entire ignorance of even a single instance wherein any such constraint was ever practised, or even thought of. On the contrary, throughout the whole system, from the lowest to the highest degree, every step is the result of the most entire freedom of thought and action." (Letter on Masonry, p. 69.)
[42] If the cowans of those days had possessed the advantage of hearing masonic addresses, from the highest quarters of honour and intelligence, which happily distinguish our own times, they would surely have displayed less hostility to the institution, and entertained a higher opinion of its virtues. His Royal Highness, the late Grand Master, on the occasion of presenting a masonic jewel to the Earl of Moira, thus described it :— " Masonry," said the royal speaker, " is one of the most sublime and perfect institutions that ever was formed for the advancement of happiness and general good to mankind, creating in all its varieties universal benevolence and brotherly love. It holds out allurements so captivating, as to inspire the fraternity with emulation to deeds of glory, such as must command, throughout the world, veneration and applause, and such as must entitle those who perform them to dignity and respect. It teaches us those useful, wise, and instructive doctrines upon which alone true happiness is founded, and, at the same time, affords those easy paths by which we attain the rewards of virtue ; it teaches us the duties which we owe to our neighbour, never to injure him in any one situation, but to conduct ourselves with justice and impartiality ; it bids us not to divulge the mystery to the public, and it orders us to be true to our trust, to be above all meanness and dissimulation, and in all our avocations to perform religiously that which we ought to do."
[43] Vide Scots' Magazine, 1755, p. 137.

last; and, indeed, it seems rather like the delirious ravings of a brain-sick head, inflamed with the fumes of enthusiasm, than a rational design to expose them. Its publication is an affront upon the judgment of the world, no less than inserting it in the Scots' Magazine, is an impeachment upon the taste of the readers of that collection.

To remove such prejudices, and in some degree to satisfy the world and inquisitive cavillers, Masons have descended to publish what opinions they maintained with respect to the great principles of human action. Their belief in God is founded upon the justest notion of his being and attributes, drawn from the light of nature assisted by revelation.[44] They never enter into the speculative regions,[45] so much cultivated by divines; what cannot be comprehended in his nature, they leave as incomprehensible. They adore his infinite Being, and

[44] Some writers, in the face of the plainest indications of Christian types in Freemasonry, will still contend that the Order is at variance with our religious duties. The Rev. H. Jones, a well meaning, but exceedingly weak person, says that, "the institution of Freemasonry should be discountenanced, because some of its principles are at variance with the gospel of Christ—One thing which very evidently clashes with the gospel is this, that while the latter requires us to do good to all men, especially unto them who are of the household of faith; but Masonry requires of its members to do good, especially to the masonic fraternity, whether they do or do not belong to the household of faith!! And what else can it be but a perversion or profanation of the scriptures, to use so frequently the words of Christ, as they are used in reference to the door of the lodge-room—' Ask and ye shall receive; seek and ye shall find'; knock and it shall be opened unto you.'" (Jones' Letters on Masonry, pp. 11, 12.) Brother Jones! Brother Jones! thou art a most accomplished logician!

[45] Namely, of religion and politics. The evil of introducing politics into Freemasonry, has been recently felt in the New World, where a political party, professedly antimasonic, raged for a few brief years, like a hurricane, and threatened to bear down all before it. It was a political party, sui generis. There was none ever before like unto it. Nor will its likeness, probably, be found in any political party to arise hereafter. The progress it made was astonishingly rapid, and in its strides it outstripped the calculations of its friends. Its influence was potent at elections, it drew into its ranks one hundred thousand electors in the State of New York; it almost divided the votes of Pennsylvania; it planted itself deeply in the soil of Massachusetts, in the New England States, and elsewhere; while in Vermont, like the rod of Aaron, it so far swallowed up all other parties, and obtained the control of the State government. Behold how great a matter a little fire kindleth. And yet it sunk as rapidly as it had risen, and now its influence is totally forgotten.

reckon it the perfection of mankind to imitate his com-
municable perfections. Their duty to their superiors, to
their neighbours, and to themselves, are all expressed in
a manner the most agreeable to the soundest morality.—
And when their actions and behaviour, which alone are
subject to human observation, and affect human society,
are conformable to such principles, no power on earth
has a right to inquire farther.[46]

The Freemason professes a particular regard to the
liberal arts, and he makes no scruple to own, that many
of his secrets have a reference to them. From these,
just notions of order and proportion are obtained, and a
true taste of symmetry and beauty is formed.[47]—And as
the transition from the beauties of the natural to those
of the moral species are so easy and apparent; if there
is any virtue, if there is any praise, instead of slander
and defamation, protection and encouragement ought to
be his reward.

Men of the greatest power and dignity, the divine and
the philosopher, have not been ashamed, in all ages, to
own their relation to this society, and to encourage and
protect it by their power and influence. But, should
this combination terminate in nothing but wickedness

[46] At the reunion of the two Grand Lodges in 1813, His Royal Highness the Duke of Kent embodied these principles in a proposition—"That
an humble address be presented to His Royal Highness the Prince
Regent, respectfully to acquaint him with the happy event of the reunion
of the two Grand Lodges of Ancient Freemasons of England—an event
which cannot fail to afford a lively satisfaction to their illustrious patron,
who presided for so many years over one of the fraternities, and under
whose auspices Freemasonry has risen to its present flourishing condition.
That the unchangeable principles of the institution are well known to His
Royal Highness, and the great benefits and end of this reunion are to
promote the influence and operation of these principles, by more extensively inculcating loyalty and affection to the sovereign, obedience to the
laws and magistrates of their country, and the practice of all the religious
and moral duties of life."

[47] How many associations, professedly designed to benefit our species,
have come into being and wasted away since the origin of Masonry. How
many have been instituted with one set of principles, and one of more
objects of fair promise, and afterwards so modified the one and varied the
other as to change the whole ground on which they first stood, lose their
moral character, and finally perish in their own corruption. Freemasonry, however, is eternal in its nature, and universal in its character.
Founded on charity and the liberal arts, no human power can shake it
from its basis; and it is the only institution in existence whose landmarks
can never be altered.

and folly, can it be imagined, either that men of honour, wisdom, and integrity, would lend their countenance to fraud, and encourage folly, merely to make the world stare? or that an association, resting on so unstable a foundation, could so long have subsisted, without the cement of mutual trust and confidence, which result from virtue and consistency alone.[48]

The Freemason, conscious of his integrity, and persuaded of the good tendency of his principles to promote the purposes of virtue and human happiness, beholds with contempt the impotent efforts of envy and ignorance, however sanctified the garb, or dignified tne title they may assume.[49]   In his lodge, which he considers as the school of justice, love, and benevolence, he is taught to oppose truth to misrepresentation, good humour and innocent mirth to sourness and grimace— the certain signs of malice and imposture.   To attend the importunate calls of his enemies, would be to interrupt his tranquillity; and, therefore, wrapt in his own innocence, he despises their impotent attacks, and for the future will disdain to enter the lists with champions so weak and ignorant, so deluded and deluding.

[48] Bro. Russell, Past Grand Master of Massachusetts, very justly observes that " the masonic institution has been and now is the same in all and every place.   No deviation ever has been made or can be made at any time from its usages, rules, and regulations.   Such is its nature, that no innovation on its customs can be introduced or sanctioned by any person, how great soever may be his authority.   Its ancient rules, usages, and customs, have been handed down, and carefully preserved from the knowledge of the world, by the members of the craft, who are solemnly bound to observe and obey them, although many of them have never been written or printed."

[49] When will Ephraim cease to vex Judah, and, under the benign influences of the gospel of peace, brotherly love, such as is recommended by the Saviour and his apostles, pervade the hearts of the children of men?   When shall the desire to secure virtue and happiness to each other absorb every other desire, and inspire every act to produce such a glorious result?   This, however, we may say of Masonry, and its bitterest enemies cannot deny the fact, that although it has been persecuted by bigotry in all ages of its existence, *it never had the character of a persecutor;* which speaks volumes in favour of the purity of its principles, and the correctness of its doctrine and discipline.

CHAPTER Iv.

AN ACCOUNT OF THE SUFFERINGS OF JOHN COUSTOS IN
THE INQUISITION AT LISBON.

WRITTEN BY HIMSELF.

—————————————with a frown
Revenge impatient rose;
He threw his blood-stained sword in thunder down,
And, with a withering look,
The war-denouncing trumpet took,
And blew a blast so loud and dread,
Were ne'er prophetic sounds so full of woe.
And ever and anon he beat
The doubling drum with furious heat;
And though sometimes, each dreary pause between,
Dejected Pity at his side
Her soul-subduing voice applied,
Yet still he kept his wild, unaltered mien,
While each strain'd ball of sight seemed bursting
from his head.   COLLINS.

I CAN justly affirm that it was not vanity that induced
me to publish the following accurate and faithful relation of my sufferings in the Inquisition of Lisbon.[1]   A

[1] The origin of the Inquisition is thus related by Fleury, in his Ecclesiastical History :—" In 1198, Pope Innocent III. sent into the southern
provinces of France two Cistertian monks to convert the Manicheans,
with which those parts swarmed; to excommunicate the obstinate, and
to command the lords to confiscate the possessions of the excommunicated,
to banish them, and punish them with severity ; with power to excommunicate the lords, and put their lands under sequestration, if they refused
obedience to the mandate.   These commissioners were afterwards called
Inquisitors.   The Dominicans subsequently received an ordinance of
thirty-seven articles, which formed the basis of the rules afterwards
observed in the tribunals of the Inquisition.   Some imagine that this
tribunal originated in a constitution made by the Pope Lucius in 1184 ,
because he commands the bishops to examine personally, or by commissioners, people suspected of heresy ; distinguishing the various degrees

strong desire to justify myself with regard to the false
accusations brought by that tribunal against me, as well
as against the Brotherhood of Freemasons, of which I
have the honour to be a member, were the chief motives
for my taking up the pen. To this I will add, that I
was very willing the whole world should receive all the
lights and informations I was capable of giving it concerning the shocking injustice, and the horrid cruelties,
exercised in the pretended holy office. Persons, who live
in countries where this tribunal is had in abomination,
will, from the perusal of the following sheets, have
fresh cause to bless Providence for not fixing their abode
among the Spaniards, the Portuguese, or the Italians.

Such of my readers as may happen to go and reside in
countries where this barbarous tribunal is established,
will here find very salutary instructions for their conduct ; and, consequently, be less liable to fall into the
hands of the unrelenting Inquisitors.

Those who, spite of all the precautions taken by them,
may yet have the sad misfortune to become their innocent victims, will here be taught to avoid the snares laid
in order to aggravate the charge brought against them.[2]
These snares ought the more to be guarded against, as
they are but too often spread by the inquisitors merely
to give a specious air of justice and equity to their iniquitous prosecutions.

For this reason, I shall first give an impartial relation

of guilt, and allotting to each its proper punishment. And he also
directs that after the church has employed its spiritual weapons, it shall
deliver criminals to the secular arm, that corporal punishment may be
inflicted on them, experience having shown," says my authority, " that the
heretics of this age care very little for either ecclesiastical censures or
spiritual punishments."

[2] The manner of prosecuting a person impeached is this : First, he is
summoned, three several times, to appear before the inquisitors ; and if,
through fear or contempt, he neglect to do this, he is excommunicated,
and sentenced to pay a considerable fine ; after which, if he should be
apprehended, a more severe sentence would inevitably be passed upon him.
The safest course, therefore, is to obey the first summons. The longer he
delays, the more criminal he appears in the estimation of the inquisitors,
even though he should be innocent of the charge preferred against him ;
for it is considered a crime of no common order to disobey the command
of the inquisitors. And, if they ultimately seize a person who has crimi-
nated himself by delay, nothing can save him from the most rigorous
punishment. An inquisitor never forgets ; time cannot obliterate any
crime ; and prescription is entirely unknown to the holy office.

of my own prosecution and sufferings on account of my
being a Freemason.   I shall add, for the satisfaction of
the curious, a succinct history of the pretended holy
office ; its origin ; its establishment in France,[3] Italy,[4]
Spain, and Portugal ; the manner how it grasped, by
insensible degrees,[5] the supreme authority now exercised

[3] Ducange tells us that the Inquisition was established in France, by
the council of Toulouse, to punish the Waldenses, and the inquisitors
were chosen from amongst the Dominicans.   It is true the tribunal of the
Inquisition was never legally settled in that country, yet inquisitors were
delegated by the pope, under the pretext of preserving purity of doctrine,
and obedience to the church.   Pope Gregory IX. appointed a commission to exercise the inquisitorial functions in several convents throughout
the kingdom.
[4] The Inquisition of Rome is composed of twelve cardinals, and some
other officers ; over which the pope presides in person.   These cardinals
assume to themselves the title of Inquisitors General throughout the
Christian world ; but they have no jurisdiction in France, and some other
Roman Catholic countries.   They are empowered to deprive or remove
all inferior inquisitors.   Popes Innocent, Alexander, Urban, Clement,
and their successors, used their most endeavours, but to no purpose, to
prevail with the Venetians to follow the example of the other states of
Italy in this particular.   The conduct of the Inquisitors was adduced by
the republic of Venice as a reason for refusing admission to that tribunal
into its territories ; for they were guilty of great disorders, preached
seditious sermons, and, upon any caprice, published crusades against the
heretics, and appeared to be more disposed to revenge themselves upon
any who had affronted them than to promote the purity of religious truth.
They seized the possessions of innocent persons, upon the false pretence
of their being heretics ; so that nothing was heard all over Italy but
loud complaints against the inquisitors.   The Senate of Venice, who
understood their interest as well as any body of men in the world, took
advantage of these disorders to justify their refusal of this tribunal.
However, Pope Nicholas IV. being noways disheartened at the fruitless
attempts of his predecessors, renewed them with so much address, that
the senate were persuaded that if they continued their opposition, they
would be forced to admit an Inquisition dependant on that of Rome ; to
prevent which, they established one by their authority, composed of both
ecclesiastical and lay judges.   This Inquisition had its own laws, which
were less rigorous than those of other nations ; and the utmost precautions were taken to prevent the disorders which had disgraced the tribunal in all other places.
[5] A remarkable instance of the assuming spirit of this tribunal occurred
in the year 1580.   The Archbishop of Milan, going on his visitation of
certain places in his diocese, which, although subordinate to him in his
spiritual capacity, were under the subjection of the Swiss cantons in
other respects, thought it necessary to make some new regulations for the
government of these churches.   The Swiss took umbrage at this conduct,
and sent an ambassador to the Governor of Milan, intreating him not to
allow the prelate to continue his visitations in any places which were
under their jurisdiction : assuring him, at the same time, that if he should

by it, not only against those considered by it as heretics, but even against Roman Catholics; how prisoners are proceeded against; the tortures inflicted on them, in order to extort a confession; the execution of persons sentenced to die; with an accurate description of the *auto-da-fé*, or gaol delivery, as we may term it;[6] together

persist in this obnoxious practice, they would expel him by force, which would necessarily destroy the harmony which it was the interest of the King of Spain to preserve. The ambassador having arrived at Milan, lodged at the house of a rich merchant of his acquaintance. The inquisitor was no sooner informed of this, than, disregarding the law of nations, he sent his officials to seize the ambassador, and deposit him in the dungeons of the Inquisition. Such an insult offered to a state in the person of its ambassador, was unprecedented; but no one dared to complain. The merchant, however, interested himself in favour of his friend, and informed the Governor of Milan of the cruel usage which the ambassador had received. The governor was alarmed at such a flagrant violation of the rights of nations, and commanded the inquisitor to set the ambassador at liberty without the slightest delay; and, to atone for the injury he had received, he paid him all imaginable honours, and complied with several demands, and particularly that the archbishop should discontinue his visitations.

[6] The learned Dr. Geddes thus describes an *auto-da-fé* in Lisbon, of which he himself was a spectator. The prisoners were first placed in the hands of the civil magistrate, and loaded with chains; and being brought before the lord chief justice, he asks them in what religion they intend to die. If they answer that they will die in communion with the Church of Rome, they have the privilege of being first strangled, and afterwards burnt to ashes. But if they die Protestants, they are burnt alive. At the place of execution there is a stake set up for every prisoner, with a good quantity of dry furze about it, and a seat about half a yard from the top. They ascend the stake by a ladder, at the foot of which two Jesuits are placed, who spend about a quarter of an hour in exhorting the professed to be reconciled to the Church of Rome; which, if they refuse to be, the Jesuits come down, and the executioner ascends; and having turned the professed off the ladder upon the seat, and chained their bodies close to the stake, he leaves them, and the Jesuits go up to them a second time, to renew their exhortation to them, and at parting tell them that they leave them to the devil, who is standing at their elbow to receive their souls, and carry them with him into the flames of hell fire, so soon as they are out of their bodies. Upon this a great shout is raised; and as soon as the Jesuits are got off the ladder, the cry is, "Let the dogs' beards be made! let the dogs' beards be made!" which is done by thrusting flaming furzes, fastened to a long pole, against their faces. And this inhumanity is commonly continued until their faces are burnt to a coal, and is always accompanied with such loud acclamations of joy, as are not to be heard upon any other occasion. The beards of the professed being thus made, or trimmed, as they term it in their diabolical sport, fire is applied to the combustibles; but as the top of the flame seldom reaches higher than the seat they sit on, they remain in misery from one to two hours; so that, the learned doctor adds, though out of

with the sufferings of many persons who fell victims to this tribunal. I likewise will add a plan of the house of the Inquisition at Lisbon, in which I was confined sixteen months, and whence I was removed to the galley, as it is called, in that city. I will describe this Portuguese galley, and the manner how prisoners are lodged and treated in both those places.[7]

I shall conclude with a comparison between the methods employed by the primitive church in order to suppress heresy and convert heretics; and those now made use of by the inquisitors (under the cloak of religion) indiscriminately towards all mankind, for the same purpose, as they pretend. I shall relate what I myself was an eye-witness of; and I will annex the remarks of many ill-fated Roman Catholics, who, as well as myself, were the innocent victims to this dreadful tribunal.[8]

I shall think it a happiness if the relation which I now offer should be found of use to the public; and shall consider it as a still greater, in case it may help to open the eyes of those who, hurried on by an indiscreet, or rather blind zeal, think it a meritorious work in the

held, there cannot possibly be a more lamentable spectacle—the sufferers crying out, as long as they are able to speak, "Mercy, for the love of God!" Yet it is beheld by people of both sexes, and all ages, with such transports of joy and satisfaction, as they do .not exhibit on any other occasion.

[7] I have inserted the greater part of the information here mentioned, amongst the notes, not only because it appears necessary to illustrate the text, but because, if placed at the end of the chapter, it would swell out this article beyond the limits assigned to it in the volume.

[8] An instance of this is found in the history of Mark Antonio de Dominis, a Venetian, who was first a Jesuit, afterwards Bishop of Segni, and at last Archbishop of Spalatro. He was considered the greatest scholar of his age; and his reading made him embrace Protestantism. He was invited into England by James I., who made him Master of the Savoy, and Dean of Windsor. The Pope was greatly annoyed at the defection of this great and good man from the Romish church, and set every engine at work to induce him to return to his native country, that he might have his revenge; and, for this purpose, the Spanish ambassador made him such splendid offers, that he was prevailed upon to return to Rome, contrary to the expostulations of all his English friends. He had no sooner arrived in the papal city, than he discovered his mistake. The pontiff did not keep one of his promises to this unfortunate man, but obliged him publicly to abjure his heresies; after which, he was seized, and cast into the dungeons of the Inquisition, where he died of a broken heart.

sight of heaven to prosecute all persons whose religious principles differ from theirs.[9]

In order to give the reader all the proof possible in the nature of the thing, that I have really undergone the tortures mentioned in the following account of my sufferings, I showed the marks still remaining on my arms and legs to Dr. Hoadly, Mr. Hawkins, and Mr. Cary, surgeons ; and I think myself particularly obliged to these gentlemen for the leave they have given me to assure the public they were quite satisfied that the marks must have been the effect of very great violence ; and that, in their situation, they correspond exactly to the description of the torture.

I am a native of Berne, in Switzerland, and a lapidary by profession. In 1716, my father came, with his whole family, to London ; and as he proposed to settle in England, he got himself naturalized there.

After living twenty-two years in that city, I went, at the solicitation of a friend, to Paris, in order to work in the galleries of the Louvre. Five years after I left this capital and removed to Lisbon in hopes of finding an opportunity of going to Brazil, where I flattered myself that I should make a fortune. But the King of Portugal, whom I addressed in order to obtain permission for this purpose, being informed of my profession, and the skill I might have in diamonds, &c., his majesty, by the advice of his council, refused my petition, upon the supposition that it would be no ways proper to send a foreigner who was a lapidary into a country abounding with immense treasures, whose value the government endeavours, by all means possible, to conceal even from the inhabitants.

Whilst I was waiting for an answer from court to my petition, I got acquainted with several substantial

---

[9] What idea ought we to form of a tribunal which obliges children, under the most rigorous penalties, to be spies upon their parents, and to discover to the merciless inquisitors, the errors, and even the trifling indiscretions to which human frailty is subject—a tribunal which will not permit relatives, even when imprisoned in its horrid dungeons, to render each other the most trifling assistance ? What disorders must such conduct produce in the bosom of a family ! An expression, however true, however innocent, may be the occasion not only of infinite uneasiness and discord, but of utter ruin ; and may cause one or more of its members to be the victims of this barbarous tribunal.

jewellers, and other persons of credit in Lisbon, who made me the kindest and most generous offers, in case I would reside among them, which I accepted, after having lost all hopes of going to Brazil. I now was settled in the above-mentioned city, equally to the satisfaction of my friends, my employers, and myself; having a prospect of gaining wherewithal not only to support my family with decency, but also to lay up a competency for old age, could I but have escaped the cruel hands of the inquisitors.

I must observe, by the way, that the inquisitors have usurped so formidable a power in Spain and Portugal,[10] that the monarchs of those kingdoms are no more, if I may be allowed the expression, than as their chief subjects. Those tyrants do not scruple to encroach so far on the privilege of kings, as to stop, by their own authority, at the post office, the letters of all whom they take it into their heads to suspect.[11] In this manner I myself

[10] The power of the Inquisition was first cemented in Spain by the marriage of Ferdinand and Isabella of Castile, in the fifteenth century. The latter had been made to promise, before her marriage, by John de Torquemada, a Dominican friar, that, in case she should be raised to the throne, she would use all possible methods to extirpate heretics and infidels. As she afterwards was queen, and brought the kingdom of Castile, by way of dower, to Ferdinand, they, finding themselves exceedingly powerful, resolved to conquer the kingdom of Grenada, and to drive back the Moors into Barbary. The Moors were accordingly subdued, and all the territories possessed by them in Spain seized, so that prodigious multitudes of them were forced to return into Africa. Nevertheless, great numbers still continued in Spain ; a circumstance owing to their having possessions or wives in this country, or their being settled in traffic there. As Ferdinand and Isabella considered that, in case they should banish these Moors from Spain, they thereby would depopulate the countries conquered by them, their majesties consented that they, as well as the Jews, should continue in it, provided they would turn Christians ; upon which those people, finding that all resistance would be in vain, embraced the Christian religion in outward appearance. But Torquemada assured the queen that this dissimulation would be extremely prejudicial to the interest of religion and persuaded her to prosecute them to the utmost ; recommending, for that purpose, the establishment of the Inquisition, to which she gave her consent ; and the Dominican was appointed Inquisitor General, and discharged his functions so much to their satisfaction, that he prosecuted, in fourteen years, above 100,000 persons, 6,000 of whom were burned at the stake.

[11] The following instance proves that the inquisitors will condemn an innocent person, rather than permit any of their accusations to be disproved. A major in a Portuguese regiment was thrown into the prison of the Inquisition at Lisbon, on a charge of Judaism, but without nam-

was served, a year before the inquisitors had ordered me to be seized ; the design of which, I suppose, was to see whether, among the letters of my correspondents, some mention would not be made of Freemasonry ; I passing for one of the most zealous members of that art, which they resolved to persecute upon pretence that enormous crimes were committed by its professors. However, though the inquisitors did not find by one of my intercepted letters that Freemasonry either struck at the Romish religion, or tended to disturb the government, still they were not satisfied, but resolved to set every engine at work, in order to discover the mysteries and secrets of Masonry. For this purpose they concluded that it would be proper to seize one of the chief Freemasons in Lisbon ;[12] and accordingly I was pitched upon as being the Master of a lodge ; they likewise cast their eye on a Warden, an intimate friend of mine, Mr. Alex-

ing the offence. After having been incarcerated two years, the inquisitors told him that he was convicted of being a relapsed Jew, which he utterly denied, protesting that he had always been a true and faithful Christian. In a word, they could not prevail with him, either by threats or promises, to plead guilty to any one of the articles of which he stood accused ; declaring that he would die with innocence, rather than preserve his life by an action which must cover him with eternal infamy. Duke d'Aveyro, then Inquisitor General, who was desirous of saving this officer, being one day upon his visitation, strongly exhorted him to embrace the opportunity he had of extricating himself; but the prisoner continuing inflexible, the inquisitor was fired, and spoke thus to him : " Dost thou imagine that we'll have the lie on this occasion ?" The inquisitor then withdrew, leaving the prisoner to his reflections on what he had heard. Surely these words employed a meaning inconsistent with the character of an upright judge, and strongly spoke the iniquitous spirit of this tribunal. To conclude, the *auto-da-fé* approaching, our victim was condemned to the flames, and a confessor sent to him. Terrified at this horrid death, he, though entirely innocent, declared himself guilty of the crime laid to his charge. His possessions were then confiscated, after which, he was made to walk in the procession, in the habit of one relapsed ; and lastly, he was sentenced to the galleys for five years.

[12] The inquisitors may seize a heretic, though he should have fled for refuge to a church or sanctuary, and the bishop himself has not the power to prevent it ; a circumstance that gives them greater power than is enjoyed by the kings of the countries where the Inquisition is established. No prelate or legate from the see of Rome can pronounce sentence of excommunication, suspension, or interdict against the inquisitors, without an express order from the pope ; and the inquisitors may even forbid the secular judges to prosecute any person, even in a suit which has been commenced by their order. Any person who shall kill, abuse, or beat an inquisitor, or an official of the Inquisition, shall be delivered over to the secular arm, and punished according to his deserts.

ander James Mouton, a diamond-cutter, born in Paris, and a Romanist. He had been settled six years before his seizure at Lisbon, in which city he was a housekeeper, and where his integrity, skill, and behaviour were such as gained him the approbation of all to whom he was known.

The reader is to be informed, that our lodges in Lisbon were not kept at taverns, &c., but alternately at the private houses of chosen friends. In these we used to dine together, and practise the secrets of Freemasonry.

As we did not know that our art was forbidden in Portugal,[13] we were soon discovered by the barbarous zeal of a lady, who declared, at confession, that we were Freemasons; that is, in her opinion, monsters in nature, who perpetrated the most shocking crimes. This discovery immediately put the vigilant officers of the Inquisition upon the scent after us; on which occasion my friend Mr. Mouton fell the first victim—he being seized in manner following:

A jeweller and goldsmith, who was a familiar of the holy office,[14] sent a friend (a Freemason also) to Mr.

[13] "Portugal," says a writer in the Freemasons' Quarterly Review, "has not been the refuge of the Mason. As in Spain, religious intolerance raised that scourge, the Inquisition, with its mummeries and horrors, seeking to coerce the mind of man within the narrowest and the vilest trammels, proving the state of bigotry into which they had sunk; and from thence the unhappy Freemason, or other liberal-minded person had not much consideration to expect; nevertheless, efforts were made, at various times, and in various places, to establish lodges; but the fears and jealousies of the bedarkened priests always interfered to prevent the spread of enlightenment, or benefit to mankind, unless they were the greatest gainers. In 1735, several noble Portuguese, with more foreigners, instituted a Lodge in Lisbon, under the Grand Lodge of England, of which George Gordon was Master; but no sooner was the slightest suspicion entertained of its existence, than the clergy determined to give the clearest evidence of their hatred to the Order by practical illustrations."

[14] The familiars are the bailiffs or catchpoles of the Inquisition. Though this is a most ignominious employment in all other criminal courts, it yet is looked upon as so honourable in the Inquisition, that every nobleman in Portugal is a familiar of this tribunal. It is not surprising that persons of the highest quality should be solicitous for this post, since the pope has granted to these familiars the like plenary indulgences as the council of Lateran gave to such persons as should go to the succour of the Holy Land against the infidels. They are the satellites of the inquisitors; they attending on them, and defending them, if necessary, against

Mouton, upon pretence that he wanted to speak with him about mending a diamond weighing four carats. They agreed upon the price; but as this was merely an artifice in order for our familiar to know the person of the said Mouton, he put him off for two days, upon pretence that he must first enquire of the owner of the diamond whether he approved of the price settled between them.

I happened to be at that time with Mr. Mouton, a circumstance which gave the highest joy to the jeweller, finding that he had got a sight, at one and the same time, of the very two Freemasons whom the inquisitors were determined to seize.

At our taking leave, he desired us to come together at the time appointed, to which we both agreed. The jeweller then made his report to the inquisitors, who ordered him to seize us, when we should return about the diamond in question.

Two days being elapsed, and my business not permitting me to accompany Mr. Mouton, he went alone to the jeweller to fetch the diamond, which was computed to be worth a hundred moidores. The first question the jeweller asked, after the usual compliments, was, "Where is your friend Coustos?" As this jeweller had before shown me some precious stones, which he pretended I should go to work upon, Mr. Mouton, imagining he was desirous of putting them instantly into my hands, replied " that I was upon 'change, and that, if he thought proper, he would go and fetch me." However, as this familiar and five subaltern officers of the Inquisition, who were along with him, were afraid of losing half their prey, they inveigled Mr. Mouton into the back shop, upon pretence of asking his opinion concerning certain rough diamonds. After several signs and words had passed between them, the oldest of the company rising up, said he had something particular to communicate to Mr. Mouton; upon which he took him behind a curtain, when, enquiring his name and surname, he told him that he was his prisoner, in the king's name.

the insults of heretics. They accompany the executioner whenever he goes to seize criminals, and must obey all orders given them by the chief officers of the Inqusition. Several privileges are allowed them, especially the carrying arms; but they are ordered to use those with discretion.

6*

Being sensible that he had not committed any crime for which he could incur his Portuguese[15] majesty's displeasure, he gave up his sword the moment it was demanded of him. Immediately several trusty officers of the Inquisition, called familiars, fell upon him to prevent his escaping; then commanded him not to make the least noise, and began to search him. This being done, and finding he had no weapons, they asked whether he was desirous of knowing in whose name he had been seized. Mr. Mouton answered in the affirmative. " We seize-you," said they, in the name of the Inquisition ;[16] and, in its name, we forbid you to speak or murmur ever so little." Saying these words, a door at the bottom of the jeweller's shop, and which looked into a narrow byelane, being opened, the prisoner, accompanied by a com-

[15] The manner in which the Inquisition was first established in Portugal appears a little fabulous. It is said to have been introduced by John Peres de Saavedra, a Spaniard. We are told that he, being expert at counterfeiting the apostolical letters, amassed by that means 30,000 ducats, which were employed by him in order to bring the Inquisition into Portugal, and that in manner following: He assumed the character of Cardinal Legate from the see of Rome ; when, forming his household of one hundred and fifty domestics, he was received in the above-mentioned quality at Seville, and very honourably lodged in the archiepiscopal palace. Advancing, after this, towards the frontiers of Portugal, he dispatched one of his secretaries to the king, to acquaint him with his arrival, and to present him with fictitious letters from the emperor, the King of Spain, the pope, and several other princes, both ecclesiastical and secular, who all entreated his majesty to favour the legate's pious designs. The king, overjoyed at this legation, sent a lord of his court to compliment him, and attend him to the royal palace, where he resided about three months. The mock legate having succeeded in his designs by laying the foundation of the Inquisition, took leave of his majesty, and departed, greatly satisfied with his achievement ; but, unluckily for himself, he was discovered on the confines of Castile, and known to have been formerly a domestic of a Portuguese nobleman. He was then seized, and sentenced to ten years in the galleys, where he continued a long time, and was at last released by Pope Paul IV. The Inquisition in Portugal was the most severe, the most rigid and cruel of any in existence.

[16] All affairs relating to the holy office are managed by the inquisitors, who, by virtue of the denunciations, informations, and accusations, brought against all sorts of persons, issue their orders for seizing and imprisoning the accused. The inquisitors receive their depositions, and if they are not to their mind, they use various kinds of tortures, in order to extort from the poor wretches such a confession as they themselves desire. It may indeed be said, that all their prisoners, how innocent soever they may be, are certain of being condemned to some kind of punishment.

missary of the holy office, was thrown into a small chaise, where he was so closely shut up (it being noon-day) that no one could see him. This precaution was used to prevent his friends from getting the least information concerning his imprisonment, and, consequently, from using their endeavours to procure his liberty.

Being come to the prison of the Inquisition, they threw him into a dungeon, and there left him alone,[17] without indulging him in the satisfaction they had promised, which was, to let him speak, immediately upon his arrival, to the president of the holy office, to know from him the reason of his detainer. On the contrary, they were so cruel to Mr. Mouton's reputation, as to spread a report he was gone off with the diamond above-mentioned. But how greatly were every one of his friends surprised and shocked at this slander! As we all entertained the highest idea of his probity, none of us would give credit to this vile report; whence we unanimously agreed, after duly weighing this matter, to go in a body to the jeweller, who was the owner of the diamond, and offer him the full payment of it; firmly persuaded that nothing but the most fatal and unexpected accident could have made him disappear thus suddenly, without giving some of his friends notice of it. However, the jeweller refused our offer in the politest manner ; assuring us, at the same time, that the owner of the diamond was so wealthy a man, that the loss of it would be but a trifle to him.

But as truth frequently breaks through all the veils with which falsehood endeavours to cloud her, this generosity in persons to whom we were, in a great measure, strangers, made us suspect some iniquitous, dark act. Our conjecture appeared but too well grounded, from the severe persecution that was immediately raised

---

[17] In these miserable places the prisoner is closed in a room about twelve feet long and ten wide, by two strong doors. The cell is generally dark, the light coming in only through a very small window at the top of the wall. This glimmering light inspires such a degree of melancholy, that the prisoner usually wishes for night, when the cell is enlightened by a small lamp. The stench of these places is most unwholesome ; for the prisoner is obliged to spend month after month in the midst of every species of filth and dirt, until the stench is so nauseous, breeding reptiles and worms, that it is a miracle how the poor wretches continue to live in the midst of so much filth.

against the Freemasons—I myself being seized four days after.

I, perhaps, should have escaped their merciless paws, had I not been betrayed, in the most barbarous manner, by a Portuguese friend of mine, as I falsely supposed him to be ; and whom the holy office had ordered to watch me narrowly.[18]   This man seeing me in a coffee-house, the 5th of March, 1742–3, between nine and ten at night, went and gave notice thereof to nine officers of the Inquisition, who were lying in wait for me, with a chaise, near that place.

I was in the utmost confusion when, at my going out of the coffee-house with two friends, the above officers seized me only.[19]   Their pretence for this was, that I had

[18] This was the usual custom.   The ties of nature were often violated to gratify the vengeance of the inquisitors.   The following is an instance of this fact :—" Alphonso Nobre, born in Villa Viziosa, and descended from one of the most ancient and illustrious families of that city, many of whom had filled those posts which, in Portugal, are bestowed on none but noble persons, and all whose ancestors could not be reproached with the least tincture of Judaism, was seized and carried to the prisons of the Inquisition of Coimbra, upon the information of persons who swore that he was not a Christian.   Some time after, his only son and daughter were seized and confined in the same prison.   These children, who were very young, impeached their father ; whether excited thereto by evil counsellors, or that the tortures had extorted the impeachment from them.   At last the unhappy father was sentenced to be burnt alive, on the depositions of his children.   The day of the *auto-da-fé* being come, the son drew near to his parent, to crave forgiveness and his blessing, but the ill-fated father replied—' I pardon you both, though you are the sole cause of my ignominious and cruel death ; as to my blessing, I cannot give it you ; for he is not my son, who makes a pretended confession of untruths, and who, having been a Roman Catholic, shamefully denies his Saviour, by declaring himself a Jew.   Go,' added he, ' unnatural son ! I beseech Heaven to pardon you !'   Being come, at last, to the stake, he discovered such great courage and resolution, made such pathetic discourses, and addressed himself with so much fervour to the Almighty, as filled all his hearers with admiration, and caused them to look upon his judges with horror."

[19] It frequently happens that the inquisitors, from an apprehension that an accused person may possibly escape from their clutches, issue their orders to seize him at once.   In such a case no asylum or privilege can protect him ; for the familiars are always sufficiently numerous to prevent a rescue.   Words can scarcely describe the extent of such a calamity.   He is perhaps seized when in company with his friend, or surrounded by his family—a father from the arms of a son, or a wife from the arms of her husband.   No person dare make the slightest resistance, or even to speak a single word in favour of the prisoner ; nor is he allowed a moment's respite to settle his most important affairs.   Thus it

passed my word for the diamond which Mr. Mouton had run away with; that I must certainly be his accomplice, since I had engaged my friends to offer to pay for the diamond; all which, added they, I must have done in no other view than to conceal my villainy. It was to no purpose that I alleged a thousand things in my own justification. Immediately the wretches took away my sword, hand-cuffed me, forced me into a chaise drawn by two mules, and in this condition I was hurried away to the prison of the Inquisition.

But, spite of these severities, and their commanding me not to open my lips, I yet called aloud to one of my friends, Mr. Richard, who had been at the coffee-house with me, and was a Freemason, conjuring him to give notice to all the rest of our Brethren and friends, of my being seized by command of the holy office, in order that they might avoid the misfortune which had befallen me, by going voluntarily to the inquisitors, and accusing themselves.

I must take notice, that the inquisitors very seldom cause a person to be seized in broad day-light, except they are almost sure that he will make no noise nor resistance. This is a circumstance they observe very strictly, as is evident from the manner in which they took Mr. Mouton. Further, they frequently make use of the king's name and authority on these occasions, to seize and disarm the pretended criminal, who is afraid to disobey the orders he hears pronounced. But as darkness befriends deeds of villainy, the inquisitors, for this reason, usually cause their victims to be secured in the night.[20]

will be seen, that persons living under the eye of the Inquisition, must necessarily be filled with apprehension; since, in order to secure themselves from its vengeance, one friend is obliged to sacrifice another; parents their children; husbands their wives, and wives their husbands, by a voluntary accusation. What kind of tribunal must that be which thus extinguishes all the sensations of tenderness and affection which nature inspires towards every relation of social life; and extends its inhumanity so far as to compel children to accuse their parents, and to become the unhappy authors of the cruelties which they are sure to suffer?

[20] When a familiar, who has been appointed by the inquisitors to seize a criminal, has found him, he merely bids him to follow his steps. All the way they go, the officer uses every artifice in his power to persuade the poor wretch to make a full confession of his guilt, in order, as he is told, to experience the mercy of the inquisitors, who are sure to liberate

The Portuguese, and many foreigners, are so apprehensive of the sinister accidents which often happen at Lisbon in the night-time, especially to a person who ventures out alone, that few are found in the streets of this city at a late hour.

I imagined myself so secure in the company of my friends, that I should not have been afraid of resisting the officers in question, had the former lent me their assistance. But, unhappily for me, they were struck with such a sudden panic, that every one of them fled, leaving me to the mercy of nine wretches, who fell upon me in an instant.[21]

They then forced me to the prison of the Inquisition, where I was delivered up to one of the officers of this pretended holy place. This officer presently calling four subalterns, or guards, these took me to an apartment, till such time as notice should be given to the president of my being catched in their snare.[22]

him, and permit his return to his family; and that if, on the contrary, he does not accuse himself, he must not expect his release from prison, until he has undergone a variety of tortures, with the almost certain prospect of being burned alive at last. In like manner, when he comes to the prisons of the Inquisition, the alcaide and his followers exhort the prisoner to confess, under the promise of being speedily restored to his friends. The prisoner is often deluded by these artifices to accuse himself of crimes which he never committed, and then, they subject him to punishment on his own confession!

[21] They were bound to do this; for it was penal to conceal, or give the prisoner advice or assistance to enable him to escape out of prison, and also to molest, by threats or otherwise, the agents of the tribunal in the discharge of their duties. If any one should speak without permission to a prisoner, or write to him, or even to give him comfort, he is liable to punishment as a fautor of heresy; as also are those who prevail upon witnesses to be silent or to favour the prisoner in their depositions; or who conceal or destroy papers which may be useful in convicting the accused.

[22] Two prisoners are seldom lodged in the same cell, because, as the inquisitors pretend, they might agree to suppress or conceal the truth; but the real motive for keeping them apart, is to extort from them, by the dreadful solitude of their confinement, an admission of the charges that are made against them. Occasionally two prisoners are allowed to be together: when a prisoner is sick, a companion is given him; and when the inquisitors have failed to induce a prisoner to admit a false charge, they then send him a companion, who artfully glides into the confidence of the prisoner, by inveighing against the inquisitors, and accusing them of injustice, cruelty, and barbarity. The unhappy victim insensibly joins in his reproaches, when the companion appears as a witness against him, and the poor deluded wretch is at once convicted on his testimony.

A little after, the above-mentioned officer coming again, bid the guards search me, and take away all the gold, silver, papers, knives, scissors, buckles, &c., I might have about me.[23] They then led me to a lonely dungeon, expressly forbidding me to speak loud, or knock at the walls; but that, in case I wanted anything, to beat against the door, with a padlock that hung on the out-ward door, and which I could reach, by thrusting my arm through the iron grates. It was then that, struck with all the horrors of a place of which I had heard and read such baleful descriptions, I plunged at once into the blackest melancholy, especially when I reflected on the dire consequences with which my confinement might very possibly be attended.[24]

I passed a whole day and two nights in these terrors, which are the more difficult to describe, as they were heightened at every little interval by the complaints, the dismal cries, and hollow groans, echoing through this dreadful mansion, of several other prisoners, my neigh-bours; and which the solemn silence of the night made infinitely more shocking. It was now that time seemed

[23] When a prisoner is placed in his dungeon, he is thoroughly searched for any books or papers that might contribute to his conviction; and to deprive him of any instrument by which he might put an end to his life, to escape the torture, of which there are too many sad examples. After his money, papers, buckles, rings, &c., have been taken from him, he is left to his own reflections. Torn from his family and friends, who are not allowed access to him, or even to communicate with him by letter, he finds himself abandoned to melancholy and despair. Innocence, in such a situation, will afford him no protection—nothing being easier than to ruin an innocent person. He is soon visited by the inquisitor and his officers, who inform him that they have been to his dwelling, and taken an inventory of all his papers, effects, and of everything there found. Indeed, they frequently seize upon the prisoner's estates, to pay them-selves, as they pretend, the fine to which the accused may probably be subjected by the holy office.

[24] The furniture of these miserable dungeons is a straw bed, a blanket, sheets, and sometimes a mattrass. The prisoner is likewise allowed a frame of wood, about six feet long and three or four wide. This he lays upon the ground and spreads his bed upon it. He has also a great earthen pot to ease nature in, an earthen pan for washing himself; two pitchers, one for clean and the other for foul water; a plate, and a little vessel with oil to light his lamp. He is not allowed, however, book or papers of any kind. Their provisions are regulated by a dietary, and are of the meanest kind. If any of the prisoners desire wine, it is sometimes allowed on a proper application. " I myself," says Coustos, " addressed the inquisitors for this purpose, and my request was granted."

to have lost all motion, and these threescore hours appeared to me like so many years.[25]

However, afterwards calling to mind that grief would only aggravate my calamity, I endeavoured to arm my soul with patience, and to habituate myself, as well as I could, to woe. Accordingly I roused my spirits; and, banishing for a few moments these dreadfully mournful ideas, I began to reflect seriously on the methods how to extricate myself from this labyrinth of horrors. My consciousness that I had not committed any crime which could justly merit death, would now and then soften my pangs; but immediately after, dreadful thoughts overspread my mind, when I imaged to myself the crying injustice of which the tribunal, that was to judge me, is accused. I considered that, being a Protestant,[26] I should inevitably feel, in its utmost rigours, all that rage and barbarous zeal could infuse in the breast of monks, who cruelly gloried in committing to the flames great num-

---

[25] Sometimes a prisoner passes several months in his cell without being brought to trial, or knowing the crime of which he stands impeached. At lenght the jailor suggests that he ought to petition for an audience. If he do this, he is conducted into the presence of his judges bareheaded. He is kept, however, in the antechamber, until the porter has given three knocks at the door of the great hall. This is a signal to the inquisitors to clear the hall, that the prisoner may not see or be seen by any improper person. This being done, the judge answers by the sound of a little bell. The prisoner is then led in, and advancing to the table, is told to kneel down and lay his hand on a closed book, and he is required solemnly to promise that he will conceal the secrets of the holy office, and speak the truth. He is then allowed to sit down, when he is strictly questioned on the subject of the charges on which he has been confined. The secretary having written down all the interrogatories, with the prisoner's replies, the latter is exhorted by his judge to spend his time, until he shall be again examined, in recollecting all the crimes he may have committed since he has arrived at years of discretion; and then, he is ordered back to his dungeon.

[26] All Protestants are deemed heretics; but the meaning of the word is much more extensive, and comprehends all persons who have spoken, or written, or taught any tenets which are contrary to the traditions of the Church of Rome. Likewise such as have been heard to speak tolerantly of the customs of other churches, or who believe that any can be saved who are not within the pale of that church. If any should disapprove of the ceremonies, usages, or customs of the church or of the Inquisition, or if they hold any heterodox opinions respecting the pope's supremacy; contemn the use of images, or read books which have been condemned by the Inquisition, they are sure to be suspected of heresy; as are also those who deviate from the customs of religion, who eat meat on fish days, or neglect confession, communion, or the mass.

bers of ill-fated victims, whose only crime was their differing from them in religious opinions, or rather, who
were obnoxious to those tigers, merely because they
thought worthily of human nature, and had in the utmost
detestation, these Romish barbarities, which are not to
be paralleled in any other religion.[27]

These apprehensions, together with the reflections
which reason suggested to me, viz., that it would be
highly incumbent on me to calm the tumult of my spirits, in order to prevent my falling into the snares which
my judges would not fail to spread round me; either by
giving them an opportunity of pronouncing me guilty,
or by forcing me to apostatize from the religion in which
I was born; these things, I say, worked so strongly on
my mind, that, from this moment, I devoted my whole
thoughts to the means of my justification. This I made
so familiar to myself, that I was persuaded neither the
partiality of my judges, nor the dreadful ideas I had entertained of their cruelty, could intimidate me when I
should be brought before them; which I accordingly
was, in a few days, after having been shaved, and had my
hair cut by their order.[28]

[27] In Poland, even so late as the year 1739, a juggler was exposed to
the torture until a confession was extracted from him that he was a
sorcerer; upon which, without further proof, he was immediately hanged;
and instances in other countries of the same thing, might be multiplied
almost without end. But this does not equal in absurdity the infatua-
tion of the Inquisition in Portugal, which actually condemned to the
flames, as being possessed by the devil, an ape belonging to an Englishman, who had taught it to perform some uncommon tricks; and the poor
animal is confidently said to have been publicly burned at Lisbon, in
conformity with his sentence, in the year 1601. (Beckmann's Ancient
Inventions, vol. i., p. 172.)

[28] A day or two after the prisoner is brought into his cell, his hair is
cut off, and his head is shaved. On these occasions no distinction is made
in age, sex, or birth. He is then ordered to tell his name and profession;
and to make a discovery of whatever he is worth in the world. To induce
him to do this, the inquisitor promises that, if he be really innocent, the
several things disclosed by him will be carefully restored; but that should
he endeavour to conceal any of his effects, and they be afterwards found,
they all will be confiscated, though he may be cleared. As most of the
Portuguese are so weak, as to be firmly persuaded of the sanctity and
integrity of this tribunal, they do not scruple to discover even such
things as they might most easily conceal, from a firm belief that every
particular will be restored to them, the moment their innocence shall be
proved. However, these hapless persons are imposed upon; for those
who have the sad fortune to fall into the merciless hands of the iniquitous

I was now led, bare-headed, to the president and four Inquisitors,[29] who, upon my coming in, bid me kneel down, lay my right hand on the Bible, and swear, in the presence of Almighty God, that I would speak truly with regard to all the questions they should ask me. These questions were: my Christian and surnames, those of my parents, the place of my birth, my profession, religion, and how long I had resided in Lisbon. This being done, they addressed me as follows :—" Son, you have offended and spoke injuriously of the holy office, as we know from very good hands ; for which reason we exhort you to make a confession of, and to accuse yourself of the several crimes you may have committed, from the time you were capable of judging between good and evil, to the present moment. In doing this, you will excite the compassion of this tribunal, which is ever merciful and kind to those who speak the truth."[30]

judges, are instantly bereaved of all their possessions. In case they plead their innocence with regard to the crimes of which they stand accused, and yet should be convicted by the witnesses who swore against them, they then would be sentenced as guilty, and their whole possessions confiscated. If prisoners, in order to escape the torture, and in hopes of being sooner set at liberty, own the crime or crimes of which they are impeached, they then are pronounced guilty by their own confession ; and the public, in general, think their effects, &c., justly confiscated. If such prisoners come forth as repentant criminals, who had accused themselves voluntarily, they yet dare not plead their innocence ; since they thereby would run the hazard of being imprisoned again, and sentenced, not only as hypocritical penitents, but likewise as wretches who accuse the inquisitors of injustice ; so that, what course soever these persons might take, they would certainly lose all such possessions belonging to them as the inquisitors had seized.

[29] The author of the Relation of the Inquisition of Goa, p. 89, et seq., Paris, 1688, writes as follows concerning the officers of the Inquisition : —" There are at Goa two inquisitors ; the first called the great inquisitor, who is a secular priest, and the second a Dominican friar. The officers called deputados draw up the prosecutions, and assist at the judgment of the prisoners. The proctor acts as the advocate of such prisoners as may desire to employ him ; but he is rather a betrayer than a defender ; for the information which he extracts from the unhappy culprit. in confidence, he always betrays to the judges. The familiars are but the bailiffs of the tribunal, who are employed in seizing suspected persons. The office is honorary, and includes persons of all conditions, even dukes and princes, who wear a medal with the arms of the Inquisition. There are likewise secretaries, apparitors, and guards or attendants to look after the prisoners, and to provide them with food and other necessaries.'

[30] A French writer, himself professing the Roman Catholic religion,

It was then they thought proper to inform me, that the diamond, mentioned in the former pages, was only a pretence they had employed, in order to get an opportunity of seizing me. I now besought them, "to let me know the true causes of my imprisonment; that having been born and educated in the Protestant religion, I had been taught from my infancy, not to confess myself to men, but to God, who, as he only can see into the inmost recesses of the human heart, knows the sincerity or insincerity of the sinner's repentance, who confessed to him; and, being his Creator, it was he only who could absolve him."

The reader will naturally suppose that they were no ways satisfied with my answer—"They declaring, that it would be indispensably necessary for me to confess myself, what religion soever I might be of; otherwise, that a confession would be forced from me, by the expedients the holy office employed for that purpose."[31]

To this I replied—"That I had never spoken in my life against the Romish religion; that I had behaved in

speaking of the various courts in Lima, says :—"The most formidable of all the tribunals is that of the Inquisition, whose name alone is sufficient to strike terror into every heart.—1. Because the informer is admitted as a witness. 2. The persons impeached never know who it is that have laid the information against them. 3. The witnesses are never confronted. Hence innocent persons are daily seized, whose only crime is to have enemies who are bent upon their destruction." (Frezier. Rel. du Voyage, p. 201.)

[31] "The pretended zeal of the inquisitors," says Coustos, in his Appendix, "for preserving religion in its purity, is merely a cloak to hide their boundless ambition, their insatiable thirst for riches, and their vindictive spirit. The Emperor Frederick invested the inquisitors with great privileges, and encouraged them to the most cruel abuse of them. All who opposed his will were deemed heretics, and judged and burnt as such. He committed to the flames, under the false pretence of heresy, so great a number of Romanists, that Pope Gregory could not forbear representing to him. in the most serious terms, that it became him to extirpate heretics only, and not the true sons of the church. The monarch in question did not foresee that the court of Rome might turn those very weapons against him, which he had employed so unjustly against a multitude of Christians. This emperor was afterwards sensible of his error, but too late ; for he himself was in 1239 impeached as a heretic, and being judged. was excommunicated as such, and his subjects freed from the allegiance they had sworn to him ; though his heresy was no more than his having opposed the unlimited power which the popes pretended to exercise over all Christians, not excepting even crowned heads."

such a manner, ever since my living at Lisbon, that I
could not be justly accused of saying or doing anything
contrary to the laws of the kingdom, either as to spiri-
tuals or temporals ; that I had also imagined the holy
office took cognizance of none but those persons who
were guilty of sacrilege, blasphemy, and such like
crimes, whose delight is to depreciate and ridicule the
mysteries received in the Romish church, but of which
I was no ways guilty."[32]   They then remanded me back
to my dungeon, after exhorting me to examine my conscience.

Three days after they sent for me, to interrogate me a
second time.   The first question they asked was—
" Whether I had carefully looked into my conscience,
pursuant to their injunction ?"   I replied—" That after
carefully reviewing all the past transactions of my life, I
did not remember my having said or done anything that
could justly give offence to the holy office ; that from
my most tender youth my parents, who had been forced
to quit France for their religion, and who knew, by sad
experience, how highly it concerns every one, that
values his ease, never to converse on religious subjects,
in certain countries ; that my parents (I say) had advised me never to engage in disputes of this kind, since
they usually embittered the minds of the contending
parties, rather than reconciled them ; further, that I
belonged to a society, composed of persons of different
religions ; one of the laws of which society expressly
forbids its members ever to dispute on those subjects,
under a considerable penalty."   As the inquisitors confounded the word society with that of religion, I assured
them, " That this society could be considered as a religious one, no otherwise than as it obliged its several
members to live together in charity and brotherly love,
how widely soever they might differ in religious prin-

---

[32] The Inquisition takes cognizance of reputed magicians, wizards, and
fortune-tellers, which abound in the south of Europe, owing to the credulity of the people.   It will be unnecessary to specify the various accusations brought forward on these occasions ; for they are all equally
absurd.   But though the prisons of the Inquisition are usually filled with
these enthusiasts, who are sometimes punished with great severity, yet
blasphemy remains unnoticed by the inquisitors.   Thus a man may offend
God with impunity, yet he must not offend an Inquisitor.

ciples." They then inquired—" How this society was called ?" I replied—" That if they had ordered me to be seized because I was one of its members I would readily tell them its name : I thinking myself not a little honoured in belonging to a society which boasted several Christian kings, princes, and persons of the highest quality among its members ; and that I had been frequently in company with some of the latter, as one of their Brethren."

Then one of the inquisitors asked me—" Whether the name of this society was a secret ?" I answered—" That it was not ; that I could tell it them in French or English, but was not able to translate it into Portuguese." Then all of them fixing, on a sudden, their eyes attentively on me, repeated, alternately, the words Freemason, or Francmaçon. From this instant I was firmly persuaded that I had been imprisoned solely on account of Masonry.

They afterwards asked—" What were the constitutions of this society ?" I then set before them, as well as I could, " the ancient traditions relating to this noble art, of which, I told them, James VI., King of Scotland,[33] had declared himself the protector, and encouraged his subjects to enter among the Freemasons ; that it appeared, from authentic manuscripts, that the kings of Scotland had so great a regard for this honourable society, on account of the strong proofs its members had ever given of their fidelity and attachment, that those monarchs established the custom among the Brethren of saying whenever they drank, ' God preserve the king and the Brotherhood ;' that this example was soon followed by the Scotch nobility and the clergy, who had so high an esteem for the Brotherhood, that most of them entered into the society.

" That it appeared from other traditions, that the kings of Scotland had frequently been Grand Masters of the Freemasons ; and that, when the kings were not such, the society were empowered to elect as Grand Master one of the nobles of the country, who had a pen-

---

[33] The Constitutions of the Freemasons, &c., for the use of the Lodge, by Dr. Anderson, p. 38, London, 1723. Some other passages here are taken from the same work.

sion from the sovereign, and received, at his election, a gift from every Freemason in Scotland."

I likewise told them—" That Queen Elizabeth, ascending the throne of England at a time when the kingdom was greatly divided by factions and clashing interests, and taking umbrage at the various assemblies of great numbers of her subjects, as not knowing the designs of those meetings, she resolved to suppress the assemblies of the Freemasons; however, that, before her majesty proceeded to this extremity, she commanded some of her subjects to enter into this society, among whom was the Archbishop of Canterbury, primate of her kingdom; that these, obeying the queen's orders, gave her so very advantageous a character of the fidelity of the Freemasons, as removed, at once, all her majesty's suspicions and political fears; so that the society has, ever since that time, enjoyed in Great Britain, and the places subject to it, all the liberty it could wish for, and which it has never once abused."

They afterwards inquired—" What was the tendency of this society?" I replied—" Every Freemason is obliged, at his admission, to take an oath, on the Holy Gospel, that he will be faithful to the king; and never enter into any plot or conspiracy against his sacred person, or against the country where he resides; and that he will pay obedience to the magistrates appointed by the monarch."[34]

I next declared—" That charity was the foundation, and the soul, as it were, of the society, as it linked together the several individuals of it by the tie of fraternal love; and made it an indispensable duty to assist, in the most charitable manner, without distinction of religion, all such necessitous persons as were found true objects of compassion." It was then they called me liar, de-

---

[34] It is strange that the skill of Masons—which was always transcendently great, even in the most barbarous times—their wonderful kindness and attachment to each other, and their inviolable fidelity in keeping the secrets of the Order, should have exposed them, in all ages, to a variety of persecutions, according to the state of party, or the alterations of government. Still it is a remarkable fact, that Masons have always been submissive to the laws of the country where they worked, although they were frequently exposed to great severities, when power wore the trappings of justice, and those who committed treason, punished true men as traitors. (MS. in British Museum.)

claring—" That it was impossible this society should profess the practice of such good maxims, and yet be so very jealous of its secrets as to exclude women from it." The judicious reader will perceive, at once, the weakness of this inference, which, perhaps, would be found but too true, were it applied to the inviolable secrecy observed by this · pretended holy office, in all its actions.[35]

They presently gave orders for my being conveyed into another deep dungeon ; the design of which, I suppose, was to terrify me completely; and here I continued seven weeks. It will be naturally supposed that I now was overwhelmed with grief. I will confess, that I then gave myself up entirely for lost, and had no resource left but in the Almighty, whose aid I implored continually with the utmost fervency.

[35] This tribunal bore some resemblance to the Vehme Gerichte of Westphalia. Mr. Palgrave, in his valuable work on the Rise and Progress of the English Commonwealth, says :—" The criminal jurisdiction of the Vehmic tribunal took the widest range. The Vehme could punish mere slander and contumely. Any violation of the ten commandments, was to be restrained by the Echevins. Secret crimes, not to be proved by the ordinary testimony of witnesses, such as magic, witchcraft, and poison, were particularly to be restrained by the Vehmic judges ; and they sometimes designated their jurisdiction as comprehending every offence against the honour of man or the precepts of religion. Such a definition, if definition it can be called, evidently allowed them to bring every action of which an individual might complain, within the scope of their tribunals. The forcible usurpation of land became an offence against the Vehme. And, if the property of an humble individual was occupied by the proud burghers of the Hanse, the power of the defendants might afford a reasonable excuse for the interference of the Vehmic power. The Echevins, as conservators of the ban of the empire, were bound to make constant circuits within their districts, by night and by day. If they could apprehend a thief, a murderer, or the perpetrator of any other heinous crime, in possession of the *mainour,* or in the very act, or, if his own mouth confessed the deed, they hung him upon the next tree. If, without any certain accuser, and without the indication of crime, an individual was strongly and vehemently suspected ; or, when the nature of the offence was such as that its proof could only rest upon opinion and presumption, the offender then became subject to what the German jurists term the inquisitorial proceeding, it became the duty of the Echevin to denounce the *leumund,* or manifest evil fame to the secret tribunal. If the Echevins and the Freygraff were satisfied with the presentment, either from their own knowledge, or from the information of their compeer, the offender was said to be *verfambt,* his life was forfeited ; and wherever he was found by the brethren of the tribunal, they executed him without the slightest delay or mercy."

During my stay in this miserable dungeon,[36] I was taken three times before the inquisitors. The first thing they made me do was, to swear on the Bible that I would not reveal the secrets of the Inquisition; but declare the truth with regard to all such questions as they should put to me; they added: "That it was their firm opinion that Masonry could not be founded on such good principles as I, in my former interrogatories, had affirmed; and that, if this society of Freemasons was so virtuous as I pretended, there was no occasion of their concealing, so very industriously, the secrets of it."

I told them, "That as secrecy[37] naturally excited curi-

---

[36] The house of the Inquisition in Lisbon, where poor Coustos was confined, is described as being a very spacious edifice. There are four courts, each about forty feet square, round which are galleries two stories high, which lead to the dormitories, or cells, in number about three hundred. Those on the ground floor are frightful dungeons, built of freestone, with arched roofs, and very dark and gloomy. The cells on the first floor are not much better. Females are commonly lodged in those of the upper story. These galleries are hid from the view by high walls, which being built only a few feet from the entrance of the cells, contribute much to their gloomy appearance. The house is so very extensive, and contains such a variety of intricate passages, that it would be impossible for a prisoner, even if he escaped from his cell, to find his way out.

[37] One of the principal parts that makes a man be deemed wise, is his intelligent strength and ability to cover and conceal such honest secrets as are committed to him, as well as his own serious affairs. And whoever will peruse sacred and profane history, shall find a great number of virtuous attempts, in peace and war, that never reached their designed ends through defect of secret concealment; and yet, besides such unhappy prevention, infinite evils have thereby ensued. But before all other examples, let us consider that which excels all the rest, derived even from God himself. Who so especially preserves his own secrets to himself, never letting any man know what should happen on the morrow; nor could the wise men in ages past divine what should befall us in this age; whereby we may readily discern that God himself is well pleased with secrecy. And although, for man's good, the Lord has been pleased to reveal some things, yet it is impossible at any time to change or alter his determination, in regard whereof the reverend wise men of ancient times evermore affected to perform their intentions secretly. The Athenians had a statue of brass which they bowed to; the figure was made without a tongue, to declare secrecy thereby. The servants of Plancus are much commended because no torment could make them confess the secret which their master entrusted them with. Likewise the servant of Cato, the orator, was cruelly tormented, but nothing could make him reveal the secrets of his master. Aristotle was demanded what thing appeared most difficult to him; he answered to be secret and silent. To this purpose St. Ambrose, in his offices, placed among the principal foundations of virtue the patient gift of silence. The wise King Solomon says, in his proverbs, that a king ought not to drink wine, because drunkenness is an

osity, this prompted great numbers of persons to enter into this society, that all the moneys given by members at their admission therein were employed in works of charity; that by the secrets which the several members practised, a true Mason instantly knew whether a stranger who would introduce himself into a lodge was really a Freemason; that, was it not for such precautions, this society would form confused assemblies of all sorts of people, who, as they were not obliged to pay obedience to the orders of the Master of the lodge, it consequently would be impossible to keep them within the bounds of that decorum and good manners which are exactly observed, upon certain penalties, by all Feecmasons. That the reason why women were excluded this society was, to take away all occasion for calumny and reproach, which would have been unavoidable, had they been admitted into it. Farther, that since women had in general been always considered as not very well qualified to keep a secret, the founders of the society of Freemasons, by their exclusion of the other sex, thereby gave a signal proof of their prudence and wisdom."[38]

They then insisted upon my revealing to them the secrets of this art. "The oath," says I, "taken by me at my admission, never to divulge them, directly or indirectly, will not permit me to do it; conscience forbids me; and I therefore hope your lordships are too equitable to use compulsion." They declared that my oath was

enemy to secrecy; and, in his opinion, he is not worthy to reign that cannot keep his own secrets; he furthermore says, that he which discovers secrets is a traitor, and he which conceals them is a faithful Brother; he likewise says, that he that refraineth his tongue keeps his soul. Therefore, I am of opinion, that if secrecy and silence be duly considered, they will be found most necessary to qualify a man for any business of importance. If this be granted, I am confident that no man will dare to dispute that Freemasons are superior to all other men in concealing their secrets from time immemorial; which the power of gold, that often has betrayed kings and princes, and sometimes overturned whole empires, nor the most cruel punishments could ever extort the secret even from the weakest member of the whole fraternity. (Coustos.)

[38] Into the systems of the spurious Freemasonry, not only men but women were admitted; because it was the opinion of the Celtic tribes, that there was in the female sex something more than commonly penetrating and clear-sighted in the discovery of future events. (Tacitus. de mor. Germ. viii.) There may be another reason why the Druids allowed women to be present at their most secret rites, which was, to season them to scenes of barbarity and blood. (Alex. ab Alex., p. 753.)

as nothing in their presence, and that they would absolve me from it.[39] " Your lordships," continued I, " are very gracious; but as I am firmly persuaded that it is not in the power of any being upon earth to free me from my oath, I am firmly determined never to violate it."[40] This was more than enough to make them remand me back to my dungeon, where, a few days after, I fell sick.

A physician was then sent, who, finding me exceedingly ill, made a report thereof to the inquisitors. These, upon their being informed of it, immediately gave orders for my being removed from this frightful dungeon into another, which admitted some glimmerings of daylight. They appointed, at the same time, another prisoner to look after me during my sickness, which, very happily, was not of long continuance.[41]

Being recovered, I was again taken before the inquisitors, who asked me several new questions with regard to the secrets of Masonry, and whether, since my abode

[39] Pope Urban IV. granted to the officers of the Inquisition the power of absolving one another, even for crimes which would have incurred a sentence of excommunication.   They are also empowered to absolve all friars, companions, and notaries of the Inquisition, from the penance which may have been enjoined them during three years ; provided they had sincerely endeavoured to procure the prosecution and punishment of persons suspected of heresy.   And if any of these agents should be slain, or die in this pursuit, the inquisitors had the power of giving them absolution for all their previous sins.

[40] This dispensing power is symbolized by the pope carrying two keys at his girdle.   One of paradise, which represents the power which he has of giving absolution ; the other of hell, which shows his power of excommunicating sinners.   And he has a third given him as an emblem of his universal knowledge, and the infallibility consequent upon it.   These three keys represent, unitedly, that the power of the pope, as God's vicegerent, is superior to all the monarchs upon earth, and includes the right of deposing them at his pleasure.

[41] During the time of actual sickness, the inquisitors are disposed to display some tokens of humanity, else their conduct is usually barbarous and severe.   They will not allow a prisoner to make the least noise, to complain, to pray, or even to sing psalms or hymns.   These are capital crimes, for which the attendants, who are always walking up and down the passages, first admonish him ; and, if he repeat the offence, they beat him severely.   An instance of this severity is given by Coustos himself. He says, a prisoner having a violent cough, one of the guards came and told him that he was not to make a noise.   The poor wretch said he could not help it ; and his cough increasing, he was a second time commanded to be silent ; and this being impossible, they stripped him naked and beat him so unmercifully, that his cough grew worse, and the blows being again repeated, he died under the infliction.

in Lisbon, I had received any Portuguese into the society. I replied "that I had not; that it was true, indeed, that Don Emanuel de Soufa, Lord of Calliaris, and captain of the German Guards, hearing that the person was at Lisbon who had made the Duke de Villeroy a Freemason, by order of the French king, Louis XV., Don Emanuel had desired M. de Chevigny, at that time Minister of France at the Portuguese court, to enquire for me ; but that, upon my being told that the King of Portugal would not permit any of his subjects to be Freemasons, I had desired two of the Brethren to wait on M. de Calliaris above-mentioned, and acquaint him with my fears ;[42] and to assure him, at the same time, that in case he could obtain the king's leave, I was ready to receive him into the Brotherhood, I being resolved not to do any thing which might draw upon me the indignation of his Portuguese majesty : that M. de Calliaris having a very strong desire to enter into our society, declared that there was nothing in what I had observed with regard to his majesty's prohibition ; it being (added this nobleman) unworthy of the regal dignity to concern itself with such trifles. However, being certain that I spoke from very good authority, and knowing that M. de Calliaris was a nobleman of great economy, I found no other expedient to disengage myself from him than by asking fifty moidores for his reception ; a demand which I was persuaded would soon lessen, or rather suppress at once, the violent desire he might have to enter into the society of Freemasons."

To this one of the inquisitors said, " that it was not

---

[42] Rank was no protection against papal power, of which there are unfortunately too many examples. Elezine, Lord of Padua, whose heresy was only too great an attachment to the Emperor Frederick, was excommunicated, and inquisitors appointed to prosecute him for this pretended crime. He was summoned to appear at Rome, and he sent an embassy to proclaim his innocence. But they were not allowed to be heard, the pope insisting that he should appear in person ; and upon his refusing to obey this order, he was declared infamous and a heretic ; a crusade was sent against him and his adherents ; and all his possessions were confiscated in favour of his brother, who had been his accuser. About the same time, the Count de Toulouse fell a victim to the same power. A crusade was declared against him, and he had no other way of extricating himself than by making mean and servile concessions ; his only crime being a strong attachment to the Emperor Frederick, who was at variance with the court of Rome.

only true that his Portuguese majesty had forbid any of his subjects to be made Freemasons, but that there had been fixed up, five years before, upon the doors of all the churches in Lisbon, an order from his holiness, strictly enjoining the Portuguese in particular not to enter into this society, and even excommunicated all such as were then, or should afterwards become members of it."[43] Here I besought them to consider, " that if I had committed any offence in practising Masonry at Lisbon, it was merely through ignorance, I having resided but two years in Portugal ; that, farther, the circumstance just now mentioned by them, entirely destroyed the charge brought against me, viz., of my being the person who had introduced Freemasonry in Portugal." They answered, " that as I was one of the most zealous partisans of this society, I could not but have heard, during my abode in Lisbon, the orders issued by the holy father." I silenced them by the comparison I made between myself and a traveller (a foreigner) who, going to their capital city, and spying two roads leading to it, one of which was expressly forbid, upon pain of the severest punishment to strangers, though without any indication or tokens being set up for this purpose ; that this stranger. I say, should thereby strike accidentally, merely through ignorance, into the forbidden road.

They afterwards charged me with " drawing away Roman Catholics of other nations residing in Lisbon." I represented to them " that Roman Catholics must sooner be informed of the pope's injunction than I, who was a Protestant ; that I was firmly of opinion that the severe orders issued by the Roman pontiff had not a

---

[43] But it may be proper to remark that if on the contrary the King of Portugal had tolerated the Freemasons, the inquisitors would have refused obedience to his mandate, as they did on other occasions. They even ventured to cite Jane, daughter of the Emperor Charles V., to appear before their tribunal, in order to be examined on some articles of faith which the inquisitors had declared to be heretical, and which were suspected to be held by one of her chief attendants. The emperor stood in such awe of the Inquisition, that he commanded his daughter, in case she thought the person accused ever so little guilty, to give her information at once, in order to avoid the sentence of excommunication, which would not only be levelled against the accused person, but also against both himself and her. In compliance with this command, the princess immediately gave in her deposition to the inquisitor-general.

little prompted many to enter among the Freemasons ; that a man who was looked upon as a heretic[44] was no ways qualified to win over persons who considered him as such ; that a Freemason who professed the Romish religion, was, I presumed, the only man fit to seduce and draw away others of the same persuasion with himself, to get into their confidence, and remove successfully such scruples as might arise in their minds, both with regard to the injurious reports spread concerning Masonry, and to the pope's excommunication, of which a vile heretic entertained an idea far different from that of the Romanists." They then sent me back to my dungeon.[45]

Being again ordered to be brought before the inquisitors, they insisted upon my letting them into the secrets of Masonry, threatening me, in case I did not comply. I persisted, as before, " in refusing to break my oath ; and besought them either to write, or give orders for writing, to his Portuguese majesty's ministers, both at London and Paris, to know from them whether anything was ever done in the assemblies of the Freemasons repugnant to decency and morality,[46] to the dictates of

[44] If a person were known to go to a Protestant place of worship, he is immediately suspected of heresy ; and also if he contracts a friendship with, or visits, or makes presents to, suspected persons. And it is a very serious crime to assist in furnishing persons accused by the Inquisition with the means of escaping, although induced thereto by the strongest ties of blood, or gratitude, or pity. This article is carried to such lengths by the inquisitors, that persons are not only forbidden to assist heretics, but are obliged to discover them, though a father, brother, husband, or wife ; and this upon pain of excommunication ; and of being obnoxious to the rigours of the tribunal, as fautors or abettors of heresy.

[45] The Romish hierarchy always entertained a great jealousy of secret societies ; which may be exemplified in the following case : The celebrated Baptista Porta having traveled into distant countries for scientific information, returned to his native home, and established a society, which he denominated the academy of secrets. This little fraternity, instituted to promote the advancement of science, soon fell under the rod of ecclesiastical oppression ; and experienced, in its dissolution, that the Romish hierarchy was determined to check the ardour of investigation, and retain the human mind in the fetters of ignorance and superstition. How, then, could Freemasonry flourish, when the minds of men had such an unfortunate propensity to monkish retirement ; and when every scientific and secret association was overawed and persecuted by the rulers of Europe ? (Laurie, p. 53.)

[46] As if they cared either for decency or morality ! Gonsalvius gives us an example which shows that vice is not the object of the inquisi-

the Romish faith, or to the obedience which every good
Christian owes to the injunctions of the monarch in
whose dominions he lives." I observed farther, " that
the King of France, who is the eldest son of the church,
and despotic in his dominions, would not have bid his
favourite enter into a society proscribed by mother-
church, had he not been firmly persuaded that nothing
was transacted in their meetings contrary to the State,
to religion, and to the church."[47] I afterwards referred
them to Mr. Dogood, an Englishman, who was born a
Roman Catholic, and was a Freemason. This gentleman had travelled with, and was greatly beloved by,
Don Pedro Antonio, the king's favourite ; "and who," I
observed farther, " having settled a lodge in Lisbon
fifteen years before, could acquaint·them, in case he
thought proper, with the nature and secrets of Ma-

tor's hatred. A poor inhabitant of Seville, who supported his family by
his daily labour, had the mortification to have his wife kept forcibly from
him by a priest, which was winked at by the Inquisition. As this man
was one day talking with some of his acquaintances about purgatory, he
happened to say:—"As to myself, I have my purgatory in this world, by
my wife being thus withheld from me by the priest." These words being
told to the ecclesiastic, he impeached the husband to the Inquisition, as
having advanced some errors relating to the doctrine of purgatory.
Hereupon the inquisitors, without once reproaching the priest for his
crime, seized the husband. The latter then was imprisoned for two
years ; and after walking in the procession at the first *auto-da-fé*, and
being sentenced to wear, during three years, the san benito in a private
prison, at the expiration of that term, he was ordered either to be continued in prison, or to be released, as the inquisitors should see fitting.
These carried their cruelties to such lengths as to confiscate, to the use
of the tribunal, the little that this unhappy creature had in the world,
and permitted the priest to still enjoy his wife, the holy lecher being pas-
sionately fond of her.

[47] In France, Masonry flourished abundantly at the above period ; and
we find an exalted Mason of that country speaking thus at the initiation
of his son :—"I congratulate you on your admission into the most ancient, and perhaps the most respectable, society in the universe. To you
the mysteries of Masonry are about to be revealed, and so bright a sun
never shed its lustre on your eyes. Pictures will be opened to your
view, wherein true patriotism is exemplified in glowing colours, and a
series of transactions recorded, which the rude hand of time can never
erase. Should your conduct in life correspond with the principles of
Masonry, my remaining years will pass away with pleasure and satisfaction. For this purpose, recal to memory the ceremony of your initiation ;
learn to bridle your tongue, and to govern your passions ; and ere long
you will have occasion to say—In becoming a Mason I truly became a
man ; and while I breathe I will never disgrace a jewel that kings might
prize."

sonry." The inquisitors commanded me to be taken back to my dismal abode.

Appearing again before them, they did not once mention the secrets of Masonry; but took notice that I, in one of my examinations, had said "that it was a duty incumbent on Freemasons to assist the needy;" upon which they asked "whether I had ever relieved a poor object?" I named to them a lying-in woman, a Romanist, who being reduced to the extremes of misery, and hearing that the Freemasons were very liberal of their alms, she addressed herself to me, and I gave her a moidore. I added, "that the convent of the Franciscans having been burnt down, the fathers made a gathering, and I gave them, upon the exchange, three quarters of a moidore." I declared farther, "that a poor Roman Catholic, who had a large family, and could get no work, being in the utmost distress, had been recommended to me by some Freemasons, with a request that we would make a purse among ourselves, in order to set him up again, and thereby enable him to support his family; that accordingly we raised among seven of us who were Freemasons, ten moidores, which money I myself put into his hands."

They then asked me "whether I had given my own money in alms?" I replied, "that these arose from the forfeits of such Freemasons as had not attended properly the meetings of the Brotherhood." "What are the faults," said they, "committed by your Brother Masons which occasion their being fined?" "Those who take the name of God in vain, pay the quarter of a moidore; such as utter any other oath, or pronounce obscene words, forfeit a new crusade;[48] all who are turbulent, or refuse to obey the orders of the Master of the lodge, are likewise fined." They remanded me back to my dungeon, having first enquired the name and habitation of the several persons hinted at a little higher, on which occasion I assured them "that the last-mentioned was not a Freemason; and that the Brethren assisted indiscriminately all sorts of people, provided they were real objects of charity."

I naturally concluded, from the behaviour of the

[48] A new crusade is two shillings and sixpence sterling.

inquisitors at my being brought before them four days after, that they had enquired into the truth of the several particulars related before. They now did not say a word concerning Masonry, but began to work with different engines.

They then employed all the powers of their rhetoric to prove " that it became me to consider my imprisonment by order of the holy office as an effect of the goodness of God, who," added they, " intended to bring me to a serious way of thinking, and, by this means, lead me into the paths of truth, in order that I might labour efficaciously at the salvation of my soul.⁴⁹ That I ought to know that Jesus Christ had said to St. Peter: ' Thou art Peter, and upon this rock I will build my church, and the gates of hell shall not prevail against it,' whence it was my duty to obey the injunctions of his holiness, he being St. Peter's successor." I replied, with spirit, and resolution, that " I did not acknowledge the Roman pontiff, either as successor to St. Peter, or as infallible ; that I relied entirely, with regard to doctrine, on the Holy Scriptures, these being the sole guide of our faith. I besought them to let me enjoy, undisturbed, the privileges allowed the English in Portugal ; that I was resolved to live and die in the communion of the church of England ; and, therefore, that all the pains they might take to make a convert of me would be ineffectual."

⁴⁹ If this were the real object of the inquisitors, how does it happen that they sometimes wreak their vengeance on dead bodies, from which the soul has departed? For it is a melancholy but well attested fact, that they prosecute individuals who have been dead for many years, and cause their bodies to be dug up to answer the accusation ; which being impossible, the bones are burnt at the ensuing *auto-da-fé*. Several instances of this might be adduced, even in our own highly favoured country. After the accession of Queen Mary, when Cardinal Pole went to the university of Cambridge, a prosecution was commenced against Bucer and Fagius, both of whom were dead. They were, however, cited by two edicts, and various witnesses brought against them. When no one would undertake their defence, they were condemned for contumacy, (ridiculous cruelty!) and on the same day sentence was pronounced before the whole university, by which their bodies were ordered to be dug up and delivered to the queen's officers. An order was afterwards sent from her majesty for inflicting the punishment. In fine, February 6, the bodies were dug up ; when a large stake being fixed in the ground in the market place, the bodies were tied to it. After this, the chests or coffins, with the bodies in them, were set up, being fastened on both

Notwithstanding the repeated declarations made by me, that I would never change my religion, the inquisitors were as urgent as ever. Encouraged by the apostacy of one of my Brother Masons, they flattered themselves with the hopes of prevailing upon me to imitate him; and, for this purpose, offered to send some English friars to me, who, they said, would instruct me,[50] and so fully open my eyes, that I should have a distinct view of my wretched condition, which, they declared, was. the more deplorable, as I was now wholly insensible of its danger.

Finding me still immoveable, and that there was no possibility of their making the least impression on me, the indulgence which they seemed to show at the beginning of my examination was suddenly changed to fury; they venting the most injurious expressions, "calling me heretic, and saying that I was damned."[51] Here I could not forbear replying, "that I was no heretic; but would prove, on the contrary, that they themselves were in error;" and now, raising their voice, "take care," cried they, with a tone of authority, "what you say." "I ad-

sides, and bound to the post with a long iron chain. The pile being fired, a great number of Protestant books were thrown into it, and these were soon consumed. Not long after, Brookes, Bishop of Gloucester, gave the like treatment, at Oxford, to the corpse of Catharine, wife of Peter Martyr, who, dying a few years before, had been buried in Christ Church, near the remains of St. Fridiswide, who was greatly venerated in that college; for the above Catharine being convicted of entertaining the same opinions as her husband, her dead body was dug up, and cast upon a dunghill. In Queen Elizabeth's reign, however, her corpse was taken from the dunghill by order of Archbishop Parker, and buried in its former place.

[50] The friars were as much under the supervision of the Inquisition as any other class; for, being delegated by the pope, for the general purpose of extirpating heresy, they were empowered to prosecute friars, as well as any other order of men. And, as we have already observed, they did not hesitate to indict kings and princes, if they stood in the way of their ambition. On such occasions, however, his holiness was always consulted; not out of respect to the high station of the person accused, but lest they should exasperate the ruling powers, and bring themselves into trouble. In a word, no person is safe from the designs of this tribunal how great soever his power may be, if he should speak contemptuously of the Inquisition, which is a more unpardonable crime even than heresy.

[51] In fact, if the poor fellow had been actually converted to their opinions, he would not have derived any benefit from the change; for such a convert is held in abhorrence by the inquisitors. And as his accuser, witnesses, and himself, are not brought face to face, his innocence is of no service; and it frequently happens that confession becomes the engine of his ruin.

7*

vance nothing," replied I, " but what I am able to prove.
Do you believe," continued I, " that the words of our
Lord Jesus Christ, as found in the New Testament, are
true." They answered in the affirmative. " But what
inference," said they, " do you draw from thence?" " Be
so good," I added, " as to let me have a Bible, and I will
inform you concerning this." I then laid before them
the passage where our Saviour says thus :—" Search the
scriptures, for in them ye think ye have eternal life, and
they are they which testify of me."[52]   Likewise the
following:—" We also have a more sure word of prophecy, whereunto ye do well that you take heed."[53]
"And yet," said I, " both the pope and your lordships
forbid the perusal of them; and thereby act in direct
opposition to the express command of the Saviour of the
world." To this the inquisitors replied:—" That I ought
to call to mind, that our Saviour says to St. Peter, and in
his name to all the popes his successors, ' I will give unto
thee the keys of the kingdom of heaven ; and whatsoever
thou shalt bind on earth, shall be bound in heaven ; and
whatsoever thou shalt loose on earth shall be loosed in
heaven.'[54]   That none but a heretic, like myself, would
dare to dispute the authority and infallibility of the pope,
who is Christ's vicar here below; that the reason of not
allowing the perusal of this book was, to prevent the
common people from explaining the obscure passages
contained therein contrary to their true sense; as was
daily the practice of schismatics and heretics, like myself."[55]   I shall omit the other controversial points that
afterwards occurred, all which I answered to the best of
my slender abilities.

One thing I can assure my reader is, that the inquisitors were not able to alter, in any manner, the firm resolution I had taken, to live and die a Protestant ; on the
contrary, I can affirm, that their remonstrances, and even

---

[52] John v. 39.
[53] Peter i. 19.   [54] Matthew xvi. 19.
[55] This was mere verbiage ; because the infallibility of the pope is fully
admitted, not only by the inquisitors, but by all other Roman Catholics ;
and therefore no charge could be founded upon it. The evident fact is,
that whatever arguments they might use, their purpose was evidently to
bring poor Coustos into condemnation, because he was in possession of
a secret, and they were determined that no one should possess a secret but
themselves.

menaces, served only to strengthen my resistance, and furnish me abundant proofs to refute, with vigour, all the arguments offered by them.

I acknowledge that I owe this wholly to the Divine Goodness, which graciously condescended to support me under these violent trials, and enabled me to presevere to the end; for this I return unfeigned thanks to the Almighty; and hope to give, during the remainder of my life, convincing testimonies of the strong impression which those trials made on my mind, by devoting myself sincerely to the duties of religion.

I was ordered back, by the inquisitors, to my dismal abode, after they had declared to me, "that if I turned Roman Catholic, it would be of great advantage to my cause; otherwise that I perhaps might repent of my obstinacy when it was too late." I replied, in a respectful manner, that I could not accept of their offers.

A few days after, I was again brought before the president of the holy office, who said:—" That the proctor [56] would read, in presence of the court, the heads of the indictment or charge brought against me." The inquisitors now offered me a counsellor, in case I desired one, to plead my cause.[57]

Being sensible that the person whom they would send me for this purpose was himself an inquisitor, I chose rather to make my own defence, in the best manner I could. I, therefore, desired "that leave might be granted me to deliver my defence in writing;" but this they refused, saying, "that the holy office did not allow prisoners the use of pen, ink, and paper." I then begged they would permit me to dictate my justification, in their presence, to any person whom they should appoint, which favour was granted me.

---

[56] A proctor is much the same in the ecclesiastical as an attorney is in the civil courts. His business is to see that the church discipline be strictly maintained, and to bring the disobedient to punishment.

[57] Counsellors and assessors in Roman Catholic countries are persons skilled in the canon and in civil law. The inquisitors consult them on all doubtful points; but follow their opinions no farther than they think proper. When a counsellor is offered to an accused person, it is generally done with a view of entrapping him into a confidential communication, which is always imparted to the judges, who make use of these persons to give authority to their decision, that the public may be induced to believe that it is according to law.

The heads of the charge or indictment brought against me, were—" That I had infringed the pope's orders, by belonging to the sect of the Freemasons, this sect being a horrid compound of sacrilege, and many other abominable crimes; of which the inviolable secrecy observed therein, and the exclusion of women, were but too manifest indications—a circumstance that gave the highest offence to the whole kingdom; and the said Coustos having refused to discover to the inquisitors, the true tendency and design of the meetings of Freemasons, and persisting, on the contrary, in asserting that Freemasonry was good in itself; wherefore the proctor of the Inquisition requires, that the said prisoner may be prosecuted with the utmost rigour; and, for this purpose, desires the court would exert its whole authority, and even proceed to tortures, to extort from him a confession, viz., that the several articles of which he stands accused are true."

The inquisitors then gave me the above heads, ordering me to sign them, which I absolutely refused. They thereupon commanded me to be taken back to my dungeon, without permitting me to say a single word in my justification.

I now had but too much leisure to reflect on their menaces, and to cast about for answers to the several articles concerning Masonry, whereof I stood accused; all which articles I remembered but too well.

Six weeks after, I appeared in presence of two inquisitors, and the person whom they had appointed to take down my defence; which was little more than a recapitulation of what I before had asserted with regard to Masonry.

" Your prisoner," said I to them, " is deeply afflicted and touched to the soul, to find himself accused (by the ignorance or malice of his enemies) in an infernal charge or indictment, before the lords of the holy office, for having practised the art of Freemasonry, which has been, and is still, revered, not only by a considerable number of persons of the highest quality in Christendom, but likewise by several sovereign princes and crowned heads, who, so far from disdaining to become members of this society, submitted, engaged, and obliged themselves, at their admission, to observe religiously the constitutions

of this noble art; noble, not only on account of the
almost infinite number of illustrious personages who
profess it, but still more so, from the sentiments of humanity with which it equally inspires the rich and poor,
the nobleman and artificer, the prince and subject; for
these, when met together, are upon a level as to rank;
are all Brethren, and conspicuous only from their superiority in virtue; in fine, this art is noble from the charity
which the society of Freemasons professedly exercises,
and from the fraternal love with which it strongly binds
and cements together the several individuals who compose it, without any distinction as to religion or birth.

" Your prisoner thinks it very hard, to find himself thus
become the victim of this tribunal, merely because he
belongs to so venerable a society. The rank and exalted
dignity of many, who have been, and still are, members
thereof, should be considered as faithful and speaking
witnesses, now pleading in his defence, as well as in that
of the Brotherhood, so unjustly accused.

" Further, could any one suppose, without showing
the greatest rashness, or being guilty of the highest
injustice, that Christian princes, who are Christ's vice-
gerents upon earth, would not only tolerate, in their
dominions, a sect that should favour the abominable
crimes of which this tribunal accuses it, but even be
accomplices therein, by entering into the society in
question.[58]

" What I have said above, should be more than sufficient to convince your lordships that you are quite
misinformed as to Masonry, and oblige you to stop all

[58] The Roman pontiffs employed every expedient to increase their
authority; and for that purpose they refused to tolerate Freemasonry,
because its free principles interfered with their views of universal dominion. Proclaiming themselves the successors of St. Peter, they assumed
an holiness and power superior to that of the apostles. Monarchs,
blinded in an ignorant age with these pretensions, strove to rival one
another in bestowing privileges on the popes, that they might obtain
their favour, until they had elevated them to the pinnacle of greatness,
and found, when it was too late, that they had become slaves to the papal
power. Some of these princes were desirous of retracing their steps, and
for that purpose offered some resistance to the holy father's will, and were
immediately declared heretics, and excommunicated; and if they persisted in their opposition they were dethroned, and their dominions given
to others, who promised obedience to the see of Rome.

prosecution against me. However, I will here add some remarks, in order to corroborate my former assertions, and destroy the bad impressions that may have been made on your lordships' minds concerning Freemasonry.

" The very strict inquiry made into the past life and conduct of all persons that desire to be received among the Brotherhood, and who are never admitted, except the strongest and most indisputable testimonies are given, of their having lived irreproachably, are further indications that this society is no ways guilty of the crimes with which it is charged by your tribunal; the utmost precautions being taken to expel from this society, not only wicked wretches, but even disorderly persons.

" The works of charity, which the Brotherhood think it incumbent on themselves to exercise towards such as are real objects of compassion, and whereof I have given your lordships some few instances, show, likewise, that it is morally impossible for a society so execrable as you have described that of the Freemasons to be, to practise a virtue so generally neglected, and so opposite to the love of riches, at this time the predominant vice—the root of all evil.

" Besides, wicked wretches set all laws at defiance, despise kings, and the magistrates established by them for the due administration of justice. Abandoned men, such as those hinted at here, foment insurrections and rebellions; whereas Freemasons pay an awful regard to the prince in whose dominions they live, yield implicit obedience to his laws, and revere, in the magistrates, the sacred person of the king, by whom they were nominated; rooting up, to the utmost of their power, every seed of sedition and rebellion; and being ready, at all times, to venture their lives, for the security both of the prince and of his government.

" Wicked wretches, when got together, not only take perpetually the name of God in vain, but blaspheme and deny him; whereas the Freemasons punish very severely, not only swearers, but likewise such as utter obscene words; and expel from their society all persons hardened in those vices.[59]

---

[59] Because the discipline of Freemasonry positively prohibits such per-

"· Wicked wretches contemn religions of every kind, turn them into ridicule, and speak in terms uworthy of the Deity worshipped in them. But the Freemasons, on the contrary, observing a respectful silence on this occasion, never quarrel with the religious principles of any person, but live together in fraternal love, which a difference in opinion can no ways lessen."—I closed my defence with the four lines following, composed by a Freemason :—

> Through trackless paths each Brother strays,
> And nought sinister can entice ;
> Now temples we to virtue raise ;
> Now dungeons sink—fit place for vice.

To which I added (in my own mind)—

> But here, the contrary is found ;
> Injustice reigns, and killing dread ;
> In rankling chains bright virtue's bound,
> And vice, with triumph, lifts its head.

"Such, my lords," continued I, "are our true and genuine secrets. I now wait, with all possible resignation, for whatever you shall think proper to decree ; but still hope, from your equity and justice, that you will not pass sentence upon me, as though I was guilty of the crimes mentioned in the indictment ; upon the vain pretence, that inviolable secrecy can be observed in such things only as are of a criminal nature."[60]

I was remanded back to my usual scene of woe, without being able to guess what impression my defence might have made on my judges. A few days after I was brought before his eminence Cardinal da Cunha, inquisi-

---

sons from being members of the society. It unites duty and interest in an indissoluble chain of sincere affection. It teaches its votaries, with one heart and one mind, to lift up their eyes to the sovereign Disposer of events, humbly imploring His most gracious assistance in all our endeavours to practise the true principles of the Order, by alleviating the distresses of the indigent, and dispensing joy and happiness to our fellow-creatures.

[60] It may be necessary to remark, at this point, that the several officers of this tribunal make oath, that they will faithfully discharge the duties of their employment, by affording the prisoner every facility to prove his innocence ; not to divulge the most minute particular relating to the Inquisition or its prisons, on any pretence whatever, on pain of the most severe punishment. On these occasions no excuse whatever is admitted, secresy being the very soul and support of the institution.

tor and director general of all the Inquisitions dependent on the Portuguese monarchy.[61]

The president, directing himself to me, declared—" That the holy tribunal was assembled purposely to hear and determine my cause; that I therefore should examine my own mind, and see whether I had no other arguments to offer in my justification." I replied—" That I had none; but relied wholly on their rectitude and equity." Having spoken these words, they sent me back to my sad abode, and judged me among themselves.

Some time after, the president sent for me again; when, being brought before him, he ordered a paper, containing part of my sentence, to be read. I thereby was doomed to suffer the tortures employed by the holy office, for refusing to tell the truth, as they falsely affirmed; for my not discovering the secrets of Masonry, with the true tendency and purpose of the meetings of the Brethren.[62]

I hereupon was instantly conveyed to the torture-room, built in form of a square tower, where no light appeared, but what two candles gave; and, to prevent the dreadful cries and shocking groans of the unhappy victims from reaching the ears of the other prisoners, the doors are lined with a sort of quilt.

The reader will naturally suppose that I must be seized with horror, when, at my entering this infernal place, I saw myself, on a sudden, surrounded by six

[61] There is a supreme council held in Lisbon, to which all the other Portuguese Inquisitions are subordinate. This tribunal consists of an inquisitor-general, who is appointed by the king, and confirmed by the pope He is empowered to nominate the inquisitors in all the countries dependent on the crown of Portugal; nor can any *auto-da-fé* be solemnized without his knowledge and concurrence. From this supreme council there is no appeal. It makes new laws at pleasure; determines all suits and contests arising between the inquisitors; punishes the ministers and officers of the Inquisition; in a word, the authority of this tribunal is so great, that every one trembles at its name; and even the king himself does not dare to complain of its decisions.

[62] It is not wonderful that this poor fellow was subjected to the torture, because one of the avowed maxims of the Inquisition is to strike terror into every one that comes under its clutches; and, for this purpose, it usually punishes with the utmost severity those who will not confess what is laid to their charge, even though they are perfectly innocent. The inquisitors are baffled by what they call the obstinacy of the prisoner, and they wreak their vengeance by torture.

wretches, who, after preparing the tortures, stripped me naked, all to my linen drawers ; when, laying me on my back, they began to lay hold of every part of my body. First, they put round my neck an iron collar, which was fastened to the scaffold ; they then fixed a ring to each foot ; and this being done, they stretched my limbs with all their might. They next wound two ropes round each arm, and two round each thigh, which ropes passed under the scaffold, through holes made for that purpose ; and were all drawn tight, at the same time, by four men, upon a signal made for this purpose.[63]

The reader will believe that my pains must be intolerable, when I solemnly declare, that these ropes, which were of the size of one's little finger, pierced through my flesh quite to the bone, making the blood gush out at the eight different places that were thus bound.[64] As

[63] This was done for the purpose of extorting a confession, on which they might act with some appearance of justice. And it sometimes happens, that though the prisoners should comply with every request, and impeach all who are charged with the same offence, it often happens that they are delivered over to the secular arm as *diminutos*, merely for omitting to name persons with whom they had not the slightest acquaintance. A most horrible instance of this is found in the case of George Francis Mela, who, having been seized by the inquisitors of Devora, made an accusation under torture of all the persons whose names he could recollect, to the number of five hundred. He had a daughter who was a nun in the convent Della Speranza, of the same city, and whenever he went to see her, it was always in the presence of some of the nuns. The unfortunate father determined to comply with all the commands of the inquisitors, under a promise of being released from prison, impeached his wife, his brothers, his children, and, amongst the rest, the nun. After going to these dreadful lengths, and when he expected to be delivered, the inquisitors quietly told him that he was condemned as a *diminuto*. Finding himself deceived, and that he must suffer, he recanted all that he had said, and declared that he had made those depositions only on the solemn promise of the inquisitors that he should be emancipated from confinement.

[64] Dean Kirwan says :—" There is no species of history which a benevolent man reads with more distress to his feelings than the history of the church. One shudders to think what scenes of blood and discord have existed at different times in the world, under the pretext of divine authority ; various and discordant parties of Christians labouring to annoy and exterminate each another, like wild beasts, with unwearied perseverance and every circumstance of the most refined barbarity ; the very shout of persecution and intolerance issuing from the pulpit of God, and the spirit and dye of the Koran transplanted into the gospel of peace. But as well might God himself be made responsible for such horrors, as the law, which expressly reproves and condemns them.

I persisted in refusing to discover any more than what has been seen in the interrogatories above, the ropes were thus drawn together four different times. At my side stood a physician and surgeon, who often felt my temples, to judge of the danger I might be in : by which means my tortures were suspended, at intervals, that I might have an opportunity of recovering myself a little.[63]

Whilst I was thus suffering they were so barbarously unjust as to declare, that were I to die under the torture, I should be guilty, by my obstinacy, of self-murder. In fine, the last time the ropes were drawn tight, I grew so exceedingly weak, occasioned by the blood's circulation being stopped, and the pains I endured, that I fainted quite away ; insomuch that I was carried back to my dungeon, without my once perceiving it.[66]

Let the answer be recollected which our blessed Lord made to his disciples, when they required him, in the true spirit of sanguinary bigotry, to command fire from heaven for the destruction of a Samaritan village, he said :—' Ye know not what manner of spirit ye are of !' The Son of Man came not to inspire principles of hatred and disunion, or cruelty and revenge ; but to fill the human bosom with mutual forbearance and affection." (Sermons, p. 190.)

[65] A most horrible account is on record of a poor girl, Mary, the daughter of Emanuel Soares, which may serve to illustrate the above account. After having constantly persisted in declaring her innocence, she was at last put to the torture, which she bore very courageously for a while ; but being overcome with the torments, she accused herself of being a Jewess. Upon this she was unbound, and suffered to put on her clothes, in order to complete her confession. But instead of persisting in what she had declared, she protested that all she had said upon the rack was untrue ; that she was an old Christian, and the sole motive why she accused herself was, lest she should die under the torture. She was then remanded back to prison ; and a few days afterwards, was again put to the torture, when she again accused herself ; and being accordingly unloosed, and carried before the inquisitors, she persisted in her innocence, and told them that it would be useless putting her to the torture, since she should certainly accuse herself falsely to escape it. She was, however, again put upon the rack ; after which she was condemned to be whipped publicly through the streets, and then banished for ten years.

[66] Severe and disgusting as the above account may appear, it is said to be exceeded by the Inquisition, which was established in the East Indies. The Jesuits themselves thus speak of it in their universal Latin and French Dictionary, printed at Trevoux :— ' The Inquisition," they say, " is very severe in India ; for although a man cannot absolutely be condemned, except by the testimony of seven witnesses, yet the depositions of slaves and young children are admitted. The prisoner is compelled to accuse himself, and is never confronted with those who swear against him. If a person happens to drop the slightest word against the church, or its

These barbarians, finding that the tortures above described could not extort any further discovery from me,
but that the more they made me suffer, the more fer-
vently I addressed my supplications for patience to heaven : they were so inhuman, six weeks after, as to expose me to another kind of torture, more grievous, if
possible, than the former.[67] They made me stretch my
arms in such a manner, that the palms of my hands were
turned outward ; when, by the help of a rope that fastened them together at the wrist, and which they turned
by an engine, they drew them gently nearer to one another behind, in such a manner that the back of each
hand touched, and stood exactly parallel one to the other,
whereby both my shoulders were dislocated, and a considerable quantity of blood issued from my mouth. This
torture was repeated thrice ; after which I was again
taken to my dungeon, and put into the hands of physi-
cians and surgeons, who, in setting my bones, put me to
exquisite pain.

Two months after, being a little recovered, I was again
conveyed to the torture-room, and there made to undergo another kind of punishment twice.[68] The reader may

ordinances, even in private conversation; or does not speak with sufficient reverence of the Inquisition, he is sure to be impeached, and, if
once impeached, his chances of escape are very trifling indeed."

[67] They justified their cruelties by such arguments as these :—that in
the Mosaic law blasphemers were condemned to be put to death ; and
that, therefore, they were obeying the will of God by slaying heretics,
who blasphemed the body of Christ, and called it only a piece of bread ;
that it became Christians to be more zealous for the true religion than
heathens for the false ; that St. Peter, by a divine power, destroyed An-
anias and Sapphira ; and that St. Paul said :—" I would they were cut
off that trouble you." How weak soever these arguments may appear,
they were used to justify the destruction of heretics, which was hence
thought to be a proceeding with which God was well pleased.

[68] However heartless and unjust the above account may appear, it is
not unparalleled in the history of persecution. Joseph Pereira Meneses,
captain-general of his Portuguese majesty's fleets in India, was ordered
by the governor of Goa to sail with his fleet to the succour of the city
of Diu, then besieged by the Arabs. Being detained by contrary winds,
the Arabs took and plundered the city before his arrival. The governor
of Goa being his enemy, seized him on his return, and condemned him to
death, on the charge of cowardice. But not being able to put him to
death without an express order from the court of Portugal, he led him
through the streets publicly, with a herald walking before, proclaiming
him a coward and a traitor ; and afterwards denounced him to the Inquisition, who overwhelmed him with an abundance of other charges,

judge of its horror, from the following description
thereof :

The torturers turned twice round my body a thick
iron chain, which, crossing upon my stomach, terminated
afterwards at my wrists. They next set my back against
a thick board, at each extremity whereof was a pulley,
through which there run a rope, that catched the ends
of the chains at my wrists. The tormentors then stretching these ropes, by means of a roller, pressed or bruised
my stomach, in proportion as the ropes were drawn
tighter. They tortured me on this occasion to such a
degree, that my wrists and shoulders were put out of
joint.

The surgeons, however, set them presently after ; but
the barbarians, not having yet satiated their cruelty,
made me undergo this torture a second time, which I
did with fresh pains, though with equal constancy and
resolution. I then was remanded back to my dungeon,
attended by the surgeons, who dressed my bruises ;
and here I continued till their *auto-da-fé*, or gaol delivery.[69]

and condemned him to be burned alive. It appears, however, that he
had a friend in one of the inquisitors, who took such steps as proved
the accusations against him to be false, and he was accordingly libe-
rated at the next *auto-da-fé*, but found himself stripped of all his possessions and quite ruined.

[69] Coustos describes this *auto-da-fé as* follows :—" The prisoners being
habited in the san benitos and pyramidal caps, the procession opened
with the Dominican friars, preceded by the banner of their order. Then
came the banner and crucifix of the Inquisition, which was followed by
the criminals, each walking between two familiars. It proceeded round
the court of the chief inquisitor's palace, in the presence of the king and
his whole court ; and then along one of the sides of Rocio Square, and
went down Odreyros Street ; when, returning by Escudeyros Street, and
up another side of Rocio Square, they came, at last, to St. Dominic's
church, which was hung, from top to bottom, with red and yellow tapestry. Before the high altar was built an amphitheatre, with a pretty
considerable number of steps, in order to seat all the prisoners and their
attendant familiars. Opposite was raised another greater altar, after the
Romish fashion, on which was placed a crucifix, surrounded with several lighted tapers and mass-books. To the right of this was a pulpit,
and to the left a gallery, magnificently adorned, for the king, the royal
family, the great men of the kingdom, and the foreign ministers to sit in.
To the right of this gallery was a long one for the inquisitors ; and between these two galleries, a room, whither the inquisitors retire to hear
the confessions of those who, terrified at the horrors of impending death
may be prompted to confess what they had before persisted in denying.

The reader may judge, from the faint description, of the dreadful anguish I must have laboured under, the nine different times they put me to the torture. Most of .my limbs were put out of joint, and bruised in such a manner, that I was unable, during some weeks, to lift my hand to my mouth; my body being vastly swelled, by the inflammations caused by the frequent dislocations. I have but too much reason to fear that I shall feel the sad effects of this cruelty so long as I live, I being seized from time to time with thrilling pains, with which I never was afflicted till I had the misfortune of falling into the merciless and bloody hands of the inquisitors.

The day of the *auto-da-fé* being come,[70] I was made to walk in the procession, with the other victims of this tribunal. Being come to St. Dominic's church,[71] my

---

they sometimes gladly snatching this last moment allowed them to escape a cruel exit. The trials of all the prisoners not sentenced to die, being read, the president of the Inquisition, dressed in his sacerdotal vestments, appeared with a book in his hand; after which five or six priests, in surplices, tapped, with a sort of wands, the heads and shoulders of the prisoners in question, saying certain prayers, used in the Romish church, when the excommunication is taken off. Then another priest went up into the pulpit to read the trials of the ill-fated persons sentenced to the flames; after which these sad victims were delivered up to the secular power, whose officers take them to the Relacaon, whither the king comes. Thus the Inquisition, to conceal their cruelties, calls in the secular arm, which condemns the prisoners to die, or rather ratifies the sentence passed by the inquisitors. This lasted till six in the morning. At last, these miserable creatures, accompanied by the familiars and priests, were conducted, under the guard of a detachment of foot, to Campo da Laa, or the Wool-field. Here they were fastened with chains to posts, and seated on pitch barrels. Afterwards the king appeared in a sorry coach, at which were ropes instead of harness. He then ordered the friars to exhort each of the victims in question, to die in the Romish faith, upon pain of being burnt alive; but to declare that such as complied with the exhortation of the priest, should be strangled before they were committed to the flames."

[70] It appears that a fortnight before the solemnization of this *auto-da-fé*, notice was given in all the churches that it would be celebrated on Sunday, 21st June, 1744; and the spectators were directed not to ridicule the prisoners, but to pray for their conversion. On Saturday, the 20th, Coustos received directions to prepare himself for the solemnity. The dresses were a yellow robe, or scapulary, striped with red; and such as were accused of sorcery had devils or flames painted on the robe, and the word WIZARD in large letters. Those who were not sentenced to die carried a yellow lighted taper in their hands. Coustos informs us that he was not included in this ceremony because he was an obstinate Protestant.

[71] In his appendix Coustos goes on to say:—" We were carried through

sentence was read, by which I was condemned to the galley, as it is termed, during four years.

Four days after this procession I was conveyed to this galley, and joined, on the morrow, in the painful occupation of my fellow-slaves. However, the liberty I had of speaking to my friends, after having been deprived of even the sight of them during my tedious, wretched abode in the prison of the Inquisition ; the open air I now breathed, with the satisfaction I felt in being freed from the dreadful apprehensions which always overspread my mind, whenever I reflected on the uncertainty of my fate ; these circumstances united, made me find the toils of the galley much more supportable.[72]

several galleries, till we came to the abode allotted us. Here were several chambers, the doors of which were open, and each of us chose that which he liked best. Each had given to him a straw bed, with blankets and sheets. Most of these things were far from clean, as an *auto-da-fé* had not been held for two years before. The women were lodged a story above us. Being thus settled, we thought ourselves the happiest persons upon the earth, though we had little to boast of. However, we were now together, and breathed the fresh air; we enjoyed the light of the sky, and had a view of a garden ; in a word, we knew that we should not be put to death ; all which circumstances proved a great consolation. The alcaide or gaoler, and his brother-keeper, brought each of us a loaf, a cake, and water sufficient for the whole company ; permitting us, at the same time, to divert ourselves, provided we did not make a noise. This was the first time we had supped in the Inquisition with any satisfaction. Having been greatly fatigued, by the ceremony described in the foregoing pages, I slept very soundly. I am to observe that, from the time of our returning from the procession, we were supported at the expense of the cardinal-inquisitor, and not at that of the mock holy office. We were soon sensible of this change of masters, not only by the advantages described above, but also by the permission allowed us, of sending to our relations and friends for such provisions as we might want, if we did not like those given us, or had not enough to satisfy our appetites. It would be the highest ingratitude in me," Coustos continues, " not to mention the very essential favours which I myself, as well as the three Brethren, my fellow-prisoners, received from the Freemasons of Lisbon. They obtained leave to visit us, and their bounty proved of the most signal advantage to us. We imagined at first, that the reason why the cardinal ordered us to be confined in this part of the prison was, to accustom us, by insensible degrees, to the open air, and to dispel the dreadful melancholy which had so long oppressed us. The true cause, however, was, that we might be the more readily conveyed to the place where we were sentenced to go ; to put into our hands a bill of the expenses which the inquisitors had been at, which, in many ca·es, were enormous."

[72] The Portuguese galley is a prison standing by the river side, and consists of two spacious rooms, which are crowded with all sorts of

As I had suffered greatly in my body, by the tortures inflicted on me in the prison of the Inquisition, of which the reader has seen a very imperfect, though faithful narrative in the foregoing sheets, I was quite unfit to go about the painful labour that was immediately allotted me, viz., the carrying water (an hundred pounds weight) to the prisons of the city. But the fears I was under of being exposed to the inhumanity of the guards or overseers, who accompany the galley slaves, caused me to exert myself so far beyond my strength, that, twelve days after, I fell grievously sick. I then was sent to the infirmary, where I continued two months. During my abode in this place, I was often visited by the Irish friars belonging to the convent of Corpo Santo, who offered to get my release, provided I would turn Roman Catholic. I assured them that all their endeavours would be fruitless, I expecting my enlargement from the Almighty alone, who, if He, in His profound wisdom, thought proper, would point out other expedients for my obtaining it, than my becoming an apostate.

Being unable, after this, to go through the toils to which I had been sentenced, I was excused, by my amply rewarding the overseers. It was now that I had full leisure to reflect seriously on the means of obtaining my liberty ; and, for this purpose, desired a friend to write to my brother-in-law, Mr. Barbu, to inform him

criminals, and replete with every species of villainous and bad characters. At the time Coustos was there, he found some of these slaves employed in the dockyard ; carrying timber, loading and unloading ships ; carrying water to the king's gardens and to all the prisons ; and to labours still more ignominious and painful. They were treated with the greatest severity, being fastened two and two by a chain, eight feet long, to their ancles. At their girdle is an iron hook, by which they might shorten or lengthen the chain at their convenience. Their heads and beards are shaved once a month ; and they wear coarse cloaks, in which they are also wrapped at night, lying on boards covered with matting. Their provision is of the meanest kind, being allowed only six pounds of salt meat for a month, besides a prescribed quantity of pulse and black biscuit. They are led early in the morning to their work, and toil incessantly till eleven ; then they dine, and labour till night, when they are led back to the galley. If any of them fall sick, they are removed to the upper room, and placed under the care of the medical attendants. If any of them offend, they are laid on their bellies, fastened to a ladder naked, and beaten by two men with a thick pitched rope. This punishment is sometimes so severe, that pieces of the flesh are torn away, which produces mortification, and sometimes death

of my deplorable state, and to entreat him humbly to address the Earl of Harrington in my favour ; my brother-in-law having the honour to live in his lordship's family. This nobleman, whose humanity and generosity have been the theme of infinitely abler pens than mine, was so good as to declare, that he would endeavour to procure my freedom. Accordingly, his lordship spoke to his grace the Duke of Newcastle, one of the principal secretaries of state, in order to supplicate for leave from our sovereign, that his minister at Lisbon might demand me as a subject of Great Britain.

His majesty, ever attentive to the felicity of his subjects, and desirous of relieving them in all their misfortunes, was so gracious as to interpose in my favour. Accordingly, his commands being dispatched to Mr. Compton, the British minister at Lisbon, that gentleman demanded my liberty of the King of Portugal, in his Britannic Majesty's name ; which accordingly I obtained the latter end of October, 1744. The person who came and freed me from the galley, by order of the inquisitors, took me before them. The president then told me, that Cardinal da Cunha had given orders for my being released. At the same time he bid me return to the holy office in three or four days.[73]

I could perceive, during this interval, that I was followed by the spies of the Inquisition, who kept a watchful eye over my behaviour, and the places I frequented. I waited upon our envoy, as likewise upon our consul, whom I informed of the commands which had been laid upon me at the Inquisition, and those gentlemen advised me to obey them. They cautioned me, however, to take a friend with me, in order that he

---

[73] These severe measures served to extinguish Freemasonry in Portugal ; and for thirty-three years it made no progress whatever. But in 1776, two members of the craft, Major Dalincourt and Don Oyres de Ornelles Paracao, a Portuguese nobleman, were incarcerated, and remained in prison upwards of fourteen months. Many inquiries were from. time to time instituted, to discover whether Masonry was in operation, under the plea of searching into conspiracies against the government ; and several arrests of distinguished personages took place at various subsequent periods, and amongst the rest Da Costa, the naturalist. But the severity of former times was not repeated, owing probably to the dispersion of the Jesuits, who were at all times the bitter and uncompromising enemies of the Order, except when they had it in their own hands.

might give them notice, in case I should be seized again. I accordingly returned to the inquisitors five days after, when the president declared—" That the tribunal would not permit me to continue any longer in Portugal, and therefore, that I must name the city and kingdom whither I intended to retire." " As my family," I replied, " are now in London, I design to go thither as soon as possible." They then bid me embark in the first ship that should sail for England ; adding, that the instant I had found one, I must inform them of the day and hour I intended to go on board, together with the captain's name and that of his ship.

A report prevailed, some days after, that one of the persons seized by the Inquisition for Freemasonry, and who had obtained his liberty by turning Roman Ca- tholic, had been so indiscreet as to divulge the cruelties exercised in this tribunal.

I now imagined that prudence required me to secure myself from a second persecution. As there was at this time no English ship in the port of Lisbon, I waited upon Mr. Vantil, the resident of Holland, and besought him to speak to the Dutch admiral to admit me on board his fleet. The resident, touched with my calamities, hinted my request to the admiral, who generously com- plied with it. I then went, together with a friend, and informed the inquisitor, that I designed to embark for England in the Damietta, commanded by Vice-admiral Cornelius Screiver, who was to sail in a few days. Upon the inquisitors inquiring the exact time when I intended to go on board, I replied, at nine o'clock the next morning. He then bid me come to him precisely at that hour; adding, that he would send some officers of the Inquisition to see me on shipboard.

These orders giving me great uneasiness, I waited upon the several gentlemen above-mentioned, when telling them the injunctions laid upon me, they advised me to act very cautiously on this occasion. I therefore thought it would be safest for me to go on board imme- diately, without giving any notice of it to the inquisi- tors.[74] We lay at anchor, after this, near three weeks before Lisbon.

---

[74] Here he felt himself safe, and out of the reach of persecution; for

8

The inquisitor no sooner found that I failed coming to him at the time appointed, in order to be conducted to the ship, than he sent out about thirty spies. Nine of these coming to inquire after me, at the house where I used to lodge, searched it from top to bottom, examining every trunk, chest of drawers, and closet. But their endeavours to find me being fruitless, some officers of the Inquisition getting into a boat, rowed several times round the three Dutch men-of-war lying at anchor. These officers imagined that if I was on board, and consequently in a place of security, I should not be afraid of showing myself—a circumstance that would have put an end to their search, which cost them some pains and expense. As I did not gratify their curiosity, and we weighed anchor a few days after, I know not whether they continued it.

Their search was so open, both at the house where I had lodged, as well as at other places, that I was soon informed of it; at which I should have been delighted, had not my joy been damped by the apprehensions I was under, lest my dear friend, Mr. Mouton, the companion of my sufferings and tortures, merely on account of Freemasonry, should likewise fall a victim to their barbarity. Speaking concerning him to the admiral, he, with the utmost humanity, gave me leave to send for him on board. He, coming accordingly next day, was received with great satisfaction by the whole ship's company, especially by myself, I having a peculiar esteem for him, which I shall ever entertain.

We set sail two days after. We had occasion to observe during our whole voyage, the true pleasure which a generous mind feels in doing a humane action, and in protecting the unhappy. This was particularly conspicuous in the admiral, he ordering the utmost care

there was no inquisition in England; although attempts were made to introduce it in the reign of Mary. " The justices of peace," says Bishop Burnet, were now everywhere so slack in the prosecution of heretics, that it seemed necessary to find out other tools; so the courts of inquisition were thought of, and a commission was given to Bonner and others to search for all who were suspected of heresy. This was carried on so vigorously in different parts of England, that the burning of heretics became common, which was looked on as an advance towards the Inquisition; but the death of Mary prevented such a project from being introduced into this free kingdom."

to be taken of us, all the time we were on board his ship ; he sometimes condescending to admit us to his table, when he would talk to us with the utmost familiarity. This distinction won us the civility of every person in the ship, which continued till our arrival at Portsmouth, where we landed ; without having been put to a farthing expense during the whole voyage.

All these favours, so generously bestowed by the admiral, call aloud for the strongest acknowledgments of gratitude.

To conclude, I arrived in London the 15th of December, 1744, after a long and dangerous voyage.

I here return thanks, with all the powers of my soul, to the Almighty, for his having so visibly protected me from that infernal band of friars, who employed the various tortures, mentioned in the former pages, in order to force me to apostatize from my holy religion.

I return our sovereign King George II. (the instrument under heaven for procuring me my liberty) the most dutiful and most respectful thanks, for his so graciously condescending to interpose in favour of an ill-fated galley-slave. I shall retain, so long as I have breath, the deepest sensations of affection and loyalty for his sacred person ; and will be ever ready to expose my life for his majesty and his most august family.

CHAPTER V.

"———————— prepare thee to cut off the flesh;
Shed thou no blood; nor cut thou less nor more,
But just a pound of flesh; if thou tak'st more,
Or less than just a pound, be it but so much
As makes it light or heavy in the substance,
Or the division of the twentieth part
Of one poor scruple; nay, if the scale do turn
But in the estimation of a hair—
Thou diest, and all thy goods are confiscate."

SHAKSPEARE.

ATTACK ON FREEMASONRY IN MALTA.[1]

THE pastoral letter of the Catholic Bishop of Malta to his diocese, on the subject of Freemasons' lodges, was issued in 1843. After the edict published against the Jews of Ancona,[2] we cannot be surprised by any act of bigotry, folly, or craft, that may emanate from the Romish Church, even in this age of information and enlightenment. The only cause for astonishment is, that

---

[1] The text of this chapter is wholly taken from the Freemasons' Quarterly Review.

[2] The above edict is given at length in the Freemasons' Quarterly Review for 1843, p. 384. But it appears to have been soon withdrawn, from the following paragraph in the Voice of Jacob:—" We have sincere pleasure in announcing, from an authentic source, that the atrocious decree of the Roman Inquisition, first issued under the authority of Leo XII., and recently put in force by the inquisitor-general of Ancona, has been again suspended. We learn from various quarters that the utmost consternation had been produced, not only throughout Italy, but everywhere in the Mediterranean; not only among the Jews, but among Protestant Christians, either subject to Catholic governments, or surrounded by Catholic populations, at this revival of the fearful Inquisition. Some misapprehension has existed as to the genuineness of the decree; we have reason to know that certain of its clauses had already begun to be acted upon."

(166)

such a document should be published in a British possession.[3]

It is not an impotent instrument of malice ; for the excitement caused amongst the ignorant population of Malta is likely to be followed by serious consequences. Denounced as a Freemason, your life is no longer safe. With the Maltese a Freemason, is now not only avoided as a mad dog, but he is in imminent danger of being treated as one. The police have been called in to protect several persons suspected as Masons. Those denounced are refused all attendance and consolation, and placed under the ban of society with their countrymen.[4]

Very few Maltese are Masons ; although some few Italian refugees have at times attended the lodge. Nearly all the members are Englishmen of great respectability, either residents here, or naval and military officers, who may be for a time stationed in the island or port. The Freemasons' lodge has been established for nearly thirty years ; therefore it is not, as the precious letter would insinuate, a thing of yesterday.[5] A branch meeting or

[3] Intolerance is confined to no country or climate ; and even Great Britain, enlightened by the successful researches of science and philosophy, is not free from its baneful influence, as we shall see in the course of the present chapter. But it is only those who can make up their minds to oppose the free practice of our holy religion, that are capable of interfering with the proceedings of Masonry.

[4] An instance of this inhumanity occurred in Gibraltar in 1840, and the honourable manner in which it was met by the Rev. Dr. Burrow, the Past Grand Master, is related in an address to him at the presentation of a masonic offering by the fraternity. A poor, but respectable Roman Catholic was refused Christian burial because he was a Freemason ; and his corpse was expelled from the Roman Catholic church as a contamination! The Past Grand Master hearing of this, offered to perform for him those sacred offices which had been refused by the clergy of his own communion, which were of course accepted ; and raised equally in the opinion of all impartial persons, the character of Masonry as an institution of Brotherly love, and of the Protestant Church as an example of toleration and humanity.

It will scarcely be believed that in the nineteenth century, in a British possession, where many of the government officers, as well as officers of regiments in garrison there, and of the ships of war in port, are Freemasons, so bigoted, calumnious and scandalous an edict should have been posted up on the doors of, and read in every Catholic church and chapel, as the following, which is termed a "Pastoral Letter," and purports to be issued by the Bishop of Malta, though, in reality, it has been concocted by the Jesuitical *clique* about him ; for it is well known his lordship is in a state of second childhood. We sincerely hope to see the

lodge is held at Senglea, for the convenience of those
living across the water, distant from Valetta.   It is to
this particularly that the Bishop refers.   The Masons
here are a very quiet and orderly class of persons, chiefly
English artisans employed in the dockyard.   No act can
have been committed that in any way deserves the slan-
ders contained in the intemperate letter of this ill-advised
old man.   It is merely conjectured that the Bishop has
published this letter to show at home how zealous a servant of the pope he is, and how watchful he is over the
interests of the church.[6]   It is a bugbear, which he has
raised for the sole purpose of exciting alarm, and of showing his power as an exorcist.[7]

" *Nos Don Franciscus Xaverius Carnana, Venerabilibus
Fratribus et Dilectis, Capitulo, Clero, Populoque Dioccsis
Melitensis, salutem in Domino Sempiternam.*

" We feel it to be the duty of our pastoral ministry to
conceal as much as possible such sins as may be committed by a few persons in secret, so that the bad example
of these may not be made known to or followed by others,
to the scandal of the church and corruption of good manners.   Up to this period this policy has been followed by

matter warmly taken up by the British press; and feel confident that
an inquiry will be made in parliament as to how the local government
ever permitted such an unlawful assu... ion of authority, understanding, as we do, that the Ecclesiastical Court signified its intention before-
hand, and why the crown lawyers have not instituted an action for
libel against all concerned.
    [6] On this point His Royal Highness the late Duke of Sussex observed,
that " the wisest and soundest policy would be to leave all religions quietly
to themselves, so long as they neither attack morality, nor subvert the
public quiet, either by their ambition or intolerance ; their variety would
not fail to produce a rivalship, useful as a balance in the scale of power,
and as an emulation to virtue.   The state has no right to exercise its
authority over the private opinions of any individual ; but merely to
notice those acts which may endanger and disturb the regularity and
good order of its civilized community."
    [7] The dignified clergy of Belgium, however, have imitated so fructify-
ing an example, and have issued an address to the inferior priests of
their several dioceses, in which they are exhorted to communicate to
their flocks, by publishing at sermon time, that the associations of Freemasons are expressly prohibited and condemned by the pope, who
rigorously forbids all persons to take any part in them, or to favour
them in any manner whatever ; and that those who so offend shall not
receive absolution, unless they positively renounce these societies !

us ; for our ecclesiastical doctrine teaches us, through the
Holy Spirit, to listen for a time silently, and, meanwhile,
search diligently :—' *audi tacens semul et quærens.*' We now
draw your attention to that iniquitous congregation, that
detestable lodge ; for we are at a loss by what epithet
to denounce a meeting held in a building in an obscure
corner of the city of Senglea. After long suffering, we
are still grieved to see that the several means which,
with evangelical prudence, we have hitherto adopted to
overturn and eradicate this pernicious society have proved
futile ; so that at length we feel ourselves under the
necessity of publicly, loudly, and energetically raising
our voice to exhort, in the name of our Lord, all our
beloved diocesans to keep far away from this infernal
meeting, whose object is nothing less than to loosen
every divine and human tie, and to destroy, if possible,
the very foundation of the Catholic Church. We also
threaten with the thunders of that church any persons
who, unhappily for them, may belong to any secret society, whether as a member, or in any way connected with,
helping or favouring, directly or indirectly, such society or
any of its acts.

" We, with anguish at heart, heard long ago, almost
immediately on its first assemblage, of the creation of this
diabolical lodge ; and being very desirous that the land
under our spiritual domination (these islands of Malta
and Gozo), should continue in ignorance of what was
doing under the veil of darkness, in an obscure part of
the city of Senglea, by a few ill-advised individuals ; and
that none of our flock should by chance, or from motives
of interest, be tempted to join this pestilential pulpit of
iniquity and error—we have as yet only adopted the
evangelical advice of secretly warning and admonishing,
hoping always that the attacks made on the human and
divine laws established among us may be foiled and become harmless ; but seeing now, that in spite of all our
silent workings, the meetings of this lodge still continue,
we openly, and with all that apostolic frankness characteristic of the Catholic clergy, in the name of God
Almighty, and of his only true Roman Catholic and
apostolic church, and authorized as we are expressly by
the papal authority, denounce, proscribe, and condemn, in
the most public manner, the instalments, unions, meet-

ings, and all the proceedings of this lodge of abominations, as being diametrically opposed to our sacred Catholic religion ; as destructive to every celestial law, every mundane authority ; contradictory to every evangelical maxim, and as tending to disorganize, put to flight, and utterly destroy whatever of religion, of honesty, and of good there may be in the holy Catholic faith, or among our peaceful citizens, under the deceitful veil of novelty, of a badly understood philanthropy, and a specious freedom.

" We therefore believe it to be our duty, most beloved diocesan, to address you under these deplorable circumstances ; to incite you to entertain the most profound horror and the deepest indignation for this lodge, union, or society, by us this day publicly condemned—to regard it as a common sewer of filth, and sink of immorality, which endeavours, although as yet in vain, to vomit hell against, to stigmatize the immaculate purity of our sacred Catholic religion.   Its pernicious orgies anticipate the overthrow of that order which reigns on earth ; promote an unbridled freedom of action unchecked by law, for the gratification of the most depraved and disorderly passions.   Do not allow yourselves to be deceived by their seducing language, which proffers humanity fraternal love and apparent reform ; but, in reality, tends to discord, universal anarchy, and total ruin, the destruction of all religion, and the subversion of every philanthropic establishment.   Their agents industriously hide their malignant intentions by deceitful and never-to-be-redeemed promises.   The great solicitude evinced to conceal every action of this society under a mask, will make you distrust its word ; for honourable undertakings are always manifest and open, courting observation and inquiry ; sins and iniquities alone bury themselves in secrecy and obscurity.   Fathers of families ! and you also to whom is intrusted the education of youth, be diligent, and be careful of your precious charge ; see that they be not contaminated by this plague spot, which, although now confined to one domicile, yet threatens to spread the pestilence among us ; scrutinize the books they read, examine the character of their associates.   It is a well-known practice of this secret society to seduce over youth under the specious pretext of communicating to

them, disinterestedly, scientific knowledge. Flee, then,
O beloved diocesan, as from the face of a venomous serpent, the society, the very neighbourhood of, and all
connection with these teachers of impiety, who wish to
confound light with darkness, trying, if possible, to obscure the former, and make you embrace and follow the
latter. You cannot possibly gain anything good from
disturbers of all rule and order, who show no veneration
for God and his religion, no esteem for any authority,
ecclesiastical or civil;—men deceitful and feigning, who,
under a show of social honesty, and a warm love for
their species, are stirring up an atrocious war with all
that can render human society honourable, happy, and
tranquil.

"Consider them as so many pernicious individuals, to
whom Pope Leo XII., in his often-repeated bulls, ordered
that no one should give hospitality—not even a passing
salute.

"Instead of such persons, bring around you honest and
just men, who 'give unto God that which is God's, and
unto Cæsar that which is Cæsar's,' endeavouring to do
their duty to God and to their neighbour.

"Finally, we absolutely prohibit persons of any grade
or condition from having any connection with this lodge,
from co-operating, even indirectly, in its establishment
or extension. We order them to prevent others from
frequenting it, or giving to its members a place of
meeting, under any pretext. We place every one under
an obligation to denounce to us all persons who may
belong to this lodge in any capacity, either as members
or agents of a secret union, founded by the Devil himself, &c.

"Datum Valettæ, in Palatio nostro Archiepiscopali, die
14 Octobris, 1843."[a]

---

[a] We have given the abridged account of the Pastoral Letter from the
Times; and offer no other comment on the above, than to express a hope,
that if the most holy (!) Lord Gregory XVI., by divine Providence the
tenant of St. Peter, on being made acquainted with the unholy conduct
of this said Don Francisco Xaverius Carnana, by the favour of God (!)
Archbishop of Rhodes, &c., &c., does not in a Christian like manner
provide for the poor lunatic, he, the said Gregory XVI., not only will
neglect his duty to a fellow-creature, but will render himself responsible
for all future acts of the wretched maniac. Blessed Freemasonry! tho

8*

A more complete specimen of Jesuitical bigotry than
the above has seldom appeared. It is, however, calculated to injure its promulgators rather than the un-
offending and widely-spread body against whom its vain
thunders have been fulminated; for it is useless for
Roman Catholics to talk of any amelioration in the
spirit of modern popery, when edicts so fierce and intolerant as the ridiculous composition in question, prove
the present existence of a rancorous spirit of persecution
and bigotry unsurpassed in the darkest ages of papal
supremacy and power.[9] In this vile document the most
atrocious calumnies are heaped upon the masonic fraternity, which is described as " the common sewer of all
filth, endeavouring, though continually in vain, to vomit
forth the things of hell against the immaculate purity of
the holy Catholic religion," and the Brethren are represented as seeking to convulse all order which reigns
upon earth.[10] The whole production is imbued with the

best proof of thy moral influence and purity is, that only maniacs and
infidels bay at the Light they comprehend not.
  [9] The following extract from W. Penn's letter to the King of Poland,
contains a beautiful lesson, which all persecutors would do well to study
attentively :—" Now, O prince," says he, " give a poor Christian leave
to expostulate with thee. Did Christ Jesus, or his holy followers, endeavour, by precept or example, to set up their religion with a carnal
sword ? Called he any troops of men or angels to defend him ? Did he
encourage Peter to dispute his right with the sword ? but did he not
say—put it up? Or did he countenance his over-zealous disciples, when
they would have had fire from heaven to destroy them that were not of
their mind ? No! but did not Christ rebuke them, saying—' Ye know
not what spirit ye are of?' And, if it was neither Christ's spirit nor
their own spirit that would have fire from heaven—Oh! what is that
spirit that would kindle fire on earth, to destroy such as peaceably follow
the dictates of their conscience ? Oh, King! when did true religion
persecute? When did the true church offer violence for religion? Were
not her weapons prayers, tears, and patience? Did not Jesus conquer
by these weapons, and vanquish cruelty by suffering? Can clubs, and
staves, and swords, and prisons, and banishments, reach the soul, convert
the heart, or convince the understanding of man? When did violence
ever make a true convert, or bodily punishment a sincere Christian?
This maketh void the end of Christ's coming. Yea, it robbeth God's
spirit of its office, which is to convince the world. That is the sword
by which the ancient Christians overcome."
  [10] " The Monita et Statuta was promulgated by the English vicars apostolic about four years before. Its character may be estimated by the
following extract :—" We (i. e. the bishops) enjoin that the Catholics
be discreetly warned against entering into the society of them who are
vulgarly called Freemasons. By a response of the sacred congregation

worst spirit of bigotry, and contains throughout the most atrocious and abominable falsehoods. It is a base libel upon the memory of that benevolent prince, who, for so many years, presided over the English portion of the ancient fraternity, a base libel upon those respected prelates of the Protestant church, who have adorned and supported the Order, and a gross libel upon the monarchs of the royal house of Brunswick, who, for so many years, have been amongst the warmest and most constant patrons.[11]

Similar edicts have been before, at various times, given to the world; whence, then, arises such bitter hostility, and why does popery dread the progress of Freemasonry? It is because the two systems contain antagonistic principles. The pure doctrines of Free-masonry — its principles of universal beneficence, its charity and brotherly love—and the truly Christian duties which its practice inculcates, are utterly at variance with that system of superstition and bigotry which, under the denomination of Catholicism, seeks to perpetuate ignorance and error, fetter the conscience, and en-slave the mind. Protestantism cherishes and promotes Freemasonry; popery would persecute and suppress it. To put the question, however, between popery and Freemasonry at issue, and to show how far the latter is calculated, as represented by the Bishop of Malta,[12] " to shake off the light yoke of religion," and "to disturb the exercise of legitimate authority," it may not be amiss to refer to the charge which is delivered to every Free-

of the holy office, July 5, 1837, it hath been declared, that a confessor cannot, lawfully or validly, grant sacramental absolution to men belong-ing to that society, in any part of the world soever, who are incorpo-rated under, and mutually bound by, the obligations of an oath of secrecy, except they absolutely, positively, and for ever abandon the aforesaid condemned society."

[11] " By toleration is meant conformity, safety, and protection, granted by the state to every sect that does not maintain doctrines inconsistent with the public peace, the rights of the sovereign, and the safety of our neighbours." (His Royal Highness the Duke of Sussex.)

[12] Let the archbishops and bishops of the Roman Catholic church take the trouble of going through the history of the past five centuries, and they will find that every time the church attempted to wound to the heart the undoubted rights of any nation, so often has she been defeated by the progress of public opinion, and compelled to seek refuge from the people over whom she wished to domineer and oppress.

mason at his initiation, and which, as comprehending the principles taught in the "detestable lodge," will, perhaps, form the best answer to the atrocious calumnies contained in the Pastoral Letter.

The Freemason is also especially exhorted to imprint indelibly on his mind the sacred dictates of *truth*, of *honour* and of *virtue*.

Masons are there particularly directed to venerate the volume of the sacred law ; upon its sanction they are obligated, and from its inspired pages all their masonic teaching is derived. This sacred volume, which is designated the first great light of Masonry, is never closed in any lodge, and the emblems of moral rectitude are at the same time displayed. Such being the principles upon which Freemasonry is founded, teaching, as it does, peace on earth and good-will towards mankind, its professors may bid defiance to the slanderous attacks of bigotry, and rest assured that the light of truth will prevail, and eventually overcome the powers of darkness.[13]

CRUSADE AGAINST FREEMASONRY IN INDIA.

The denunciations against Freemasonry, in the two last overland Spectators, are almost verbatim those of the worst of the pope's, and the most bigoted of the Inquisition's. Take the following as a specimen :

" If, then, the meaning of the inscription be, that the Christian, the Hindoo, the Mahometan, and the Parsee,

[13] **Magna est veritas et prævalebit.** It is wonderful to consider how effectually the shield of protection has been thrown over Freemasonry in every contest to which it has been subjected. Prejudice and malevolence united have frequently endeavoured to overwhelm it, but it has always risen triumphant over the severest persecutions ; and, what is more, has come out of every contest without the slightest speck to sully the purity of its glorious badge." Its principles are stainless, and nothing can prevail against it. As Dr. Burnes very justly observed, in his address to the Brethren of the lodge at Poonah, July 30, 1844, " it is an institution based on that never-failing charity which upholds universal love, calms the troubled sea of our evil passions, and leaves a smooth surface, in which all men, who are sincere and conscientious worshippers of God, and unexceptionable in their moral conduct, may unite, bless each other, and rejoice in practically realizing the sublime sentiment, that

" God hath made mankind one mighty Brotherhood ;
Himself their Master, and the world their lodge."

are all, according to, or notwithstanding their respective creeds, the approved and beloved children of God, we cannot help saying, and we do so with grief and bitterness of spirit, that the grand native hospital of Bombay is founded upon a lie.

"The doctrines set forth in the course of it by the Provincial Grand Master of Masons, is entirely opposed to the Holy Scriptures ; and, alas! that it was so, a number of the most distinguished gentlemen of Bombay who were present, gave it their unanimous, their cordial concurrence ; not one faithful voice was heard to raise itself in that large assembly of professing Christians against language which, if believed and acted upon, must unavoidably lead to eternal misery.

"The Freemasons' 'charity' is unconnected with Christ; it is not, therefore, surprising that it is not exercised for His glory ; it can never, then, be acceptable in the sight of the Almighty.

"I have now proved, as I proposed at the commencement of this letter, the Provincial Grand Master's doctrine of our holy religion.

"Freemasonry may do for a world of sin and corruption, for vain people to amuse themselves with, but, being un-Christian, it can lead to nothing but gross deception and everlasting misery. It is a thing of sin and evil in the face of it ; an engine of Satan ; a tool much beloved of him—the arch enemy of God and man, and it is wonderful how any man of sense and discernment can, for a moment, be taken with it."

"There is also no manner of use in it ; for the Bible teaches us everything. Were Freemasonry a system

---

" Something similar to this is the language of a French writer, towards the close of the last century. "The Freemasons," he says, "in almost every country have been charged with the design of destroying the religion, and abolishing the government. In consequence of this they have often been persecuted, and especially in Italy, where the popes have issued dreadful fulminations against the Order. The senate of Venice, and the King of Sardinia, have banished its members from their states ; some years ago the Queen of Hungary chased them from her dominions ; in Holland their assemblies were prohibited by manifestoes posted at the corners of the streets. Precautions have been taken to prevent their increasing in the empire of Russia ; and, finally, at Berne, in Switzerland, they have been compelled on oath to renounce their allegiance to Freemasonry."

which operated as an auxiliary to Christianity, as Masons would have us believe, and some other persons are led to think. there would be no objection to it; but that the direct contrary is the fact, there can be no sort of doubt. Its mystery, its closeness, its ostentation, are all emblematical of the pride, selfishness, and ungodliness of the natural, unregenerate man. Its object is temporal advantage only, and it rejects the Lord Jesus; whereas, the foundation of Christianity is 'Jesus Christ, and he crucified;' and the rule, 'let your light so shine before men that they may see your good works, and glorify your Father which is in heaven.' Every man, therefore, who has at heart the great concerns of eternity, will eschew Freemasonry, and esteem it, what in good truth it is, with its profane pageantry—an abomination in the sight of God."

Now, putting charity out of the question, although it might be some consideration to a person professing himself a Christian minister, to say nothing of the chance of exposure, we submit that a sensible man, and a peaceful preacher, would have avoided such observations as these, inasmuch as they are like a two-edged sword, cutting both ways, and likely very materially to frustrate rather than to advance the business of converting the heathen, which should be paramount to all other with a missionary. We think the reverend gentleman has neither shown the wisdom of the serpent, nor the innocence of the dove, in giving vent to them.[15]

---

[15] It is truly wonderful that individuals should exist who can have the hardihood to risk their reputation by a public condemnation of what they have no opportunity of understanding; their arguments are sure to turn against themselves, because they are grounded on erroneous data, being the offspring of prejudice or idle conjecture; and we would recommend all such inconsiderate persons to read the following masonic definition of truth, before they place themselves in such an unfortunate position:—" Truth is the foundation of virtue. He who walks by its light, has the advantage of the meridian sun; while he who spurns it, is involved in clouds and darkness. There is no way in which a man strenghtens his own judgment, and acquires respect in society, so surely as by a scrupulous regard to truth. The course of such an individual is a straightforward course. He is no changeling, saying one thing to-day and another to-morrow. Truth is to him like the mountain landmark to the pilot; he fixes his eye upon a point that does not move, and he enters the harbour in safety. On the contrary, one who despises truth, and loves false-

The labourer is worthy of his hire ; but it is implied that he is to do the work of his Master, not only zealously, but discreetly and peaceably ; and as Christians deeply and devoutly attached to the creed of our forefathers, we ask the Missionary Society, which deputed this gentleman to Bombay, whether they sanction the indulgence of his outpourings against a number of the most distinguished gentlemen of Bombay, to the manifest injury of that solemn and sacred cause to which he has bound himself, and whether that great cause can be advanced by his proclaiming those distinguished gentlemen " anti-Christians?" Can he now hope for success in his missionary efforts?[16] Well may the Hindoo, the Parsee, and Mahometan, tell him to go and convert the most distinguished of his own countrymen before he intermeddles with them !

With respect to the extracts which have been given from the Provincial Grand Master's speech, there is not one which ·has not been either misquoted or misrepresented ; and this is the less justifiable, as he expresses his fear that neither he (the Provincial Grand Master) nor any of the fraternity may be at liberty to reply !

To mercilessly attack a person who, from peculiar circumstances, is unable to defend himself from the violence, is a thing so dastardly, as to be stamped with the universal detestation of mankind.[17] Of a piece with it

hood, is like a pilot who takes a piece of drift-wood for his landmark, which changes with every changing wave. On this he fixes his attention, and being insensibly led from his course, strikes upon some hidden reef, and sinks to rise no more."

[16] We answer, no. The missionary duties admit of no contention—no compromise. Christian institutions are not proper objects of attack to the Christian minister, and least of all to the missionary, who ought to be an example of patience, gentleness, courtesy, and every other virtue, and to conciliate esteem by kindness and forbearance, rather than provoke hostility and foster rivalry, by the indulgence of envy or jealousy, or the exhibition of an intolerant and persecuting spirit.

[17] The persecution of Masonry in the United States during the Morgan excitement was intended to destroy its existence. The prejudices of the people were excited—the energies of the entire Union were fearfully arrayed against it—and all in vain. Its purity was its protection ; and the Grand Master of Ohio, in an address to the Grand Lodge in 1845, said :—" It affords me pleasure to be able to announce to you my belief, that the Order of Freemasonry now enjoys throughout our country, and especially within our jurisdiction, an exemption from the malign influences of envy and detraction, in a degree rarely before experienced ; that it is

is the calumny thrown upon Masonry by many who are
fully aware that the Brethren are bound by their obligation to a secrecy which would be broken were they to
attempt to disprove the slander which is thrown upon
their doctrines ;[18] a slander not fixed upon them with
even the semblance of justice, but hurled with blind and
bigoted fury against a system of which the slanderers
know nothing, and can have, therefore, no just grounds
for either praise or censure.[19]   I am sure that no man
endowed with that beautiful charity so eloquently dilated
upon by St. Paul, could, or would, raise his voice against
the internals of a system of which he is ignorant —

keeping pace with the onward progress of civilizaton and art, and gradually making its way into the favourable consideration of an unprejudiced
and intelligent community. Lodges which, long since, fell into listless
suspense, are arousing themselves to active duty, and burnishing anew
their jewels which had become dim from long neglect and disuse ; and
new lodges are springing into being in districts where hitherto our rites
have been wholly unpractised and unknown."   •
    [18] And what right have our opponents to expect an honest man to
break his word ?   Every person's secrets are a sacred deposit—they rest
between him and his God.   And no one, but least of all, a professor of
religion, has authority to demand a revelation of those secrets ; because
it would involve a breach of faith, a renunciation of principle, and a stain
on the veracity and honour. Mat. Lewis saw this in its best light, when,
in one of his dramas, he represents a person tampering with a servant to
betray some confidence which had been reposed in him.   The conversation conclu les with the servant asking his interlocutor—" Can you keep
a secret ?" He replies—" Faithfully."   And the servant very properly
replies—" As faithfully can I."   This is the answer which should invari-
ably be given to all such unreasonable querists.
    [19] A writer in Moore's Masonic Magazine says :—" It is often asked, if
the secrets of Masonry be of any value, why not make them known ? If
they be useless, why guard them with such scrupulous and sensitive care ?
We do not complain of the motive which prompts these inquiries. We
are not disposed to regard them as impertinent or unnatural. It is not
within the province of the will alone, that men derive the power or the
disposition to think or to question. It is in the nature of the human
mind itself. The Almighty has implanted in the soul of man desires that
must be gratified, and faculties of thought which are ever active in investigating the nature and uses of things." This is well, but there is a point
beyond which it is indecent to go. When men inquire into secrets which
cannot be betrayed without running into sin, they exceed their duties,
and must not complain if they be disappointed in the object of their
inquiry. But it is the province of the minister of the gospel to direct
mankind into the paths of virtue ; and therefore he is not only over-
stepping the boundaries of duty, but of prudence also, when he ventures
to make improper inquiries into the secrets of Freemasonry ; because if
he should succeed in inducing a weak Brother to comply with the
request, he would be the means of leading him into deadly sin.

whose externals all must acknowledge to be founded upon the plain and evident will of God, as revealed in His holy word.[20] " Pure religion and undefiled before God and the Father," says St. James, " is this—to visit the fatherless and widows in their affliction, and to keep himself unspotted from the world." Who will deny that this is the very basis on which Masonry is founded ? Let. him who would do so, look to our schools for the nurture of the young, our asylum for the shelter of the aged, and the countless acts of individual charity whose very fount and spring is Masonry.[21] To him who does deny it, the tongue of the widow and fatherless—the voice of destitute age, and unprotected youth, snatched from misery, ruin, and despair, and fostered in the maternal bosom of Masonry, will rise above the futile effort at detraction, and cry : " Thou liest"—knowingly and wantonly in the face of facts which he who runs may read ; may see stamped upon every stone of that beautiful fabric, whose pinnacles glitter in the sun to the glory of our God, and the benefit of our fellow-men.

Is Freemasonry unconnected with Christ ? does it reject the Lord Jesus, as some would intimate ? I deny it firmly, zealously, truly. Does the Christian divine leave unread and unstudied the Old Testament, with its hallowed poetry, its splendid imagery, and mystic types, the forerunners of that more full and perfect day which was to dawn upon the benighted heart of man?

[20] Nothing can be clearer than this proposition. Every rite and ceremony bears a reference to the usages of holy writ, and the doctrines are all drawn from the same fountain. If I were to subjoin a catalogue of the texts of scripture which are referred to in the several degrees of Masonry, there would scarcely be a single book unquoted ; and in many cases the illustrations would embrace entire chapters both of the Old and New Testament.

[21] There is no single institution in existence which embraces so many and various displays of benevolence ; and therefore the Free and Accepted Mason experiences more of that pleasing degree of satisfaction which always attends the dispensations of benevolence, than any other man. Instances of the rapturous emotions of joy and gratitude which animate the bosoms of those on whom benefits have been conferred, are frequent to the members of those boards which are the authorized dispensers of masonic benevolence, and excite in their own bosoms a corresponding sentiment of unfeigned delight. Inopi beneficium bis dat qui dat celeriter.

No! useful—pre-eminently so—is that record of God's dealings with his people, to the proper understanding of his infinite grace, and man's great salvation.[22] The science of Masonry stands in the same relation to Christianity ; or, perhaps, more correctly speaking, it is the spiritual essence of the old law, not extending to the height and sublimity of the new covenant, but a step in advance—not in the spiritual meaning of the old law, but of man's interpretation of it : a more spiritual, and, therefore, more correct reading of it than that followed by the mass of the people, who looked more to the letter, and understood not that fulfilling of the law, as defined by Christ, when he declared the law broken by him who even gazed on a woman to lust after her. If they to whom this exceeding knowledge was communicated, concealed it from those whose tongue was more ready to scoff than pray, and communicated it to those, and those alone, who loved their God with all their heart, and their neighbour as themselves, does it follow that that secrecy was sinful ?

None know but the initiated, how beautifully Masonry harmonizes with the doctrines of the +.[23] As the mystical types and allegory of the old law became plain upon

[22] An intelligent Brother has furnished me with the following curious illustration :—" After our Lord's resurrection, the disciples changed their day of assembling together, or as we should call it, their lodge day, from the seventh to the first day of the week ; and on that day Jesus Christ appeared to Mary, and directed her to go to his Brethren, and inform them that he was about to ascend to the grand lodge above, into the presence of Him who was both his Father and their Father ; and on the same day at evening, when they were assembled (which custom has been preserved among ourselves, Masons' lodges being usually held in an evening), the doors being shut where they were assembled for fear of the Jews, or in other words, the lodge being closely tyled for fear of cowans, came Jesus and stood *in the midst* of them, making use of that masonic greeting—Peace be with you. Our Brethren would naturally feel surprised at the presence of a stranger, standing like the point within a circle, when the lodge was closely tyled ; but when he had given them proofs, by showing them those signs of distress in his hands and his side, that he was their Brother, and a partaker of the same hope ; when he displayed the wound produced by some sharp-pointed instrument in his naked left breast, they hailed him as a Brother, and received at his hands the divine benediction."

[23] It is rather strange that a Brother should be found, who can persuade himself that Masonry contains no reference to religion, when the very first step which he made in advancing to the floor of the lodge, was attended with an acknowledgment that he believes in an omnipresent

the rising of the Sun of Christ, so has that day-spring from on high cleared the mists which, I confess, hung upon our beautiful science.[24] Reject Christ! I am certain every real Mason's heart will swell with indignation at the foul charge.

Masonry is also accused of ostentation. Oh! were the deep sense of degradation which that seeming ostentation inspires thoroughly known, the world would own that the ostentation of Masonry is but humility.

Despite the attacks of foes, the indiscretion of friends, and the lapse of time, Masonry still prospers, and still shall prosper, on earth, until the Great Architect of the Universe shall, in his infinite goodness, translate it into the heaven of heavens, where we shall no longer see through a glass darkly, but face to face.

ATTACK ON MASONRY IN IRELAND.

The "Tablet" weekly Catholic newspaper has ejected a shower of abuse upon the devoted heads of ALL Protestants and ALL Freemasons,[25] which may require a few words in reply. On the 20th of July, 1844, this *censor morum* of bishops, priests, laymen, Protestants, and Freemasons, thought fit to publish his censures—to fulminate

Deity, and that he puts his trust in that great and omnipotent Being to shield him from danger, and to remove his apprehensions of evil; and when the first lesson which was taught him at his initiation, was to persevere in the constant study of the Holy Bible, as the sacred source of his faith and hope, and containing the only certain information on a subject the most interesting to a responsible agent; and to practise the three great duties of morality, the first and most important of which is, his duty to God.

[24] We allegorize the building of the temple thus:—" The stones were carved, marked, and numbered in the quarry from whence they were hewn; the timber was prepared and marked in the forest; and when brought to Jerusalem and put together, each part fitted with such perfect exactness, as made it appear rather the work of the Great Architect of the Universe, than an exertion of human skill." Every Christian is a stone in this spiritual edifice, which, when properly modelled and polished by the exercise of religion and the practice of morality, and fitted for translation to a celestial building, he is cemented with his perfected Brethren, by charity, into a beautiful temple prepared on earth, and put together in heaven.

[25] That worthy coadjutor of the Tablet, the Rev. Mr. Burke, has received a signal castigation from the pen of a "Catholic Freemason," in an article that appeared lately in the Nenagh Guardian, which is extremely well written, and calculated to apply an antidote to the poison which the Tablet has spirted on all within its influence.

his anathemas and to pronounce his excommunications in the following quaint, but ignorant enunciations:—
" Who are—and who are not excommunicated? ALL Protestants of course." "And ALL Freemasons? Many loyal and contented Freemasons pass generally for Catholics."[26]

But, thank God! exclaims a "Catholic Freemason," such is not the creed of the Roman Catholic church; our church never did teach the condemnation of the invincibly ignorant; therefore ALL Protestants are not excommunicated.[27]

Many thousands have entered " secret societies," who never saw or heard of the papal decrees against Freemasons. If there be any such who have entered " secret associations" in ignorance, of any doubts upon the matter —I have known many—the Roman Catholic church never did affirm that such persons are excommunicated; therefore ALL Freemasons are not excommunicated.[28]

[26] The Archbishop of Tuam has issued a fulminating letter against the Freemasons, addressed to a Roman Catholic priest in Canada, a copy of which I subjoin. " Rev. dear Sir,—Having been informed by you, that there are in Canada some misguided Catholics who, striving to justify the practices of Freemasonry, scruple not to assert that it was sanctioned by priests and bishops in Ireland, allow me to tell you that this was never the case; and that those men are only aggravating their disobedience to the church by the additional guilt of calumny; I have had extensive acquaintance, not only with the present race of ecclesiastics, but also with some of those venerable men of more ancient standing, some of whom are no more, and I can confidently state, that neither in this city, nor in any other part of Ireland, was the bond of Masonry sanctioned by any other portion of the clergy. That Freemasons' lodges were then more numerous and frequent than now, may be true; but their existence, in contempt and defiance of the repeated denunciations of the clergy, cannot be brought as an argument of their sanctioning the system, more than the prevalence of other evils, against which they do not cease to raise their voices, could be adduced as a proof of similar connivance. I am, &c. To the Rev. J. H. M'Donough."

[27] The liberal professors of the Roman Catholic system of religion are incapable of giving their sanction to the encroachments of a persecuting church. And though some of the more precise members of our Order might be prevailed on, by the admonitions of a respected priest, to withdraw their membership from the Order, yet they would not become parties in the oppression of those who, from motives equally conscientious, still hold on their allegiance to the lodge. Freedom of opinion, in this respect, is surely neither criminal, nor at variance with any precept in the gospel of Christ. It will be unnecessary to add, that the reply in the text was written by a Roman Catholic Brother.

[28] The wiseacres of the Tablet prove their point thus:—an infidel is a

In polemical antagonism, and political discussion, individual considerations should be merged, lest truth and
justice might suffer from deference to personal feeling,
or mistaken courtesy. Truth requires that I should state
the fact, that nearly all objectors appear to be not only
totally unacquainted with Freemasonry,[29] but to exhibit
the vague hostility of preconceived opinions and feelings
on the subject, founded upon certain erroneous notions
they seem determined to carry out at all hazards, rather
than yield to the charitable disposition of ascertaining
the truth, and showing lenity towards supposed misguided neighbours. They boldly assert their own chi-
merical fancies, as if derived from authority which no-
where supports them. Many appear to be enthusiasts,
who, in the public display of their zeal for religious morality, form hasty, if not uncharitable conclusions, and
hazard opinions upon subjects they never cared to understand.[30]

man—but a Freemason is a man—and therefore a Freemason is an infidel! whence they deduce this *admirable* syllogism :—An infidel is excommunicate—but a Freemason is an infidel—and therefore a Freemason is
excommunicate. Such reasoning as this is considered sound and conclu-
sive when applied by prejudice to our sublime institution !

[29] Because those who are acquainted with the Order find nothing ob-
jectionable either in its doctrine or discipline. And for this reason it is
that worthy men are invited to enter the society, that they may have an
opportunity of ascertaining whether their preconceived notions be borne
out by facts. And it is to the credit of Freemasonry that such an ex-
periment has in all cases been successful. Even those Brethren who have
been induced to leave it under any temporary cause of disgust, have not
been able to lay the blame on any defect in the system, as it is practised
in the lodges. The reasons for their defection have been merely personal,
arising out of a dispute with an individual Brother, or an objection to
some local arrangement, but never from a want of purity in the construction of the Order.

[30] One of the existing causes of this unholy crusade against Freemasonry is envy. From this source the uninitiated antimasons of the
United States, about twenty years ago, were led to vent their spleen by
such remarks as these, which have been extracted from a periodical of
the day. "The *blushing honours* of Masonry continue to adorn the
names of legislators and magistrates. It is not too much to suppose that
the unhallowed oaths of Masonry have a corrupt influence on their hearts.
Men who will consent to stand out arrayed in the high priesthood of an
Order notoriously sworn to keep each other's secrets, in all cases whatsoever, and to obey each other's signs of distress at the hazard of life,
without stopping to inquire into the nature of that distress, whether it
be right or wrong, are called Freemasons—*the most ancient and honourable fraternity of Freemasons* Call them by what name you will, adorn

Before proceeding further I must repeat, in order to
save all misconception, that I utterly repudiate the slightest opposition to lawful authority.   I deem it necessary
also to state that I use the words *prohibit* and *condemn* in
restricted senses, and not indiscriminately, after the manner of the "Tablet."[31]   The church or our bishops may
prohibit anything, on account of abuse or misuse, without condemning it as immoral.   In England our bishops
have felt it necessary to use their discretion in prohibiting our clergy from losing their time attending public
theatres, oratorios, concerts, and balls, which are not on
that account condemned as immoral.   In England members of the theatrical profession are admitted to the
sacraments—in France they are denied Christian burial.
As a layman my object is not to expound the laws of the
church, but simply to disprove the arrogant and uncharitable assumptions, the monstrous lay-censorship of
the "Tablet," and gratuitous allegations in respect of
British Freemasons, Odd Fellows, Rechabites (Temperance), Ancient Druids, and the like convivial and charitable "secret societies," having no concern with either
politics or religion.[32]

them with private virtues, with public usefulness, with intellectual attain-
ments, nevertheless such men deserve to be pointed at in their most excellent titles, in their pontifical mitres and robes, and to be distrusted in
the impartial discharge of official duties."

[31] It is to be regretted that men so learned and distinguished as the
bishops of any church, should suffer themselves to be so far led away by
prejudice, as to fulminate anathemas against an institution which numbers in its ranks so many of the higher classes, who have been as well
educated, and are consequently as capable of judging as themselves.   The
princes and peers of any community are an ample guarantee that the societies which they patronize do not contain any elements which are hostile to its social institutions, or at variance with the precepts of religion
or sound morality.   This ought to furnish the ecclesiastical dignitaries
with an incontrovertible evidence of the purity of proceedings, which, if
their sacred station renders the propriety of their personal participation
in them doubtful, should be sufficient to exempt the Order from suspicion, and relieve it from the disheartening effects of official interference.

[32] That the decrees of the pontiffs were not provoked by the illegal
opinions, and anti-christian dogmas, propagated by British Freemasons,
no one can assert ; that they were not published specially to extirpate
British Freemasonry, which repudiates the very opinions and doctrines
condemned, may be safely affirmed, without danger of trenching upon
ecclesiastical ground.   Have, then, our bishops, in consequence of the
political occurrences in Canada, impugned in the letter of the Roman
Catholic Archbishop of Tuam, and the late combination of trades' unions

FIRST OBJECTION.—*An Oath ; Truth, Justice, and Judgment.*—That a secret oath is forbidden by the pontifical constitutions, therefore immoral.

That an oath or affirmation should be conformable to the words of Jeremiah (iv. 7), " Thou shalt swear, saith the Lord, in truth, in justice, and in judgment."

Our Christian doctrine teaches, that by the commandment—" Thou shalt not take the name of the Lord thy God in vain"—are forbidden, "all false, rash, and unnecessary oaths .... breaking of lawful oaths or vows, and making or keeping unlawful ones."

An oath is lawful, "when God's honour, our own, or neighbour's good requires it."

Therefore the oath or affirmation of a Freemason, Odd Fellow, Rechabite (Temperance), Ancient Druid, and the like, who swear to keep secret that of which they have no foreknowledge, and who are compelled to take an oath without previously knowing the import before admission, are deficient in those requisite attributes; therefore rash and immoral.

NOT SO,—

Because oaths are sanctioned by scripture,[33] and no council of the church has ever condemned the taking

in England and Ireland, condemned in their pastorals, felt it necessary to include in their denunciations, British Freemasons, Odd Fellows, Rechabites, Ancient Druids, Foresters, and other harmless, charitable, and convivial societies, few, if any of which are known to be bound by oaths, with such like combinators and conspirators? No clergyman will afford a more positive solution of this question, than a reference to the Alia Observanda, by which he is guided. (F. Q. R. 1845, p. 17, written by the intelligent author of the above portion of the text.)

[33] Thus Abimelech called upon Abraham to " swear unto him by God." (Gen. xxi. 23.) This kind of oath appears not only to have been generally in use in the time of Abraham, but also to have descended through many generations and ages in the East. When Mr. Bruce was at Shekh Ammer, he entreated the protection of the governor in prosecuting his journey. Speaking of the people who were assembled together at this time in the house, he says (Travels, vol. i. p. 148) : " The great people among them came, and, after joining hands, repeated a kind of prayer, of about two minutes long, by which they declared themselves and their children accursed, if ever they lifted up their hands against me in the field or in the desert ; and in case that I, or mine, should flee to them for refuge, they would protect us at the risk of their lives and fortunes ; or, as they emphatically expressed it, to the death of the last male child among them."

of an oath ; and there is no proof that Freemasons are
compelled to take an oath ; for there are many other
secret societies to which members are bound by promise
only, or by subscription to the rules and regulations.

Because the tenor of the oath or affirmation attributed to Freemasons must be of the same import as that
imposed upon every member of her majesty's privy council, secret committees of the houses of parliament, and
courts-martial ; those required at the Bank of England
and East India House, binding parties to keep secret
whatever may be brought before them in future in their
respective capacities;[34] freemen of municipal corporations, and the like ; and apprentices, who are sometimes
bound by oath to keep their masters' secrets ; also direc-
tors and members of comme cial unions and associations
are sworn to secrecy of the future, of which they have
no foreknowledge, and without previously knowing the
import of those oaths. Such oaths being deemed in
strict accordance with Christian morals, so must be those
of a Freemason, and the like.

Because between them there is no distinction in effect,
the only difference being, that one is a judicial oath, imposed by the laws, and compulsory, the other is extra
judicial, not forbidden by the laws, sanctioned by the
custom of ages, by millions of the great and good from
time immemorial, bishops and clergymen innumerable,
never compulsory, and always voluntary ; therefore in
strict accordance with the laws of Christian morality.[35]

[34] In the United States every public body was filled with members of
the fraternity ; and this created so much jealousy, as to form one of the
many causes of the great persecution. Thus, a writer against the Order
said : " If the names of the members of every Chapter in the Union could
be obtained, it would be found that at least the same proportion of their
members hold public offices, and receive annually a greater amount of
money than any other body of men." In another periodical it is stated,
that "the Royal Arch Chapter of Pittsburg contains fifty members,
eight of whom receive from the public treasury, by way of salary for the
offices they hold, $11,400 annually." The writer then goes on to say :
" Let the people look seriously at this matter, and ask themselves whether
all this is the effect of mere accident, or whether it is not brought about
by a systematized plan of operations, arranged and settled upon within
the walls of a lodge-room ?"

[35] The ancient mode of taking an oath appears to have been by lifting
up the hand to heaven, as if calling upon God to attest the truth of that
which is affirmed. (Gen. xiv. 22.) And this method appears to have had

Because every candidate is obliged to submit to a rigorous examination, and fully instructed upon the serious nature of his obligations previous to admission ; therefore in perfect accordance with the laws of good morals.

Because the oaths attributed to Freemasons are said to be found in books, though said to be published without authority ; therefore cannot be said to be hidden, or not foreknown, in accordance with the laws of good morals.

Because the previous knowledge and import (alone) of an oath does not constitute the act a moral one, which may otherwise be immoral ; nor does the extra judicial character (alone) make that immoral which might be in other respects moral, any more than that the judicial character (alone) of an oath would cause that to be a moral act which might be otherwise immoral.[36] This has been proved by the numbers who suffered death in the reigns of Henry VIII. and his successors, for conscientiously refusing to take the judicial oath of supremacy in the ecclesiastical affairs of Dissenters and the Roman Catholic church, then imposed by the penal laws.

SECOND OBJECTION.—*Want of Necessity.*—That secret societies are unnecessary; secret signs are unnecessary;

the sanction of the Divinity ; for when God promised to bring his people into the land of Canaan, he is said to have lifted up his hand. (Exod. vi. 8 ; Nehem. ix. 15.) This custom appears to have been practised even by those nations which had renounced the worship of the true God. Thus, we read in Virgil—

"Suspiciens cœlum, tenditque ad sidera dextram."

And thus, also, when Agamemnon makes his oath—

"To all the gods his sceptre he uplifts."

[36] These absurd charges against the Masonic oath were carried to a most ludicrous excess in America ; and the English Mason will be amused with the following mendacious extract from a periodical, published in 1834 : "Every Mason, when initiated in every degree, takes an oath. Thus, the Entered Apprentice swears three oaths ! the Fellowcraft, six ! the Master Mason, seventeen !!! the Mark Master, seven (the notes of admiration must be imagined) ; the Past Master, eleven ; the Most Excellent Master, eight ; the Royal Master, eleven ; the Royal Arch, seventeen ; Select Master, five ; Knight of the Red Cross, seven ; Knight Templar, eight ; Knight of the Christian Mark, three ; Knight of the Holy Sepulchre, one ; Secret Master, one ; Illustrious Order of the Cross, twenty-four ; Elected Knights of Nine, one ; Knight of the Sun, sixteen, etc., etc., up to the forty-third degree of Grand Inspector General."!!!!!!!

secret oaths or affirmations are unnecessary; and Freemasonry is unnecessary, though alleged to be instituted for convivial and charitable purposes, but tending to useless, ruinous, and extravagant expenditure, leading men into scenes of riot, drunkenness, and debauchery. Therefore, Freemasonry, secret oaths, secret signs, and secret societies, being unnecessary, are immoral.

NOT SO,—

Because, neither the church in any council, nor any code of morals, affirms that want of necessity alone constitutes that to be immoral which is otherwise moral.

Because such acts have not before been deemed unnecessary or immoral, which the custom of ages has established, as well as the constant practice of millions, from time immemorial over the whole world, by potentates and princes, bishops, priests, and laymen—the great and the good of all nations.[37]

Because the edicts of the popes, prohibiting and condemning the " sect " of Freemasons and other secret societies, " bound by an oath in an impenetrable bond of secrecy," from Clement XII., in 1737, to that of our present " Vicar of Christ," have become obsolete from disuse, the term of duration and force, according to the canon law, having expired, without republication—in this country, I believe, unlawful, and the urgency therefore having generally long since ceased, by the utter extinction of most of the obnoxious and wicked combinations against Christianity and the laws of civil society.[38]

[37] It was common among the ancients to swear by the head. Thus Virgil—
" Per caput hoc juro, per quod pater ante solebat."
(Æn. ix. 300.)
So, also Horace, reproaching Barine, says—
" ———— sed tu, simul obligasti
Perfidum votis caput." (Carm. l. ii. 8.)
Some used to swear by the ashes of their parents. The form of this oath has been preserved in Propertius. (B. ii. 20.)
" Ossa tibi juro per matris, et ossa parentis;
Si fallo, cinis, heu ! sit mihi uterque gravis."
Homer also mentions the same thing. See also, Juv. Sat. vi. 17, and also, Horace, Carm. l. ii. 9.
[38] A French writer, speaking of Freemasonry, says :—" The profound silence which Freemasons observe, the air of mystery which is spread

Because such denunciations against the wicked ten ets of infidel, atheistical, anti-social, anti-Christian, and anti-Catholic sects, and unnecessary secret societies, some calling themselves "Freemasons," as "Illuminati," "Carbonari," "Communists," "Orangeists," and the like, if they exist anywhere, never were professed or promulgated by Freemasons, Odd Fellows, and the like in these realms, being exclusive of any interference in politics or religion, convivial and charitable brotherhoods, innocent in themselves, and perfectly legal, obliged by the constitutions to denounce as criminal, treason and murder.[39]

Because the argument of want of necessity, ruin, riot, debauchery, tendency to evil, and the like, if allowed to the full extent, according to the words of scripture, "if thy eye offend thee, pluck it out;" "if thy arm offend thee, cut it off," or that the abuse were an argument for disuse, would shut up all our theatres, public houses, gin shops, distilleries, &c., forbid the use of money, &c., which cannot be denied are all so many awful instruments in the hands of the devil, for damning millions of souls. This argument goes even further, as, I believe,

over all their actions, has not ceased to prejudice against them some minds whose self-love is offended, and who cannot bear that themselves should be kept in ignorance of what passes in this assembly of Brethren. These think they have a right to believe them guilty of a species of crimes, which might well draw down upon the lodge the avenging flames which formerly consumed five abominable cities. It is doubly unjust to attack, or reproach so many illustrious men who have ranked themselves on the lists of the Freemasons. We may assure ourselves that the abominable crimes, which none but a vile imagination could suspect them of, had never any access to the lodges; and it is sufficient to oppose to the appearance of it, the character of the illustrious men I have just referred to, whose known integrity ought to shame the foul accuser, and whose delicacy incontestibly proves it a falsehood; for it is not likely, whatever oath they might have taken, that it could prevent their flying precipitately from this Babylon, at the first appearance of such a monstrous excess."

[39] And therefore a distinguished member of the Massachusetts legislature, during the Morgan excitement, advocated the appointment of a committee to investigate whether the Order were really guilty of the alleged crime. He was a Mason of the highest order, and cheerfully placed the matter upon this test. "Only show that the practices of Masonry are noxious and deleterious to the body politic; and how respectable so ever they may be, or however sanctioned by antiquity, it becomes the imperious duty of the legislature, as the legitimate guardian of the rights of the people, to suppress it by legal enactment."

exemplified by some Brahmins; would deprive religion itself of its efficacy; in fact, deprive man of the most valuable endowments from his Creator, will, memory, and understanding, the perversion of which causes all the sins of the world.[40]

Because the letters and pastorals of the English and Irish bishops, which incidentally only cited the authority of the papal edicts against "the sect," and other unlawful secret societies—those edicts not having been published in this country, and having become obsolete, it is reasonable to presume that such letters and pastorals were directed against political Freemasonry in Canada, where, during the late insurrection, the secrecy of Freemasonry was said to have been abused and violated by the cowardly partisans of revolution—against White Boys, Ribbonmen, and the like political secret societies in Ireland, and against the trades' combinations and unions in England, and by no means intended to condemn Freemasonry, as practised in these realms, as unnecessary or immoral.[41]

[40] If nothing were lawful but what was absolutely necessary, ours would be but a miserable world to live in. Literary talent would be circumscribed within a very narrow compass; science might be consigned to oblivion; the fine arts be suffered to decay; and we should return to the state, almost savage, of the first inhabitants of this island, who dwelt in dens, and caves, and wretched hovels; who had no clothing, and lived upon roots and raw flesh; and in case of danger, as Dio Nicæus tells us, " would plunge themselves in deep morasses up to their necks, and there continue many days together without sustenance, and then retiring and hiding themselves in the woods, they fed on the bark and roots of trees." The above objection is altogether puerile, and unworthy the advocacy of a man of sense.

[41] Bro. Gourley, in an address to the Grand Lodge of Massachusetts, has the following excellent sentiments, which are worthy of more extensive circulation:—" That there are bad, as well as good men, who belong to our institution, has never been denied. But this assertion may be made, with equal truth, of every association of men that ever existed. When it can be said of all, who profess to be the disciples of religion, that they are pious, honest, and benevolent, it will alone be time to accuse Masonry of the delinquencies of Masons. But when our institution is attacked, as being, in its design, hostile to the peace and order of society, it is but reasonable that we should be heard in our defence against so unjust a reproach. Look upon those men who have patronized Masonry, and say whether they have been inimical to the public happiness? Was Washington an enemy to his country, or to mankind? Why should I not mention the name of this illustrious man? He was a Mason, and loved the craft. What Mason is there, then, let me ask you, in the language of Mark Anthony over the dead body of Cæsar, what reason is

THIRD OBJECTION.—*Secrecy.*—That secrecy, being " a test of evil," prohibited and condemned by the church, a secret society, secret sign, password or watchword, ceremonies and degrees, and a secret oath (or affirmation), being rash and unlawful, tending to evil, are therefore immoral.

That the oath (or affirmation) to secrecy, attributed to Freemasons and the like, obliging them to keep secret whatever may occur within the lodge, [a most extraordinary objection], being an usurpation of the power delivered by Christ to his apostles and their successors, " what ye shall bind on earth shall be bound also in heaven," (St. Matt.,) which imposes an inviolable secrecy upon all things revealed in the confessional, to be broken only in heaven—is therefore impious and immoral.

That " secret societies" are anti-social, anti-Catholic, and anti-Christian, inasmuch as they are by " secrecy placed beyond the control of the lawful authority" of magistrates, and of the church ; therefore dangerous and immoral.

That under the secrecy of Freemasons revolutions have been perpetuated, and states overthrown ; therefore destructive and immoral.

NOT SO,—

Because in no council of the church have secrecy, a secret society, a secret sign, or a secret oath (or affirmation), been " prohibited or condemned as being immoral," otherwise if " secrecy were a test of evil" always, secrecy might be alleged against numberless societies, associations, commercial unions, and others ; even the annual meeting of the Catholic clergy in May, where none but a priest of the mission, not even their bishop is admitted.[42] Freemasons, in fact, meet not more secretly

there, then, that you should forget him ? None whatever. He was the glory of his country, both as a warrior, a legislator, and a Mason ; and, therefore, his services will never be forgotten."

[42] An answer to the above plea is found in that excellent illustration contained in the lectures of Masonry.—" Of all the arts which Masons possess, the art of silence, or secrecy, particularly distinguishes them. Taciturnity is a proof of wisdom, and is allowed to be of the utmost importance in the different transactions of life. The best writers have declared it to be an art of inestimable value ; and that it is agreeable to

at the Freemasons' Tavern, and other lodges at other public places and taverns all over the world.

Because a " secret sign" is no more than the password or watchword in the army and navy; by which brothers or friends may be known from strangers or foes. Secret degrees and ceremonies are merely a test of merit, and for the exclusion of bad characters.[43] They are of the greatest antiquity, and sanctioned by custom everywhere.

Because an oath (or affirmation) to keep secret a crime would be contrary to the constitutions of Freemasonry, which forbids such concealment, or of treason or murder.[44]

the Deity himself, may be easily conceived from the glorious example which He gives, in concealing from mankind the secret mysteries of His providence. The wisest of men cannot pry into the arcana of heaven; nor can they divine to-day what to-morrow may bring forth."

[43] " From the period at which I reached the summit of what is called ancient Masonry," says Col. Stone, " I have held but one opinion in relation to masonic secrets; and, in that opinion, I have always found my intelligent Brethren ready to concur. It was this—that the essential secrets of Masonry consisted in nothing more than the signs, grips, passwords, and tokens, essential to the preservation of the society from the inroads of impostors; together with certain symbolical emblems, the technical terms appertaining to which served as a sort of universal language, by which the members of the fraternity could distinguish each other, in all places and countries where lodges were instituted, and conducted like those of the United States. The Freemasons' Monitor says —' Did the particular secrets, or peculiar forms prevalent among Masons, *constitute the essence of the art*, it might be alleged that our amusements were trifling, and our ceremonies superficial.' But this is not the case. The Rev. Salem Town, long the Grand Chaplain of the Royal Arch Chapter of New York, whose book on Speculative Masonry has been sanctioned by the highest masonic officers in the country, expressly declares, that *our leading tenets are no secrets*. And again, by a full and fair exposition of our great leading principles, *we betray no secrets*." (Letters on Masonry, p. 71.)

[44] The above writer thus defends the Order against certain calumnies which were prevalent in his time:—" Is it to be believed," he says, " that men of acknowledged talents and worth in public stations, and of virtuous, and frequently religious habits, in the walks of private life—with the holy Bible in their hands, which they are solemnly pledged to receive, as the rule and guide of their faith and practice—and under the grave and positive charge from the officer administering the obligation, that it is to be taken in strict subordination to the civil laws—can understand that obligation, whatever may be the peculiarities of its phraseology, as requiring them to countenance vice and criminality, even by silence? Can it for a moment be supposed that the hundreds of eminent men—the hundreds of eloquent divines—the tens of thousands of the most intelligent and virtuous of the community—with oaths upon their consciences, can be guilty of any such iniquities as the Masons are charged with?"

Because there is no parallel between the secrecy of the confessional and the secrecy of Freemasonry, the one being a religious, the other a temporal affair.

Because most of such societies are secret only in name, opened to all the inhabitants of the globe, good character and morals being the only test, to all potentates and magistrates, to bishops and priests, if they were not forbidden by their own ecclesiastical regulations.

Because it is notorious that all revolutions said to have been aided by Freemasons, would have occurred if Freemasonry had never existed.

Because it is a common vulgar error to class " secrecy" with " evil," some persons forming false notions of secrecy, either from prejudice or under the influence of preconceived opinion by which they deceive themselves, as well as others. The morbid imaginations of such persons cannot separate secrecy from darkness— an oath to keep secret the affairs of Freemasonry, from an oath to keep secret crimes, conspiracies, assassinations, and murder, in face of the axiom, " an oath bindeth not iniquity." A secrecy over which they have thrown certain romantic, horrible fancies of deep, dismal, dungeon gloom, phantoms of their own creation in weak and distorted intellects.[45] This absurd self-created conscientiousness would object to oaths altogether, as the Quakers, who appeal to scripture in support of these scruples—" But 1 say unto you, not to swear at all," St. Matt. v. 33. In Leviticus, xix. 12, however, it is said— " Ye shall not swear by my name to deceive." Which explains the meaning of the above as understood by all Christians. In Deut. vi. 30, and x. 20, is said—" Thou

---

[45] A paper was circulated, some time since, under the following head : —" Decisions of the holy Apostolic See concerning the Society of Freemasons. Addressed to the Most Holy Father." It states that ecclesiastical punishments have been decreed by Roman pontiffs against the Freemasons ; and that a doubt has arisen whether any person, repenting of having taken the oath, can be admitted to the sacrament of penance. On inquiring how the conference ought to act, the reply of the sacred congregation was, " taking things as proposed, it is not permitted." A doubt having arisen as to the words *not permitted*, if implying the invalidity of the absolution, the sacred congregation replied in the affirmative. The document is signed—ANGELUS ARGENTI, Notary of the sacred Roman and Universal Inquisition. See the F. Q. R., 1845, p. 285.

shalt swear by his name." In Num. xxx. 3—"That
man that voweth a vow to the Lord, shall not break his
word,"[46] Which clearly shows that oaths are lawful for
lawful purposes. Will, then, any man affirm, that the
oath attributed to Freemasons is for an unlawful purpose—therefore immoral ?

FOURTH OBJECTION.—*Want of Authority.*—That any
oath (or affirmation) being extra-judicial, not imposed or
commanded by the laws of the land, is illegal, and being
imposed without authority, is immoral.

NOT SO,—
Because the constitutions of Freemasonry are accommodated to the laws of every country,[47] and the present
code of British Freemasonry was renewed a few years
ago by a committee of the ablest lawyers of the day,
under the Grand Mastership of His Royal Highness the
late Duke of Sussex, whose name alone ought to have
been a sufficient guarantee against the monstrous assertions of the " Tablet." In all Acts of Parliament
against secret societies, secret oaths, associations, &c.,
British Freemasons are specially exempted—therefore
not " illegal."
Because it is a false assumption involved in this objection, that the swearing of an extra-judicial oath is a
compulsory act, compulsory, like too many of the numerous judicial ones, which cause persons to swallow them
as being " mere matters of form," or " custom-house
oaths," often without due regard to the whole truth, or

---

[46] It was common with the Jews to swear by Jerusalem; and, therefore, the altar, the temple, and Jerusalem, as objects of their vows, are
frequently expressed in their writings. In the Gemmara, it is laid down,
as an orthodox doctrine, that a Jew cannot be justified till he has made
his vow on something which has been offered up at Jerusalem.

[47] At the revival of Masonry, the Grand Lodge set out with a declaration, that " it is not in the power of any man or body of men, to make
any alteration or innovation in the body of Masonry, without the consent
first obtained of the Grand Lodge." And on the 25th November, 1723,
the Grand Lodge in ample form resolved, " that any Grand Lodge, duly
met, has a power to amend or explain any of the printed regulations in
the Book of Constitutions, while they break not in upon the ancient rules
of the fraternity. But that no alteration shall be made in the printed
Book of Constitutions without leave of the Grand Lodge." And this
fundamental principle has always been strictly adhered to.

the serious binding nature of the act.[48] The oath attributed to Freemasons is perfectly voluntary, and no one would be admitted whose vanity or pride had urged him to differ with his Christian neighbours, and had created for himself a false conscience upon a received opinion, or whose conscience revolted at an act sanctioned by the scriptures, the practice of all times, by the greatest and most pious men of ages past and present. Quakers, Moravians, and others, are, however, protected in their religious scruples by an affirmation when requisite; therefore this oath or affirmation cannot be alleged to be deficient in authority, or to be immoral.

FIFTH OBJECTION.—*Liberty and Equality.*—That the pernicious principles of a spurious liberty, and levelling equality, as propagated by Freemasonry, are subversive of all social order in society, destructive of all good government, and opposed to the influence of true religion; therefore impious and immoral.

NOT SO,—

Because the liberty practised and promulgated in the lodges, is that natural liberty, secured by the laws of nature, compatible with the laws of nations, communities, and individuals, acknowledging no enemy more dangerous than licentiousness in any form. The liberty of Freemasonry is subordidate to reason, to immutable justice, by which it must ever be supported; to conscience, and a regard for the public welfare, by which it must be directed; friendly to order and to peace. The liberty and equality of Freemasonry are understood in a sense entirely moral, and foreign to politics. The Abbé Barruel, too, has exempted British Freemasonry from the charge of establishing the wild notions of liberty, he asserts to have been taught in the lodges of certain "secret societies" on the continent. Therefore, the natural and judicious liberty of Freemasonry is neither impious nor immoral.[49]

---

[48] In some countries it is said to have been a custom to place the right hand upon the throne in attestation of an oath; and in others it was laid upon the altar. With us the right hand is laid upon the holy Bible. Juvenal says, that in his time atheists could *intrepidos altaria tangere*, or, in other words, could forswear themselves without trembling.

[49] After the work of Barruel had been subjected to the test of criticism,

9*

Because the equality of Freemasonry has no relation to the distinctions of civil order, trenches not upon the possession of riches or dignities. Freemasonry considers men of all ranks only with regard to the connection which unites them as members of one universal Brotherhood.[50] The equality of Freemasons is one of those virtues, recommended by religion and morality, as is said by an eminent writer, "such institutions weaken pride, without

however, he was very much inclined to retract his exception of the English lodges, while writhing under the lash which he had so freely inflicted upon others. He says (Hist. Jac. vol. iv. obs. iv.)—"Dr. Griffiths declares, that my position is wholly erroneous when I say, that equality and liberty form the essential and perpetual creed of the Freemasons. Here I was tempted to recognize a brother dupe; but he had his reasons for appearing to be better informed than I was. He then speaks of a communication opened between the Grand Lodges of London and Berlin, 1776; and Berlin, he says, was at that era the very focus of convergence for every ray of modern philosophy; and then, he asks, were these embassies mere child's play, or were there Timoleons concealed in the lodges? I candidly confess, that had I known of these communications with the very centre of sophistry, so far should I have been from retracting my proofs of the conspiracy of the Freemasons, that I should have given them a stronger term. I can also assure him, that I would not have generalized to such an extent, my exception in favour of the Masonry of the Grand Lodge of London, had I been informed that it could possibly have contained members so inimical to kings as that Timoleon, who assassinated his brother Timophane, for that same cause of hatred to royalty in which the elder Brutus became the executioner of his children, and the younger Brutus the murderer of Cæsar, his benefactor. Let English Masons defend themselves against the imputations of Dr.Griffiths; but every reader will perceive that the method he has adopted to prove that my position was erroneous is rather extraordinary; for, according to his assertions, *if I am culpable, it is of having generalized my exception too much in favour of those to whom I thought no guilt could attach.*"

[50] We are all equal by our creation, but much more so by the strength of our obligation. We meet on the level, and part on the square. These, and other similar masonic aphorisms, will explain the nature of our equality. "I conceive no valid reason," says an eloquent transatlantic brother, "why Masonry should be fettered down by any sectarian or local feeling whatsoever. I would have it untrammelled, unadulterated, unstipendiary; the sphere of its active usefulness only circumscribed by the limits of its universality. It would then be godlike within the range of its glorious latitude. Regard it as you will, it is, under any aspect, a most benignant and elevated conception; everywhere busy, erecting schools and infirmaries and asylums, for the destitute. the unfortunate, and the oppressed; hushing the sob of the fatherless little one, and causing the widow's heart to sing for joy! It is abroad. upon its errand of beneficence, in every country, and climate, and kingdom under heaven; wherever charity can be exercised—wherever suffering can be alleviated—wherever good can be done. It is around us, and about us; in every whisper of mercy, in every movement of love."

destroying subordination," which recal the rich and the magistracy to sentiments of natural equality, without injuring the legal power of the latter, and the respect due to their functions, and is of the highest advantage to morality and happiness, rendering them permanently useful.[51] The Freemason desires to make but one great family of the whole human race under the Great Architect of the Universe, the Almighty Creator, and to induce mankind, on moral considerations, to regard and treat. each other as brothers. In the moral sense of the term must be understood this equality, that among Masons there are no strangers, and man is everywhere at home, whatever may be the race to which he belongs, or the land in which he is born. This equality, then, is not of that destructive or levelling description which would drag down the prince from the high station in which birth or fortune may have placed him, in order to degrade him to the level of the simple citizen; nor does it pretend falsely to raise a beggar, or even a simple citizen, beyond the sphere of his own merits: therefore the principles of equality taught by Freemasonry are neither impious nor immoral.

[51] Dean Kirwan has a beautiful passage on this subject. He says:— " I open the gospel, and there I cannot find a trace of countenance to intemperate and uncharitable zeal, even in support of essential truths; witness the instant and indignant rebuke of that sanguinary and intolerant spirit in which all the Jew appeared, manifested by him, against the wretched inhabitants of an unbelieving village; witness his tender and indefatigable effort to remove the prejudices of the woman of Samaria; how he accommodated himself to that prejudice, the better to remove it; spoke the very language of her errors, in search of an occasion to insinuate truth. Through the whole course of his ministry his first object was to propagate a benevolent spirit, and to mend the human heart. Listen to his words :—' Blessed are the peacemakers, for they shall be called the children of God. Blessed are the merciful, for they shall obtain mercy. Blessed are the meek, the poor in spirit, the pure of heart. Blessed are all those who hunger and thirst after righteousness!' It is the simple, but fervent eulogy of every relative virtue, and every bond of blissful intercourse between man and man."

MASONIC INSTITUTES,

BY

VARIOUS AUTHORS.

CONTENTS.

PAGE

Dedication v

Introductory Essay on the Masonic Literature of the Eighteenth
Century. By the Editor. 243

LECTURE I.

On the Rise and Progress of the Order. Anon.   **264**

LECTURE II.

A Defence of Masonry. By Dr. Anderson, S. G. W. . . 274

LECTURE III.

On the Advantages enjoyed by the Fraternity. By Martin
Clare, Esq., D. G. M. 292

LECTURE IV.

On the Connection between Masonry and Religion. By the
Rev. Charles Brockwell, A. M. 303

LECTURE V.

On the Social Virtues of Freemasonry. By Isaac Head, Esq. 312

LECTURE VI.

A Search after Truth. Anon. 321

LECTURE VII.

On Masonic Light, Truth, and Charity. By Thomas Dunc-
kerly, Esq., P. G. M. 335

CONTENTS.

LECTURE VIII.

The Moveable Jewels illustrated by the Aid of Moral Geometry. Anon. 348

LECTURE IX.

On the Government of the Lodge. By John Whitmash, Esq., W. M. 361

LECTURE X.

On the Design of Masonry. By John Codrington, Esq., D. P. G. M. 375

LECTURE XI.

On the Masonic Duties. By the Rev. R. Green. . . . 389

LECTURE XII.

On Brotherly Love. By the Rev. John Hodgets, A. M. . 405

LECTURE XIII.

On the Value of Masonic Secrets. By the Rev. Daniel Turner. 416

MASONIC INSTITUTES.

INTRODUCTION.

REMARKS ON THE MASONIC LITERATURE OF THE
EIGHTEENTH CENTURY.

"————— absentum qui rodit amicum ;
Qui non defendit, alio culpante ; solutos
Qui captat risus hominum, famamque dicacis ;
Fingere qui non visa potest ; commissa tacere
Qui nequit ; hic niger est, hunc tu, Romane, caveto."
HORACE.

I⸱ will be in the recollection of every reader of Sir
Walter Scott's inimitable novels—and by this description
I include every person in her Majesty's dominions who
possesses the slightest pretensions to taste—that, in the
preface to "The Antiquary," his third prose publication,
he said :—" I have now only to express my gratitude to
the public for the distinguished reception which they
have given to works that have little more than some
truth of colouring to recommend them, and to take my
respectful leave *as one who is not likely again to solicit their
favour.*" And yet, a very short period after this announce-
ment, he delighted his admirers with the charming
fiction of " Rob Roy," which he introduced by saying—
" when the editor of the following volumes published,
about two years since, the work called ' The Antiquary,'
he announced that he was for the last time intruding
upon the public in his present capacity. He might
shelter himself under the plea that every anonymous writer
is, like the celebrated Junius, only a phantom, and that,
therefore, although an apparition of more benign, as well

as much meaner description, he cannot be bound to
plead to a charge of inconsistency. A better apology
may be found in imitating the confession of honest Bene-
dict, that when he said he would die a bachelor, he did
not think he should live to be married. The best of all
would be, if, as has eminently happened in the case of
some distinguished contemporaries, the merit of the work
should, in the reader's estimation, form an excuse for the
author's breach of promise." And this was followed up
by a rich series of classical productions which leave us
no reason to regret that the promise was not kept.

Now, although the editor of the following series of
Masonic Works has no pretensions to shelter himself
under the plea of writing anonymously, yet, if it were required, he might find ample justification for obtruding
himself once more upon the public on the authority of
such a great example; although it would be the height
of presumption on his part to entertain an idea of being
worthy to occupy a place even at the feet of Gamaliel.
But it is scarcely necessary to apologize for a re-appear-
ance in the humble and unpretending character of an
editor, whose duty is simply to point out what is excellent, to illustrate what is obscure, and to show the
adaptation of the argument to the age in which the
authors flourished, as well as to trace the gradual modification and improvement with which the taste of modern
times has invested the sciences or works which he has
undertaken to supervise.

At the close of the seventeenth century, Freemasonry
had suffered a very serious declension from its former
proud position in society. The number of lodges in the
south of England, actually working, was reduced to four,
and these consisted of so few members as to be quite insufficient for any practical purpose; although the author
of the "Ahiman Rezon" asserts that "there were, at
that time, numbers of old Masons in and adjacent to
London, from whom the *ancient* Masons received the old
system free from innovation."

This, however, is doubtful; for, if better Masons had
existed, they would not have been overlooked, and it
should rather appear that Masonry had suffered a total
eclipse, and had been shorn of its chief excellencies by
neglect or misapprehension during the two preceding

reigns. It is highly probable that very few Masons existed at that period who were acquainted with the " Master's Part," because the third degree was seldom conferred except as the reward of very great scientific merit, or long continued and faithful services to the craft.

The ancient Charges and Constitutions were sought out and digested into form ; for the new Grand Lodge foresaw that to ensure the permanent interests of Masonry, it was necessary to place the Order in as elevated a position as possible. Under an anticipation that the revived institutions would have great difficulties to encounter, the details were made as unexceptionable as circumstances would admit. A solid foundation was laid, that the superstructure might be stable and enduring ; and presumed objections were boldly met, or provided against by a series of judicious regulations which awakened curiosity and cemented the union of the fraternity, without trenching on the ancient landmarks of the Order.

But the great obstacle which they encountered, enunciated itself in the apparently simple inquiry, *Cui bono ?* What is the object of the society? This was a question which required a prompt and decisive reply.[1] If it were a newly-invented institution, its claims on the public would sustain no higher rank than those of any temporary association which rose on the surface of society, floated with the current for a brief period, and then sunk and was heard of no more. The fundamental distinction of Freemasonry was based on its antiquity; and, unless that could be clearly established, its permanency was problematical. The consideration of this point occupied the serious attention of the Grand Lodge, at its quarterly communications; and at length, it was unanimously resolved to lay before the public a succinct history of Freemasonry from the earliest times, that its reputation might be established on the sure pillar of historic truth, from which there could be no appeal.

To promote this object, Dr. Anderson, the Junior

---

[1] The French Masons answered this question in their lectures thus:— " Francmaçonnerie contribue à rendre l'homme plus parfait, ou plus heureux. plus sociable, ou plus humain."

Grand Warden, was directed, by an official resolution of the Grand Lodge, to "collect copies of the old Gothic Constitutions, and digest them into a better method."[2] When he had accomplished this undertaking, his labours were committed to the examination of a committee of fourteen learned Brethren, and the result is described in the following resolution:—" At a Grand Lodge holden on the 25th March, 1722, the said committee of fourteen reported that they had perused Brother Anderson's manuscript, viz., the history, charges, regulations, and Master's song; and, after some amendments, had approved of it. Upon which the Lodge desired the Grand Master to order it to be printed."[3]

The details of this process were, however, attended with an evil equally unforeseen and irremediable. Some few fastidious Brethren, distrusting the wisdom of the Grand Lodge in authorizing the above measure, which was found necessary for the general welfare of the craft took the alarm, and several very valuable MSS. concerning the fraternity, their lodges, regulations, charges, secrets, and usages, particularly one in the handwriting of Nicholas Stone, the warden under Inigo Jones, were too hastily burnt, that these papers might not fall into improper hands.

The commentator on Dr. Anderson's book thus judiciously remarks on this rash and unnecessary proceeding, by which a series of evidences, whose value to the fraternity can neither be ascertained nor supplied, were irrecoverably lost :—" The rash act may be ascribed to a jealousy in these over-scrupulous Brethren, that committing to print anything relating to Masonry would be injurious to the interests of the craft. But surely such an act of *felo de se* could not proceed from zeal according to knowledge !"

Enough, however, remained to give character and consistency to the Order ; and we do not find that its claims to a remote antiquity were ever again called into

---

[2] " At a Grand Lodge, September 29, 1721, the Grand Master and the lodge finding fault with all the copies of the old Gothic Constitutions, ordered Brother Anderson to digest the same in a new and better method." From the Minutes.

[3] A similar resolution was passed in 1735, when a new edition of the "Book of Constitutions" appeared.

question. It continued gradually to increase in numbers and respectability, under the judicious guidance of its noble Grand Masters ; and at length attained so high a rank as a social institution, as to excite into action numerous imitations, which rose into a temporary notice, but failed to establish themselves in the opinion of the public. These were generally free and easy convivial societies ; and assumed the names of Grand Volgi, Grand Kaiheber, Hurlothrumbians, Ubiquarians, Gormagons, whom Hogarth has ridiculed so admirably, Hiccubites, Scald Miserables,[4] and many others of facetious memory, all of which descended, one after the other, in solemn procession to the tomb of the Capulets, and their peculiarities are shrouded in a common mausoleum.[5]

Meanwhile our noble Order kept on the noiseless tenor of its way, uninjured by occasional volleys of small shot from the pop-guns of its feeble opponents ; and not af-

[4] I copy the following burlesque extract from a broad sheet printed in ridicule of masonic processions :—" The remonstrance of the R. W. the Grand Master, &c., of the Scald Miserable Masons.—Whereas, by our manifesto some time past, dated from our lodge in Brick-street, we did, in the most explicit manner, vindicate the ancient rites and privileges of this society, and by incontestible arguments, evince our superior dignity and seniority to all other institutions ; nevertheless, the Freemasons still continue to arrogate to themselves the usurped titles of Most Ancient and Honourable, in open violation of truth and justice ; still endeavour to impose their false mysteries on the credulous and unwary, under pretence of being part of our brotherhood ; and still are determined, with drums, trumpets, gilt chariots, and other unconstitutional finery, to cast a reflection on the primitive simplicity and decent economy of our ancient annual peregrination. We therefore think proper, in justification of ourselves, publicly to disclaim all relation or alliance whatsoever with the said society of Freemasons. as the same must manifestly tend to the sacrifice of our dignity, the impeachment of our understanding, and the disgrace of our solemn mysteries."

[5] " Several of these clubs or societies have, in imitation of the Freemasons, called their club by the name of lodge, and their presidents by the title of Grand Master, or Noble Grand. Hence the meanest club think they have a right to the freedom of communication among themselves equal to any unchartered society, though composed of the most respectable persons. Nor is the custom or constitution of the country unfavourable to this opinion. And whereas, a great number of those clubs or societies, without scripture or law to recommend them, have existed and multiplied for several years past, no wonder Freemasonry should meet with encouragement, as being the only society in the universe which unites men of all professions, believing in the Almighty Creator of all things, in one sacred band." (Ahiman Rezon, 28th ed. 1813.)

fected even by the heavy ordnance of more potential
adversaries.

"The world was in pain
The secrets to gain."[6]

But their most abstruse speculations were incomprehensible and absurd, as may be gathered from the following
conjectures of the witty Dean of St. Patrick's. On the
symbols he thus expresses himself in his usual felicitous
manner:—" A bee, in all ages and nations, has been the
grand hieroglyphic of Masonry, because it excels all
other living creatures in the contrivance and commodi
ousness of its habitation or comb. The Egyptians paid
divine worship to a bee under the outward shape of a
bull, the better to conceal the mystery ; which bull, by
them called apis, is the Latin word for a bee. The
enigma representing the bee by a bull consists in this—
that, according to the doctrine of the Pythagorean lodge
of Freemasons, the souls of all the cow kind transmigrate
into bees : what modern Masons call a lodge was, for the
above reasons, by antiquity, called a hive of Freemasons.
And, for the same reasons, when a dissension happens in
a lodge, the going off and forming another lodge is called
to this day swarming."[7] I have extracted the *honey* from
what the satirical dean has said on the subject.

It is ingenious and witty, but his reverence is totally
at fault, as he is also in his account of the signs and
tokens of Masonry.—"Now as to the secret words and

[6] This curiosity respecting the secret pursuits of our lodges, is still a
very powerful feeling in the uninitiated world ; and there are many vili-
fiers of the Order who would gladly penetrate the veil, if they possessed
the means of accomplishing their object surreptitiously. A clever writer
in the " London Magazine" (De Quincey), who had suffered himself to be
obnubilated by the wild dreams of Professor Buhle, speaks of Masonry
as a problem *sub judice*, and classes it with other outstanding problems
in history, which furnish occasion for the display of extensive reading
and critical acumen. In reference to persons, *e. g.*, What became of the
ten tribes of Israel ? Did Brennus and his Gauls penetrate into Greece ?
In reference to things ; as—Who built Stonehenge ? Who discovered
the compass? What was the golden fleece ? Was the siege of Troy a
romance, or a grave historic fact? Who wrote the letters of Junius?
In reference to usages ; as the May-pole and May-day dances, &c., &c.
In reference to words ; as, whence came the mysterious labarum of Constantine ? Among the problems of the first of these classes, says the
above writer, there are not many more irritating to the curiosity than
that which concerns the well-known Order of Freemasons.

[7] Swift's Works. Ed. 1766, vol. xii., p. 253.

signals used among Masons," he says, "it is to be observed that in the Hebrew alphabet there are four pair of letters, of which each pair are so like, that, at the first view, they seem to be the same. Beth and Caph, Gimel and Nun, Cheth and Thau, Daleth and Resch; and on these depend all their signals and gripes. Cheth and Thau are shaped like two standing gallowses of two legs each; when two Masons accost each other, one cries Cheth, the other answers Thau; signifying that they would sooner be hanged on the gallows than divulge the secret. Then again, Beth and Caph are each like a gallows lying on one of the side posts, and, when used as above, imply this pious prayer—May all who reveal the secret hang upon the gallows till it fall down. This is their Master secret, generally called the Great Word. Daleth and Resch are like two half gallowses, or a gallows cut in two. at the cross stick on the top, by which, when pronounced, they intimate to each other that they would rather be half hanged than name either word or signal before any but a Brother, so as to be understood. When one says Gimel, the other answers Nun; then the first again, joining both letters together, repeats three times Gimel-Nun, Gimel-Nun, Gimel-Nun; by which they mean that they are united as one in interests, secresy, and affection."[8]

But to be serious. Freemasonry was too deeply imbedded in the cement of its native merits to heed these desultory facts, how pointed soever the satire might be which was launched against it.

The dearth of masonic publications in these times may be accounted for, by supposing that the scientific Mason felt himself so secure in his stronghold as to consider that his position needed no apology. If the outer defences of the science were attacked, he considered them of little exclusive importance, as they would stand or fall with the intelligence of the age. And retiring into the inner works of morality and the cardinal virtues, he made his stand; and, if the purity of these were questioned, he appealed to masonic practice and masonic charity, and placed himself on the strong basis afforded by the theological virtues of Christianity, which he knew

[8] Swift's Works, vol. xii. p. 250.

to be impregnable, because their observance needed neither justification nor defence.   And as it was not a proselyting system, the Brethren were perfectly satisfied in the quiet enjoyment of their privileges, without offering them to the acceptance of others, or refusing the participation of them to any worthy friend who voluntarily sought admission into the society.   Indeed, the reasons of the fraternity, at that period, for their literary abstinence were publicly stated to be these—that "considering the flourishing state of our lodges, where regular instruction and suitable exercises are ever ready for all Brethren who zealously aspire to improve in masonical knowledge, new publications are unnecessary on a subject which books cannot teach."[9]

It must be further considered, that at this period, polite literature was only just in its dawn, and had not yet shed that full effulgence of light over the world which was destined to dissipate the almost Gothic ignorance that distinguished the early part of the reign of Anne, when rank and title were considered the rivals of learning and science; and, as was observed by Johnson, "that general knowledge which now circulates in common talk, was then rarely to be found.   Men, not professing learning, were not ashamed of ignorance; and in the female world any acquaintance with books was distinguished only to be censured."[10]   And hence the manners of men were so unrefined, that they took pleasure in amusements which we, of the present age, are unable to reconcile with the dictates of humanity or the precepts of religion.   Hard drinking, bull and cock fighting, bear baiting, and other similar diversions, were not confined to the lower classes of society, but formed a point of attraction to gentlemen of the highest quality in the kingdom, and it was not esteemed dishonourable for females to be present at these disgusting exhibitions.[11]

[9] See Constitutions, Ed. 1784, note, sub anno 1783.
[10] Lives of the Poets, vol. ii.
[11] But though it is clear, from existing records, that the Brethren did not generally indulge in any excessive degree of intemperance, or carry their convivialities to an unreasonable height, yet it is no less true, that the cheerful glass was accompanied by toasts, and sentiments, and songs; and, in too many instances, this formed the chief business of the meeting. From the by-laws of an old lodge at Lincoln, over which Sir Cecil Wray presided, it appears that the fine for any breach of discipline was "a bot-

The fraternity at length discovered that the dignified bearing which they had hitherto observed towards their adversaries, was too exclusive. It was showing too great an indifference—not to say contempt—for public opinion, and gave the enemies of Masonry an advantage, of which they did not fail to profit, and objections were urged by rival institutions with a pertinacity which it was found necessary to combat from the press.[12] Charges and Addresses were, therefore, delivered by Brethren in authority, on the fundamental principles of the Order, and they were printed, to show that its morality was sound, and not in the slightest degree repugnant to the precepts of our most holy religion. These were of sufficient merit to ensure a wide circulation amongst the fraternity, from whence they spread into the world at large, and proved decisive in fixing the credit of the institution for solemnity of character, and a taste for serious and profitable investigations.

Another cause of the dearth of Masonic publications in the early days after the revival of Masonry, existed in the difficulties under which composition laboured ; for the style of the English language had not attained to all the purity of which it was susceptible till it became refined by the literary labours of Addison and Steele.

tle of wine, to be drank by the Brethren present ;" and there is reason to believe that this was the usual custom.

[12] It was the absence of authentic writings which furnished the heresiarch Weishaupt with his chief arguments ; and bad and inconclusive as they were, his disciples received them with the greatest avidity. " I declare," says he, " and I challenge all mankind to contradict my assertion, that no man can give any account of the Order of Freemasonry, of its origin, of its history, of its object, nor any explanation of its mysteries and symbols, which does not leave the mind in total uncertainty on all these points. Every man is entitled, therefore, to give any explanation of the symbols, and any system of the doctrines, that he can render palatable. Hence have sprung up that variety of systems which, for twenty years have divided the Order. The simple tale of the English, the fifty degrees of the French, and the knights of the Baron Hunde, are equally authentic, and have equally had the support of intelligent and zealous Brethren. These systems are, in fact, but one. They have all sprung from the blue lodge of three degrees ; take these for their standard, and found on these all the improvements by which each system is afterwards suited to the particular object which it keeps in view. There is no man nor system in the world which can show, by undoubted succession, that it should stand at the head of the Order." On such sophisms did Weishaupt found his claims to credence ; and, strange to say, they were received by the multitude as orthodox and irrefutable.

10

This may be gathered from the fate of the most popular work of the day. I allude to Collier's Essays on various subjects, which display an inelegance of diction, notwithstanding their extensive circulation, that detracted from their value, and caused them to be laid aside when the harmonious cadences and flowing language which distinguished the "Spectators" had improved the literary taste of the age. The occasional productions of eminent Masons were amongst the earliest efforts of this happy reformation in our language; and we may appeal to them with the assured confidence that their claims will not be disallowed.

The attempted exposure of Freemasonry was not confined to verbal insinuations, or vague conjectures respecting its tendency and design ; but displayed itself by numerous experiments on the credulity of the public, in a series of pamphlets professing to reveal the secret practices of its private meetings ; and from the rapidity with which they appeared, it should seem that the object of the authors was answered by an ample and remunerative consumption. Their insane pretensions to the extinction of the Order, were, however, not verified ; for it steadily maintained its place in public opinion, and the reiterated attacks of its opponents, couched, as they were, in coarse and slovenly language, and founded on assumptions which were proved to be untrue, failed to make the slightest impression on the majestic form of Freemasonry,[13] and her numbers and influence increased

---

[13] A German author, in the " Freemasons' Lexicon," which-is now in course of translation for the " Freemasons' Quarterly Review," by Bro. G. Watson, says :—" When it is maintained by the world that the books which are said to have been written by oppressed Freemasons, contain the secrets of Freemasonry, it is a very great error. To publish an account of the ceremonies of the lodge, however wrong that may be, does not communicate the secrets of Freemasonry, no more than that the liturgy of the church contains true religion. Neither are any of the printed rituals correct, because they are printed from memory, and not from a lodge copy. In Europe there are at least eleven different rituals ; and if every one of them was printed correctly, it could contain only a small portion of the forms of Freemasonry. Neither has any one, who has been admitted into the higher degrees, published the secrets of those degrees. Enquiries into the history of the Order, and the true meaning of its hieroglyphics and ceremonies by learned Brethren cannot be considered treason, for the Order itself recommends the study of its history, and that every Brother should instruct his fellows as much as possible."

in proportion with the virulence of those who sought to weaken her defences by an insidious conspiracy against the beneficent objects of her association.[14]

It will only be necessary to enumerate these pretended exposures, to show the animus by which the warfare was actuated and maintained.[15] And, strange to say, it commenced at a period when Freemasonry was in a state of comparative inactivity, during the reign of Charles II. The following catalogue of these spurious publications may be acceptable :—

1676. A short Analysis of the unchanged rites and ceremonies of Freemasons.
1685. The Paradoxical Discourses of Fr. Mercur. van Helmont, concerning the macrocosm and microcosm of the greater and lesser world, and their union.
1686. An account of the Freemasons. By Dr. Plot.
1698. A short Charge. O. D. A. A. M. F. M. K. O.
1709. The Secret History of Clubs, with their original.
1712. Observations and Enquiries relating to the Brotherhood of the Freemasons. By Simon Townsend.
1724. The Grand Mystery of the Gormagons.
1724. The Grand Mystery of Freemasons discovered; wherein are the

[14] Thus a writer in the " Craftsman," No. 563, published April 16th, 1736, having asserted that those who hanged Capt. Porteous at Edinburgh were all Freemasons, because they kept the secret so inviolably, an allusion to it was introduced in the secretary's song, as follows :—

" In vain would D'Anvers show his wit,
Our slow resentment raise,
What he and all mankind hath writ,
But celebrates our praise.
His wit this only truth imparts,
That Masons have firm faithful hearts."

[15] A writer of the period thus complains of the spirit that pervaded the the opponents of Masonry :—" But though we envy not the prosperity of any society, nor meddle with their transactions and characters, we have not met with such fair treatment from others ; nay, even those that never had an opportunity of obtaining any certain knowledge of us, have run implicitly with the cry; and, without fear or wit, have vented their spleen in accusing and condemning us unheard—untried ; while we, innocent and secure within, laugh only at their gross ignorance and impotent malice. Have not people in former ages, as well as now, alleged that the Freemasons in their lodges raise the devil in a circle, and when they have done with him, that they lay him again with a noise or a hush, as they please? How have some diverted themselves with the wild story of an old woman between the rounds of a ladder! Others will swear to the cook's red-hot iron or salamander for making an indelible character on the new-made Mason, in order to give him the faculty of taciturnity. Sure such blades will beware of coming through the fingers of the Freemasons!"

several questions put to them at their meetings and installations, as also their oath, healths, signs, and points to know each other by ; as they were found in the custody of a Freemason who died suddenly ; and now published for the information of the public.

1725. Observations and Critical Remarks on the new Constitutions of Freemasonry.

1725. The Secret History of Freemasonry ; being an accidental discovery of the ceremonies made use of in the several lodges, upon the admission of a Brother as a Free and Accepted Mason, &c.

1726. The Freemasons' Accusation and Defence, in six genuine letters between a gentleman in the country and his son, a student in the Temple ; wherein the whole affair of Masonry is fairly debated, and all the arguments for and against the Fraternity are curiously and impartially handled.

1726. The Post Boy ; a genuine discovery of Freemasonry.

1728. The Flying Post.

1731. Masonry Dissected ; being a universal and genuine description of all its branches, from the original to this present time ; giving an impartial account of their regular proceeding in initiating their new members in the whole three degrees of Masonry, viz., the Entered Prentice, Fellow Craft, and Master. By Samuel Prichard, late member of a constituted lodge.[16]

1736. The Freemasons' Vade Mecum.[17]

1737. The Mystery of Masonry.

1737. The Secrets of Masonry made known to all men. By Samuel Prichard.

1737. The Mysterious Reception of the celebrated society of Freemasons ; containing a true account of their ceremonies.

1738. Masonry further Dissected. By Samuel Prichard.

1738. La Friponnerie laïque des pretendus esprits-forts, en Angleterre, ou Remarques de Philéleuthère de Leipsig, sur le discours de la liberté de penser. Translated into English, by Richard Bentley.

1745. The Testament of a Freemason.

1747. L'Adepte Maçon, ou le vrai secret des Francs Maçons. Printed in London.

1750. Jachin and Boaz, or an authentic key to the door of Freemasonry, both ancient and modern ; calculated not only for the instruction of the new-made Mason, but also for the information of all who intend to become Brethren, &c.

[16] This was boldly avowed to be the genuine catechism of Freemasonry, which was communicated only by conference from one lodge to another, or from one Brother to another ; and this is the reason why we have so many different forms of the masonic catechism, although in spirit there is no material difference in any of them. As a religious catechism contains a summary of all that is taught by that religion, so our catechism contains the essence of Freemasony ; but it is not to be understood without the teacher taking great pains to instruct the student, nor without having been previously taught in a lodge, and being able to reflect upon and remember the instructions there given. This work was answered by Dr. Anderson.

[17] The Vade Mecum was condemned by the Grand Lodge as a piratical and silly publication, done without leave ; and the Brethren were warned not to use it, nor encourage the sale thereof.

1751. Le Maçon démasqué ou le vrai secret des F. M. mis au jour dans toutes ses parties avec sincérité et sans deguisement. Printed in London.

1752. The Thinker upon Freemasonry.

1754. The Point of a Mason, formed out of his own materials.

1754. The Masons' Creed.

1754. The Ghost of Masonry.

1755. Manifesto and Masons' Creed.

1755. Discovery of the secrets of Masonry. Printed in the Scots' Magazine.

1759. The Secrets of Masonry Revealed, by a disgusted Brother. Containing an ingenious account of their origin, their practices in the lodge, signs and watchwords, proceedings at the making, &c.

1760. A Master Key to Freemasonry; by which all the secrets of the society are laid open, and their pretended mysteries exposed to the public, with an accurate account of the examination of the Apprentice, Fellowcraft. and Master, &c.

1763. Allegorical Conversations Organized by Wisdom.

1764. An Institute of Red Masonry.

1764. Hiram, or the Grand Master Key to the door of both ancient and modern Freemasonry; being an accurate description of every degree of the Brotherhood, as authorized and delivered in all good lodges. Containing more than any other book on the subject ever before published. By a member of the Royal Arch.

1765. Shibboleth, or every man a Freemason.

1766. Solomon in all his Glory, or the Master Mason; being a true guide to the inmost recesses of Freemasonry, both ancient and modern. Containing a minute account of the proceedings, &c. By T. W. Translated from the French original, published at Berlin; and burnt by order of the King of Prussia, at the intercession of the Freemasons.

1767. The Three distinct Knocks; or the door of the most ancient Freemasonry opened to all men, neither naked nor clothed, barefooted nor shod. Being an universal description of all its branches, from its first rise to the present time, as it is delivered in all lodges. By W. O. V. M.

1767. The Secret Mysteries of the High Degrees of Masonry Unveiled; or the true Rose Croix. Translated from the French.

1768. Masonry the way to hell. A sermon, wherein is clearly proved, both from reason and scripture, that all who profess the mysteries are in a state of damnation.

1769. The Freemason stripped naked; or the whole art and mystery of Freemasonry made plain and easy to all capacities, by a faithful account of every secret from the first making of a Mason, till he is completely master of every branch of his profession. By Charles Warren, Esq., late Grand Master of a regularly constituted lodge in the city of Cork.

1770. Art Royal du Chevalier de Rose Croix. Printed in London.

1788. Les Jesuites chassés de la Maçonnerie et leur poignard brisé par les Maçons. La Maçonnerie Ecossaise comparée avec les trois Professions et la secret des Templiers du 14ᵉ Siècle. Meté des quatre voeux de la compagnie de Saint Ignace et des quatre grades de la Maçonnerie de St. Jean. Printed in London.

1792. Freemasonry of the Ladies, or the grand secret disclosed.

1792. The Veil Withdrawn; or the secret of the French Revolution explained by the help of Freemasonry.

The above list, with the heavy works of Barruel and Robison, published at the latter end of the century, occasionally reinforced by articles in popular periodicals, will serve to show that Freemasonry was considered like some gigantic Polyphemus, against whom it was esteemed honourable to shiver a lance, even though the recoil should be injurious to the assailant. Many of these productions were too absurd to be noticed; others carried their own refutation along with them; while a few there were which it was thought expedient to refute by sober argument, and a brief display of the real objects of the institution, and of the manner in which they were carried into practical effect by the general regulations of the society.

Notwithstanding the number of these spurious publications, and the pertinacity with which they were obtruded on public notice, very few of their authors succeeded in obtaining any credit amongst right-minded men. How plausible soever they were introduced; even though the veracity of their contents were asserted on oath before the civil magistrate,[18] few converts were made by their instrumentality; for what credit could be attached to the affidavit of a man who solemnly swore that he had revealed the secrets which, by his own acknowledgment, he had already sworn as solemnly to conceal; the difficulty was insurmountable; and the fraternity enjoyed the inextricable dilemma in which the perjurers were placed.

The fabricators appear to have been sensible of this dilemma, and, to neutralize its effects, they dedicated their lucubrations to the fraternity, for the purpose of inspiring a confidence that they contained the genuine secrets of the Order, as actually practised in the tyled recesses of the lodge.[19] This ingenious pretext, however,

[18] Thus we find affixed to Prichard's book the following affidavit:—
" Jur. 13, die Oct. 1730, coram me R. Hopkins.—Samuel Prichard maketh oath that the copy hereto annexed is a true and genuine copy in every particular."

[19] Prichard inscribed his work to the " Right Worshipful and Honourable Fraternity of Free and Accepted Masons.—Brethren and Fellows,— If the following sheets, done without partiality, gain the universal ap-

was unsuccessful, because it was known to be a fiction. For how could that be made public for the use of the lodges, which, as it was openly avowed, the Brethren had entered into the most solemn obligations to preserve inviolate :—and how could they be secrets which were thus openly displayed? It was finally concluded that these publications did not contain any correct information on the mysteries of the craft; or, if a few grains of wheat were mixed amongst a mountain of chaff, they could not be extracted, because they were not distinguishable by an unpractised examiner. Like the Roman ancilia, truth and falsehood assumed an appearance so similar to each other, that it was not possible to ascertain the difference between them ; and therefore they were alike considered undeserving of the slightest confidence.

These pretenders might find occasional readers, but it was not with a view of gaining information or acquiring any knowledge of the peculiarities of an institution which was open to every honest and virtuous inquirer ; but perhaps with a design of ascertaining what new absurdities were offered to the digestion of the public. Idlers at a coffee-house might take up one of these pamphlets to wile away a vacant hour ; and they would resign it with about the same degree of edification which would have followed a perusal of the erudite tales of the fairies. They considered "this swarm of pamphleteers who stole each an hour, as wasters of human life, and would make no other difference between them, than between a beast of prey and a flight of locusts ;" and it is probable the verse in Pope's paraphrase of Homer would frequently occur to such a casual reader :—

> " Who dares think one thing and another tell,
> My heart detests him as the gate of hell."

A cotemporary thus describes the claims which such writers have to veracity :—" To these compositions is required neither genius nor knowledge, neither industry nor sprightliness, but contempt of shame and indifference

plause of so worthy a society, I doubt not but their general character will be diffused and esteemed among the remaining polite part of mankind ; which, I hope, will give entire satisfaction to all lovers of truth ; and I shall remain with all humble submission, the fraternity's most obedient humble servant, Samuel Prichard."

to truth are absolutely necessary. He who, by a long
familiarity with infamy, has obtained these qualities, may
confidently tell to-day what he intends to contradict to-
morrow; and he may fearlessly affirm what he knows he
shall be obliged to recant." In a word, the men who
could thus deliberately violate a solemn engagement were
justly considered infamous; for, in all ages, this shameless prostitution of principle to the purposes of gain, has
been met by the reprobation of mankind.[20]

On the other hand, supposing the absurd pretensions
of these books to have been well founded, how did their
authors propose that the reader should be benefited by
their perusal? He could not make his appearance at a
lodge without the risk of being discovered and branded
as an impostor,[21] a character which would not have ad-

[20] The author of "Multa Paucis for Lovers of Secrets," does not wonder "that so many have attempted to publish these impenetrable mysteries
of the fraternity, under various pretences, in order to satisfy the curious."
But, he adds, the readers of them "were not altogether ignorant of the
innumerable volumes published by the eminent and learned of this fraternity, whereby Britain is become mistress of all the arts and sciences;—
of the surprising progress Masonry and architecture have made in Great
Britain since the time of those two remarkable architects—Inigo Jones and
Sir Christopher Wren; or of the flourishing condition of lodges all the
world over, and their craving the patronage of our noble Grand Master
of England. Therefore, the authors of these pamphlets were rightly
judged to be either false pretenders, or very stupid, ignorant fellows,
little versed in that noble science."
[21] The ill-disguised curiosity of the cowan appears to have been a never-
failing source of amusement to our Brethren of the last century. I
remember an anecdote to this effect was told with great glee by the
Brethren with whom I was in the habit of associating at the earliest
period of my initiation. A Quaker Mason formed one of an indiscriminate
company of cowans at an inn, where the landlord was a Brother. Numerous
jokes were cracked at the expense of the fraternity, and the Quaker was
called upon to show them the Masons' sign. One of the company offered
to give him a bottle of wine if he would comply with their wishes; and,
at length, though with much apparent reluctance, he agreed, on condition
that the wine should be immediately produced, and the individual consented to receive the communication privately; the Quaker adding—
"Friend, if thou dost not confess to the company that I have shown thee
a Freemason's sign, I will pay for the wine myself." The proposition
was too reasonable to be refused, and the curious candidate for Masonic
knowledge retired into another room with his formal friend. When
there, the following dialogue took place :—
    Quaker.—" So, friend, thou art desirous of seeing a Freemason's sign?"
" I am." " Canst thou keep a secret?" " Try me." " Good! Thou
knowest that our friend Johnson (the innkeeper) is a Mason?" " I do."
" Very well." Then taking him by the arm he led him to the window

vanced his credit either in his public or private capacity.
He could not have displayed his knowledge even amongst
his friends in the fraternity, because the searching question—simple though it appear to be—"Where were you
made a Mason?" would have removed the veil, and laid
his unauthorized pretensions bare, to his eternal shame.
In a word, no benefit whatever could be derived from
these publications, even supposing them to be true; and
the dilemma was insurmountable.

" Cui non conveniat sua res, ut calceus olim,
  Si pede major erit, subvertet; si minor, uret."—Hor.

Some kind of reply was, at length, found necessary,
and it was soon forthcoming. The first that appeared on
the stage as an apologist was the distinguished author
of the "History of Masonry," Dr. Anderson.[22] It is
true he had been preceded by a few masonic pamphlets,
but they were not of a controversial character, and had
been published simply to show from authority, the tendency of masonic teaching. Thus, in 1721, Dr. Desaguliers,[23] the late Grand Master, issued, in a printed form,

" Dost thou see that ramping lion which swings from yonder upright post?"
"To be sure I do—it is our landlord's sign." "Good! Then, friend,
our landlord being a Freemason, thou art satisfied that I have shown thee
a Freemason's sign, and thy bottle of wine is forfeited. For thy own sake
thou wilt keep the secret." He returned into the room with a look of
astonishment, confessing that he had received the desired information;
and the mystery, which he purposely observed, tempted others to pur-
chase the secret at the same price.

[22] A writer who styles himself Euclid, and uses the signature of the
forty-seventh proposition, under date 1738, thus characterizes this admirable defence :—" Some think the ingenious defender has spent too much
learning and reasoning upon the foolish Dissection that is justly despised
by the fraternity, as much as the other pretended discoveries of their
secrets in public newspapers and pasquils, all of a sort; for all of them
put together do not discover the profound and sublime things of old
Masonry; nor can any man, not a Mason, make use of those incoherent
smatterings, interspersed with ignorant nonsense and gross falsities,
among bright Brothers, for any purpose but to be laughed at."

[23] Bro. Desaguliers was born at Rochelle in 1683, and was the son of a
French Protestant refugee. While he was an infant, his father brought
him into England, and gave him an excellent education at Oxford. The
Duke of Chandos made him his chaplain; and he was afterwards chaplain to the Prince of Wales. He introduced the practice of reading
public lectures on experimental philosophy in London; and made several
improvements in mechanics, which he communicated to the Royal
Society. He was a member of several foreign academies; and published
many scientific works.

10*

an oration which he had pronounced in Grand Lodge, in
the presence of the Duke of Montague and his officers.
A few years later, a similar oration was delivered in the
Grand Lodge at York, and another at Caernarvon, both
of which were considered of sufficient merit to appear
before the public. In 1735, the celebrated address of
Martin Clare, J. G. W., was issued. He had been already
authorized to revise the lodge lectures, which difficult
task he accomplished to the satisfaction and edification
of the Brethren.[24]

In 1738 appeared Dr. Anderson's celebrated defence.
It was a most learned and masterly production, and completely demolished poor Prichard, who, however, mus-
tered sufficient courage to reply, but his overthrow was
so complete, that his new pamphlet fell dead from the
press, and found few purchasers. The defence contains
an admirable vindication of the ceremonies, which Prichard had wofully travestied, for the purpose of exposing
the institution to ridicule; and his attempt was successful amongst people of doubtful character, who possessed
no claims to an honourable participation in the mysteries;
and, like the fox in the fable with the unattainable
grapes, rejoiced in the existence of a pretext for pro-

[24] I find, in an ancient Minute book belonging to the Witham lodge at
Lincoln, the following record of a practice in use when Sir Cecil Wray,
Bart., who was D. G. M. of the Order in England, held also the office of
Master of this private lodge :—"Dec. 4, 1733. Sir Cecil Wray, Bart.,
Master. Several of the by-laws were read, as also Bro. Clare's discourse
on S. M. and G. F. Then the Master went through an examination as
usual.

"Aug. 6, 1734.—Sir Cecil Wray, Bart., D. G. M., Master. Several
of the by-laws and regulations out of the book of Constitutions, as also
Bro. Clare's discourse relating to P—d, were read, after which the Master went through an examination, and the lodge was closed with a song.

"Jan. 6, 1735.—Sir Cecil Wray, Bart., the Master, went through an
examination ; and Bro. Clare's lecture made to a body of Free and Accepted Masons, assembled at a quarterly communication held near Tem-
ple-bar, Dec. 11, 1734, was read by Bro. Becke." It is clear from these
entries that Martin Clare's lectures were enjoined by authority. The
warrant of the above lodge was dated Sept. 7. 1730, and numbered, in
the Grand Lodge books, thirty-eight. I find, however, in a list of lodges
appended to the first edition of the "Pocket Companion," published in
1736, the number seventy-three erroneously assigned to it, for it stands
thirty-eight in all the engraved lists published by the grand lodge, and
several others in my possession. There was another lodge which met at
the Angel, in "The Bailywick of Lincoln," under a warrant dated Dec.
28, 1737 ; but I am ignorant of the number.

nouncing sentence against it. But the matter terminated
otherwise with persons of judgment and discrimination.
The manly and straightforward arguments used by Dr.
Anderson, produced conviction in the mind of every
reader, and made many converts. The consequence was,
that the reputation of the Order was increased by the ad-
hesion of rank and talent; and the very next quarterly
communication, after its appearance, was attended by the
officers of ninety-two lodges, instead of about sixty, as
had been previously the average number. And at the
succeeding Grand Lodge, it was ordered that the laws
should be strictly executed against all irregularities, or
whatever else might tend to break the cement of the
fraternity.

This period was also marked by the extension of the
craft throughout England; and new lodges were established in every town of importance. Hence it was found
necessary to appoint Provincial Grand Masters to regulate the affairs of the craft in districts at a distance from
the metropolis, to prevent the introduction of innovations, and to preserve an uniformity of practice in the
country lodges.

In the following year a work was published called
" The Beginning and First Foundation of the most worthy Craft of Masonry." This was intended to prove its
antiquity; which had been scarcely questioned, because
the evidences were easily accessible that showed its existence in England many centuries before the art of print-
ing was invented; and the subtleties of special pleading,
or as Hudibras expresses it, a power to

" _____ distinguish and divide
A hair 'twixt south and southwest side;
On either which he would dispute,
Confute, change hands, and still confute,"

had not then obtained such complete possession of the
mind as to induce men to advance arguments in support
of a theory, with unanswerable proofs of its soundness
before their eyes. This pamphlet does not appear to
have created much sensation, because its object was
simply to assert a fact which had never been formally
denied.

About this time, Freemasonry excited considerable attention on the continent of Europe, by the squabbles and

disputes which existed amongst the adherents of the numerous masonic adventurers who swarmed in France and
Germany, and offered its privileges to the acceptance of
good and bad in every class, merely to increase their numbers ; and the fulminations of the Vatican were imitated
and followed up by the denunciations of Protestant states
and political associations on all secret societies which
were based on the principles promulgated by Freemasonry.   The States General of the United Provinces, the
magistrates of Berne, and the ministers of the Associated
Synod of Scotland, did not disdain to unite in the unholy
crusade. These violent proceedings produced a masterly
pamphlet from an English Mason, called, " An Apology
for the Free and Accepted Masons," which attained, as
it well deserved, such an extensive circulation, both in
England and on the continent, as alarmed the Holy See,
and produced a papal decree, by which it was censured,
condemned, prohibited, and ordered to be burnt publicly
by the minister of justice in the street of St. Mary supra
Minervam. This decree, as might have been expected,
increased the popularity of the pamphlet ; and it was
subsequently reprinted in various forms, and transcribed
into almost every work of any note on the subject of
Freemasonry during the remainder of the century.

It will be unnecessary to enumerate all the masonic
publications which distinguished the eighteenth century,
because many of them were mere transcripts of Anderson, Calcott, and Hutchinson ; and the ensuing pages
will contain most of the original works of merit that
were printed during that period.[25] Suffice it to say, that
the literary labours of our Brethren who lived in the early
times, when Freemasonry had been regenerated and
placed on a new and more diffusive basis, are equal to

.

[25] The original writers on genuine Masonry in this age were in reality
very few, although the publications, professing to treat on the subject, appear to be numerous, particularly on the continent. The three authors
above-named possess the merit of originality ; Smith was a copyist to a
certain extent, and hence some parts of his book are useless. Dunckerley,
and a few others, have left behind them some lectures of great value,
inasmuch as they show the true character of Freemasonry at the revival.
Martin Clare's lodge-lectures are lost—at least they have escaped my researches, and I have never had the good fortune to meet with them.
Almost all the other masonic works of that period were mere transcripts
of one or other of the above.

the best compositions of the age ; and some of them are not inferior to the Spectators and Tatlers which have borne successfully the scrutinizing test of criticism for upwards of a century, and promise to be standard works so long as our national taste for purity of style and elegance of diction shall remain uncorrupted.

LECTURE I.

ON THE RISE AND PROGRESS OF FREEMASONRY.—NO DATE.

> Hail, mystic science, seraph maid!
> Imperial beam of light!
> In robes of sacred Truth array'd,
> Morality's delight.
> O give me Wisdom to design,
> And Strength to execute;
> In native Beauty e'er be mine,
> Benevolence thy fruit.   DR. PERFECT.

IN the history of mankind there is nothing more re-markable than that Masonry and civilization, like twin sisters, have gone hand in hand together. The orders of architecture[1] mark their growth and progress; dark, dreary, and comfortless were those times when Masonry had not laid her line, nor extended her compass.[2] The race of man in full possession of wild and savage liberty sullen and solitary, mutually offending and afraid of each

---

[1] A free and easy proportion, united with simplicity, seem to constitute the elegance of form in building. A subordination of parts to one evident design forms simplicity; when the members thus related are great, the union is always very great. In the proportion of a noble edifice, you see the image of a creating mind result from the whole, the evident uniformity of the rotunda, and its unparalleled simplicity, are probably the sources of its superior beauty. When we look up to a vaulted roof, that seems to rest upon our horizon, we are astonished at the magnificence more than at the visible extent.

[2] Our Brethren of the last century entertained an unvarying opinion that Masonry was coeval with the creation of the world. And they not only applied it to operative architecture, but also to the moral principles included in the six precepts of Adam, and the seven injunctions laid on the Noachidæ, which they considered to be the basis of what we call speculative Masonry. Indeed, these precepts constituted the foundation of natural religion, and were recognized by the very first synod of Christianity, which enjoined on all the disciples of Christ, that they should "abstain from meats offered to idols, and from blood, and from things strangled, and from fornication." (Acts xv. 29.)

other; hid themselves in thickets of the woods, or dens, and caves of the earth. In these murky recesses, these sombrous solitudes, the Almighty Architect directed Masonry to find them out;[3] and pitying their forlorn and destitute condition, instructed them to build houses, for convenience, defence, and comfort.[4] The habitations they then built were of the Rustic, or Tuscan order, which, as a prototype of their manners, was an artless

---

[3] In a work called "Multa Paucis for Lovers of Secrets," published in 1763, the rise and progress of Masonry are thus described:—"The origin of Masonry is indisputably traced from the creation of the universe; for after the Almighty Architect had finished his grand design in making all things good, and. according to geometry, Adam, the first of all the human race, did soon discover this noble science, by surveying the works of God in his state of innocency; and although he fell through disobedience, and was expelled from that lovely arbour into a wide world, he still retained the knowledge thereof, and communicated the same to his offspring. For Cain, his first-born, after he had committed the murder of his brother Abel, for which God drove him into the land of Nod, he showed his early skill in Masonry by building a strong city, and called the same after the name of his first son, Enoch. The offspring of his descendant, Lamech, are very remarkable, viz., Jabal was the inventor of huts and tents; Jubal was the inventor of music; Tubal Cain was the inventor of metals. The offspring of these ingenious craftsmen are traced by historians for many centuries after, but as it cannot be warranted from scripture this may suffice. Seth, the patriarch of the other part of mankind, with his offspring, Enos, Cainan, Mahalaleel, Jared, and Enoch, were the better instructed in geometry by Adam's living among them, until the year of the world 930."

[4] The natural progress of the works of men is from rudeness to convenience, from convenience to elegance, and from elegance to nicety. The first labour is enforced by necessity. The savage finds himself incommoded by heat and cold, by rain and wind; he shelters himself in the hollow of a rock, and learns to dig a cave where there was none before. He finds the sun and the wind excluded by the thicket, and when the accidents of the chase, or the convenience of pasturage, lead him into more open places, he forms a thicket for himself, by planting stakes at proper distances, and laying branches from one to another. The next gradation of skill and industry produces a house, closed with doors, and divided by partitions; and apartments are multiplied and disposed according to the various degrees of power or invention; improvement succeeds improvement, as he that is freed from a greater evil grows impatient of a less, till ease, in time, is advanced to pleasure. The mind, set free from the importunities of natural want, gains leisure to go in search of superfluous gratifications, and adds to the rise of habitation the delights of prospect. Then begins the reign of symmetry; orders of architecture are invented, and one part of the edifice is conformed to another, without any other reason than that the eye may not be offended. The passage is very short from elegance to luxury. Ionic and Corinthian columns are soon succeeded by gilt cornices, inlaid floors, and petty ornaments, which show rather the wealth than the taste of the possessor.

imitation of coarse and simple nature. Yet rude and in-elegant as they were, they had this happy effect: that by aggregating mankind, they prepared the way for im-provement.[5] The hardest bodies will polish by collision, and the roughest manners by communion and intercourse. Thus by degrees they lost their asperity and ruggedness, and became insensibly mild and gentle. Masonry beheld and gloried in the change; and, as their minds softened and expanded, she showed them new lights, and con-ducted them to new improvements.[6]   .

[5] It may be observed here that some of our Brethren consider ancient Masonry to have been exclusively an operative institution; some believe it was speculative; while others understand it as a judicious admixture of both. Anderson treats it throughout his elaborate history as an operative fraternity. Laurie observes, speaking of the Egyptian archi-tecture: "In Egypt, and those countries of Asia which lie contiguous to the favoured kingdom, the arts and sciences were cultivated with success, while other nations were involved in ignorance. It is here, therefore, that Freemasonry would flourish; and here only can we discover marks of its existence in the remotest ages." Faber says in his work on Pagan Idolatry: "All the most remarkable ancient buildings in Greece, Egypt, and Asia Minor, were ascribed to the Cabirean or Cyclopean Masons; and in the present day the Freemasons, with all their formalities, are wont to assist at the commencement of every public edifice. Finally, their affectation of mysterious concealment closely resembles the system of the Epoptæ in all ages and countries, particularly that of the bards, when their religion no longer reigned paramount. These last are proba-bly the real founders of English Freemasonry." A Scottish Mason writes to me in these words: "Originally the study of Freemasonry was confined to operative masons, and was a secret means of conferring the freedom of that craft. All other crafts had something similar; but whe-ther Masonry was the oldest, or had the best system, all the others are nearly obliterated. It is of little consequence when this system of giving the freedom was got up, whether in the middle ages, or whether it was formed on one more ancient; but there is no occasion for any more than three degrees, and I doubt if any other be ancient." Bro. Stephen Jones insists that the institution is speculative. "The solemnity of our rites," he observes, "which, embracing the whole system of morality, cannot fail to include the first principles of religion, from which morality is best derived, necessarily calls our attention to the Great Architect of the Uni-verse, the Creator of us all. The masonic system exhibits a stupendous and beautiful fabric, founded on universal piety. To rule and direct our passions; to have faith and hope in God, and charity towards man, I consider as the objects of what is termed Speculative Masonry." While Preston considers Freemasonry as a science arising out of the union of both. See the Illustrations of Masonry, Book i. s. 4. Under these cir-cumstances, every Brother must be left to his own judgment.

[6] Here we have primitive Masonry identified with operative architec-ture; and there can be no doubt but they were considered to advance hand in hand towards perfection.

The Tuscan mansions please no more, in the Doric order they aimed at something more high and noble; and taking their idea of symmetry from the human form divine, adopted that as their model. At that era their buildings, though simple and natural, were proportioned in the exactest manner, and admirably calculated for strength and convenience.[7]

It can be no matter of astonishment, that men who had formed their original plan from nature, should resort to nature for their lessons of ornament and proportion, to complete their labors. The eye that was charmed with the fair sex, the heart that was conscious of woman's elegance and beauty, would instantly catch the idea from thence, and transpose the lovely form in perfect symmetry, to complete the column he was then studying. Accordingly, the Ionic order was formed after the model of a beautiful young woman, with loose dishevelled hair, of an easy, elegant, flowing shape.[8]

Thus human genius, which we have seen in the bud, the leaf, the flower, ripened to perfection, and produced the fairest, richest fruit; every ingenious art, every liberal science, every moral and social virtue, that could delight, exalt, refine, adorn, edify, or improve mankind.[9]

[7] The first recognized style of building has been distinguished by the name of Cyclopæan, and its general character was—immense blocks without cement, which were put together with such exactness as to seem an entire mass. Schneider, editor of Vitruvius, says, that the style which was called Insertum meant large stones, with smaller ones inserted between them. This was the most ancient manner of building, and was sometimes called Antiquum.

[8] The Ionians, says Vitruvius, tried to invest their edifices with the greatest delicacy and elegance. Instead of taking for a model the body of a man, as had been done in the composition of the Doric order, they were regulated by that of a woman. With a view of making their columns more pleasing, they made the height eight times the diameter. They also made flutings to imitate the folds of the female dress, and the volutes represented the curls which hung on each side of the face. This order of architecture was hence called the Ionic.

[9] If the God of Israel inspired Bezaleel and Aholiab with wisdom and knowledge in all manner of workmanship, the God of nature has not been wanting in his instructions to the fowls of the air. The skill with which they erect their houses, and adjust their apartments, is inimitable. The caution with which they hide their abodes from the searching eye, or intruding hand, is admirable. No general, though fruitful in expedients, could build so commodious a lodgement. Give the most celebrated artificer the same materials, which these weak and inexperienced creatures use;—let a Jones, or a Wren, or a Demoivre, have only some rude stones or uncouth

Now it was that Masonry put on her richest robes, her most gorgeous apparel, and in the Corinthian order displayed a profusion of ornaments, the principal parts of which were eminently conspicuous in Israel's holy temple. She displayed the torch and enlightened the whole circle of arts and sciences. Commerce flew to her on canvas wings, fraught with the treasures and produce of the universe. Painting and sculpture exerted every nerve to decorate the building she had raised, and the curious hand of design contrived the furniture and tapestry—Geometry, Music, Astronomy—Virtue, Honour, Mercy, with an infinite variety of masonic emblems were wrought thereon; but none shone more conspicuous than MORALITY, CHARITY, and BROTHERLY-LOVE.[10]

sticks, a few bits of dirt or scraps of hair, a lock of wool, or a coarse sprig of moss; and what work would they produce? We extol the commander who knows how to take advantage of the ground; who, by every circumstance, embarrasses the forces of his enemy, and advances the success of his own. Does not this praise belong to the feathered leaders? who fix their pensile camp on the dangerous branches that wave aloft in the air, or dance over the stream? By this means the vernal gales rock their cradle, and the murmuring waters lull the young, while both concur to terrify their enemies, and keep them at a distance. Some hide their little household from view, amidst the shelter of entangled furze. Others remove it from discovery in the centre of a thorny thicket. And by one stratagem or another they are generally as secure as if they intrenched themselves in the earth.

[10] But the permanent triumphs of Freemasonry were reserved for the Christian architect. Every one who has an eye to see and a soul to feel, must, on entering the cathedrals of York, Lincoln, or Winchester, or in contemplating the majestic front of Peterborough, experience impressions of mingled solemnity and delight, such as none but similar edifices are capable of producing. If he should enquire when were these extraordinary specimens of architectural skill, rivalling in their execution and surpassing in sublimity the proudest structures of Athens and Rome, erected, what would be his astonishment, had he not previously ascertained the fact, on being told in reply, that they were built during the dark ages, when but few even of the clergy could read, and scarcely any of them could write their own names; when nobles lay upon straw, and thought a fresh supply of clean straw in their chamber, once a week, a great luxury; when monarchs usually travelled on horseback, and when they met, wrestled with each other for the amusement of their courtiers; then it was that those Freemasons, whose names have not reached us, and whose manners and course of instruction are merely conjectured, raised buildings almost to the clouds, with stones, most of which they might have carried under their arms. Rude men, untaught by science, applied the principles of arcuation, of thrust, and of pressure, to an extent that would have made Wren and Jones tremble. Men ignorant of metaphysical theories, so blended forms and magnitudes, light and shade, as to

Were I to take a general survey of the Order of Free-masonry, a field of unbounded space would open to the view, replete with more beauties than the most fanci-ful pencil can delineate, or poet describe, assisted by all the flowers of metaphor. But time will not permit me to investigate the ground plan of the fabric. I shall, therefore, take an allegorical view of the building and mode of introduction.

Virtue crowned with a wreath of laurel, dressed in a robe of the palest sapphire, girt round her waist by an azure zone, on which peculiar emblems were richly em-broidered in blue, purple, and crimson, formed the mosaic work, or ground plan of the building.

Wisdom, Justice, Truth, Mercy, and Benevolence, as pillars of the purest marble, supported the portal, over which, on a magnificent dome of a quadrangular form, the principles of the establishment were delineated by Religion and Morality, together with certain hierogly-phics descriptive of the Order.[11]

The entrance was guarded by two sentinels, who had something in their looks so awful, that strangers recoiled at the sight of them. Their names were Temperance, and Fortitude, the former held a bridle, the latter a spear. Notwithstanding their aspect was so forbidding,

---

produce the artificial infinite and the real sublime. Men, who lived in the grossest superstition, erected temples for the worship of God, which seem as if intended. to rival in durability the earth on which they stand; and which, after the lapse of several ages, are still unequalled, not only in point of magnificence of structure, but in their tendency to dilate the mind, and to leave upon the soul the most deep and solemn impressions. (See the Eclectic Review.)

[11] Like the tabernacle of Moses and the temple of Solomon, the ancient oratories of the gods abounded with hieroglyphics, which were descriptive of the system of religion used by the nations where such buildings were erected. The prophet Ezekiel has described them as containing " every form of creeping things and abominable beasts, and all the idols of the house of Israel, pourtrayed upon the wall round about." (Ezek. viii. 10.) This is a true picture of the inner chambers and sanctuaries of the Egyptian temples, the tombs, and mystic cells, according to the descriptions which modern travellers have supplied. The walls are cover-ed with representations, sculptured, or painted in vivid colours, of sacred animals, and of gods represented in the human form and under various circumstances, or in various combinations of the animal and human forms. These things now appear more conspicuously in the tombs than in the temples, perhaps because the decorations of the latter have suffered more from the hand of man.

yet when a candidate approached, conducted by Honour
and Perseverance, their countenance was softened by affability to serene courtesy.

Having passed the sentinels and entered the building,
Honour and Perseverance presented him to Brotherly-
love, who, after discharging the duties of his office, led
him to a beautiful transparent arch, descriptive of the
six days' work of the creation; on the right side of the
arch stood Charity, her eyes were blue, beautiful, and
piercing; in one hand she held a chalice of wrought
gold, in the other a censer of incense. One the left
stood Contemplation; her looks were directed towards
heaven; a large folio book lay open in the centre,[12] on
the back of which was written in letters of gold, THE
HOLY BIBLE. Here Brotherly-love delivered him to the
care of Faith, Humility, and Hope. The former had her
head invested with a circle of rays, which threw a bright
lustre on all around her; she bore a shield of divine
workmanship, and went foremost. Humility, clothed in
a vesture of a dark sober hue, which trailed the ground,
walked slowly by her side. Hope had in her hand an
opening bud, fresh and fragrant as the morning rose: by
those he was conducted to an elderly personage, who
still appeared fresh and vigorous, she had a meek and
contented aspect, having a staff in her hand, on which she
sometimes leaned. Her name was Prudence, from whom
he received peculiar instructions respecting the institution.

Leaving her, they ascended, by easy steps, towards
the GRAND HALL; near the entrance, on an elevated
throne, sat a comely matron in her bloom, well dressed,
but without art, and crowned after a very beautiful
manner: her name was Happiness, to whom he was presented by Hope. She received him most cheerfully, and
introduced him to the liberal arts and sciences, by whom
he was led into the hall, and after being regularly initiated, he was invested by Innocence with the ensign of the
Order.

[12] None but Masters' lodges are opened on the centre. Apprentice and
craft lodges are of a mixed composition, including Brethren who have
taken part or all of the degrees. They do not, therefore, present to the
view a masonic equality. The Masters, however, are all equal—they
meet on the level, and part on the square; and maintain the same relation
towards each other as the centre does to the circumference of a circle.

Sacred and profane history concur with respect to this institution, and allow it to be coeval with human society. In all ages, and in all countries, we find men of the most exalted situations in life, as well as those of the most enlightened characters, have been anxious to be invested with the badge of innocence, and to have their names enrolled as Brethren of the Order. Always considering the society of FREEMASONS as the safeguard of the state, the defence of the country, the welfare of the nation.[13]

Having slightly touched on the origin of the institution, and mode of introduction, the principles may be conveyed to you in a few words, BROTHERLY-LOVE, RELIEF, and TRUTH. Were I to take a retrospective view of those principles, it would only be recapitulating a subject with which you are well acquainted.[14] Allow me, however, to call your attention to the excellence and utility of FREEMASONRY from that all-informing science, on which it is founded—GEOMETRY, and bring to your recollection a figure which is generally delineated on the master's tracing board, namely, the 47th proposition of the first book of Euclid, proving that the square subtending a right angle is equal to the squares on the sides that form the right angle ;[15] from the construction of the figure it is evident, that the triangles within the squares are reciprocally equal, and also, that the squares on the sides forming the right angle are equal to the square subtending the right angle. Pythagoras, the inventor of this proposition, which is the foundation of geometry, in grateful testimony for the happy discovery, is said to have sacrificed an hecatomb to the Muses.

[13] Such has been the masonic character in all ages, where bigotry has not intervened to sully its brightness ; and invested with this high recommendation, it has been honoured with the patronage of princes and nobles, who have considered the fraternity as a certain protection to the throne, whenever it might be assailed by disloyalty and sedition.

[14] In fact, the principles of Masonry are like to a well-drawn circle, unbounded in their extent and universal in their application.

[15] Vitruvius ascribes this theorem to Pythagoras. (Vitruv. Archit. IX. 1.) By the use of it he taught his disciples how to make a gnomon or square thus : take three rods, one of them three feet long, another four, and a third five ; with these form a triangle ; and if to each of these rods be adscribed a square, that which is three feet in length will make an area of nine ; that of four feet will make sixteen ; that of five will make twenty-five. Hence it will appear that the areas of the two former are exactly equal to that of the latter.

But Freemasons consider geometry as a natural logic;[16] for as truth is ever consistent, invariable, and uniform, all truths may and ought to be investigated in the same manner. Moral and religious definitions, axioms, and proportions, have as regular and certain a dependence upon each other as any in physics or the mathematics.

As the figure above-mentioned depends on the connection of the several lines, angles, and triangles which form the whole; so FREEMASONRY depends on the unanimity and integrity of its members, the inflexibility of their charitable pursuits, and the immutability of the principles upon which the society is established. The position is clear, and, therefore, in a synthetical sense we demonstrate, that some of our Brethren, from their exalted situation in life, rolling in their chariots at ease, and enjoying every luxury, pleasure, and comfort, may with strict propriety be considered as standing on the basis of earthly bliss, emblematic of the greater square, which subtends the right angle.[17] Others whom Providence hath blessed with means to tread on the flowery meads of affluence; are descriptive of the squares which stand on the sides which form the right angle. The several triangles inscribed within the squares, are applicable to those happy beings, who enjoy every social comfort, and never exceed the bounds of mediocrity. Those, who by application to peculiar arts, manufactures, and commerce, from their several productions not only add to the wealth of the nation, and to the happiness of the exalted, but have the heartfelt satisfaction of administer-

---

[16] Iamblichus informs us that the Egyptians acquired a knowledge of geometrical problems from their custom of annually measuring their whole country in consequence of the landmarks being obliterated by the overflowing of the Nile. (Iambl. c. xxix. p. 144.) But some ascribe geometry to the joint investigations of the Egyptians and Chaldeans, which were augmented by the learning and application of Pythagoras; for Proclus (in Eucl. l. ii.) affirms that he was the first who elevated geometry into a liberal science, by considering the principles more sublimely than Thales and others—his predecessors in this study. And Timæus adds that he first brought geometry to perfection.

[17] We are told by Apollodorus that Pythagoras sacrificed a hecatomb to the muses in gratitude for the invention of this problem; but Plutarch says it was only a single ox; and even this is questioned by Cicero, because it was inconsistent with his doctrines, which forbad the shedding of blood. Porphyrus says that he only sacrificed an ox kneaded from flour ; while Gregory Nazianz thinks the ox was made of clay.

ing to the wants of the indigent and industrious, may, with strict justice, be compared to the angles which surround and support the figure, whilst the lines which form it, remind us of those unfortunate Brethren, who, by a series of inevitable events, are incapable of providing the common necessaries of life, until aided by our cheerful and ever-ready assistance.[18]

Hence from the corollary we draw an axiom in Masonry; for by connecting the several lines together, and bringing the unfortunate and industrious into compact with the affluent and exalted, we form a figure descriptive of the true basis on which our ancient Brethren raised the superstructure of FREEMASONRY. A basis which no mortal power can shake ; THE BOSOM OF ALL GENTLE CHARITY ; that heaven-born virtue, is the attribute divine of GOD OMNIPOTENT ; a sublime emotion, that fully demonstrates the existence of our spiritual being, and animates us to the glorious certainty of immortality.

[18] The use of the 47th proposition of Euclid is as ancient in Masonry as the Vesica Piscis, the application of which was kept a profound secret by the Masons in all ages. We find this expressive symbol immediately after the revival in 1717, used as a Mason's signature or mark, although it was not adopted as the cognizance of a Past Master until after the Union in 1813.

LECTURE II.

A DEFENCE OF MASONRY, OCCASIONED BY A PAMPHLET
CALLED MASONRY DISSECTED. BY DR. ANDERSON. A. D.
1730.

> "———————————— manibus date lilia plenis ;
> Purpureos spargam flores, animamque nepotis
> His saltum accumulem donis, et fungar inani
> Munere."
>
> VIRGIL.

AMONG the extraordinary discoveries of the present
age, nothing has been received with more delight and
exultation than a few sheets written, it seems, without
partiality, called Masonry Dissected. The grand secret,
which has long withstood the batteries of temptation ;
that neither money, the master key of the heart ; nor
good liquor, that unlocks the very soul ; nor hunger,
that breaks through stone walls ; nor thirst, a sore evil
to a working Mason, could bring to light ; has at last
been disgorged upon oath, to the great easement of a
tender stomach, the eternal scandal of the fraternity, and
the good of the public, never to be forgotten. The design was no less than to disburden a loaded conscience,
to acquaint the world that " never did so ridiculous an
imposition appear amongst mankind ; and to prevent so
many innocent persons being drawn into so pernicious a
society." What could induce the dissector to take that
oath, or the magistrate to admit it, shall not at this time
be decided. However, I must give the world joy of so
notable a discovery, so honourable, so circumstantiated !
A mighty expectation was raised, and, without doubt,
is wonderfully gratified by this course of anatomy. " It
must be this," the public will doubtless say, " it can be
nothing else. It is as we always supposed, a whimsical
cheat, supported by great names to seduce fools, who,

once gulled out of their money, keep the fraud secret to draw in others."

I confess, I cannot come into this method of arguing, nor is it, in my opinion, a fair way of treating a society, to run implicitly with the cry, without examining whether these reproaches are founded upon any thing in the mystery, as now represented, either wicked or ridiculous. For that stupid imputation of drawing in fools for the sake of their money, can have no weight in the present case. Since the fraternity, as it now stands, consists principally of members of great distinction, much superior to views so sordid and ungenerous. But for once, let this dissection contain all the secrets of Free-masonry; admit that every word of it is genuine and literally true, yet, under all these concessions, under all the disadvantages and prejudices whatever; I cannot but still believe there have been impositions upon mankind more ridiculous, and that many have been drawn into a society more pernicious.

I would not be thought agitated on this occasion, as if I were any way concerned whether this dissection be true or false; or whether the credit of Freemasonry be affected by it or not. These considerations can give me no trouble. My design is to address to the sensible and serious part of mankind, by making a few impartial remarks upon this dissection, without contending for the reputation of Masonry on the one hand, or reflecting upon the dissector on the other.

The formidable objection which has given offence to the better part of men, is the copy of the oath as it lies in the dissection. It has been a matter of admiration, that so many persons of great piety, strict conscience, and unspotted character, should lay themselves under so solemn an obligation, under penalties so terrible and astonishing, upon a subject so trifling and insignificant. To obviate this objection I observe, that the end, the moral, and purport of Masonry, as described in the dissection, is, "to subdue our passions; not to do our own will; to make a daily progress in a laudable art; to promote morality, charity, good fellowship, good nature, and humanity."[1] This appears to be the substance, let

[1] Anderson terms these pursuits "the substance of Masonry;" and, in-

11

the form or vehicle be ever so unaccountable. As for
the terms relating to architecture, geometry, and mathematics, that are dispersed throughout the dissection, it
would be strange if a society of such a denomination
could subsist wholly without them ; though they seem,
to me at least, to be rather technical and formal, yet
delivered perhaps by long tradition, than essentially attached to the grand design.

Now, where is the impiety—where the immorality,
or folly,[2] for a number of men to form themselves into a
society, whose main end is to improve in commendable
skill and knowledge ; and to promote universal beneficence and the social virtues of human life, under the
solemn obligation of an oath ?   And this, in what form,
under what secret restrictions, and with what innocent
ceremonies they think proper ?

This liberty all incorporate societies enjoy without
impeachment or reflection. An apprentice is bound to
keep the secrets of his master ; a freeman is obliged to
consult the interest of his company, and not to prostitute
in common the mysteries of his trade.   Secret committees and privy councils are solemnly enjoined not to
publish abroad their debates and resolutions.   There appears to be something like Masonry, as the dissector
describes it, in all regular societies of whatever denomination.   They are all held together by a sort of cement,
by bonds and laws that are peculiar to each of them,
from the highest to the little clubs and nightly meetings
of a private neighbourhood.   There are oaths administered, and sometimes solemn obligations to secrecy.
There are a master and two wardens, and a number of
assistants, to make what the dissector may call, if he
pleases, a perfect lodge in the city companies.   There is
the degree of entered prentices, master of his trade, or
fellowcraft and master, or the master of the company.
There are constitutions and orders, and a successive and

deed, they constitute invaluable landmarks which never have been, nor
ever can be altered.
    [2] It is not to be believed that the dissector really saw either impiety,
immorality, or folly, in the pursuits of the fraternity at their private
meetings.   His object appears to have been the public sale of his principles ; and it was doubtless remunerative.

gradual enjoyment of offices, according to the several rules and limitations of admissions.[3]

But it is replied, that the general design of Masonry may be commendable, or at least innocent, and yet carried on to the same advantage without the solemnity of an oath, especially pressed under such dreadful penalties. In answer to this I observe, that the question is not whether the purpose of Masonry may be as well served without an oath, but whether an oath, in the present case, be lawful, and may be taken with a good conscience. To solve this difficulty, I shall introduce the opinion of Bishop Sanderson,[4] the most judicious casuist that ever treated upon the subject of oaths, who says :—" When a thing is not by any precept or interdict, divine or human, so determined ; but every man, *pro hic et nunc*, may at his choice do or not do, as he sees expedient, let him do what he will, he sinneth not. As if Caius should swear to sell his land to Titius, or to lend him a hundred crowns ; the answer is brief, an oath in this case is both lawful and binding."

Now, I would know what precept, divine or human, has any way determined upon the contents of the dissection ? And whether the general design of Masonry, as there laid down, is not at least of equal benefit and importance to the public with the lending of an hundred crowns to a private man ? The answers to these questions are obvious, and the consequence is equally plain, that an oath upon the subject of Masonry is at least justi-

---

[3] In reality it was so. "The Master Masons in the middle ages were chiefly foreigners, incorporated by royal authority. When the foundation of an abbey was meditated, these artisans removed themselves in great numbers to any spot in any part of the kingdom. The ecclesiastics were the only men of science at that time. The Freemasons were blessed by the pope, and were first encouraged in England by Henry III., where they were constantly employed till the close of Gothic architecture. They had become masters of its geometrical principles, and were associated together as a distinct fraternity under a Master and Wardens. At the building or rebuilding of our cathedral churches they removed from one province to another by lodges. Their constitution and internal government were strictly regular ; and from the peculiar privileges which they obtained upon their first institution, they were enabled to conceal their art and modes of practice from the rest of the world. And this accounts for the general coincidence and character maintained throughout each era of the pointed style."

[4] De Obligatione Juramenti. Prælect. iii. s. 15.

fiable and lawful.   As for the terror of the penalty, the
world, upon that occasion, is commonly mistaken ; for
the solemnity of the oath does not in the least add to the
obligation ; or, in other words, the oath is equally binding without any penalty at all.   The same casuist has
this expression :—" A solemn oath of itself, and in its own
nature, is not more obligatory than a simple one, because
the obligation of an oath arises precisely from this, that
God is invoked as a witness and revenger, no less in a
simple oath than in the solemn and corporal ; for the invocation is made precisely by the pronunciation of the
words, which is the same both in the simple and solemn,
and not by any corporal motion or concomitant sign in
which the solemnity of the oath consists."[5]   I write to
intelligent readers, and therefore this citiation wants not
to be explained.

But further, if the oath in the dissection be taken by
all Masons upon their admission, no member of the fraternity, upon any pretence whatever, dares violate the
obligation of it without incurring the guilt of perjury ;
even supposing that Masonry were more trifling and indifferent than in the dissection it may appear to be.   And
therefore if the conduct of the dissector has staggered
the conscience of any one of the Brotherhood concerning
the observation of that oath, and has induced him to
trifle and play with the force of it, I hope he will desist
betimes, lest he becomes actually forsworn.[6]

Having taking off the weight of the great objection,
I shall now endeavour to remove an imputation which
has been often urged with great confidence, viz., that the

[5] Prælect. v. s. 12.

[6] The case is thus determined by the same casuist. (Ibid. iv. s. 11.)
"A voluntary oath is the more binding for being voluntary, because there
is no straiter obligation than that which we take willingly upon ourselves." And in another place the casuist is more particular. " Where
a matter," he says, " is so trivial that it is not worth the deliberation of
a wise man, nor matters a straw whether it be done or not done : as to
reach up a chip, or to rub one's beard ; or for the slightness of the matter is not much to be esteemed : as to give a boy an apple, or to lend a
pin ; an oath is binding in a matter of the least moment, because weighty
and trivial things have a like respect unto truth and falsehood.   And
farther, because every party swearing is bound to perform all he promised
as far as he is able, and as far as it is lawful.   But to give an apple
to a boy is both possible and lawful, he is bound, therefore, to perform it,
and ought to fulfil his oath." (Ibid. iii. s. 15.)

principles and the whole frame of Freemasonry is so very weak and ridiculous, as to be a reflection upon men of the least understanding to be concerned in it. And now, say the merry gentlemen, it appears evidently to be so by the dissection, which discovers nothing but an unintelligible heap of stuff and jargon, without common sense or connection.[7]

I confess I am of another opinion, though the scheme of Masonry, as revealed by the dissector, seems liable to exceptions. Nor is it so clear to me as to be fully understood at the first view, by attending only to the literal construction of the words; and for aught I know, the system, as taught in the regular lodges, may have some redundancies or defects, occasioned by the ignorance or indolence of the old members. And, indeed, considering through what obscurity and darkness the mystery has been delivered down, the many centuries it has survived, the many countries and languages and sects and parties it has run through, we are rather to wonder it ever arrived to the present age without more imperfection. In short, I am apt to think that Masonry, as it is now explained, has in some circumstances declined from its original purity. It has run long in muddy streams, and, as it were, underground; but notwithstanding the great rust it may have contracted, and the forbidding light in which it is placed by the dissector, there is still

---

[7] This is a very common charge against the Order by those who are ignorant of its design. It is scarcely within my province to answer objections, but I cannot dismiss the above observation without asking those who think Freemasonry "ridiculous and absurd," a few simple questions. Are gravity of demeanour and seriousness of deportment ridiculous? Are brotherly love and charity absurd? Are dissertations on the theological and cardinal virtues miserable stuff? Are prayer and praise to the Great Architect of the Universe unintelligible jargon? Are the sublime types of Christianity with which the Old Testament abounds ridiculous and absurd? The Order of Freemasonry then can be neither ridiculous nor absurd, because it abounds in all the above characteristics. And more than this; Freemasonry has not a single emblem—and they are numerous—a single ceremony, or a single reference, but what is consonant with the general principles of religion. Would Freemasonry, do such sceptics believe, be so extensively patronized by the noble, the learned, and the good, if it were, "an unintelligible heap of stuff and jargon, without common sense or connection." It is not to be believed. Every possible evidence contributes its aid to prove the purity and usefulness of the Order; and no testimonies exist that can establish a contrary opinion.

much of the old fabric remaining; the essential pillars
of the building may be discovered through the rubbish,
though the superstructure be overrun with moss and ivy,
and the stones, by length of time, be disjointed. And,
therefore, as the bust of an old hero is of great value
among the curious, though it has lost an eye, the nose,
or the right hand; so Masonry, with all its blemishes
and misfortunes, instead of appearing ridiculous, ought,
in my humble opinion, to be received with some candour
and esteem, from a veneration to its antiquity,

I was exceedingly pleased to find the dissector lay the
original scene of Masonry in the East, a country always
famous for symbolical learning supported by secrecy;
and I could not avoid immediately thinking of the old
Egyptians, who concealed the chief mysteries of their
religion under signs and symbols, called hieroglyphics.
So great was their regard for silence and secrecy that
they had a deity called Harpocrates,[8] whom they respected with peculiar honour and veneration.[9] A learned
author has described this idol thus :—" Harpocrates, the
god of silence, was represented with his right hand
placed near the heart, covered with a skin before, full
of eyes and ears, to signify that many things are to be
seen and heard which ought not to be spoken. And
among the same people, their great goddess Isis, the
same as Minerva, the goddess of strength and wisdom
amongst the Greeks, had always the image of a sphinx
placed in the entrance of her temples;[10] because their

[8] I must observe here, although I think I have made the same remark
elsewhere, that Mr. Wilkinson doubts this appropriation. In his " Manners and Customs of the ancient Egyptians," he says, that " the sign
adopted by the Egyptians to indicate silence is evidently shown, from the
sculptures on their monuments, to have been given by *placing the hand
over the mouth*, and not, as generally supposed, by approaching the finger
to the lips ; and the Greeks erroneously concluded that the youthful
Harpocrates was the deity of silence, from his appearing in this attitude ;
which, however humiliating to the character of a deity, was only illustrative of his extreme youth, and of a habit common to children in every
country, whether of ancient or modern times."

[9] Vide Imagines deorum, a Vincentio Chartario.

[10] The sphinx was used abundantly in the approaches to the Egyptian
temples for the above reason. The avenues leading to the temple of
Carnac were filled with them. A traveller, quoted by Goguet, says :—
" This palace shows itself by many avenues formed by rows of sphinxes,
the head turned to the inside of the alley. These figures, which are each

secrets should be preserved under sacred coverings, that they might be kept from the knowledge of the vulgar, as much as the riddles of Sphinx."

Pythagoras, by travelling into Egypt, became instructed in the mysteries of that nation ; and here he laid the foundation of all his symbolical learning. The several writers that have mentioned this philosopher,[11] and given an account of his sect and institutions, have convinced me fully that Freemasonry, as published by the dissector, is very nearly allied to the old Pythagorean discipline; from whence, I am persuaded it may, in some circumstances, very justly claim its descent. For instance, upon the admission of a disciple, he was bound by solemn oath to conceal the mysteries from the vulgar and uninitiated. The principal and most efficacious of their doctrines, says Iamblichus,[12] were ever kept secret amongst themselves ; they were continued unwritten, and preserved only by memory to their successors, to whom they delivered them as mysteries of the gods. They conversed with one another by signs, and had particular words, which they received upon their admission, and which were preserved with great reverence as the distinction of their sect ; for, it is the judicious remark of Laertius, as generals use watchwords to distinguish

twenty-one feet high, are distant from each other about the space of two paces. I have walked in four of these avenues, which ended at so many gates of the palace. I know not whether there were any more, because I only made half the circuit of that edifice, which appeared extremely spacious. I counted sixty sphinxes in the length of an alley, ranged opposite to an equal number, and fifty-one in another." Other travellers have told us that in one avenue they had the head of a bull ; in another, they were represented with a human head ; in a third with a ram's head. On approaching them the visitor is inspired with astonishment ; their enormous size strikes him with wonder and respect to the gods to whom they were dedicated. The immense colossal statues which are seated at each side of the gate, seem guarding the entrance to the holy ground.

[11] Vid. Iamblichus ; vit. Pyth. Laertius ; vit. Pyth. Porphyry. Clem. Alex. Strom., &c., &c.

[12] The words of Iamblichus were to this effect : The principal and most efficacious of their doctrines were never divulged, but kept with exact echemythia towards the uninitiated. They were never committed to writing, but transmitted to their successors by oral communication, as the sacred mysteries of the gods. And thus nothing of consequence went abroad from them. Their exoteric doctrines were only known within the walls ; and if by chance any cowan, or profane, or uninitiated person was found amongst them, they conversed with each other solely by symbols, which the stranger could not comprehend. (C. 17.)

their own soldiers from others, so it is proper to communicate to the initiated peculiar signs and words as distinctive marks of a society. The Pythagoreans professed
a great regard for what the dissector calls the four principles of Masonry, viz., a point, a line, a superficies, and
a solid ; and particularly held that a square was a very
proper emblem of the Divine Essence ; the gods, they
say, who are the authors of everything established in
wisdom, strength, and beauty, are not improperly represented by the figure of a square.[13]

Many more instances might be produced, would the
limits of my design admit; I shall only observe that
there was a false Brother, one Hipparchus,[14] of this sect,
who, out of spleen and disappointment, broke through
the bond of his oath, and committed the secrets of the
society to writing, in order to bring the doctrine into contempt. He was immediately expelled the school as a
person most infamous and abandoned—as one dead to all
sense of virtue and goodness ; and the Pythagoreans,
according to their custom, made a tomb for him, as if he
had been actually dead. The shame and disgrace that
justly attended this violation of his oath, threw the poor
wretch into a fit of madness and despair, so that he cut
his throat, and perished by his own hands ; and, which
surprised me to find, his memory was so abhorred after
his death, that his body lay upon the shore of the island
of Samos, and had no other burial than in the sands of
the sea !

The Essenes among the Jews were a sort of Pythagoreans, and corresponded in many particulars with the
practice of the fraternity, as delivered in the dissection.
Thus, when a person desired to be admitted into their
society, he was to pass through two degrees of probation,
before he could be a perfect master of their mysteries.
When he was received into the class of novices, he was
presented with a *white garment;* and when he had been
long enough to give some competent proofs of his secrecy
and virtue, he was admitted to further knowledge ; but
still he went on with the trial of his integrity and good
manners, and then was fully taken into the society.[15]

[13] Vid. Proclus in Euclid, l. xi. def. 2, 34.   [14] Clem. Alex. Strom. v.
[15] The Essenes, like the Pythagoreans, kept a perfect silence at table ;

But before he was received as an established member, he was first to bind himself by solemn obligations and professions,[16] to do justice, to do no wrong, to keep faith with all men, to embrace the truth, to keep his hands clear from theft and fraudulent dealing; not to conceal from his fellow-professors any of the mysteries, nor to communicate any of them to the profane, though it should be to save his life; to deliver nothing but what he received, and to endeavour to preserve the principle that he professes. They eat and drink at the same common table; and the fraternity that come from any other place are sure to be received there. They meet together in an assembly, and the right hand is laid upon the part between the chin and the breast, while the left hand is let down straight by their side.

The cabalists, another sect, dealt in hidden and mysterious ceremonies.[17] The Jews had a great regard for this science, and thought they had made uncommon discoveries by means of it. They divided their knowledge into speculative and operative. David and Solomon, they say, were exquisitely skilled in it, and nobody at first presumed to commit it by writing. But what seems most to the present purpose is, that the perfection of their skill consisted in what the dissector calls "lettering of it," or by ordering the letters of a word in a particular manner.[18]

and if ten of them sat together, no one was allowed to speak except by permission of the other nine. Nor could he be interrupted by words, although signs were allowed to be used for that purpose. They imitated the Pythagoreans also in another practice: the period which necessarily intervened between their first admission and their full initiation was five years, four of which were years of trial. The commencement of their probation was signified by their reception of dolabellum, perlzoma, and vestem albam; i. e., a spaddle, an apron, or girdle for the loins, and a white robe. They second year they were admitted to a participation in some of the exoteric secrets. If any one broke his oath, a hundred Essenes were assembled together, and he was formally expelled, which usually ended in his death.

[16] Philo de vita contemp. Josephus Ant. l. viii. c. 2.

[17] See Basnage's Hist. of the Jews, and Collier's Dict. on the word cabala.

[18] The cabala was transmitted from father to son, and from one generation to another, by tradition; and the Jews considered it as a sort of reparation for the loss of knowledge at the fall. They teach that their forefathers received the cabala at four several times by immediate revelations from heaven. First, it was communicated to Adam, who, being

The last instance I shall mention is that of the Druids in our own nation, who were the only priests among the ancient Britons.[19] In their solemnities they were clothed in white; and their ceremonies always ended with a good feast. Pomponius Mela relates of them, that their science was only an effort of memory; for they wrote down nothing, and they never failed to repeat many verses which they received by tradition.[20] Cæsar observes that they had a head or chief, who had sovereign power. This president exercised a sort of excommunication, attended with dreadful penalties, upon such as either divulged or profaned their mysteries. Thus, with reasonable allowance for distance of time, place, and other intermediate accidents, the preceding collections discover something, at least, like Masonry, if the dissection contains any such thing.

Whatever reflections may attend the following re-

very sad and sorrowful after his expulsion from the garden of Eden, and the consequent forfeiture of the confidence of his Creator, the angel Raguel was commissioned to appear unto him, not only to administer comfort, but also to give him such instructions as might repair the knowledge which he had lost by disobedience. This instruction the Jews call their cabala, which was lost a second time at the deluge, and again on the plain of Shinar, and was restored to Abraham. It was again lost during the Egyptian captivity, and communicated to Moses at the burning bush. The idolatry of the Jews in the Promised Land, caused it to be once more withdrawn, and it was revealed to Solomon in a dream, when he preferred wisdom to riches. The cabala was again lost at the Babylonish captivity; and, according to Jewish tradition, it was restored to Esdras, who, by God's command, withdrew himself into the wilderness forty days, attended by five scribes, and there wrote two hundred and four books, whereof the first one hundred and thirty-four were publicly read, but the other seventy were delivered to the Levites, and these they pretend to contain the secrets of their cabala.

[19] Vid. Cæsar. Com. l. vi. Sammes. Brit. b. i. c. 4.

[20] Those things which regarded the internal discipline of the Druids, and the mysteries of their religion, were conducted with the greatest privacy. "Docent multa, nobilissimos gentis," says P. Mela, "clam, et diu, vicenis annis, in specu, aut in abditis saltibus." (l. iii. c. 2.) And their effectual regard to secrecy is forcibly pointed out by what the author immediately adds—"Unum ex iis, que præcipiunt, in vulgus effluxit." The attentive ear of curiosity had been able to catch only one of their institutional triads. Cæsar also mentions the solicitude of the Druids, lest their discipline should be exposed to public view; and their religious meetings, though covered by the inaccessible grove, were holden in the night, as well as at noon.

Medio cum Phœbus in axe est,
Aut cœlum nox atra tenet.
Lucan. Pharsal. l. iii.

marks, arising either from an overflow of wit or ill-nature, I shall be unconcerned, and leave them wholly to the mercy of the serious reader ; only desiring them to remember that no more ought, in any case, to be expected than what the nature of it will reasonably admit. I own freely, I received a great pleasure in collecting, and was frequently surprised at the discoveries that must evidently occur to an observing eye. The conformity between the rites and principles of Masonry, if the dissection be true, and the many customs and ceremonies of the ancients, must give delight to a person of any taste and curiosity ; to find any remains of antique usage and learning preserved by a society for many ages without books or writing, by oral tradition only.

The number three is frequently mentioned in the dissection ; and I find that the ancients, both Greeks and Latins, professed a great veneration for that number. Theocritus[21] thus introduces a person who dealt in secret arts :—" Thrice thrice I pour, and thrice repeat my charms." Again in Ovid :[22]—" Verbaque ter dixit : thrice he repeats the words." And in Virgil :[23]—" Necte tribus nodis ternos, amarilli, colores : three colours in three knots unite." Whether this fancy owes its original to the number three, because containing a beginning, middle, and end, it seems to signify all things in the world ; or whether to the esteem the Pythagoreans and other philosophers had for it, on account of their triad or trinity ; or, lastly, to mention no more opinions, to its aptness to signify the power of the gods, who were divided into three classes, celestial, terrestrial, and infernal, I shall leave to be determined by others. The gods, however, had a particular esteem for this number, as Virgil asserts —" Numero deus impare gaudet : unequal numbers please the gods." We find three fatal sisters, three furies, three names and appearances of Diana—" Tria virginis ora Dianæ : three different forms does chaste Diana bear."[24] The sons of Saturn, among whom the empire of the world was divided, were three. And for the same reason we read of Jupiter's fulmen trifidum, or three-forked thunderbolt ; and of Neptune's trident, with

[21] Idyll. B. See the Landmarks of Masonry, vol. i. lect. ix.
[22] Metam. l. vii.
[23] Ecl. viii.   [24] Virgil. eclog. viii. Æneid. l. iv.

several other tokens of the veneration they had to this particular number.

A peculiar ceremony belonging to the oath, as declared by the dissector, bears a near relation to a form of swearing among the ancients, mentioned by a learned author.[25] The person who took the oath was to be upon his bare knees, with a naked sword pointed to his throat, invoking the sun, moon, and stars to be witnesses to the truth of what he swore.[26]

A part of the Mason's Catechism has given occasion to a great deal of idle mirth and ridicule, as the most trifling and despicable sort of jargon that men of common sense ever submitted to. The bone-box and the tow-line have given wonderful diversion. I think there are some verses in the last chapter of the book of Ecclesiastes, which in some manner resemble this form of expression. I shall transcribe them, with the opinion of the learned upon them, without making any particular application. The passage is as follows:[27]—" In the day when the keepers of the house shall tremble ; and the grinders cease because they are few ; and those that look out at the windows be darkened ; and the doors shall be shut up in the streets ; when the sound of the grinding is low ; and he shall rise up at the voice of the bird ; and all the daughters of music shall be brought low ; or ever the silver cord be loosed, or the golden bowl be broken, or the pitcher be broken at the fountain, or the wheel broken at the cistern." The expositors upon these verses are almost unanimous in their opinion,[28] that they ought to be thus explained :—The keepers of the house are the shoulders, arms, and hands of the human body ; the grinders are the teeth ; those that look out at the windows are the two eyes ; the doors are the lips ; the streets are the mouth ; the sound of the grinding is the noise of the voice ; the

---

[25] Alexander ab Alexandro. l. v. c. 10.

[26] The Druids had a similar custom. It was a necessary duty of the bards to *unsheath the sword* against those who had forfeited their obligation by divulging any of the secrets of the Order. In this respect their custom was the same as that of all other nations. Thus, in the introduction to Llywarch Hen, we find that the custom was to " call upon the delinquent three times, proclaiming that *the sword was naked against him.*" The same ceremony was used in the Eleusinian mysteries.

[27] Eccles. xii. 3, 4, 6.

[28] Bishop Patrick, Smith, Foster, Melancthon, &c.. &c.

voice of the bird is the crowing of the cock; the daughters of music are the two ears; the silver cord is the string of the tongue; the golden bowl is the pia mater; the pitcher at the fountain is the heart, the fountain of life; the wheel is the great artery; and the cistern is the left ventricle of the heart.[29]

There could not possibly have been devised a more significant token of love, friendship, integrity, and honesty, than the joining of the right hands—a ceremony made use of by all civilized nations, as a token of a faithful and true heart. Fides, or Fidelity, was a deity among the ancients, of which a learned writer[30] has given this description:—The proper residence of faith or fidelity was thought to be in the right hand, and therefore this deity was sometimes represented by two right hands joined together; sometimes by two little images shaking each other by the right hand; so that the right hand was esteemed by the ancients as a sacred symbol. And agreeably to this are those expressions in Virgil—" En dextra fidesque ;" as if shaking by the right hand was an inseparable token of an honest heart. And again—" Cur dextræ jungere dextram non datur, et veras audire et reddere voces ?" That is, why should we not join right hand to right hand, and hear and speak the truth?

" In all contracts and agreements," says Archbishop Potter,[31] " it was usual to take each other by the right hand, that being the manner of plighting faith. And this was done either out of respect to the number *ten*, as some say, there being ten fingers on the two hands; or because such a conjunction was a token of amity and concord; whence at all friendly meetings they joined hands as a sign of the union of their souls. It was one of the cautions of Pythagoras to his disciples—'take heed to whom you offer your right hand;' which is thus explained by Iamblichus,[32] 'take no one by the right hand but the initiated, that is, in the mystical form, for the vulgar and profane are altogether unworthy of the mystery.' "[33]

---

[29] The above passage contains such an admirable illustration of the tropical hieroglyphic, that I cannot forbear calling particular attention to it.   [30] Chartarius in lib. ut supra.
[31] Ant. of Greece, vol. i. p. 251.   [32] In vit. Pythagoras.
[33] The exact words of Iamblichus are very expressive :—" Give not

The dissector frequently taking notice of the number *seven*, I instantly recurred to the old Egyptians, who held the number seven to be sacred; more especially they believed that whilst their feast of seven days lasted, the crocodiles lost their inbred cruelty. And Leo Afer, in his description of Africa, says, that in his time the custom of feasting seven days and nights, was used for the happy overflowing of the Nile. The Greeks and Latins professed the same regard for that number, which might be proved by many examples.

The accident by which the body of Master Hiram was found after his death, seems to allude, in some circumstances, to a beautiful passage in the sixth book of Virgil's Æneid. Anchises had been dead for some time, and Æneas, his son, professed so much duty to his departed father, that he consulted witht he Cumæan sibyl, whether it were possible for him to descend into the *shades below*, in order to speak with him. The prophetess encouraged him to go; but told him he could not succeed, unless he went into a certain place and plucked a *golden bough* or *shrub*, which he should carry in his hand, and by that means obtain directions where he should find his father. The words are well translated by Dryden, viz. :—

```
——————————————in the neighbouring grove
There stands a tree; the queen of Stygian Jove
Claims it her home; thick woods and gloomy night
Conceal the happy plant from mortal sight.
One bough it bears, but wondrous to behold,
The ductile rind and leaves are radiant gold;
This from the vulgar branches must be torn,
And to fair Proserpine the present borne,
Ere leave be given to tempt the nether skies;
The first thus rent, a second will arise,
And the same metal the same room supplies.
The willing metal will obey thy hand,
Following with ease.
```

your right hand easily : that is, draw not towards you improper and uninitiated persons by giving them your right hand; for to such as have not been long tried by repeated disciplines and doctrines, and who have not proved themselves fit to participate in the mysteries by a quinquennial silence and other trials, the right hand ought not to be given." Pythagoras had a similar moral reference to the right foot. One of his symbols was—" Pluck off your right shoe first, but put your left foot first into the basin ;" by which he exhorted his disciples to active prudence. The *right* represented good actions, which ought to be performed; and the *left* bad ones, which ought to be laid aside and rejected.

Anchises, the great preserver of the Trojan name, could not have been discovered but by the help of a *bough*, which was plucked with great ease from the tree; nor, it seems, could Hiram, the Grand Master of Masonry, have been found, but by the direction of a *shrub*,[34] which, says, the dissector, came easily up. The principal cause of Æneas's descent into the shades was to inquire of his father *the secrets of the Fates*, which should some time be fulfilled among his posterity. And in like manner the occasion of the Brethren searching so diligently for their Master was, it seems, to receive from him *the secret word of Masonry*, which should be delivered down to their fraternity in after ages.[35] This remarkable verse follows :—

> Præterea jacet exanimum tibi corptus amici,
> Heu nescis!

> The body of your friend lies near you dead,
> Alas, you know not how!

This was Misenus, that was murdered and buried, *monte sub ærio*, under a high hill; as, says the dissector, Master Hiram was.[36]

[34] In the Jewish Talmud there is an account of the death of Hiram, in unison with the above tradition. So says M. Laurens, in his Essais sur le F. Maçonnerie. But be that correct or not, the shrub or sprig of acacia, here referred to, cannot be the acacia of modern botanists. The word, as we use it, is entirely allegorical, and there are some doubts whether it was ever applied by Masons to a shrub till the beginning of the last century.

[35] The Hebrews attributed mystical powers to certain secret words which they called Tetragrammaton, and these were esteemed ineffable. In like manner the Pythagoreans venerated the Tetractys, a word which was very early corrupted in the pagan world to JAO, JAVE, JUBA, JOVAH, &c. Warburton mentions some secret words which were used in the Eleusinian mysteries. " When the ceremony," says he, " of initiation was over, then came the Aporreta, and delivered the hymn called the Theology of Idols. After this the assembly was dismissed with these two mysterious words, *KOГ϶, OMΠAΞ*, which have been variously translated, and constituted the secret tokens by which the initiated made themselves known to each other.

[36] An intelligent and highly respected friend and Brother, who feels inclined to understand our allegories astronomically, writes to me thus on the above subject:—" Whatever might have been the absolute origin of the mysteries of the spurious Freemasonry, I have no doubt but they ended in a mythological death of the sun ; and, that finally they merged into a celebration of the vernal equinox, when the sun was about to give more light and vigour to the earth for the next six months. At one time I thought to connect the solar murderers with the opposition made

But there is another story in Virgil that stands in a
nearer relation to the case of Hiram, and the accident by
which he is said to have been discovered, which is this :—
Priamus, King of Troy, in the beginning of the Trojan
war, committed his son Polydorus to the care of Polym-
nestor, King of Thrace, and sent with him a great sum
of money.   But after Troy was taken, the Thracian, for
the sake of the money, killed the young prince and privately buried him.   Æneas, coming into that country,
and *accidentally plucking up a shrub that was near him on the
side of a hill*, discovered the murdered body of Polydorus.
Thus Dryden :—

> Not far a rising hillock stood in view,
> Sharp myrtles on the sides and cornels grew ;
> There while I went to crop the sylvan scenes,
> And shade our altar with the leafy greens,
> *I pulled a plant ;* with horror I relate
> A prodigy so strange and full of fate,
> Scarce dare I tell the sequel.   From the womb
> Of wounded earth, and caverns of the tomb,
> A groan, as of a troubled ghost, renew'd
> My fright ; and then these dreadful words ensued—
> Why dost thou thus my buried body rend ?
> Oh spare the corpse of thy unhappy friend !

The agreement between these two relations is so
exact, that there wants no further illustration.

We are told that a sprig of cassia was placed by the
Brethren at the head of Hiram's grave ;[37] which refers to
an old custom of those eastern countries of embalming
the dead, in which operation cassia was always used,

by some of the winter signs to his progress towards the summer ones; but
I could never satisfy myself on that point.   The weeping for Tammuz is
said to have taken place at the summer solstice, when the sun commenced
his retreat ; and it is possible that mysteries were also celebrated then,
although I have only turned my attention to those connected with our
more direct traditions."

[37] In more modern times a sprig of laurel or rosemary was used for the
same purpose.   Thus Misson, in his Travels, says :—" When the funeral
procession is ready to set out, they nail up the coffin, and a servant presents the company with sprigs of rosemary ; every one takes a sprig and
carries it in his hand till the body is put into the grave, at which time
they all throw in their sprigs after it."   Sometimes, however, other herbs
were substituted, as appears from the following passage in an old play—

———— our showre shall crowne
His sepulcher with olive, myrh, and bayes,
The plants of peace, of sorrow, victorie.

At present, flowers of any description are placed *in the coffin*.

especially in preparing the head, and drying up the
brains, as Herodotus more plainly explains. The sweet
wood, perfumes, and flowers, used about the graves of
the dead,[38] occur so frequently in the old poets, that it
would be tedious to mention them.[39] Ovid thus describes the death of the phœnix :[40]

> Upon a shady tree she takes her rest,
> And on the highest bough her funeral nest
> Her beak a jc t alon, build ; the j v tre ws thereon
> Balm, *cassia*, spikenard, myrrh, and cinnamon ;
> Last on the fragrant pile herself she lays,
> And in consuming odours ends her days.

[38] The Grecian graves were always marked by a shrub called πούος,
or a garland of herbs. In honour of the dead they threw boughs and
leaves upon the grave ; as Euripides says they did to Polyxena when she
died ; for in latter times, if a man had won a race or the like, they had a
custom to bedeck his valiant corpse with boughs and leaves of myrtle, as
in Euripides, Elect. v. 510. Whether there was any allusion to the golden
bough of Virgil in all this, I will not say. In Italy they had the same
customs ; for Varro says :—" Ad sepulchrum ferunt frondes." And they
not only cast leaves upon the graves, but also strewed them with garlands,
as will appear by the words of Minutius Felix to Octavius—Coronas
etiam sepulchris denegati, &c. See Archæol. Attic. l. v. c. 32.

[39] Speaking of nocturnal funerals, an old writer says :—" Certainly, (in
my poor opinion, as I have already said,) they, i. e., blank, nocturnal
funerals are unfit for the noble, who have ensignes and markes of honour
to display, and should so have spent theyr time, that theyr luciflorian
deeds should not need, after theyr deceases, to fear either speech or light.
A custome so old and venerable, that Cicero, in his short commentarie
or annotation upon this fragment of the lawes of the twelve tables—*Ne
longæ coronæ nec acerræ prætereantur*, hath these memorable words—Illa
jam significatio est, laudis ornamenta ad mortuos pertinere ; quod *coronam*
virtute partam, et ei qui peperisset, et ejus parenti sine fraude esse im-
positam lex jubet. And to this honourable rite of placing the *garland*
or crown, which the deceased Roman gentleman had atchieved by his ver-
tue and valor, upon his funeral beare, herse, or coffin, there hath, here
among us in these parts of the world, and in the latter times, from the
decay of the empire of Rome, commendablie succeeded the use of coats
of arms, and other ornamental ceremonies at funerals."

[40] Metam. l. xv.

LECTURE III.

ON THE ADVANTAGES ENJOYED BY THE FRATERNITY.
BY MARTIN CLARE, ESQ., M. A., JUNIOR G. WARDEN, 1735.

> Hail to the craft! at whose serene command
> The gentle arts in glad obedience stand ;
> Hail, sacred Masonry ! of source divine,
> Unerring sovereign of the unerring line ;
> Whose plumb of truth, with never-failing sway,
> Makes the joined parts of symmetry obey ;
> Whose magic stroke bids fell confusion cease,
> And to the finished orders gives a place ;
> Who calls vast structures from the womb of earth,
> And gives imperial cities glorious birth.
> To works of art her merit not confined,
> She regulates the morals, squares the mind ;
> Corrects with care the sallies of the soul,
> And points the tide of passions where to roll.
>
> CUNNINGHAM.

THE chief pleasures of society, viz., good conversation, and the consequent improvements, are rightly presumed, Brethren, to be the principal motive of our first entering into, and then of propagating our craft,[1] wherein those advantages, I am bold to say, may be better met with than in any society now in being ; provided we are not wanting to ourselves, and will but consider, that the

---

[1] A reverend Brother, belonging to the Grand Lodge of Alabama, echoes these sentiments. He says :—" Masonry inculcates morality and benevolence. She teaches us to reverence the name of God, to curb irregular passions and appetites, and to be good and loyal subjects of the government ; but she does not profess to change the heart and prepare man for a better life, although, in her instructions, she directs to that God who can pardon sin, constantly reminding us that the same eye which watches the sun, moon, and stars, searches the inmost recesses of the heart, and will eventually bring into judgment every thought, word, and action."

basis of our Order is indissoluble friendship, and the cement of it unanimity and brotherly-love.[2] That these may always subsist in this society, is the sincere desire of every worthy Brother ; and, that they may do so in full perfection here, give me leave to lay before you a few observations, wherein are pointed out those things which are the most likely to discompose the harmony of conversation, especially when it turns upon controverted points. It is, Brethren, a very delicate thing to interest one's-self in a dispute, and yet preserve the decorum due to the occasion. To assist us a little in this matter, is the subject of what I have at present to offer to your consideration ; and I doubt not but the bare mention of what may be disagreeable in any kind of debate, will be heedfully avoided by a body of gentlemen, united by the bonds of Brotherhood, and under the strictest ties of mutual love and forbearance.[3]

By the outward demeanour it is that the inward civility of the mind is generally expressed ; the manner and

[2] Dalcho, an American Grand Master of Masons, in his official oration (p. 19), directs the Brethren to " love the whole human species, but particularly those who are united by the mystic union. When the deep sighs of poverty assail your ear," he continues, " stretch forth the hand of relief, and chase necessity and want from a Brother's door. If afflicted by misfortune, comfort their souls, and soothe them to tranquillity. And if they are exposed to danger, give them your assistance. It is this sympathy with the pleasures and pains, with the happiness and misfortunes of our fellow-men, which distinguishes us from other animals, and is the source of all our virtues."

[3] Nothing could have been better chosen than this subject for a lecture from a grand officer in the infancy of the new grand lodge, and when the Brethren, fresh from other societies, where debates were carried on without regard to the personal feelings of the disputants, would be inclined to introduce into Masonry the same pertinacious and forbidding custom, which is utterly at variance with the fundamental principles of the craft. The ancient charges of Masonry were applied to counteract this unsocial practice. Thus, in the first edition of Anderson's Constitutions, we find the following directions for behaviour in the lodge :—" You must not hold private committees, or separate conversation, without leave from the Master ; nor talk anything impertinent ; nor interrupt the Master or Wardens, or any Brother speaking to the chair ; nor act ludicrously while the lodge is engaged in what is serious and solemn ; but you are to pay due reverence to the Master, Wardens, and Fellows, and put them to worship. No private piques, no quarrels about nations, families, religion, or politics, must be brought within the door of the lodge ; for as Masons we are of the oldest Catholic religion, and, of all nations, upon the square, level, and plumb ; and, like our predecessors in all ages, we are resolved against political disputes, as contrary to the peace and welfare of the lodge."

circumstances of which, being much governed and influenced by the fashion and usage of the place where we live, must, in the rule and practice of it, be learned by observation, and the carriage of those who are allowed to be polite and well-bred.   But the more essential part of civility lies deeper than the outside, and is that general good-will, that decent regard and personal esteem for every man, which makes us cautious of showing, in our carriage towards him, any contempt, disrespect, or neglect.   It is a disposition that makes us ready on all occasions to express, according to the usual way and fashion of address, a respect, a value and esteem for him, suitable to his rank, quality, and condition in life.   It is, in a word, a disposition of the mind visible in the carriage, whereby a man endeavours to shun making another uneasy in his company.

For the better avoiding of which, in these our conventions, suffer me, Brethren, to point out to you four things, directly contrary to this the most proper and the most acceptable conveyance of the social virtues, from some one of which, incivility will generally be found to have its rise, and of consequence that discord and want of harmony in conversation, too frequently to be observed.

The first of these is a natural roughness, which makes a man uncomplaisant to others ; so that he retains no deference, nor has any regard to the inclinations, temper, or condition of those he converses with.   It is the certain mark of a clown, not to mind what either pleases or offends those he is engaged with.   And yet one may sometimes meet with a man in clean and fashionable clothes, giving an absolute, unbounded swing to his own humour herein, and suffering it to jostle and overbear everything that stands in its way, with a perfect indifference how people have reason to take it. This is a brutality every one sees and abhors.   It is what no one can approve, or be easy with ; and therefore it finds no place with those who have any tincture of good breeding—the end and design of which is, to supple our natural stiffness, and to soften men's tempers, that they may bend and accommodate themselves to those with whom they have to do.[4]

⁴ This observation was intended to illustrate that significant masonic

Contempt is the second thing inconsistent with good-breeding, and is entirely averse to it. And if this want of respect be discovered, either in a man's looks, words, or gesture, come it from whom it will, it always brings uneasiness and pain along with it; for nobody can contentedly bear to be slighted.

A third thing of the like nature is censoriousness, or a disposition to find fault with others. Men, whatever they are guilty of, would not choose to have their blemishes displayed and set in open view. Failings always carry some degree of shame with them; and the discovery, or even imputation of any defect, is not borne by them without uneasiness.

Raillery must be confessed to be the most refined way of exposing the faults of others; and, because it is commonly done with some wit, in good language, and enter-tains the company, people are apt to be. led into a mistake, that where it keeps within fair bounds there is no incivility in it. The pleasantry of this sort of conversation introduces it often, therefore, among people of the better sort; and such talkers, it must be owned, are well heard, and generally applauded by the laughter of the standers-by; but it ought at the same time to be considered, that the entertainment of the company is at the cost of the person who is painted in burlesque characters, who therefore cannot be without some uneasiness on the occasion, unless the subject, on which he is rallied, be matter of commendation; in which case the pleasant images which make the raillery, carrying with them praise as well as sport, the rallied person, finding his account in it, may also take a part in the diversion.

But as the right management of so nice a point, wherein the least slip may spoil all, is not every body's talent, it is better that such as would be secure of not provoking others, should wholly abstain from raillery, which by a small mistake, or wrong turn, may leave,

symbol, the chisel, which demonstrates the advantages of discipline and education. The mind, like the diamond in its original state, is unpolish-ed; but as the effects of the chisel on the external coat soon present to view the latent beauties of the diamond, so education discovers the latent virtues of the mind, and draws them forth to range a large field of matter and space, in order to display the summit of human knowledge, our duty to God, our neighbour, and ourselves.

upon the mind of those who are stung by it, the lasting memory of having been sharply, though wittily, taunted, for something censurable in them.[5]

Contradiction is also a sort of censoriousness, wherein ill-breeding much too often shows itself. Complaisance does not require that we should admit of all the reasonings, or silently approve of all the accounts of things, that may be vented in our hearing. The opposing the ill-grounded opinions, and the rectifying the mistakes of others, is what truth and charity sometimes require of us; nor does civility forbid, so it be done with proper caution and due care of circumstance. But there are some men who seem so perfectly possessed, as it were, with the spirit of contradiction and perverseness, that they steadily, and without regard either to right or wrong, oppose some one, and perhaps every one of the company, in whatsoever is advanced. This is so evident and outrageous a degree of censuring, that none can avoid thinking himself injured by it.

All sort of opposition to what another man says, is so apt to be suspected of censoriousness, and is so seldom received without some sort of humiliation, that it ought to be made in the gentlest manner, and couched in the softest expressions that can be found, and such as, with the whole deportment, may express no forwardness to contradict. All possible marks of respect and good-will ought to accompany it, that whilst we gain the argument, we may not lose the good inclinations of any that hear, and especially of those who happen to differ from us.[6]

---

[5] This was guarded against by an earnest charge to the candidate at his initiation, and being frequently repeated, was likely to make a permanent impression. In a charge which was delivered at this period, we find the following passage:—" In the lodge you are to behave with all due decorum. lest the beauty and harmony thereof should be disturbed and broken. You are to be obedient to the Master and presiding officers, and to apply yourself closely to the business of Masonry, that you may the sooner become a proficient therein, both for your own credit and for that of the lodge. . . . . Nothing can be more shocking to all faithful Masons, than to see any of their Brethren profane or break through the sacred rule of their Order; and if any are found capable of doing so, their initiation is sincerely regretted."

[6] This was symbolized by the prohibition of metal tools at the building of King Solomon's temple, which " was built of stone made ready before it was brought thither, so that there was neither hammer, axe, nor any tool of iron heard in the house while it was in building" (1 Kings vi. 7):

And here we ought not to pass by an ordinary, but a very great fault, that frequently happens in almost every dispute, I mean that of interrupting others while they are speaking. This is a failing, which the members of the best-regulated confraternities among us have endeavoured to guard against in the by-laws of their respective societies, and is what the right worshipful person in the chair should principally regard, and see well put in execution.[7] Yet as it is an ill practice that prevails much in the world, and especially where less care is taken, it cannot be improper to offer a word or two against it here.

There cannot be a greater rudeness than to interrupt another in the current of his discourse; for if it be not impertinence and folly to answer a man, before we know what he has to say, yet is it a plain declaration that we are weary of his discourse; that we disregard what he says, as judging it not fit to entertain the society with; and is, in fact, little less than a downright desiring that ourselves may have audience, who have something to produce better worth the attention of the company. As this is no ordinary degree of disrespect, it cannot but give always a very great offence.[8]

The fourth thing, Brethren, that is against civility, and therefore apt to overset the harmony of conversation, is captiousness. And it is so, not only because it often produces misbecoming and provoking expressions and

emblematical of the harmony and peace which subsisted amongst the workmen in their respective lodges.

[7] It is his especial duty to do this; for which reason he is symbolically classed with the two great luminaries of the sky, because he ought to rule and govern his lodge with the same order and regularity as the sun rules the day and the moon the night. This duty is intimated by the jewel with which he is invested. It teaches him, and all who see it glittering on his breast, to regulate their actions by rule and line, and to harmonize their conduct by the principles of morality and virtue. And he is to be assisted in the performance of his responsible duties by his two chief officers, who are enjoined to promote good order and regularity; and by a due regard to the laws in their own conduct, to enforce obedience to them in the conduct of others.

[8] Such irregularities, however, are sure to accompany a lack of discipline, without an uniform attention to which no society can expect to be permanently successful; and discipline can only be supported in all its beauty, and all its efficacy, by pursuing, in an undeviating course, that line of conduct which is marked out by the wisdom of our superior governors, and laid down, in broad characters, in the book of constitutions.

behaviour in a part of the company, but because it is a tacit accusation and a reproach for something ill taken from those we are displeased with. Such an intimation, or even suspicion, must always be uneasy to society; and as one angry person is sufficient to discompose a whole company, for the generality, all mutual happiness and satisfaction cease therein on any such jarring. This failing, therefore, should be guarded against with the same care, as either the boisterous rusticity and insinuated contempt, or the ill-natured disposition to censure, already considered and disallowed of. For as peace, ease, and satisfaction are what constitute the pleasure, the happiness, and are the very soul of conversation; if these be interrupted, the design of society is undermined, and in that circumstance, how should brotherly-love continue? Certain it is, that unless good order, decency, and temper be preserved by the individuals of society, confusion will be introduced, and a dissolution will naturally, very quickly, follow.[9]

What, therefore, remains is to remind the Brethren that Masons have ever been lovers of order. It is the business of their particular profession to reduce all rude matters to truth. Their aphorisms recommend it. The number of their lights,[10] and the declared end of their

[9] To prevent this result, various laws have been at different times enacted by the Grand Lodge. The general Grand Royal Arch Chapter of the northern States of America, promulgated at the latter end of the last century some excellent practical regulations, which cannot be too strongly recommended. "It shall be incumbent on the Grand High Priest, King, and Scribe, severally to improve and perfect themselves in the sublime arts and work of Mark Masters, Past Masters, Most Excellent Masters, and Royal Arch Masons; to make themselves masters of the several masonic lectures and ancient charges; to consult with each other, and with the Grand High Priests, &c., of other States, for the purpose of adopting measures suitable and proper for diffusing a knowledge of the said lectures and charges, and an uniform mode of working, in the several chapters and lodges throughout this jurisdiction; and the better to effect this laudable purpose, the aforesaid grand officers are severally hereby authorized and empowered to visit and preside in any and every chapter of Royal Arch Masons, and lodge of Most Excellent, Past or Mark Master Masons, throughout the said States, and to give such instructions and directions as the good of the fraternity may require, *always adhering to the ancient landmarks of the Order.*"

[10] The prophet Daniel says (xii. 3):—" Those who are wise shall be shining with light, and those who shall influence others to do justly, shall shine eternally as the stars." Solomon expresses the same thought by

coming together, intimate the frame and disposition of mind wherewith they are to meet, and the manner of their behaviour when assembled.

Shall it, then, ever be said that those, who by choice are distinguished from the gross of mankind, and who voluntarily have enrolled their names in this most ancient and honourable society, are so far wanting to themselves and the Order they profess, as to neglect its rules? Shall those who are banded and cemented together, by the strictest ties of amity, omit the practice of forbearance and brotherly-love?[11] or shall the passions of those persons ever become ungovernable, who assemble purposely to subdue them?

We are, let it be considered, the successors of those, who reared a structure to the honour of Almighty God, the Grand Architect of the world, which for wisdom, strength, and beauty hath never yet had any parallel.[12]

saying, that " the head of the wise is of the purest gold." (Cant., v. 11.) Jesus Christ announces that "the just shall shine as the sun in the kingdom of his Father." (Matt. xiii. 43.)

[11] Or to express all in one word—Charity, on which our science is based. This is an evident proof, if we had no other, that Freemasonry is not an offshoot from the mysteries of heathenism, which knew nothing of this heaven-born virtue. They deified faith and hope, and many other virtues and vices, but charity was excluded from their creed. They had none of those buds and blossoms, and fruit of charity, which Freemasonry now possesses. Orphan schools, asylums for the destitute, and funds of benevolence were unknown. Not a single individual amongst the innumerable dii minorum gentium, not even the bona dea, answer to the character of charity. The Assyrians, and a few other nations, had indeed a subordinate deity, called Beneficium ; but it was a selfish deity, and worshipped only as the dispenser of benefits to the devotee. The only approach which the mythology of heathen nations made to this virtue, was in the personification of the three graces, which were called Charities. They were supposed to preside over kindness and other good offices; and were represented naked, because kindnesses ought to be done with sincerity and candour. Their hands were joined, to signify that kindness amongst friends ought to be unceasing and perpetual. But this is a very imperfect resemblance to the charity of our noble Order, which " beareth all things, believeth all things, hopeth all things."

[12] And without wisdom to contrive, strength to support, beauty to adorn, no piece of architecture can be completed. These pillars, therefore, refer to the three governors of the lodge. The pillar of wisdom represents the Worshipful Master, whose business it is to *contrive* the most proper and efficient means of instructing and improving the Brethren in Masonry. The pillar of strength refers to the Senior Warden, whose duty it is to *support* the authority, and facilitate the designs of the Master, and to see that his commands are carried into effect. The

12

We are intimately related to those great and worthy spirits, who have ever made it their business and their aim to improve themselves, and to inform mankind.[13] Let us, then, copy their example, that we may also hope to obtain a share in their praise. This cannot possibly be done in a scene of disorder: pearls are never found but when the sea is calm; and silent water is generally deepest.

It has been long, and still is, the glory and happiness of this society, to have its interest espoused by the great, the noble, and the honoured of the land. Persons who, after the example of the wisest and the grandest of kings, esteem it neither condescension or dishonour to patronize and encourage the professors of the craft.[14] It is

pillar of beauty is the Junior Warden, whose duty it is to *adorn* the work with all the powers of his genius and industry; to promote regularity amongst the Brethren by the sanction of his own example, that pleasure and profit may be the mutual result. Thus, by the united energies of these three representatives of wisdom, strength, and beauty, Freemasonry is established, firm as a rock in the midst of the ocean, braving the malignant shafts of envy and detraction; its summit gilded with the rays of the meridian sun, though storms may beat eternally on its basis.

[13] This is intimated by the jewel which distinguishes the Senior Warden. It demonstrates that we are descended from the same stock, partake of the same nature, and share the same hope; and that though distinctions among men are necessary to preserve subordination, yet no eminence of station can make us forget that we are Brethren, and that he who is placed on the lowest spoke of Fortune's wheel may be entitled to our regard; because a time will come, and the wisest knows not how soon, when all distinctions. but that of goodness, shall cease, and death, the grand leveller of all human greatness, shall reduce us all to our original elements—dust and ashes.

[14] A writer in an American periodical (Bro. H. Brown, Esq., barrister at law), thus expresses his opinion of the true influence and operation of Masonry:—" Masonry has continued to flourish. It has pervaded almost every portion of the habitable globe, and extended its salutary influence to the distressed in every climate, unnerved the warrior's arm on the shores of our inland seas, and converted the uplifted tomahawk's sanguinary blow into a fraternal embrace. Even the mighty Tecumseh felt its influence, and amid the carnage of battle, the groans of expiring victims, and the cries of savage torture, stepped from his ranks to save a fallen foe—because he was a Brother. And well it may. Freemasonry regards no man for his worldly wealth or riches. It is, therefore, the internal and not the external qualifications which we cherish and admire. The hand that grasps a spade, and the hand that wields a sceptre, are equally entitled to our friendly grip. No matter whether an African or an Indian sun may have burned upon him—no matter in what disastrous battle his liberties may have been cloven down—no matter if, like Laza-

our duty, in return, to do nothing inconsistent with this favour; and being members of this body, it becomes us to act in some degree suitable to the honour we receive from our illustrious head.

If this be done at our general meetings, every good and desirable end will very probably be promoted among us. The craft will have the advantage of being governed by good, wholesome, and dispassionate laws;[16] the business of the grand lodge will be smoothly and effectually carried on; your grand officers will communicate their sentiments, and receive your opinions and advice with pleasure and satisfaction; particular societies will become still more regular, from what their representatives shall observe here. In a word, true and ancient Masonry will flourish; and those that are without, will soon come to know that there are more substantial pleasures to be found, as well as greater advantages to be reaped, in our society, orderly conducted, than can possibly be met with in any other bodies of men, how magnificent soever

rus, he has lain at the rich man's gate, and the dogs have licked his sores, the moment he enters a lodge of Free and Accepted Masons, the distinctions of wealth, of rank, and of power, flee before him, and he finds himself among friends and Brothers, ready to assist, defend, and protect him."

[16] These distinctions have not been withdrawn from the Order. Bro. Tenison, a celebrated barrister in the sister isle, said, in an address to the Brethren:—"The higher orders and well-informed classes were coming forward to seek the honours of Masonry. Why? because they were convinced that it did not contain anything derogatory to the dignity of a gentleman, unworthy the acceptation of a free citizen, contrary to the conscientious scruples of a believing Christian, or opposed to that allegiance which is due to our sovereign lady the Queen. But, on the other hand, its ordinances and discipline have been productive of the happiest effects, by cementing in personal friendship people of different creeds and countries, and uniting in the sacred sympathies of social life those who, in this distracted land, would otherwise be divided through the discordant materials of politics or party. Yes, my Brethren, persons of property and intelligence are now pressing forward to assist in the resuscitation of our lodges, encouraged by the hope of doing good, regardless of the supineness of mere nominal Masons, and despising the hostility of those who are unbound by—

> Honour's sacred tie, the law of kings;
> The noble mind's distinguishing perfection;
> That aids and strengthens virtue where it meets her,
> And imitates her actions where she is not—

would crumble in the dust a fabric built for the shelter of infant destitution or aged decay, and which presents a common centre, where all can associate without being disturbed by a difference of opinion."

their pretensions may be.   For none can be so amiable
as that which promotes brotherly-love, and fixes that as
the grand cement of all our actions; to the performance
of which we are bound by an obligation, both solemn
and awful, and that entered into by our own free and
deliberate choice; and as it is to direct our lives and
actions, it can never be too often repeated, nor too
frequently inculcated.

LECT·URE IV.

ON THE CONNEXION BETWEEN FREEMASONRY AND RELIGION.
BY THE REV. C. BROCKWELL, A. M.   PUBLISHED 1749.

"The constitutions of the Freemasons have an extensive circulation, and the ablest writers, both in the last and present century, have expressed the most favourable opinion of the institution; while the most dignified and illustrious characters, both in church and state, in almost every country in Europe, have given it a sanction, and continue to patronize and protect the regular assemblies of the fraternity."—PRESTON.

THE principal intention in forming societies is undoubtedly the uniting men in the stricter bands of love; for men, considered as social creatures, must derive their happiness from each other; every man being designed by Providence to promote the good of others, as he tenders his own advantage; and by that intercourse to secure their good offices, by being, as occasion may offer, serviceable unto them.[1]

Christianity, in general, never circumscribes our benevolence within the narrow confines of fortune, profit, or personal obligation; and, in like manner, Freemasonry teaches us not to restrain our love to our next neighbour

---

[1] This is the very design of Masonry. Mutual love, mutual instruction, and mutual assistance, form the substantial basis of the fabric. It is an institution where virtue is inculcated and morality rewarded. I have no hesitation in saying, that in addition to the science taught by Freemasonry, it stands unrivalled by any other institution in its inculcation of morals. It teaches the duties which we owe to God, our neighbour, and ourselves. It teaches morality, equality, and integrity; and also to speak as well of our Brethren in their absence as in their presence (a most valuable lesson in these times,) because when present they are able to defend themselves. These are a few of the moralities which Freemasonry inculcates. And it is by an adherence to such principles that lodges flourish, while decay and dissolution are sure to follow a disregard of them! This is the true secret on which the prosperity of Freemasonry depends.

only, this being merely a point of conveniency—nor to
our acquaintance solely, this being the effect of inclination purely to gratify ourselves. We are not to caress
our friends only; because gratitude and common justice
require even that at our hands—nor yet those especially
from whom we expect to receive benefit; for this interest
and policy will prompt us to—nor our relations only, for
this the ties of blood and mere nature dictate—nor are our
love and charity limited to them particularly who are of
the same church or opinion with us; for by the very
same reason that we are induced to believe ourselves in
the right, they may imagine themselves so too; and what
we may judge to be a perfection among ourselves, they
may condemn as a blemish. However in some points,
or modes of worship, we may differ or dissent from each
other, yet still the lodge reconciles even these. There
we all meet amicably, and converse sociably together;
there we harmonize in principles, though we vary in
punctilios; there we join in conversation, and inter-
mingle interests; there we discover no estrangement of
behaviour, nor alienation of affection—we serve one
another most readily in all the kind offices of a cordial
friendship. Thus are we united, though distinguished—
united in the same grand Christian fundamentals, though
distinguished by some circumstantials—united in one
important band of brotherly-love, though distinguished
by some peculiarities of sentiment.[2]

Freedom of opinion thus indulged, but its points never
discussed, is the happy influence under which the unity[3]

***

[2] This constitutes one of the excellencies of Masonry, and tends, more
than any other, to recommend the science to the favourable consideration
of mankind. The absence of all discussion connected with politics, is
the great peculiarity by which the Order is distinguished. A Masons'
lodge is a sanctuary wherein religious discord or political dissension can
never be suffered to prevail. And however these plague-spots in society
may vex all other communities, there is a line drawn by Masonry round
the external avenues of the lodge, which forbids their approach. In the
ceremonial of opening, which was used in the last century, this peculiarity
was clearly expressed. The formula distinctly prohibited "all cursing,
swearing, and whispering; all improper, profane, and unmannerly conversation; together with all religious and political disputes; under no
less penalty than what the by-laws shall inflict, or a majority think
proper."

[3] Unity was ever considered a grand characteristic of the Order, and
to preserve it from innovation it was ordained, and made a permanent

of this truly ancient and honourable society has been preserved from time immemorial. And whoever is an upright Mason, can neither be an atheist, deist, or libertine;[4] for he is under the strictest obligation to be a good man, *a true Christian*, and to act wth honour and honesty, however distinguished by different opinions in the circumstantials of religion. Upon which account Masonry is become the centre of union,[5] and the means of conciliating friendship among men that might have otherwise remained at a perpetual distance; causing them to love as Brethren, as heirs of the same hope, partakers of the same promises, children of the same God, and candidates for the same heaven.

We read that when Tertullus pleaded against Saint Paul, the chief accusation whereon he founded his plea, was his being ringleader of the sect of the Nazarenes— and this sect (said the Jews) we know that everywhere it is spoken against. And wherefore was this sect so spoken against? Was it from any evil they knew of its professors? or from mere ignorance or blind prejudice? We find nothing of the former, but undoubted proof of the latter. And this I take to be pretty much our case in respect to Masonry, as flowing from the same corrupted principles. I have had the honour of being a member of

article in the Act of Union, A. D. 1813, that—" There shall be the most perfect unity of obligation, of discipline, of working the lodges, of making, passing, and raising, instructing and clothing Brothers; so that but one pure unsullied system, according to the genuine landmarks, laws, and traditions of the craft, shall be maintained, upheld, and practised, throughout the masonic world."

[4] An atheist or an infidel cannot, without a full renunciation of his errors, gain admittance into a masonic lodge. Our preliminary ceremonies would prove a sufficient test for his exclusion; for what atheist would be willing to acknowledge the existence of a God, or that a reliance on his providence will afford protection in all cases of difficulty or danger? What infidel will admit the possibility of a future state of rewards and punishments? Both of which must be unequivocally acknowledged on the very threshold of Masonry; and without an open avowal of these introductory points, no person can be admitted within the sacred inclosure of the lodge as a candidate for initiation.

[5] Here we have a reference to that universal symbol, the point within a circle. Nothing can more clearly express that "centre of union," by which Masonry is distinguished. It is the one institution, which gives laws to all others; which, by a kind of centripetal force, gravitate round it. and preserve their respective distances and reciprocal movements, as the planets of a system revolve round the sun.

this ancient and honourable society many years, have sustained many of its offices, and can, and do aver, in this sacred place, and before the Grand Architect of the World, that I never could observe aught therein, but what was justifiable and commendable, according to the strictest rules of society; this being founded on the rules of the gospel,[6] the doing the will of God, and the subduing our passions, and highly conducing to every sacred and social virtue.[7] But not to insist on my own experiences, the very antiquity of our constitution furnishes a sufficient argument to confute all gainsayers;[8] for no combination of wicked men, for a wicked purpose, ever lasted long. The want of virtue, on which mutual trust and confidence is founded, soon divides and breaks them to pieces. Nor would men of unquestionable wis-

---

[6] It was the universal belief of these early times, derived from a much higher antiquity, that Masonry was strictly dependant on the rules of the gospel. This principle was acknowledged in the very first edition of the Ancient Charges, published by Anderson in 1723. The learned doctor there says : "The Freemasons had always a book in manuscript, called the Book of Constitutions, of which they have several very ancient copies remaining, containing not only their charges and regulations, but also the history of Masonry from the beginning of time." He then gives a copy of these charges, commencing with the memorable words : "In ancient times the Christian Masons were charged to comply with the Christian usages of each country where they travelled or worked." The author of the above lecture, therefore, was quite correct in saying, that speculative Masonry was founded on the rules of the gospel of Christ.

[7] The well-trained Brother will immediately recollect that lucid passage which instructs him in the duty of self-abandonment, where he is taught to confess that his object in becoming a Mason was not to follow the dictates of his own inclination, but to "rule and govern his passions, to keep a tongue of good report, and to practise silence or secrecy; because taciturnity is a proof of wisdom, and an art of inestimable value, which is proved to be an attribute of the Deity, by the glorious example which he gives in concealing from mankind the secret mysteries of his providence. The wisest of men cannot penetrate into the arcana of heaven, nor can they divine to-day what to-morrow may bring forth."

[8] Thus, so early as the year 1357, the charges and regulations of Freemasonay were revised and meliorated, as an old record thus explains: "In the glorious reign of King Edward III., when lodges were many and frequent, the Grand Master and his Wardens, at the head of the Grand Lodge, with the consent of the lords of the realm, then generally Freemasons ordained : 1. that for the future, at the making or admission of a Brother, the constitutions and proper charges and monitions should be read by the Master or Warden, &c." These regulations consist of five articles, concluding thus : "For this cause, principally, have these congregations been ordained, that as well the lowest as the highest should be well and truly served in this art. Amen. So mote it be."

dom, known integrity, strict honour, undoubted veracity, and good sense (though they might be trepanned into a foolish or ridiculous society, which could pretend to nothing valuable) ever continue in it (as all the world may see they have done, and now do), or contribute toward supporting and propagating it to posterity.

As to any objections that have been raised against this society, they are as ridiculous as they are groundless;[9] for what can discover more egregious folly in any man, than to attempt to vilify what he knows nothing of? At that rate, he may, with equal justice, abuse or calumniate anything else that he is unacquainted with. But there are some peculiar customs among us; surely these can be liable to no censure: hath not every society some peculiarities, which are not to be revealed to men of different communities? But some among us behave not so well, as might be expected: we fear this is too true, and are heartily sorry for it: let us, therefore, every one try to mend one. But even this objection is of no weight with a man of ingenuity and candour; for if the unworthiness of a professor casts a reflection upon the profession, it may be inferred, by parity of reasoning, that the misconduct of a Christian is an argument against Christianity. But this is a conclusion which I presume no man will allow; and yet it is no more than what he must subscribe to, who is so unreasonable as to insist on the other.[10]

[9] When the author wrote the above, he little thought that, in his own country, zealots would arise even amongst the fraternity, who would denounce this pure and excellent society; and yet, in less than a century, we find a reverend zealot, of the name of Bradley, in the United States, who terms himself a seceding Brother, writing some stupid things against the Order, which he concludes in these words: "A lying spirit is abroad, and speaks through all masonic presses, and this spirit inflames all who hate the truth, and will make them wax worse and worse, till sudden destruction shall overwhelm these workers of iniquity, to the astonishment of every beholder. *Then Masonry will rise no more* to trouble Zion, and spread delusion amid civilized nations." (Odiorne's Opinions, p. 42.) And another red hot bigot, called James Hawker, who was president of the Antimasonic State Convention of New York, predicted that "Freemasonry has received its death-blow, and it will finally crumble into ruin, and sink into oblivion. Idle prognostics of the like nature, which have not been verified by fact, are numerous in the antimasonic writings of America, and of which, I have no doubt, the authors are now heartily ashamed.

[10] "Were the wicked lives of men admitted as an argument against the

12*

Upon the whole, then, it appears that the rules of this
society have a direct tendency to render conversation
agreeable, as well as innocent; and so to influence our
practice, as to be useful to others, and profitable to ourselves; for to continue in amity, and maintain a fair correspondence, to be disposed reciprocally to all offices of
humanity, and to act upon mutual terms of benevolence,
which are the characteristics of Christianity, are, likewise,
the cement of this society. And how good it is to assist,
comfort, and relieve the oppressed, I need not now observe.   Nor is it less obvious, how pleasant it is to contribute to the innocent delight, and promote the lawful
advantage of one another; and always to converse with
security, without even the least suspicion of fraudulent,
injurious, or malicious practices.

Now, in order to cherish and promote this harmony
within doors and without, let us first lay hold on the
surest means to stop the mouth of detraction, by endeavouring to lead a pure and unblemished life.   Let us
consider, my Brethren, that not the reputation of one
only, but that of the whole society, is affected by a
Brother's misbehaviour.   Invested as we are with that
distinguishing badge,[11] which at this day is the glory of
the greatest potentates upon earth, we should scorn to

religion they profess, the wisest and most judicious establishments might
be exposed to censure. It may be averred in favour of Masonry, that
whatever imperfections are found among its professors, the institution
countenances no deviation from the rules of right reason. Those who
violate the laws, or infringe on good order, are kindly admonished by secret monitors; when these means have not the intended effect, public reprehension becomes necessary; and at last, when every mild endeavour to
effect a reformation in their conduct is of no avail, they are expelled the
lodge, as unfit members of the society." (Preston. Illust. b. i. s. 7.)

[11] The masonic apron is said to be more ancient than the badge of any
other honourable institution. It was used before the Greeks or Romans
had a name. The Argonautic expedition is generally believed to be only
a figurative account of the deluge; and the apron is unquestionably older
than that event; it was, therefore, worn before the establishment of the
spurious Freemasonry. We are certain, from undeniable authority, that
the apron was the first species of clothing with which mankind were acquainted, and was adopted before the expulsion of our great progenitors
from the garden of Eden. When they had violated the original compact,
their eyes were opened to a sense of guilt and shame, and they saw that
they were naked. Decency suggested the necessary expedient of covering
themselves with aprons. It is, therefore, said with great propriety that
" the apron is more ancient than the golden fleece or Roman eagle."

act beneath the dignity of the Order. Let us, then, walk worthy of our vocation, and do honour to our profession.

Let us rejoice in every opportunity of serving and obliging each other; for then, and only then, are we answering the great end of our institution. Brotherly love, relief, and truth,[12] oblige us not only to be compassionate and benevolent, but to administer that relief and comfort which the condition of any member requires, and we can bestow without manifest inconvenience to ourselves. No artful dissimulation of affection can ever be allowed among those who are upon a level; nor can persons, who live within compass, act otherwise than upon the square, consistently with the golden rule, of doing as they would be done by. For among us, every one is, or should be, another self; so that he that hates another must necessarily abhor himself also; he that prejudices another, injures his own nature; and he that doth not relieve a distressed Brother, starves a member of his own body: but then this relief is not to be bestowed upon the idle, indolent, and extravagant; but upon the unfortunate, industrious, successless Brother.[13]

Let us next remember, the regulations of this society are calculated not only for the prevention of enmity, wrath, and dissension, but for the promotion of love, peace, and friendship; then here surely conversation

[12] Milton has the following beautiful allegory on truth :—"Truth came into the world with her divine Master, and was a perfect shape most glorious to look upon. But when he ascended, and his apostles after him were laid asleep, there straight arose a wicked race of deceivers, who, as the story goes of the Egyptian Typhon with his conspirators, how they dealt with the good Osiris, took the virgin Truth, hewed her lovely frame into a thousand pieces, and scattered them to the four winds of heaven. Ever since that time the friends of Truth, such as durst appear, imitating the careful search that Isis made for the mangled body of Osiris, went up and down gathering up limb by limb still as they could find them."

[13] It will be recollected that charity, in its most restricted sense, when it means simply benevolence and relief, is not confined to the act of giving money, because some who are willing to exercise it have none to spare. It has been well observed, that every human being has something to give. If silver and gold he have none, he yet possesses a power of producing happiness in some way or other. There is a variety in the necessities of mankind which affords to every member of society an opportunity of communicating something, which some of his fellow-creatures want. Beneficence is not confined to opulence. There is other indigence besides want of bread; there are alms in every hand; there are charities in the power of poverty.

must be attended with mutual confidence, freedom, and complacency. He who neither contrives mischief against others, nor suspects any against himself, has his mind always serene, and his affections composed. All the human faculties rejoice in order, harmony, and proportion; by this our society subsists, and upon this depends its wisdom, strength, and beauty. Let, therefore, no narrow distinctions discompose this goodly frame, or disturb its symmetry.[14] But when good and worthy men offer themselves, let them ever have the first place in our esteem. But as for the abettors of atheism, irreligion, libertinism, infidelity, let us, in the words of the prophet, shake our hands from them, just as a person would do who happens to have burning coals or some venomous creature fastening upon his flesh. In such a case none would stand a moment to consider, none would debate with himself the expediency of the thing, but instantly fling off the pernicious incumbrance; instantly endeavour to disengage himself from the clinging mischief; so should every upright Mason from such perilous false Brethren.

There is one essential property which belongs to our craft, that had like to have slipped me, and which, however condemned, is highly worthy of all applause; and that is secrecy.[15] All that should be disclosed of a lodge

---

[14] Dean Kirwan has expressed this sentiment beautifully. He says: "I open the gospel; I see there living benevolence uniting the Jew and the Gentile, annihilating the distinction of Greek and barbarian, and delivering up to the execration of the head and the heart every prejudice and passion that stood in the way of general union and felicity. I see it pointing out to man the greatness of his origin and distinction; the dangers of worldly prosperity; the utility of afflictions; the merit of submission and patience; the necessity of rigorous privations; and thus kindling in his soul the glorious ambition of an imperishable good. I see it uniting him to his fellow by one common worship and one common hope; and moulding all the people of the earth into the nature of one family, and that family into one heart."

[15] "Secrets," says Taylor, in Calmet, "may be considered as various. Some are known to a few, but are unknown to the many; some are kept closely a long time, but are revealed in proper season; some are kept entirely, totally, and never are revealed: some are of a nature not to be investigated by us; and some so far surpass our powers, that however familiar their effects may be to our observation, yet their principles, causes, progresses, and distributions, exceedingly perplex our understanding, and confine us to probabilities, inference, and conjecture." These observations will apply to the secrets of Freemasonry.

is this, that in our meetings we are good-natured, loving, and cheerful one with another. But what are these secrets? Why, if a Brother in necessity seeks relief, it is an inviolable secret, because true charity vaunteth not itself. If an overtaken Brother be admonished, it is in secret, because charity is kind. If, possibly, little differences, feuds, or animosities should invade our peaceful walls, they are still kept secret; for charity suffereth long, is not easily provoked, thinketh no evil. These, and many more (would time permit) which I could name, are the embellishments that emblazon the Mason's escutcheon. And as a further ornament, let us add that aromatic sprig of cassia, of letting our light so shine before men, that they may see our good works; and that whereas they speak against us as evil doers, they may, by our good works, which they shall behold, glorify God, and dismiss their uncharitable opinions of the Order.

LECTURE V.

ON THE SOCIAL VIRTUES OF FREEMASONRY, DELIVERED
IN THE LODGE, NO. 151, AT HELSTON, IN CORNWALL,
BY ISAAC HEAD, ESQ. A. D. 1752.

" In the lodge, Masons always call each other Brother, and the poorest
among them, even the serving Brethren, dare not address them by any
other title, although they may fill the highest offices of the state, or even
be monarchs. Out of the lodge, in the presence of strangers, the word
Brother may be dropped ; but when a Brother meets a Brother out of the
lodge, and no other person is present, then the title must not be omitted.
It must be much more agreeable to every Brother to be called by that
endearing name, than to be addressed by the title of your excellency or
Mr., as well in the lodge as out of it, when no strangers are present. No
one hath a Brother except he be a Brother himself."

Freemasons' Lexicon.

As I have the honour of being distinguished by a badge
of office in this regularly constituted lodge, I have made
choice of this opportunity to assure you that I will use
my best endeavours to execute the trust which you have
reposed in me with freedom, fervency, and zeal: and I
beg the favour of your attention for a few minutes, while
I exhort you to consider, with a becoming seriousness,
some useful hints which concern all of us. And first, I
beg leave to recommend an unwearied diligence and
assiduity in the great work wherein you are immediately
concerned; to be upon your guard at all times and on all
occasions, especially before strangers, who will certainly
watch every opportunity to extract from you that secret[1]

---

[1] An anonymous writer in Moore's Freemasons' Magazine (vol. iii. p.
359), well observes—" if you wrench from the heart of a Mason the secret of his Brother, from that same heart you may blot out the image of
his God, the vows made to a confiding wife, or the duty he owes to his
children, to country and to home. The betrayer of secrets is a moral
renegade, too foul for the atmosphere of honour ; he is the Judas of
friendship, and the assassin of character."

which has for ages and generations been hid from those who are unqualified to receive it. The proper observance and diligent exe:ution of this part of your duty will recommend you to the notice of the world in general, and the regard of this lodge in particular.[2]

Be ye also careful, my Brethren, to avoid every action which has the least tendency to brand you with the odious name and character of a covetous man, which our holy Brother, the Apostle Paul, has with great reason declared to be idolatry. For what, my Brethren, can be expected from the man who makes gold his hope, and places his confidence in his riches? what! but that he will be deaf to the cries of the destitute orphan, and entreaties of the distressed widow? Let the contrary disposition prevail with us, and let not our charity be circumscribed within a narrow circle; but, like that glorious luminary which opens the day, dispense its kindly influence to all around us.[3] Indeed, if we are good Masons, we cannot be cap-

---

[2] The mystery of Masonry has, indeed, in all ages, been an object of great curiosity. "We never hear the word mystery," says a modern writer, "without thinking of the old English term MAISTERIES, e. g., the maisterie of the Merchant Taylors, the maisterie of the cordenniers (cordwainers), and of other arts and trades. In fact, the term is still currently used in the city of London; and *the art and mystery of——* occurs in the indentures of apprenticeship used in most branches of business; meaning that which may be a difficulty, or even an impossibility to a stranger or a novice—to a person only beginning to consider the subject—but which is perfectly easy and intelligible to a master of the business, whose practice and whose understanding have been long cultivated by habit and application. Or, mystery may be defined, a secret; and a secret will always remain such to those who use no endeavours to discover it. We often hear it said, such a person holds such a mode of accomplishing such a business a secret. Now imagine one who wishes to know this secret; he labours, he strives, but unless he proceed in the right mode, the object still continues concealed. Suppose the possessor of this secret shows him the process, teaches him, gives him information, &c., then that secret is no longer mysterious to him; but he enjoys the discovery and profits accordingly; while others, not so favoured, are as much in the dark respecting this peculiar process as he was."

[3] Our late Bro. Inwood thus beautifully pourtrays this duty.—" Seek the cottage of affliction, where misery reigns with her iron rod; lay the arm of masonic affection, which is the very arm of Christian love, beneath the neck of thine afflicted Brother; support his drooping head, and cheer his afflicted heart; cover him with the garment of kindness and friendship; administer to him the cordial cup of brotherly affection; and however great or small may be thy ability, always remember that a cup of wine, or even a drop of water, given in the name, and with the heart of a Brother, shall in nowise be forgotten."—The French lodge directions are

able of abusing the means with which Providence has supplied us to do good unto all men, as opportunity shall offer, and in a more especial manner the miserable and distressed. These are objects which not only deserve our commiseration, but also claim relief at our hands ; let the grand principles of brotherly-love, relief, and truth at all times distinguish us in the world, and ever prevail amongst us. This compassionate temper cannot fail of obtaining the love and esteem of all good and wise men ; and, what is of infinitely greater importance, the approbation of that gracious Being whose favour is better than life.[4]

Let us also be resolutely fixed in the great duty of sobriety, and not suffer liquor to get the ascendancy of our reason; it is reason, my Brethren, informs us that we are creatures every·way adapted to and fitted for society ; and that God has given us knowledge and understanding superior to other beings on the habitable globe, who all tend by a natural impulse to answer in their respective spheres the end of their creation ; and shall the creatures thus fulfil, with the greatest regularity, the different purposes to which Providence assigned them, and man, the glory of this lower world, pervert the gracious designs of his Creator in appointing proper liquids to satisfy his thirst, and exhilarate his heart, by abusing the means and forgetting the end of their appointment, use them beyond the bounds of moderation, and thereby render himself equal, I had almost said inferior, even to the beastly swine ? Did we but rightly and seriously consider the many mischiefs to which this vice exposes us, we should certainly be very cautious of

somewhat similar—" Si un F∴ tombe malade, vous le visiterez. S'il est pauvre, vous le secourrez et vous tâcherez qu'il l'ignore. Vous le consolerez, vous ferez des demarches pour lui. Vous le releverez à ses propres yeux. Vous empêcherez qu'il ne se decourage."

[4] The charity or relief of Masons has always been as evident as their brotherly-love ; and is admitted by those who were in other respects averse to the institution. In a French work, published in 1745, with the avowed intention of annihilating Freemasonry by the disclosure of its occult secrets, this benevolent principle is fully conceded. The passage is too long for citation in this place. It commences with an acknowledgment that " la manière dont les F∴ M∴ assistent leurs pauvres merite d'être rapportée ;" and then he goes on to explain the particulars, which are very creditable to Freemasonry. (L'Ordre des Francs Maçons trahi, v. 191.)

drinking to excess, well knowing the fatal consequences which attend it, that it lays our reason asleep, and rouses the many, too often, predominant passions which disturb the mind of man.[5]

And whilst we are careful to avoid the shameful sin of drunkenness, let us at the same time remember that we are in duty bound to abstain from another vice, which is too common in the present age; I mean the detestable practice of swearing by, and invoking the solemn name of the great and glorious God on the most trifling occasions.[6] This vice, my Brethren, has not one motive or

[5] However such directions as these might be considered unnecessary in these temperate days, they were not altogether useless in the last century, when hard drinking was esteemed a fashionable accomplishment, even by the best society. For instance, it has been said that Sir Richard Steele spent half his time in a tavern. In fact, he may be said to have measured time by the bottle; as, on being sent for by his wife, he returned for answer, that "he would be with her in half a bottle." The same has been said of that great genius, Savage; and Addison was dull and prosy till he was three parts tipsy. It is also recorded of Pitt, but I cannot vouch for the truth of it, that two bottles of port wine per diem were his usual allowance, and that it was to potent Bacchus he was indebted for the almost superhuman labour he went through during his short, but actively-employed life. His friend and colleague, Harry Dundas, afterwards Lord Melville, a clever man also in his way, went the pace with him over the mahogany; and the joke about the speaker in his chair, after they had dined together, cannot be forgotten. Pitt could see no speaker, but his friend, like Horace with the candle, saw two. Sheridan, latterly without wine, was a driveller. He sacrificed to it talents such as no man I ever heard or read of possessed; for no subject appeared to be beyond his reach. I knew him when I was a boy, and thought him then something more than human. The learned Porson would get drunk in a pothouse—so would Robert Burns the poet; and Byron drank brandy and water by buckets-full. Fox was a thirsty soul, and drank far too much wine for a politician; yet, like Nestor, over the bowl he was always great. A large collection of evidence to this effect may be found in the Bacchanalia Memorabilia of Fraser's Magazine. It may be easily conjectured, that with such examples before them, the Masons could scarcely be expected to escape contamination.

[6] Another vice was strictly forbidden in the ancient regulations of the craft, as appears from an old MS. in the British Museum, which Mr. Halliwell admits may be safely dated in the tenth century. The M. M. will not be displeased to find the prohibition of such ancient standing.

Thou schal not by thy maystres wyf ly
Ny by thy felows, yn no maner wyse,
Lest the craft wolde the despyse;
Ny by thy felows concubyne,
No more thou woldest he dede by thyne.
Yef he forfete yn eny of hem,
So y-chastcd thenne most he ben;
Ful mekele care mygth ther begynne,
For such a fowlo dedely synne.

inducement, that I know of, to support the practice of
it. Is it practised by the great vulgar? It is forbid by
the positive command of an Almighty God, who is ever
jealous of his honour, and will not hold any guiltless who
taketh his holy name in vain. This vice is a scandal to
society, and degrades the man below the level of the
brutal tribe, who all join with the feathered choir in the
praises of their great Creator. Let us, therefore, keep
a constant watch upon the door of our lips. Let us, if
it be possible, live peaceably with all men; let us keep
our passions in constant subjection; by this means we
shall be enabled to demonstrate to the world that we are
good men and true, that we aim at no other character
than that of piety towards God, and unfeigned love to
one another.[7] Love, my Brethren, is the bond of per-
fectness; it is this divine temper which enables us to
preserve the unity of the spirit in the bond of peace, and
makes us like him, who is the pure and inexhaustible
fountain of it. Stand fast in one spirit, and be perfectly
joined together in the same mind, and in the same judgment; let us consider that this is a duty incumbent on
us, that it is recommended to our notice and imitation by
our great Leader and Exemplar, who came to seek and
to save that which was lost, and laid down his life even
for his enemies.[8] What a powerful motive and induce-

---

[7] This sentiment is preserved in the masonic lectures of the United
States of America. In Cross's Chart, (p. 41,) we find the following :—
" As our lectures admonish, let us imitate the Christian in his virtuous
and amiable conduct ; in his unfeigned piety to God ; in his inflexible
fidelity to his trust ; that we may welcome the grim tyrant death, and
receive him as a kind messenger sent from our Supreme Grand Master to translate us from this imperfect to that all-perfect, glorious, and
celestial lodge above, where the Supreme Architect of the Universe
presides."

[8] I quote a beautiful passage, illustrative of the effects of this virtue,
from the address of Bro. Burnes, Prov. G. M., Bombay, in 1840. He
said to the Brethren of the Lodge of Perseverance, of which he was the
W. M. : "We have but to proceed, my Brethren, in the goodly structure,
whose foundation is brotherly-love; and if, in addition to working together in unity of purpose, sinking all trivial points of collision in the great
and common aim of advancing Masonry and improving ourselves, we
admit only, as participators in our labours, men under the tongue of
good report, well vouched for, and true; animating them, by steady example, to walk uprightly—to live within compass, and act upon the
square ; and instilling into them the great masonic precept of VERITATEM
SEQUI, BENEFICERE ALIIS : to follow after true knowledge for just and

ment have we in this unparalleled instance of Divine love opened to our view for our instruction and government in this state of trial, unto which we shall do well if we take heed as unto a light shining in a dark place. And I hope there is not one member of this community who does not endeavour, to the utmost of his power, to discharge this duty as it behoves every good and wise man ; and that there are not any amongst us who are not truly sensible of the necessity we lie under to fulfil this great, this important part of an obligation, which is an indissoluble bond by which the particular members are united and cemented in one body. Let us support and recommend this great and laudable virtue by examples worthy the imitation of mankind. This is the most effectual method we can pursue to silence the ill-natured suggestions of the proud, the wicked, and the vain part of our species, who, though they are by no means proper to be members of our well-governed community, yet must by this means be induced (as it were forcibly) to own, and secretly to admire, the benign influence of that love and unity which naturally produce peace and harmony amongst Brethren.[9]

I must also beg leave to recommend a proper regard to be paid to the laws, constitutions, and orders of our

practical objects, and to do all the good they can to their fellow-creatures ; we need not doubt that we shall be achieving one of the chief ends of our creation ; and may humbly hope that the blessing of the Almighty Master will continue to descend upon us."

[9] Under such a beautiful view of the nature and design of Freemasonry, is it not both disgusting and unfair to hear an opponent, who has been regularly initiated, make use of such an argument as follows, which he well knew had no foundation in fact? "It is not a little difficult satisfactorily to prove anything in relation to a topic which is sometimes operative, sometimes speculative, a mechanic art, or a liberal science ; which is sometimes the very essence of Christianity, and sometimes the way of wonning the faculty of magic ; a religion in which all men agree, and the art of foreseeing things to come ; which, in fine, bows the knee sometimes in solemn invocation to the Deity, and teaches its pupils to become good and perfect without the help of fear or hope. Such a farrago," continues this author, " of absurdity is ancient Freemasonry : and yet, if it have any distinguishing and uniform characteristic, it is this, viz., it acknowledges a God without the reception of divine revelation." (Freemasonry by a Master Mason, p. 237.) It is gratifying to know that, when the excitement was at an end, the author of the above work had the good sense to renounce his erroneous judgment of Free masonry.

most ancient and honourable fraternity,[10] and due defer
ence and respect to the particular officers thereof in their
respective places, whose business it is to carry them into
execution; and I hope the only contention among you
will be a laudable emulation in cultivating the royal
art,[11] and striving to excel each other in every thing
which is great and good. Let us convince the unbelieving multitude that no private, sordid, or lucrative views
can ever prevail upon us to admit into the number of
those who are acquainted with the knowledge of our
mysteries, the unworthy, the profane, or contentious part
of mankind;[12] but that we will stand fast in that liberty
with which God hath blessed us, and join, with one heart,
and one voice, in excluding such wolves from our peaceable fold. In a word, let all of us endeavour, in our respective stations, so to regulate our whole conduct, as
not to give just occasion for offence in anything.[13] Let

[10] The G. M. of the State of New York, in his annual address to
the Brethren, June, 1843, made the following correct observation :—
"The ancient constitutions and landmarks of our Order were not made
by us. We have voluntarily put ourselves under them, as our predecessors have done for ages before us. As they are, we must conform to
them, or leave the institution—*but we cannot alter them.* The regulations
of the Grand Lodge, which are made by ourselves, must be in conformity
with the constitutions of the Order."

[11] The D. G. Master's Song embodies this sentiment :

> Again, my lov'd Brethren, again let it pass,
> Our ancient firm union cements with the glass:
> And all the contention 'mong Masons shall be,
> Who better can work, or who better agree.

[12] Under some constitutions, this regulation extends to visitors. I·
the Laws of the Grand Lodge of Texas, it is provided " that all Masons
in good standing, *who can produce satisfactory evidence* that they have
been regularly initiated, passed, and raised, in a regularly constituted
lodge, working under the sanction of the Grand Lodge of France, or in
a regularly constituted lodge, working in the ancient rite of Heroden of
Scotland, otherwise known as the Scottish rite, shall be admitted as
visitors, and may be affiliated in any lodge in this republic, by their observing the usual ceremony in such cases made and provided."

[13] " We are aware," says a writer in the Westmeath Guardian, for May,
1844, " that many of the clergy have objections to the Masonic Order,
on account of the well-maintained secrecy of the institution; and we
quarrel not with them on that point. We profess not to know the mysteries of the craft, and, of course, are not prepared to defend them. It
would be well if others, equally ignorant, but more assuming, observed
so prudent a taciturnity. We are only inclined to think that an institution which has enrolled amongst its members men of the highest standing. deepest learning, and most unimpeachable integrity in all civilized

us be submissive to superiors, courteous and affable to
equals, kind and condescending to inferiors ; and let our
whole deportment testify for us that we have formed our
lives upon the perfect model of God's revealed will, exhibited to us in the Holy Bible ;[14] that this book is the
basis of all our craft, and that it is by this piece of divine
furniture, so essential to our society, that we are taught
wisdom to contrive in all our doings such means as may
conduce to his honor, and the salvation of our immortal
souls ; strength to support us in all difficulties and distresses ; and beauty to polish the rough unhewn block
of the mere natural man, and bring it into the likeness
of our Maker.[15]   Let us run with patience the race that
is set before us, and by an unwearied perseverance in
well-doing, put to silence the ignorance and malice of
foolish men ; and the wise and great will think it no
disparagement to be influenced by our example, when
we shall let our light shine before men, that they, seeing
by our good works, may be also induced to glorify the

communities, nay, which monarchs even have not deemed it beneath their
lofty lineage to join, cannot contain, in its code of rules, anything that is
vicious in theory, or pernicious in practice."
[14] An American writer regrets that there should be found, in the ranks
of Masonry, men that profess to reverence the Holy Bible, and yet do
daily what the Bible forbids, and then excuse themselves by saying, " Masonry is not a Christian institution." These constitute a class of enemies,
far worse than any other with which the institution has to contend. From
an unwillingness to expel them from the lodge, and from a hope of being
instrumental in their reformation, they have frequently been retained, till,
by their improper conduct, the Order has been brought into disrepute, and
many worthy persons prevented from entering into it. " The truth is,"
this writer continues, " no one, I firmly believe, can be a good Mason,
unless he be a good Christian ; and every good, experimental, and practical Christian, is, in principle and practice, a Mason ; though, it may
be, he is entirely unacquainted with the peculiar arts and mysteries of
Masonry." (Masonic Mirror, vol. ii., p. 2.)
[15] This is a beautiful illustration of the manner in which the pillars that
support the lodge are strengthened and furnished with vitality by the
First Great Light ; and shows how applicable Freemasonry is to the
Christian system of salvation. When would Jewish Masonry, or even
the law of Moses itself, teach anything which would be adopted on the
consideration that it would lead to happiness in another world ? The
religion of the Jews was limited to temporal rewards, and there appears
considerable doubts whether they were acquainted with the doctrine of a
future state. It is evident that a great and influential party amongst
them absolutely denied it ; and, therefore, when an eminent Mason applies
the symbols of the craft, as above, to promote the work of salvation, it is
evident that he makes them subservient to the purposes of Christianity.

Supreme and Almighty Architect of the universe. Let us approve ourselves faithful stewards of those things committed to our charge, that whensoever it shall please our great Creator to demand of us an account of those talents which He, in his infinite wisdom, has thought fit to bestow upon us, we may be found ready to render it up with joy, may have our loins girded up, and our lights burning, and we ourselves be as men waiting for the kingdom of God, and in that morning when the Sun of Righteousness shall arise with healing on his wings, we may be allotted to a house not made with hands, in the happy regions of eternal day—may hear this welcome salutation of the Redeemer in the presence of men and angels—" Well done, thou good and faithful servant; thou hast been faithful in a few things ; I will make thee ruler over many things : enter thou into the joy of thy Lord."[16]   O happy day ! when the faithful shall outlive the world and all its fading glories, shall see the sun, moon, and stars obliterated from the concave of heaven, and himself employed, swallowed up in the never-fading glories of a boundless eternity.

[16] Here we have a full exemplification of the happy results of Christian Masonry, when it is practised through the influence of the theological virtues. Those who are sceptical as to its Christian reference, seeing the dilemma in which they are placed by the existence of these virtues in Masonry, meet the difficulty by questioning their right to be classed amongst the symbolical illustrations of the craft. But there would be many other things to dispose of, before the direct Christian references could be got rid of. The numerous types of Christ must be struck out ; the G. A. O. T. U. must be expelled ; the text, " seek, and ye shall find," etc., must be expunged ; the two St. Johns, the great parallels of the Order, must be renounced ; and the Vale of Jehoshaphat, with its Christian allusions, must be cast overboard ; for all these, and many more, were contained in the earliest lectures known.

LECTURE VI.

A SEARCH AFTER TRUTH.   DELIVERED AT GLOUCESTE⟨R⟩
BEFORE THE LODGE, NO. 95.   A. D. 1752.

" As sometimes Democritus said, the truth lyeth in profundo and in
abdito, dark and deep as the bottom of a pit; it will take some time,
yea, and cunning, too, to find it out, and bring it to light."—BISHOP
SANDERSON.

" The greatest of characters, no doubt, would be he who, free from all
trifling accidental helps, could see objects through one grand immutable
medium, always at hand, and proof against illusion and time, reflecting
every object in its true shape and colour, through all the fluctuations of
things."—LAVATER.

THERE is a tendency towards knowledge in every
mind. The reason of man is still active and fruitful,
still in pursuit of wisdom, and fitted for generous and
enlarged ideas; it should be our business, therefore, to
find out our own peculiar bent, and then to give it a
proper culture and polish.[1] For arts and sciences are

[1] This able address was doubtless occasioned by the peculiar circumstances in which Freemasonry was placed at that particular period. The
author, whose name has escaped my researches, had evidently in view,
when he urged the Brethren, with such earnestness and zeal, to persevere
in their search after Truth, the unhappy divisions which deformed the
continental Masonry, and brought on those heavy proscriptions which
impeded its progress in many European countries. The prince, Charles
Edward Stuart, after his ineffectual attempt upon the crown of England,
appears to have given himself up to the delusions of the fabricated degrees of Masonry, and the adventurers, who inundated France and Germany, found in him a ready patron. Ramsay in the former country, and
Hunde in the latter, carried on their respective systems under his patronage; and the name of Masonry soon became, which it was never intended
to be, associated with magic, theosophy, alchymy, the raising of spirits,
and the discovery of hidden treasures. Rumours of its unpopularity under
the ban of the Pope, the council of Berne, and the King of France,
reached this country, and the Lodges were cautioned against the admission of innovations in the regularity of their proceedings. A grand lodge

not attained instantaneously; reading, contemplation, variety of objects, and diversity of conversation, are necessary rightly to inform our judgment, and to enlarge our sense of things; these are the channels by which knowledge is conveyed, by which the inward vigour of our souls, though variously exerted, not only forms the hero, the patriot, the saint, and the philosopher, but also the husbandman and the mechanic; and hence arise true wisdom, strength, and beauty, in all our designs.[2] For knowledge and application, or industry, are like two parallel lines, they are always progressive and equidistant, and, though they are both generated by points, may be potentially, though not practically, continued *ad infinitum*.[3] We find that it was some centuries before the alphabet, brought by Cadmus out of Phœnicia into Greece, consisting only of sixteen letters, was perfected into that of twenty-four; and[4] that the Egyptians, whom the scriptures allow to be skilled and mighty in wisdom, and whom profane authors unanimously testify to have been the parents of all philosophical knowledge, knew no more of geometry than plain measuring, and such rules as were in common use to them in particular, because the bounds of their lands were annually disturbed by the overflowing of the Nile; perhaps, in time, a further contemplation of their drafts and figures helped them to discover many excellent and wonderful proper-

was convened for the revision of the constitutions; and it was provided that " the Grand Master, with his deputy, Grand Wardens, and Secretary, shall, at least once, go round and visit all the lodges about town, during his mastership," for the purpose of ascertaining whether any irregularities were practised in the symbolical lodges, because the masonic authorities of this country were determined to avoid the evils which accompanied the continental deviations from pure masonic truth.

[2] The author introduces the supporting pillars of Masonry very judiciously, at the commencement of his discourse, as the immoveable foundation on which his reasoning is to be built; for, in the figurative language of the craft, without wisdom to contrive, strength to support, and beauty to adorn, no piece of architecture can be esteemed perfect, whether it be a temple, a palace, a literary composition, or an entire science. Freemasonry, as an universal system, is supported by these pillars, and so is an individual lodge. The Doric, Ionic, and Corinthian columns support the literal building, while their representatives, wisdom strength, and beauty uphold the speculative edifice; and lead the industrious and obedient Brother to a building not made with hands, eternal in the heavens.

[3] Herod. lib. v.   [4] Acts, vii. 22, and 1 Kings, iv. 30.

ties belonging to them, which speculations were continually improving; but they were entire strangers to those more abstruse theorems and analytical methods which were afterwards known. Most of the Jews, in the time of David, and part of Solomon's reign, were so ignorant of the liberal sciences, that the building of the temple was chiefly owing to the skill of Tyrian workmen,[5] and in particular to the superior knowledge of a Master of our ancient fraternity, whom Solomon made overseer of all the artists;[6] the son of a woman of the daughters of Dan, and his father was a man of Tyre, skilful to work in gold, in silver, in brass, in iron, in stone, and in timber; in purple, in blue, in fine linen, and in crimson; also to grave any manner of graving, and to find out every device which should be put unto him. The wisest of kings was not ashamed to receive his assistance, to seek for knowledge wherever she might be found, and to make a proper use and improvement of it. And, indeed,[7] Solon, Plato, and Pythagoras,[8] and from them the Grecian literati in general, in a great measure, were obliged for their learning to Masonry, and the labours of some of our ancient Brethren.[9] They fetched

[5] It is a common error to ascribe the building of the temple, and consequently the promulgation of Operative Masonry, to the Jews; for they were profoundly ignorant of the art. It was the Tyrians—the Dionysiacs —that erected that superb edifice, and after it was completed, carried the art and mystery of Masonry into every region of the globe. About two hundred and fifty years after that event, we find corporations of architects existing under the patronage of Numa' Pompilius, the second King of Rome. The evidences of the transactions of these colleges are lamentably deficient; but there is quite enough to show that they were conducted on the same principle as the masonic lodges of the present day.

[6] 2 Chron. ii. 14.

[7] Herod. lib., i. Plutarch vit. Sol. Disc. sur la Myth. des Anc. p. Ramsay, p. 16.

[8] Mr. Clinch, in his Essay on Freemasonry, published in the Anthologia Hibernica for 1794, has enumerated, at great length, the points of resemblance between Freemasonry and the system of Pythagoras; but though he has been successful in pointing out a remarkable coincidence between them, he has no authority for concluding that the former originated from the latter.

[9] Many of our Brethren are in doubt whether Freemasonry was derived from the heathen mysteries, or the mysteries from it. "I have a notion," says Professor Robison, "that the *Dionysiacs of Ionia* had some scientific secrets, viz., all the knowledge of practical mechanics which was employed by the architects and engineers, and that they were really a masonic fraternity." Bro. Knapp, in a work entitled the Genius of Masonry, or a

their knowledge from afar, and borrowed their philosophy
from the inscriptions of Egyptian columns, and the hiero-
glyphical figures of the sacred pillars of Hermes. And
we are told[10] that the Babylonians kept their astronomical observations engraven on bricks;[11] and Democritus
is said to have transcribed his moral discourses from a
Babylonish pillar;[12] not to insist upon the use of those

Defence of the Order, on a view of the late discoveries in Egypt, says:—
" These distinguished men," meaning Champollion and others, " who have
embarked with so much of that zeal which is necessary for the accomplishment of any great object, will, we trust, be permitted to draw aside the
veil of Isis, which has covered her mysteries so long that the world began
to despair of ever seeing the glories it concealed. Behind this veil I have
long thought was concealed our masonic birth. I now fully believe it.
There was the cradle of Masonry; no matter by what name it was called;
no matter by whom it was employed." Fellows was of the same opinion.
He says:—" I will endeavour to unravel the intricate web in which the
mystery of Freemasonry is involved, by tracing it back to its source; and
by showing its intimate connection and similitude to institutions more
ancient, put it beyond a doubt, that *it sprang from, and is a continuation
of, the rites and ceremonies observed in those establishments* (the heathen
mysteries)." And in another place he says:—" I conceive it (Freemasonry) to be no other than the forms and ceremonies of the ancient pagan
religion." A learned and practical Brother writes to me thus:—" There
can be no doubt that *the ceremonials still used in the first degrees have
been founded on the ancient Egyptian and Eleusinian religious mysteries;*
and it is probable that in Egypt and Eleusis the members were not Operative, but Speculative Masons. But our knowledge of these degrees is
understood to have come to us through the Dionysian artificers who
assisted at Solomon's temple, and who merely adopted the secret religious
ceremony as a mode of receiving individuals into their architectural fraternity—a means towards an end." Now, in opposition to the above
reasoning, it is a fact universally admitted, that the idolatrous mysteries
sprang up in the time of Nimrod, and were evidently modelled on a plan
which had preceded them. They were founded on the principle of exalt-
ing the creature on the prostration of the Creator; and the crafty hiero-
phants, termed indifferently the Cabiri, the Corybantes, the Idei Dactyli,
incessantly devoted to this purpose, travelled over the known world to
reorganize the celebrations of every colony, to elevate themselves into
objects of religious commemoration, and to stamp the mysteries with a
character productive of every revolting and impious practice. It is true,
they imitated Masonry in the mechanical outline, yet they could never
emulate its purity, because they rejected its fundamental principle—the
knowledge and acknowledgment of a true and only God.

[10] Plin. lib. vii.   [11] Clem. Alex. lib. i.
[12] " The most ancient way," says Stillingfleet, " of preserving any monuments of learning in those elder times, was by inscriptions on pillars,
especially among the Egyptians, as is evident from the several testimonies
of Galen, Proclus, Iamblichus, and the author of the book called Sapien-
tia secundum Egyptios, adjoined to Aristotle, who all concur in this, that
whatever laudable invention they had among them, it was inscribed on

which Seth (according to Josephus)[13] erected, the one of brick, and the other of stone, upon which he engraved his astronomical inventions, so that neither fire nor water might consume them, understanding, from a prediction of Adam, that there would be a general destruction of all things, once by the violence and multitude of waters, and once by the rage of fire.[14] Therefore, let no one ever presume to think himself perfect in wisdom, but let us continually endeavour to attain higher degrees, by every lawful and laudable method, to go step by step in a regular manner, and readily to make use of all those advantages the labours and studies of others generously afford us.[15] Inquire, therefore, I pray thee, of the former age, and prepare thyself to the search of their fathers; shall not they teach thee, and tell thee, and utter words out of their heart?[16] I said I will be wise, but it was far from me; that which is far off and exceeding deep who can find out? But yet, let us use our endeavours, and let nothing discourage us to fetch our knowledge, though from afar, still remembering to ascribe righteousness to our Maker.

From these considerations it will appear that man has a natural right to indulge speculation, and make researches after truth;[17] under this restriction, that he does

---

some pillars, and those preserved in their temples, which were instead of libraries to them." (Orig. Sacr. b. i. c. 2.) Homer says : " they had also pillars or obelisks, on every side os which was delineated the whole of their knowledge." The same thing may be found in Eusebius. (Hist. Syn. c. 2.) He says, that the Greeks received their knowledge from the Atlantians, who left it in that country engraven on pillars and obelisks.

[13] Joseph. lib. i.

[14] The ancient masonic tradition of this event, as we learn from an old MS. in the British Museum, is as follows :—After giving an account of the children of Lamech, the writer goes on to say :—" These children knew that God would take vengeance for sin either by fire or water; wherefore they did write these (the seven liberal) sciences on two pillars of stone, that they might be found after that God had taken vengeance ; the one was of marble, and would not burn ; the other was latres (brick) and would not drown, or perish by water ; so that the one would be preserved and not consumed, if God would that any people should live upon the earth."

[15] Job viii. 8—10.   [16] Eccles. vii. 23.

[17] A search after truth is the peculiar employment of Masons at their periodical meetings ; and, therefore, they describe it as a divine attribute, and the foundation of every virtue. To be good men and *true*, is the first lesson we are taught in Masonry. On this theme we contemplate, and

not exercise himself in inquiries that surpass his faculties, but in those adapted to his capacity; with an intent
to improve, to the best advantage, whatever he is capable of knowing; by joining in the language both of
heaven and earth, and of the whole universe, which,
with one common voice, proclaim the glory of God.

God has created nothing in vain, but has established
the most exact agreement and fitness between every
faculty and its object. He has granted somewhat to
answer all our passions. As he has created us subject to
hunger and thirst, so, at the same time, he amply provided
us wherewith to gratify these two appetites. It is the
nature of the soul to think; and it is not to be supposed
that he has left this natural passion, this strong desire of
knowledge, without some attainable ends: therefore, man
has certainly a natural right to inquire after those ends;
and, upon inquiry, we shall find that they are properly
varied and diversified, so as to answer the various genii,
or inclinations, of men's minds, whether they have a
more peculiar turn to the useful arts, or to the more abstract and deep researches of learning and science. The
same earth answers the inquiries both of the husbandman
and geometrician, and the same heavens, those of the
sailor and astronomer.

Besides, the study and contemplation of truth is absolutely necessary for us in this mortal state; by this our
hearts are improved, our manners are regulated, and
society enriched. How useful was this to the various
nations of Asia in the more early ages of the world,
and how much reason have they to lament the want of it
now![18] Then they were polite and cultivated, now ig-

by its dictates endeavour to regulate our conduct; influenced by this
principle, hypocrisy and deceit are unknown in the lodge; sincerity and
plain dealing distinguish us; while the heart and tongue join in promoting the general welfare, and rejoicing in each other's prosperity.

[18] " If antiquity merits our attention, and demands our reverence,"
says Dr. Dodd, in his celebrated Oration, A. D. 1775, " where will the
society be found that hath an equal claim. Masons are well informed,
from their own private and interior records, that the building of Solomon's temple is an important era from whence they derive many mysteries of their art. Now, be it remembered, that this great event took
place above a thousand years before the Christian era; and consequently
more than a century before Homer, the first of the Grecian poets, wrote,
and about five centuries before Pythagoras brought from the East his
sublim system of masonic instruction, to illuminate our Western World."

norant and barbarous. Methodical rules of proportion
and exactness of symmetry not only strongly appeared
in their architecture, painting, and sculpture, but was as
visible also in their civil affairs. And it is to man's diligence, and his careful pursuit and inquiry after things,
that we are now indebted for a thousand advantages that
escaped the discovery of former ages. By this the mag-
net directs the sailor more surely, even time itself is
measured more accurately, and new wonders are daily
discovered by the help of our glasses, among God's
works in the heavens and on the earth.[19] We shall find
also that Providence seems to direct this active principle
to be continually employed, since all contrivances are
not hit upon at once; but some were owing to curious
researches of former ages, some reserved for these latter
times, and some *quæsita* yet remain for future generations.

But, as the eye is not satisfied with seeing, nor the
ear filled with hearing,[20] as hunger and thirst, though
they are daily gratified, daily return, so this passion, this
desire of knowledge, though it is delighted with the discovery of every new truth, yet still seems to be uneasy

[19] Bro. Goodacre, in concluding his series of public lectures on astronomy, thus illustrated this countless host:—" Let us," said he, " compare
the great solar system (of which this earth forms so inconsiderable a
part) to the single habitation of a family in a thinly peopled district; the
brightest of the stars, Lyra and Sirius, and others of the first magnitude,
though distant from us millions of millions of miles, are our nearest neighbours; the less brilliant of the visible stars are similar scattered dwellings at somewhat greater distances; the small groups, such as Pleiades
and the Dolphin, are the little hamlets of our vicinity; while the brighter
and more crowded portions of the milky way, are the villages and towns
dispersed throughout the country; yet these eight or ten millions of suns
make but one region—one firmament. Aided by the telescope, in those
lucid spots called nebulæ, are brought to view thousands of such firmaments, each perhaps separated from our region of stars, by spaces as
much exceeding the distances of the stars from us, as the mighty ocean
exceeds the little brook that divides two hamlets; and some of these
firmaments are so distant, that the combined radiance of millions of suns
never reaches our vision; nay, it is only presented as a faint streak of
light to the most powerful telescope. Yet is not this infinitude? This
assemblage of myriads of firmaments—each firmament composed of
millions of suns—and each sun, with its respective system, capable of
sustaining millions upon millions of millions of created beings—forms
but a mere speck amidst the boundless regions of existence throughout
which the Eternal reigns."
[20] Eccles. i. 8.

after somewhat farther, after higher perfection, after a
happy hereafter; that then we may be perfect in knowledge, that then we may be fully enlightened. But to be
now too curious or inquisitive, how or after what manner, would be vain, if not wicked; presumptuous inquiries often lead us into error, bewilder, if not ruin, us;
our faculties have their proper bounds, and God has said
to them as he did to the sea, hitherto shalt thou go, and
no farther. Should we once attempt to transgress this
salutary law, we shall soon find that in much wisdom is
much grief, and that he that imprudently endeavoreth to
increase such knowledge, increaseth sorrow.[21]

We ought not, therefore, vainly to endeavour at inquiries that surpass our faculties, but rather meditate on
those that are adapted to our capacity.

There seems to be a regular gradation in nature. As
in numerical figures each has a power of filling a certain
space, and, was there to be wanting any one, the rest
could not maintain a gradual progression; so this is visible also of the creatures on earth; some having barely
being, as earth, air, and water, here these rest; some
that, besides being, have life, as vegetables, these are
next in a regular succession; some that, besides life, have
sense and perception, as brute animals, rising still higher
in order and proportion; some that, besides sense, have
reason and cogitation, as men, to whom God has given
the superiority in the animal world. The brute part of
the creation comes nearest the human, and borders upon
it, and therefore they are endued with something like
reason, though it does not amount to it, and this we usually call instinct, the powers and extent of which are variously regulated, but confined within certain bounds,
beyond which it was never known to pass. We men are
also under rules and restrictions; we rise next to the
angelic beings; beings, perhaps, as much superior to us
as we are to brutes; for naturally we know no more of,
nor can comprehend properly, by the utmost extent of
mere reason, the strong power, the real nature, the various offices and appointments of even the lowest rank of
them, which borders upon man, than we may venture to
suppose the beasts do of us; how much less of the high-

[21] Eccles. i. 18.

est. which may probably be exalted, as near as finite creatures can, to an infinite Deity; and then how immensely far from fully comprehending the essence and perfection of that Deity! Behold he puts no trust in his servants, and his angels he chargeth with folly;[22] how much less on them who dwell in houses of clay, whose foundation is in the dust, which are crushed before the moth? They are destroyed from morning to evening, they perish for ever without any regarding it. Doth not their excellency which is in them go away; they die even without wisdom. For canst thou, by the most sublime speculations, by the most exalted powers of human understanding, find out God? Canst thou find out the Almighty to perfection? It is as high as heaven, what canst thou do? deeper than hell, what canst thou know?[23] The measure thereof is longer than the earth, and broader than the sea.[24] It is he that sitteth upon the circle of the earth, and the inhabitants thereof are as grasshoppers, that stretcheth out the heavens as a curtain, and spreadeth them out as a tent to dwell in.[25] We must, therefore, cover our eyes, as the seraphim mentioned by Isaiah did, before his divine Majesty.[26] Our curiosity must be conducted with moderation, lest we become vain in our imaginations, and our foolish hearts, instead of being enlightened, be further darkened. For who hath measured the water in the hollow of his hand? and meted out the heaven with a span, and comprehended the dust of the earth in a measure, and weighed the mountains in scales, and the hills in a balance?[27]

The deep things of God none but the Spirit of God has ever searched out; and though this Holy Spirit hath graciously afforded us depths and hidden treasures of knowledge, yet its intention seems to be this, to direct us how to proceed, and what to believe and hope for, but not entirely to lift up that veil which deprives us of the true knowledge of superior things. Providence has afforded

---

[22] Job iv. 18.   [23] Ibid. xi. 7.
[24] In this lecture Masonry is inculcated so judiciously, that none but the fraternity can possibly divine which part of it refers to the Order. The above reference to the extent of the lodge would be overlooked by every careless reader, although it is a landmark of great importance in pointing out the universality of Masonry.
[25] Isai. xl. 22.   [26] Ibid. vi. 2.   [27] Ibid. xl. 12.

us objects enough suited to the power of our faculties, which may exercise all the industry, and skill, and parts, of the most learned and wise, and which may make them better and more happy. These, then, and these only, let us diligently search after, and let us improve, to the best advantage, whatever we are capable of knowing, either by promoting our own or the general good. Let us willingly be confined within this our proper circle, and have respect only to this useful centre. For, if we pretend to go farther, and should amuse ourselves with some faint glimpse of superior things, yet we shall soon find even that glimpse is but as the lightning, no sooner seen than lost: philosophy is quite at a stand, and our reasonings and reflections quite uncertain.[28]   Thus, upon this principle, the wise and curious artist (allowing for the meanness of the comparison) when he could not draw sorrow to the life, drew it with a veil over its face, that imagination might supply the defects of the pencil. And, therefore, our constitutions wisely forbid any disputations in every regular lodge about such matters, and direct only to the contemplation of useful arts and sciences, not to pursue studies or speculations which may not be only barren and unfruitful, but rather dangerous and destructive ; but that, according to the rules of architecture in our well-built fabric, there should be solidity and convenience, order and decorum ; that we should contemplate nature and the works of God, in order to make them serviceable to ourselves and our fellow-creatures, that we all may be more sensible of our Creator's favours and blessings to us.

So as to ascribe righteousness to our Great Benefactor, by joining in the language both of heaven and earth, and the whole universe, which, with one common voice, proclaim the glory of God.

---

[28] To the same effect Pope said :—

> " A little learning is a dangerous thing,
> Drink deep, or taste not the Pierian spring;
> There shallow draughts intoxicate the brain,
> But drinking largely sobers us again."

And nothing can more perfectly apply to the science of Freemasonry. The greatest pretenders are those who have acquired only a superficial knowledge of the Order. A drum is a large instrument, and makes a great noise, but alas, it is hollow !

The soul of man seems to be made, as it were, on purpose to contemplate the works of God ; for this end it can
discern, think, and reason ; therefore, both duty and gratitude oblige us to set forth the glories of our great Creator. This should be the alpha and omega, the beginning
and end of all our enquiries. We should learn by arithmetic, that as numbers proceed from unity ; by geometry,
that as magnitudes arise from an indivisible point ; by
philosophy, that as all causes are owing to one first
cause ; by astronomy and mechanics, that as all motions
and movements depend upon one first mover :[29] so that
of all things there is but one infinitely wise and powerful
Maker, Director, and Preserver; and consequently, that
for all things we are to worship and to give divine honour but to one God, and to let glory only surround his
great and awful name.

Let even the earth teach us and the sea declare unto
us the doctrine of obedience; the one continually moves
in its proper orb, and the waves of the other, though
seemingly unruly, yet never pass those bounds decreed
them. When out of the south cometh a whirlwind, or
cold out of the north, when, by the breath of God, frost
is given, and the breadth of the waters is straitened ;[30]
or when, by watering, he wearieth the thick cloud, let
us reflect that it is turned round about by his counsels,
that they may do whatsoever he commandeth them upon
the face of the world, in the earth, either for correction,
or for mercy. As day unto day uttereth speech,[31] and
night unto night showeth knowledge, let us admire the
majesty of God wrote in characters of light, and let the

[29] In ancient Masonry the study of the seven liberal sciences was
strongly recommended ; and their origin was untruly attributed to
Euclid. The following passage from an ancient masonic MS. will illustrate this observation :—

> Through hye grace of Crist yn heven,
> He (Euclid) commensed yn the syens seven ;
> Gramatica ys the furste syens y-wysse,
> Dialetica the secunde so have y-blysse,
> Rethorica the thrydde, withoute nay,
> Musica ys the fowrthe, as y you say,
> Astromia ys the v, by my snowte,
> Arsmetica the vi, withoute dowte,
> Gemetria the seventhe maketh an ende,
> For he ys bothe meke an bende.

In more modern times, however, geometry is made the fifth science.

[30] Job xxxvii. 9.   [31] Ps. xix. 2.

13*

solemn gloom of darkness suggest to us that our race
will soon be run, and our eyes closed in its certain shades.
Lift up your eyes on high, and see who hath created
these things, that bringeth out their host by number,
that calleth them all by their names, by the greatness of
his might.[32] And then, when we behold the sun as it
shineth, or the moon walking in brightness, let not our
hearts be secretly enticed to adore those glorious luminaries, nor let our mouths kiss our hands by way of worship.[33] But, rather, when the one riseth in the east, and
rejoiceth as a giant to run its course ; as men, and more
particularly as Masons, let us be taught to go forth to our
labour ; and, when it sets in the west, let us be thankful
for the approaching necessary rest, and for those wages
or rewards we are assured of, for performing well the
duty of the day ; and that, upon emergent occasions,
Providence has still left us the glimmering light of the
other to direct our paths. Though we often meet with
a various chequer of seeming good or evil in this mortal
state,[34] yet let us never pretend to censure what God
doth, or to amend his work, or to advise Infinite Wisdom ;
but, rather, to believe their ends and purposes are right
and just ; for, shall the thing formed say to him that
formed it, why hast thou made me thus? let the animal
world and their endowments crowd in a throng of glories
and admiration upon our minds : and, as to ourselves, let
us, unless we will be worse than irrationals, with David,
continually say, I will praise thee, O God, I am fearfully
and wonderfully made : marvellous are thy works, and
that my soul knoweth right well.[35] Let even our own
inventions teach us, let the compass mark our ways, let
the square direct our actions, the plumb-line form us upright, and the level moderate our desires, and make them
regular and even. Let us often reflect to whose sacred
influence all our contrivances, all our sciences, are pri-
marily owing ; and let us ascribe to the Father of Lights
every good and every perfect gift,[56] and offer unto him a
solemn sacrifice of praise and thanksgiving. We find

---

[32] Isai. xl. 26.   [33] Job xxxi. 26.
[34] A most beautiful vein of Masonry runs through the whole of this
lecture ; and we cannot but admire the tact and delicacy with which it is
introduced and embodied in the argument.
[35] Ps. cxxxix. 14.   [36] James i. 17.

that even the light of nature taught the wiser heathens this easy duty.[37] For it is said of Pythagoras that he offered an hecatomb on his finding out the proportion of the longest side of a right-angled triangle to the other two ;[38] and that Thales sacrificed an ox to the gods, for joy that he had hit on a method of inscribing a rectangled triangle within a circle. In everything, therefore, remember that thou magnify his work, which men behold. Every man may see it: men may behold it afar off.[39] For the minutest insect may instruct us, even a blade of corn may be considered as a type of our resurrection; for that which thou sowest is not quickened except it die.[40] Therefore, though our bodies be deprived of life by natural accidents, or by the violence of men, yet we may thus assure ourselves of their being raised again, when this corruptible shall put on incorruption, and this mortal shall put on immortality, when the veil shall be entirely taken away, and we shall see and conceive a new scene of wonders.

The most learned and studious, without this sort of knowledge, is only a naked superficies, is more devoid of real wisdom than the most illiterate, upright man, who perceives enough to be convinced that the fear of the Lord is true wisdom, and that to depart from evil is understanding.[41]

The principles upon which this society is established, the regulations by which it is supported, are founded upon this strong, this lasting basis, our speculations hereby become more than a pleasing amusement, by being also a mental improvement, and a practical good to ourselves and others. Offices of humanity, benevolence, and unanimity, are not only hereby deduced, and every social pursuit, not only the justifiable, but likewise the laudable appears amongst those that are good men and true; but

[37] Diog. Laer. in Pythag.
[38] Apollodorus says, that on the invention of this theorem, Pythagoras sacrificed a hecatomb to the Muses in the joy of his heart. Plutarch, however, thinks it was only an ox, and that for a very different problem, viz., concerning the area of a parabola. As Pythagoras was averse to bloody sacrifices, it is more probable that Cicero and Porphyry may be more correct when they say, that the ox which he offered to the Muses was made of baked flour.
[39] Job xxxvi. 24, 25.   [40] 1 Cor. xv. 36.
[41] Job xxviii. 28.

they continually endeavour also, in every particular, and in the whole, to convince that the works of the Lord are great, not the atheist only, but all other careless, incurious, unthinking creatures of the human species.

Reason and freedom are our own, and may they eve. continue so to us! both are privileges received from God, and therefore all our concurrent endeavours should be to make a right use of them to our own benefit, and to the glory of him that gave them.

And let us bless God for our further improvement as Christians; and with our patron, St. John, though he wept much at first, because no man was found worthy to open and to·read the book, neither to look thereon, nor to loose the seven seals thereof, let us be comforted that the Lamb of God, which is also called the Lion of the tribe of Judah, the Root of David, hath come forth, and prevailed to open the book, to loose the seals, and to manifest to men the will of God.[42] By which glorious revelation, they that properly wait upon the Lord shall renew their strength,[43] they shall mount up with wings as eagles, they shall run and not be weary, they shall walk and not faint, they shall glorify his name on earth, and he will glorify them eternally in heaven, when we shall not see only in part, or as through a glass darkly,[44] for in the city of the living God there is no need of the sun, neither of the moon, to shine in it, for the glory of God enlightens it, and the Lamb is the light thereof.[45]

[42] Rev. v. 4, 5.   [43] Isai. xl. 31.
[44] 1 Cor. xiii. 12.   [45] Rev. xxi 23.

LECTURE VII.

ON MASONIC LIGHT, TRUTH, AND CHARITY.   BY THOS.
DUNCKERLEY,[1] ESQ., P. G. M., BEFORE THE LODGE AT
PLYMOUTH.   A. D. 1757.

" The two principles of light and darkness cannot be said to have beginning, but are co-eternal ; yet the light swalloweth up darkness, as the
day doth the night. The flagrat or operation of darkness is the wrath
of God, and the flagrat or manifestation of light is his love. These make
one triumphant kingdom, wrestling to exalt the sublime joy of the holy
and divine freewill of God."—TEUTONIC LECTURES.

LIGHT and truth being the great essentials of the royal
craft, I shall begin this discourse with that awful message which St. John delivered to the world, that " God

[1] Brother Dunckerley was the natural son of King George II., and was
born in the year 1724. In his early youth he evinced the germ of those
high talents which afterwards raised him to such eminence, although his
education does not appear to have been regular. Being without resources,
as the king, it is believed, was kept in ignorance of his existence, he was
suffered to enter the navy as a man before the mast; and, although his
conduct was perfectly regular and praiseworthy, he never attained any
higher rank than that of a humble warrant officer, and he remained in the
service nearly thirty years without knowing the secret of his birth. At
length, however, it was disclosed on the death-bed of a lady who was
privy to the fact; but the king's indisposition, and his demise a few weeks
subsequent to the revelation, prevented poor Dunckerley from deriving
any advantage from a personal intercourse with his father. The case
was, however, represented to George III., who assigned to him a pension
and apartments in Hampton Court for his residence. He now became a
law student, and was in due course called to the bar, where his talents
soon advanced him to distinction. He assumed the royal arms, with the
bar sinister, and was sometimes designated by the name of Fitz George.
His masonic zeal was unparalleled, and elevated him to offices of trust
and confidence ; and the assiduity which he displayed in the discharge
of their duties, was equally honourable to himself, and beneficial to the
craft. He held the office of Prov. G. M. and G. Sup. of the Royal Arch
for fourteen provinces ; and was also the G. M. of the Templars, Kadosh,
and Rose +. In addition to a taste for the fine arts, his knowledge was

is light, and in him is no darkness at all ;" and that we are not worthy of the true fellowship unless we walk in the light, and do the truth. O, sacred light! whose orient beams make manifest that truth which unites all good and faithful Masons in a heavenly fellowship.

This sublime part of Masonry is that firm basis on which is raised the shaft of faith, that supports a beautiful entablature of good works. It is the foundation of a superstructure unbounded as the universe, and durable as eternity.[2] To attempt a description of this stupendous fabric may seem presumptuous in me, who have been so few years a Mason; but as, my Brethren, you have been pleased to request it, give me leave to assure you that I am truly sensible of the honour; and though there are several among you who, by knowledge and long experience, are well qualified for such an undertaking, yet, as

sound, and his researches into the true design of speculative Masonry extensive. His reputation was so great, that every difficult question which elicited more than one opinion in Grand Lodges, was always referred to him, and his decision was delivered with such consummate judgment and tact, as to be satisfactory to all parties. It will be readily believed, therefore, that he was an universal favourite; and advanced the character of Masonry by the influence of his example, amongst those who held it in little estimation; and the number of lodges in the provinces under his superintendence was considerably augmented. His services were rewarded with the rank of Past G. W., and he died at Portsmouth, in the year 1795.

[2] "The venerable institution of Masonry," says a Committee of the Grand Lodges of the United States, in their report of May, 1843, "was planned in wisdom, and established on the firm and unshaken foundations of love and friendship, in ages long since rolled away. These foundations were laid broad and deep, by those master spirits of yore, who, we trust, are now conversant with other scenes in that blissful and immortal lodge, which no time can remove. They constructed the temple of the choicest materials of past ages, and it is ours to embellish it with the finest ornaments of modern times. Masonry is, therefore, venerable with age. It nobly lived in the hearts of those worthy spirits of ancient days, before even science had thrown her beams over the world, or put forth the embodied expressions of her glory in the combination of letters into words; this fair fabric of masonic splendour was planned, and reared, and finished for eternity. It has withstood the shocks of time, the revolutions of ages, the concussion of empires, and the convulsions of hostile, contending nations. She has passed safely through the dark ages of superstition and bigotry; has come forth from the furnace purified from those stains which the conduct of unworthy men had fixed upon the bright escutcheon of her character; she has put on her beautiful garment, and, shining with renewed accessions of splendour, she stands among us in the firm majesty of war-worn grandeur, like the lofty Apennines sublimely towering to heaven."

it is my duty to execute your commands, I shall cheerfully begin the work, and humbly hope by patience and
industry to make some amends for the little time I have
served.

The light and truth which St. John takes notice of in
his message to the world being a principal part of sublime Masonry, I have, as I observed before, taken it for
the subject of my discourse on this solemn occasion.[3] I
entreat you to hear me with attention; and whatever
deficiencies you may discover in this essay, impute to
inexperience, and admonish me with brotherly love, that
while I am pleading the cause of truth I may be free
from error.

God said, let there be light; and there was light.[4]
Without it the rude matter of the chaos, though brought
into form, would still have been to little purpose. Let
your light so shine before men, that they may see your
good works, was the advice of Him that was a light to
lighten the Gentiles. Our lights are not hid, but placed
on candlesticks; and these are silent monitors, continu-

[3] It is said in the Trismegistic Books, that "there hath ever been one
great intellectual light, which hath always illuminated the mind ; and the
union of light and mind is nothing else but the spirit, which is the bond
of all things."

[4] Respecting the origin of light or Masonry there are a variety of opinions. Preston says :—"From the commencement of the world we may
trace the foundation of Masonry. Ever since symmetry began, and harmony displayed her charms, our Order has had a being." On the other
hand, Laurie affirms, that "while a certain class of men, a little over anxious for the dignity of their Order, have represented Freemasonry as
coeval with the world ; others, influenced by an opposite motive, have
maintained it to be the invention of the English Jesuits ; others, that it
arose during the crusades, &c." Amongst our transatlantic Brethren,
these opinions are equally various. Grand Master Dalcho affirms, that
"the origin of Masonry may be dated from the creation of the world."
De Witt Clinton, however, another Grand Master, entertained a very
different opinion. In a masonic address to the Brethren, delivered Sept.
29, 1825, he observed :—"Enthusiastic friends of our institution have
done it much injury, and covered it with much ridicule, by stretching its
origin beyond the bounds of credibility. Some have given it an ante-
diluvian origin ; while others have represented it as even coeval with the
creation ; some have traced it to the Egyptian priests, and others have
discovered its vestiges in the mystical societies.of Greece and Rome.
The erection of Solomon's temple, the retreats of the Druids, and the
crusades to the Holy Land, have been at different times specified as the
sources of its existence. The order, harmony, and wonders of the creation, the principles of mathematical science, and the producing of architectural skill, have been confounded with Freemasonry."

ally intimating to us, that as the ancient and honourable badge[5] we wear has placed us above the rest of mankind, so all our duties to our heavenly Master, our fellow-creatures, and ourselves, should be formed and contrived by the wisdom of God's word; strengthened and supported by love, truth, and charity; and beautified and adorned by honesty, temperance, and true politeness. All Masons that are, or ever have been, were shown the light; and though they cannot forget it, yet, alas! how faintly does it shine in the hearts of too many! how is its lustre sullied, and splendour diminished, by the folly, stupidity, and madness of irreligion and impiety![6]

[5] In denial of the antiquity of Freemasonry. De Quincy asserts :—" I affirm it as a fact, established upon historical research, that before the beginning of the seventeenth century, no traces are to be met with of the Rosicrucian or masonic orders; and I challenge any antiquarian to contradict me." Colonel Stone says :—"The main superstructure, in its history and traditions, and its pretensions to antiquity, are founded, to a very considerable degree, in fraud and imposture." A third adds :— " Let Freemasons give up their vain boastings, which ignorance has foisted into the Order, and relinquish a fabulous antiquity rather than sacrifice common sense." These testimonies are balanced by the authority of Anderson, Desaguliers, Calcott, Hutchinson, Preston, and a host of worthy and intelligent Brethren, who have asserted the antiquity of the Order. Even Lawrence Dermott, who has been unfairly quoted by Stone, in his severe philippic, as having recorded his testimony against this fact, says :—" It is certain that Freemasonry has existed from the creation, though probably not under that name; that it was a divine gift of God; that Cain and the builders of the city were strangers to the secret mysteries of Masonry; that there were but four Masons in the world when the deluge happened, &c." A correspondent of my own, whose opinions are entitled to great respect, says :—" I do not dispute that Masonry was encouraged by Athelstan ; but I deny that the Masonry of that day was anything akin to the Freemasonry of the eighteenth and nineteenth centuries. I have very great doubts if the present mode of initiation was introduced prior to the eleventh or twelfth century ; and even I have strong grounds for thinking that it suffered much modification in the fourteenth century."

[6] Archbishop Tenison has given a brilliant description of this light.— " Nothing is in nature so pure and pleasant, and venerable as light, especially in some reflections or refractions of it, which are highly agreeable to the temper of the brain. By light God discovereth his other works ; and by it he hath pleased to shadow out himself; and both secular and sacred writers have thence taken plenty of metaphors, dipping, as it were, their pens in light, when they write of Him who made heaven and earth. Iamblichus, in his book of the Egyptian Mysteries, setteth out by LIGHT, the power, the simplicity, the penetration, the ubiquity of God. R. Aben Levita, supposeth light to be the garment of God ; it having been said by David, that he clothed himself with it. Maimonides

These are the persons of whom St. John says:—" They went out from us; but they were not of us; for if they had been of us, they would no doubt have continued with us; but they went out, that they might be made manifest that they were not all of us." And thus it is that those who depart from the light bring an evil report on the craft.

As in the sight of God we are all equally his children, having the same common parent and preserver—so we, in like manner, look on every Freemason as our Brother; nor regard where he was born or educated, provided he is a good man, an honest man, which is "the noblest work of God."

A laudable custom prevailed among our ancient Breth ren: after they had sent their donations to the general charities,[7] they considered the distresses of those in particular that resided in their respective neighbourhoods, and assisted them with such a sum as could be conveniently spared from the lodge.[8]   I repeat it, that

supposeth the matter of the heavens to have risen from the extension of this vestment of divine light. Eugubinus supposeth the divine light to be the empyrean heaven, or habitation of God. And this he thinketh to be the true Olympus of the poets, so called because it shineth throughout with admirable glory. St. Basil calleth the light of God not sensible but intelligible; and conceiteth that, after that first uncreated. the angels are a second and created light. Such sayings, though they have in them a mixture of extravagance, yet, in the main, they teach the same with scripture, that God is light; or that there is nothing in the creation so fit an emblem of him, and so fit to be used in his appearance to the world." (Idol. c. 14.)

[7] The preamble to the first code of laws issued by the Committee of general Charity, A. D. 1729, was expressed in the following words :—" By the original order and constitution of nature, men are so made and framed, that they of necessity want one another's assistance for their mutual support and preservation in the world ; being fitted by an implanted disposition to live in societies, and establish themselves into distinct bodies, for the more effectual promulgating and propagating a communication of arts, labour, and industry, of which charity and mutual friendship is the common bond ; it is in this respect only that all the human race stand upon a level, having all the same wants and desires, and are all in the same need of each other's assistance, as by this common cement every one is bound to look upon himself as a member of this universal community ; and especially the rich and great; for the truly noble disposition never shines so bright, as when engaged in the noble purposes of social love, charity, and benevolence."

[8] It was ordered by the Grand Lodge in 1724, that in order to promote the charitable disposition of the Freemasons, and to render it more extensively beneficial to the society, each lodge should make a collection,

brotherly love, relief, and truth, are the grand principles of Masonry; and as the principal part of the company are unacquainted with the original intention of this society, it may be proper for their information, and your instruction, that I explain those principles, by which it is our duty in particular to be actuated.

By brotherly love, we are to understand that generous principle of the soul which respects the human species as one family, created by an all-wise Being, and placed on this globe for the mutual assistance of each other. It is this attractive principle, or power, that draws men together and unites them in bodies politic, families, societies, and the various orders and denominations among men. But as most of these are partial, contracted, or confined to a particular country, religion, or opinion; our Order, on the contrary, is calculated to unite mankind as one family: high and low, rich and poor, one with another; to adore the same God, and observe his law.[9] All worthy members of this society are free to visit every lodge in the world; and though he knows not the language of the country, yet by a silent universal language of our own, he will gain admittance, and find that true friendship, which flows from the brotherly love I am now describing.

At that peaceable and harmonious meeting he will hear no disputes concerning religion or politics; no swearing; no obscene, immoral, or ludicrous discourse; no other contention but who can work best, who can agree best.[10]

according to their ability, to be put into a joint stock, lodged in the hands of a treasurer at every quarterly communication, for the relief of distressed Brethren that shall be recommended by the contributing lodges to the Grand Officers from time to time.

[9] " Though I speak with the tongues of men and of angels and have not charity, I am become as sounding brass and a tinkling cymbal. And though I have the gift of prophecy, and understand all mysteries and all knowledge ; and though I have all faith, so that I could remove mountains, and have not charity, I am nothing. And though I bestow all my goods to feed the poor, and though I give my body to be burned, and have not charity, it profiteth me nothing." (1 Cor. xiii. 1—3.)

[10] One of the objections urged against Masonry in those times was, " that Masons being not more religious, nor more knowing than other men, what benefit can they derive from the proceedings of their lodges ?" which was thus answered at the time (1738) by Euclid—" It is true that although a 'odge is not a school of divinity, yet the Brethren are taught

To subdue our passions, and improve in useful scientific knowledge; to instruct the younger Brethren, and initiate the unenlightened, are principal duties in the lodge;[11] which, when done, and the word of God is closed, we indulge with the song and cheerful glass, still observing the same decency and regularity, with strict attention to the golden mean, believing with the poet, that—

> "God is paid when man receives,
> T' enjoy is to obey."

Let me travel from east to west, or between north and south, when I meet a true Brother I shall find a friend, who will do all in his power to serve me, without having the least view of self-interest; and if I am poor and in distress, he will relieve me to the utmost of his power, interest, and capacity. This is the second grand principle; for, relief will follow where there is brotherly love.

I have already mentioned our general charities as they are at present conducted;[12] it remains now that I con-

there the great lessons of their ancient religion—morality, humanity, and friendship; to abhor persecution, and to be peaceable subjects under the civil government wherever they reside. And as for other knowledge, they claim as large a share of it as other men in their situation."

[11] The above writer thus expresses himself on this point also; and his testimony is valuable, because it is addressed to Dr. Anderson, and inserted at the end of the second edition of his Constitutions; and shows the opinion of the craft at the revival of Masonry respecting some of its fundamental doctrines.—" The ancient lodges," says he, " were so many schools or academies for teaching and improving the arts of designing, especially architecture; and the present lodges are often employed that way in lodge hours, or else in agreeable conversation, though without politics or party feeling; and none of them are ill employed, have no transactions unworthy of an honest man or a gentleman, no personal piques, no quarrels, no cursing and swearing, no cruel mockings, no obscene talk, or ill manners; for the noble and eminent Brethren are affable to the meanest; and these are duly respectful to their betters in harmony and proportion; and though on the level, yet always within compass, and according to the square and plumb."

[12] Our general charities are now in a very flourishing state. The Schools for Boys and Girls, the Fund of Benevolence for Widows and distressed Brethren, the Annuity Fund for aged Brethren. and the Asylum for worthy aged and decayed Freemasons, are all amply supported. In the schools, sixty-five boys, and the same number of girls are educated and clothed. The funded property of the girls' school is about 16,000*l*., and its income 1600*l*. a-year, including 150*l*. annually from the Grand Lodge. The funded property of the boys' school is not so much; it

sider particular donations given from private lodges, either to those that are not Masons, or to a Brother in distress. And first, with respect to our benevolent fund ; perhaps it is better to be distributed in small sums, that more may receive the benefit, than to give it in larger sums, which would confine it to few.

With regard to a Brother in distress, who should happen to apply to a lodge, or to any particular member for relief, it is necessary that I inform you in what manner you are to receive him. And here I cannot help regretting, that such is the depravity of the human heart, there is no religion or society free from bad professors, or unworthy members; for as it is impossible for us to read the heart of man, the best regulated societies may be imposed on, by the insinuations of the artful, and hypocrisy of the abandoned. It should, therefore, by no means lessen the dignity and excellency of the royal craft, because it is our misfortune to have bad men among us, any more than the purity and holiness of the Christian religion should be doubted, because too many of the wicked and profligate approach the holy altar.

Since, therefore, these things are so, be careful whenever a Brother applies for relief, to examine strictly whether he is worthy of acceptance; inquire the cause of his misfortunes, and if you are satisfied they are not the result of vice or extravagance, relieve him with such a sum as the lodge shall think proper, and assist him with your interest and recommendation, that he may be employed according to his capacity, and not eat the bread of idleness. This will be acting consistent with truth, which is the third grand principle of Masonry.

amounts only to 8500l.. and the annual income is about 1150l., including 150l. from the Grand Lodge. The funded property of the royal masonic annuity fund is 3500l., and the annual income, including 400l. from the Grand Lodge, is 1300l. The number of annuitants, at 20l. a-year each, is now thirty. The funded property of the asylum is about 3450l., and its annual income from other sources 400l. To this institution the Grand Lodge contributes nothing. The number of annuitants on the asylum is at present only four ; because since the establishment of the annuity fund it has declined to receive any more candidates, reserving itself until the " temple" is built, and anticipating the union of both charities. The sums annually voted by the Board of Benevolence to distressed Brethren and the widows of Masons amount to about 750l., and its funded property is 12,000l. ; and that of the Board of General Purposes about 6000l.

Truth is a divine attribute, and the foundation of all masonic virtues; to be good men and true, is part of the first great lesson we are taught; and at the commencement of our freedom, we are exhorted to be fervent and zealous in the practice of truth and goodness. It is not sufficient that we walk in the light, unless we do the truth.[13] All hypocrisy and deceit must be banished from us—sincerity and plain dealing complete the harmony of the Brethren, within and without the lodge; and will render us acceptable in the sight of that great Being, "unto whom all hearts are open, all desires known, and from whom no secrets are hid." There is a charm in truth that draws and attracts the mind continually towards it; the more we discover, the more we desire, and the great reward is, wisdom, virtue, and happiness. This is an edifice founded upon a rock, which malice cannot shake, or time destroy.

What a secret satisfaction it is to Masons, when, in searching for truth, they find the rudiments of all useful knowledge still preserved among us, as it has descended by oral tradition from the earliest ages! and to find, likewise, this truth corroborated by the testimonies of the best and greatest men the world has produced! But this is not all, the sacred writings confirm what I assert, the sublime part of our ancient mystery being there to be found; nor can any Christian Brother be a perfect Mason that does not make the word of God his study. Indeed, we own all Masons·as Brothers, be they Chris-

---

[13] This advice is precisely the recommendation of our holy religion. We must not only have faith, but we must keep the commandments; for although our best works can *merit* nothing, they will be rewarded, because they are the means ordained by God to show the purity of our faith. They are the only test by which we can ascertain whether our religion produces its proper effect in the heart. A tree can only be known by its fruit. The tree which never bears fruit, or bears bad and cankered fruit, which is the same thing, would be properly rooted up and cast into the fire. In like manner, if we bear no fruit, or if we bear evil fruit, God will cut us down, and cast us into the fire—the fire that never will be quenched. Thus St. John, one of the great parallels of Masonry, tells us that if we say we believe in Christ, and yet do not obey his commandments, the truth is not in us. "Let no man deceive you," he goes on to say, "he only that doeth righteousness, is righteous." Our faith, therefore, must show itself by its fruits; it must work by love, or in other words, according to that great masonic and Christian precept, by doing to others as we would have them do to us.

tians, Jews, or Mahometans[14] (for Masonry is universal,
and not strictly confined to any particular faith, sect, or
mode of worship); all Masons, I say, of whatever religious
denomination, who rule their passions and affections, and
square their actions accordingly, are acknowledged by us
as Brothers;[15] but, for our parts, the holy scripture is to be
studied by us, and occasionally read and consulted.[16]

[14] A very severe struggle has recently taken place on the continent to
exclude Jews from the lodges; but it will fail, because at variance with
the true and universal spirit of Masonry. On the 3rd of March, 1842,
this very important matter respecting the admission of Brethren of the
Israelitish persuasion, in possession of proper certificates, was brought
forward before the Grand Lodge at Berlin, and led to very animated
debates. After many eloquent speeches, made with a spirit of Christian
liberality, by Brothers Schmuckert, Klug, Schmidt, Vater, Loest, and
Messerschmit in favour of the law; and Brothers Von Blomberg, Marot,
and Van Rœder, expressing their opposition to the law: arguing that a
Brother in possession of a certificate from an acknowledged masonic
lodge, is entitled to admission, but in many cases a lodge has the power
to refuse admittance; and they contended that as Christianity is the foundation of Masonry, it is necessary to strive against the prevailing opinion,
that Masonry encourages infidelity. The Most Worshipful Grand Master
thought that the question, " whether persons belonging to the religion of
Moses should be admitted as Masons, depends solely on the rites of which
the different fraternities have been established. According to the rites,
the Grand Mother Lodge of the Three Globes is founded and based on
Christian principles, and consequently the membership of a person not
belonging to the Christian church is not admissible; but it is characteristic of our system to be just and tolerant as to the opinion of others.
It is not the object of the Grand Lodge not to acknowledge as Masons
such whose ceremonies are not based on the rites of the Christian church,
and we do not wish it to be considered that we publicly or secretly deny
them as Free and Accepted Masons." On this subject there has been a
recent correspondence between the Earl of Zetland and the Grand Master
of the Grand Lodge of Berlin, which has ended in severing the connection
between them.
[15] This is according to the spirit of our constitution, which binds every
Brother to belong to that religion in which all good men ought to agree,
viz., to be a good man and a true citizen, and in all his transactions with
the world to reduce to practice the principles of honour and probity.
Under this feeling, it is hoped, that the German lodges which refuse to
receive an Israelite into their tyled recesses, will see their error, and
rescind the obnoxious law. In all English lodges, Jews are received as
members, except in the German lodge. London, which works after the
system of Zinnendorf; but even it admits them as visitors.
[16] Or in other words, a Christian is bound to practise Masonry as a
Christian institution. All other Masons are equally bound to adore the
one God, the Creator of heaven and earth; for an infidel or an atheist is
ineligible for admission. Even the spurious Freemasonry had a similar
requisition; and all the great heathen philosophers admitted the existence
of a Supreme Being, who created and governs the world.

Since without light we cannot perceive the beauty and excellency of truth, and since we are certain that no man can be a worthy Brother who is wanting in either, it may not be improper at this time to draw the character of him who walks in the light, and does the truth, and who, according to St. John's account, is worthy of the true fellowship.

As we call any building or piece of architecture perfect, which hath all its parts, and is finished and completed according to the nicest rules of art; a Brother is is, in like manner, said to be a good Mason who has studied and knows himself, and has learnt and practises that first and great lesson of subduing his passions and his will, and tries to the utmost of his power to free himself from all vices, errors, and imperfections; not only those that proceed from the heart, but likewise all other defects of the understanding which are caused by custom, opinion, prejudice, or superstition; he who asserts the native freedom of his mind, and stands fast in the liberty that makes him free; whose soul is (if one may so express it) universal, and well contracted, and who despises no man on account of his country or religion; but is ready at all times to convince the world that truth, brotherly-love, and affording relief, are the grand principles on which he acts.

His whole life will be conformable and agreeable to that true light, the law of God, which shines clear to his heart, and is the model by which he squares his judgment.[17] In his outward behaviour he will be very careful

[17] The Rev. Bro. T. Eyre Poole, P. G. Chap. of the Bahamas, has given a lucid explanation of this principle in his sermon on the creation of light :—" From what we are taught by the lectures and workings of our lodges, we see that Masonry, in its most sacred sense, is a science of light, a bright beam, a noble and holy system of practical religion, which derives its excellence from, and would ever direct its children to, the first grand source of all light—the mighty God, the everlasting Father, the Prince of Peace. How, then, do we endeavour to be affected by it ? Did we embrace, and do we estimate it, professedly and abstractedly, without concern about its internal excellencies, which, if duly practised and studied according to our time and abilities, must help us to be better Christians? Did we unite ourselves with it, or do we behave as if we united ourselves with it, as a mere society to be desired and followed solely for its exclusive charity and peculiar mysteries? Heaven forbid! At our initiation we professed to believe; and we have been, in the course of our regular advancement, subsequently taught and made to know, that

not to give private or public offence, and (as far as appears to him right) will strictly comply with the laws, the customs, and religious institutions of the country in which he resides.   To all mankind he will act upon the square, and do to others as he would have them do unto him.   He will be firm and consistent with himself, and continually in expectation and on his guard against all accidents to which this life is exposed ; and in particular he will by a well-spent life be daily preparing for death, that final period of human action, which sooner or later will take us hence, to give a strict account of our stewardship and the improvement of our talents.[18]

In fine, all good Masons should be pious, prudent, just, temperate, and resolutely virtuous.

From what I have advanced, and from these our ancient charges, I hope it is evident to every one present, that it is the duty of every Mason to live soberly, righteously, and godly ; or, according to the words of the Evangelist, he should walk in the light, and do the truth.

Continue, my Brethren, to persevere in principles that are disinterested, and I doubt not but you will find this room, which we have now opened and dedicated to Masonry, constantly resorted to by the wise, the faithful, and the good.

the principles of Order are founded upon the never-failing base of revealed light, or true religion. And we cannot, moreover, forget how imperatively it insists upon and prizes the daily practice of every social, moral, and religious virtue. It is, consequently, our most serious duty, as professors of this light, undeviatingly to comply with its important, excellent, and solemn obligations." I cannot allow the present opportunity to passs without strongly recommending the above sermon to the notice of the fraternity.

[18] To this lecture was subjoined the following prayer, written by Bro. Dunckerley, which, with some modifications, is at present used in our lodges :—Most holy and glorious Lord God, thou Architect of heaven and earth, who art the giver of all good gifts and graces, and hast promised that, where two or three are gathered together in Thy name, Thou wilt be in the midst of them : in Thy name we assemble and meet together, most humbly beseeching Thee to bless us in all our undertakings, to give us Thy Holy Spirit, to enlighten our minds with wisdom and understanding, that we may know and serve Thee aright, that all our doings may tend to Thy glory and the salvation of our souls ; and we beseech Thee, O Lord God, to bless this our present undertaking and to grant that this, our Brother, may dedicate his life to Thy service, and be a true and faithful Brother among us ; endue him with divine wisdom, that he may, with the secrets of Masonry, be able to unfold the mysteries of godliness and Christianity. This we humbly beg in the name, and for the sake of Jesus Christ, our Lord and Saviour. Amen.

Let us consider the intention of our meetings; let submission to your officers, and brotherly love to each other, be shown by your diligent attendance in the lodge; and be very careful to inquire into the characters and capacities of those who are desirous to be admitted among you.[19]

Study the constitutions and charges, and improve in the fifth science,[20] as far as your abilities and several avocations will permit. Have universal benevolence and Charity for all mankind; and wherever you meet your necessitous Brethren dispersed, relieve them to the utmost of your ability, remembering, notwithstanding, not to do things that may really prejudice yourselves or families.

"Let us by well-doing put to silence the ignorance of foolish men. As free, but not using our liberty for a cloak of maliciousness, but as the servants of God. Honour all men, love the Brotherhood, fear God, honour the king."

[19] This is a most important direction. The old proverb says:—" tell me your company, and I will tell you your character." A more than usual care is necessary in Freemasonry, because secret societies are more influenced by the reputation of their members than any other. For, independently of the ill-fame which is sure to accompany an institution that is indifferent in the choice of associates, the evil influence of bad example is too alarming to be overlooked. Who can touch pitch and remain undefiled? who can associate with vicious companions and preserve their virtue uncontaminated? Example is all-powerful, either for good or evil; and therefore it is of the utmost importance, both to the members individually and to the institution in general, that the greatest circumspection should be used with respect to the admission of candidates for initiation. Bro. Dunckerley saw it in the last century, when innovations in the ritual, as well as unprincipled conduct in a host of masonic adventurers, deformed the continental Masonry; and it is equally necessary in these days, when pure Masonry is practised in the lodges, and the Order has established a reputation for high principle and universal philanthropy, which requires to be guarded with the most zealous care.

[20] The fifth science is geometry; and the explanations of it formed a principal business of the second lecture, as used at the above period.

14

LECTURE VIII.

THE MASONIC JEWELS ILLUSTRATED BY THE AID OF
MORAL GEOMETRY. ANONYMOUS.

> " Lo, where our silent emblems breathe
> Their sacred influence o'er the soul,
> In mystic order ranged : while round the whole
> A starry zone the sister virtues wreathe.
> Ye, who by compass, square, and line,
> Those hidden truths can well divine,
> To all besides unknown."   RODWELL WRIGHT.

THE mighty Pillars on which Masonry is founded, are those whose basis is Wisdom, whose shaft is Strength, and whose chapiter is Beauty.[1] The Wisdom is that which descends from above, and is first pure, then peaceable, gentle and easy to be entreated, full of mercy and good fruits, without partiality, and without hypocrisy.

The Strength is that which depends on the living

---

[1] It will be observed here that a distinction appears to have been made by our Brethren of old between the pillars supporting Masonry and those which support the lodge. The latter are indeed called by the same names, but the reference is different, although they may be considered types of each other. The lodge thus constructed is aptly described by Bro. Bancks, in an Ode on Masonry, written before 1738 :—

> Behold the lodge rise into view,
>   The work of industry and art :
> 'Tis grand, and regular, and true,
>   For so is each good Mason's heart.
> Friendship cements it from the ground,
> And secresy shall fence it round.
>
> A stately dome o'erlooks the East,
>   Like orient Phœbus in the morn ;
> And *two tall pillars in the West*
>   At once support us and adorn.
> Upholden thus the structure stands,
> Untouch'd by sacrilegious hands.

God, who resisteth the mighty, and scattereth the proud in the imaginations of their hearts; who giveth us power to resist and to escape all temptation, and to subdue our evil appetites. A strength which is a refuge to the distressed, a bond of unity and love amongst Brethren, and of peace and quiet in our own hearts.

Our Beauty is such as adorns all our actions with holiness; is hewn out of the rock, which is Christ, and raised upright with the Plumb-line of the Gospel; squared and levelled to the horizontal of God's will, in the holy lodge of St. John;[2] and such as becomes the Temple, whose maker and builder is God.

On sobriety your pleasure depends; on regularity your reputation, The ungovernable passions and uncultivated nature of man, stand as much in need of the Square and Compass to bring them into order, and to adorn us with the beauty of holiness, as those instruments of Masonry are necessary to bring rude matter into form, or to make a block of marble fit for the polished corners of the temple.

Those societies dwindle away and vanish which are not contrived, supported, and adorned with the wisdom, strength, and beauty of our most ancient and honourable Order, where nobility is ennobled, where knowledge is improved, and where conversation is rendered useful, as Masons and rational creatures draw no design, but on the Trestle-board of a good intention. Though we are all free and on the Level, yet it is our duty to keep always within Compass, and to conduct ourselves according to the Square and Plumb.[3]

---

[2] Here is a most distinct and lucid description of primitive Masonry applied to the best and most holy feelings of every Christian Mason. Nothing can be more illustrative of the belief of our Brethren of the last century on this great point; and I would draw general attention to it, because I am inclined to believe it to be a quotation from a lecture of very ancient date. And for this reason it was ordained in the famous charter of Cologne that, "although in the exercise of charity and benevolence, we neither regard country nor religion, yet we consider it both necessary and prudent to initiate no one into our mysteries except those who, in the society of the uninitiated and unenlightened, profess the Christian religion."

[3] A reverend Mason of the last century thus beautifully applies these jewels :—" By these he learns to reduce rude matter into due form, and rude manners into the more polished shape of moral and religious rectitude; becoming thereby a more harmonious corner-stone of symmetry in

There is no conversation more useful than that which promotes morality, charity, good-fellowship, good-nature, and humanity. Society has harmony in the very word, but much more in the application of it ; for it is to it we owe all arts and sciences. Until the dust and cobwebs of a man's study are brushed off him by conversation, he is utterly unfit for human society. A good genius not cultivated this way, is like a rich diamond, whos beauty is indiscernable till polished.

Prudence is the queen and guide of all other virtues . the ornament of our actions ; the Square and Rule of all our affairs. Faith, Hope, and Charity are the three principal graces by which we ascend to the Grand Celestial Lodge, where pleasures flow for evermore.

Let every true Mason knock off every evil disposition by the Gavel of righteousness and mercy ; measure out his actions by the Rule of one day ; fit them to the Square of prudence and equity ; keep them within the bounds of the Compass of moderation and temperance ; adjust them by the true Plumb-line of Gospel sincerity ;[4] bring them up to the just Level of perfection ; and spread them abroad with the silent Trowel of peace.

These implements of architecture form the jewels of Masonry, which, under the name of Geometry,[5] was

the structure of human society, until he is made a glorified corner-stone in the temple of God, made without hands, eternal in the heavens. In the lodge he learns to apply the square of justice to all his actions ; the level of humanity and benevolence to all his brother men ; and by the plumb-line of fortitude to support himself through all the dangers and difficulties of this our fallen, feeble state."

[4] The plumb is an instrument used by operative masons for adjusting uprights, and is one of the moveable jewels of speculative Masonry. If a building is not exactly upright, it is insecure, and cannot stand ; so the Mason who is not upright in his life and conduct, will suffer in his reputation, and cannot long sustain an upright character ; while he who is just, and maintains his integrity, will shine as the stars in the firmament, and as the sun for ever and ever.

[5] The old Constitutions of Masonry affirm that " while Noah, Shem, and Heber, diverted themselves at Ur in mathematical studies, teaching Peleg the father of Rehu, father of Serug, father of Nachor, father of Terah, father of Abraham, a learned race of mathematicians and geometricians ; and they expatiate on Abraham's great skill in geometry, and of his teaching it to many scholars, though all the sons of the free born only." See Anderson's Constitutions, p. 7, ed 1738.

practised by many an ancient, wise, and worthy Brother.[6] Let us, then, enquire how the symbolical meaning of these implements will harmonize with the morality which is deducible from the principles of this comprehensive science.

A point is an inactive affective disposition or inclination to the several duties of man, and is the beginning of every active duty. It is also the beginning of every advantage, profit, pleasure, or happiness, that flows from the observation or performance of such a duty.

The flowing of a point generates a line. A line is therefore any duty in general, or any reward, profit, or pleasure annexed to such duty. Lines are of two sorts; right and perfect, or crooked and imperfect. A crooked or imperfect line is an inconstant, interrupted, or imperfect duty.

A right line is a duty persisted in with constancy; or any uninterrupted advantage, profit, pleasure, or happiness. That which hath no dependance on any other thing to make it perfect, is perfect in itself, and is a right line. Every divine command is a right line, and also the sincerity with which such a command ought to be performed.[7] Every line representing a duty to be performed may be supposed to contain all the particular branches of that duty; for the branches or parts of any duty must of consequence make up the whole duty itself.

The flowing of a line generates a surface.[8] A surface,

[6] Dr. Anderson has embodied these in his Master's Song :—

> At length the Grecians came to know
> Geometry, and learned the art,
> Pythagoras was raised to show,
> And glorious Euclid to impart.
> Great Archimedes too appear'd,
> And Carthagean masters bright;
> Till Roman citizens uprear'd
> The art of wisdom and delight.

[7] It is worthy of notice that in most languages the word which is used in a direct sense to indicate straightness of course or perpendicularity of position, is also employed in a figurative sense to express uprightness of conduct. Such are the Latin *rectum*, which signifies at the same time a right line, and honesty or integrity; the Greek ὀρθός which means straight, and also equitable, just, and true ; and the Hebrew tsedek, which, in a physical sense, denotes rightness, straightness, and, in a moral sense, that which is right and just. Our own word RIGHT, partakes of this peculiarity.

[8] A sect of the Pythagoreans held that a body consists of one point ; the point by fluxion makes a line ; the line by fluxion makes a superfi-

therefore, is perfect duty.   Duty is either theoretical or practical.   The sum of theoretical duty is the whole system of divine commands.   Practical duties are those commands as existing in practice.

In the consideration of theoretical duties, if we suppose each line of divine command to be of equal magnitude, and to be placed directly upon each other, they will form a surface, containing the whole system of divine law, and this surface will be a square; for the length and breadth of the law are equal.   But if we suppose these laws or duties each one to be of lesser or greater magnitude than the other, it will follow that the whole system of divine laws is as a right lined triangle whose base is equal to its altitude.

Every duty in practice, if perfect and complete, is a square surface; for every part of the practice of that duty should be supported by a line of sincerity, of equal length with the duty itself; for any duty is of the same length or extent with the sincerity with which it should be performed.   The truth of this depends on the supposition that all the parts of any duty are of equal length.   What obedience the supreme legislature enjoins is exactly of the same length or extent as that will, by which it is enjoined.   And every part of that obedience is built or founded on that very same will; wherefore obedience to any one particular command is as a square or a triangle.

Whatever line stands in need of some other lines to make all its parts perfect, will be as a square or a triangle.   Every right lined triangle whose base is equal to its altitude, is equal to a rectangle or oblong square, whose length is equal to twice its breadth.[9]   Whence

cies; the superficies moved to thickness makes a solid.   Another sect contended that of the two principles, the monad and duad were made numbers; of numbers were made points, lines, superficies, and solids.   Thus solid bodies are produced of numbers, and contain fire, water, earth, and air, which comprise the proportions that constitute perfect harmony.

[9] Of quadrangular figures, the Pythagoreans believed that the Divine Essence was represented by a square; because rectitude imitates inflexibility, and equality, firm power; for motion proceeds from inequality, and rest from equality.   The gods, therefore, who are authors of all consistent things which move in order and regularity, are not improperly represented by the figure of a square.   The right angle was a symbol of the female deities Ceres, Vesta, and Rhea.

the magnitude of such an oblong square is as the magnitude of the whole divine law in theory. In this proportion was the breadth and height of Solomon's temple, so that the very walls in this respect were an emblem of the divine law.

A plain angle is the mutual inclination to each other of two lines which touch one another in a plane, and so as not to make one right line. Or rather it is the space contained betwixt them and the arch of a circle, described from one right line to the other, from the point of their meeting as a centre.[10]

The perfect sincerity of one right line to another forming an angle, is as the line of that angle, the line of duty being radius. An acute angle is imperfect sincerity. An obtuse angle is injustice. Join sincerity perfectly to any duty, and it forms justice; and is equal to an angle of ninety degrees.

A triangle is a plain surface contained by three right lines. An emblem of friendship. An equilateral triangle is perfect friendship. The base of a triangle may be as a duty, the perpendicular as the sincerity of performance, and the hypothenuse as the advantage arising from the performance. If the duty of sincerity flow equally, the advantage will flow equally.

A solid hath length, breadth, and thickness; and is generated by the flowing of a superficies.[11] A solid, then,

[10] It is very extraordinary, but true, for it is recorded in the Ayen Akbery that the ancient Hindoos were fully acquainted with the occult properties of the circle ; for they pronounced the proportions between the diameter and circumference to be as 1250 to 3927 ; which is very near the quadrature of the circle as given by Metius many centuries afterwards. For the purpose of obtaining this result, it was necessary to inscribe in a circle a polygon of 768 sidès, which they could not have performed without a knowledge of the properties of a circle, and the extraction of the square root to the ninth power, each to ten places of decimals. A wonderful acquisition of geometrical knowledge for those early ages.

[11] The followers of Pythagoras thus philosophize on these known principles of geometry, which they assimilate with their favourite science of numbers :—" Monad hath the nature of the efficient cause, Duad of passive matters ; and after the same manner as they produced numbers which consist of them, they composed the world also, and all things in it. A point is correspondent to the monad, for the monad is indivisible as well as the point, and is the principle of numbers as the point is of lines. A line is correspondent to the duad, both are considered by transition. A line is length without breadth, extended between two points. A superfi-

is the whole system of divine laws, as existing in prac·
tice. For if every duty in practice and perfection is a
superficies, it will follow that when they are all laid one
upon each other, there will be formed a solid; and this
solid will be a rectangled triangular pyramid, whose altitude, and the length and breadth of its base, are all
equal.[12] For the length, breadth, and height of the whole
law in practice must be equal.

The application of these principles to the moveable
jewels of Masonry will show their moral adaptation to
the daily purposes of social life.

It was asserted by Aristotle, "that he who bears the
shocks of fortune valiantly, and demeans himself uprightly, is truly good, and of·a square posture without
reproof." Now he that would smooth himself into such
a perfect square posture, should often try himself by the
perfect Square of justice and equity. For " thou shalt
love the Lord thy God with all thy heart, with all thy
mind, with all thy soul, and with all thy strength; and
thy neighbour as thyself; by doing to all men as we
would they should do unto us."[15]

cies corresponds to the triad ; besides length, whereby it was a duad, it
receives a third distance, breadth. Again, setting down three points,
two opposite, the third at the junction of the lines made by the two, we
represent a superficies. The solid figure and the body, as a pyramid,
answer the tetrad, if we lay down three points and set over them another
point, behold the pyramidical form of a solid body which hath three
dimensions, length, breadth, and thickness." See more of this in Stanley's
Life of Pythagoras.

[12] The quadrangular pyramid was anciently supposed to contain many
mysterious and symbolical references. It allegorized the soul, or the principle of immortality. And this opinion was not peculiar to the Pythagoreans, but was admitted in Egypt, India, China, and the extremest
regions of the west. The high altar of Vitzliputzli in Mexico was pyramidical, as was also the celebrated temple at Nankeen.

[13] This is the true doctrine of Christianity, for its founder declared that
these two duties included all the philosophy and religion of Jew, Gentile,
or Christian. And it was the salutary effect of such precepts that induced the theosophists and illuminists of the last century to banish them
from Freemasonry. It was with a view to the expulsion of Christianity
from the Order, that Knigge, in an epistle to his coadjutor Zwack said,—
"The Jewish theosophy was a mystery, like the Eleusinian or the Pythagorean, unfit for the vulgar. And thus the doctrines of Christianity were
committed to the Adepti, in a disciplina arcani. By these they were
maintained like the vestal fire. They were kept up only in hidden societies, who handed them down to posterity ; *and they are now possessed by
the genuine Freemasons.*" But he goes on to say, "I have put meaning

This Square, if well applied, will perfectly show where the Gavel[14] and the Chisel should be employed, and how far their use is necessary. But that we may make no mistake in the application of the Square,[15] it will be necessary to show the nature of its construction, and then its use will be easy.

The Square, then, is the theory of universal duty, and consisteth of two right lines, forming an angle of perfect sincerity, or ninety degrees ;[16] the longest side is the sum of the lengths of the several duties we owe to the Supreme Being ; the other is made up of the lengths of the

to all these dark symbols, and have prepared both degrees, introducing beautiful ceremonies, which I have selected from among those of the ancient communions, combined with those of the Rosaic Masonry; and hence it will appear that we are the only true Christians. But all *this is only a cloak to prevent squeamish people from starting back.*"

[14] "The mallet or hammer used by the Master and Wardens in regulating the lodge, is called a gavel, and sometimes a Hiram. It is used by the operative mason to break off the corners of the rough ashlar, and thus fit it the better for the builder's use, and is therefore adopted as a symbol in speculative Masonry, to admonish us of the duty of divesting our minds and consciences of all the vices and impurities of life, thereby fitting our bodies, as living stones, for that spiritual building not made with hands, eternal in the heavens. Hence, too, we see the propriety of adopting the gavel as the instrument for maintaining order in the lodge. For, as the lodge is an imitation of the temple, and each member represents a stone thereof, so, by the influence of the gavel, all the ebullitions of temper, and the indecorum of frivolity, are restrained, as the material stones of that building were, by the same instrument, divested of their asperities and imperfections." (American Lectures.)

[15] The square is one of the working tools of a fellowcraft, and the jewel of the W. M. Its use amongst operative masons is to lay lines and prove horizontals, that the stones of a building may be accurately placed in their respective positions. To the speculative Mason it is an emblem of morality and justice ; and as, by the application of the square, the stability of the building is proved; so by the application of the principles of morality and justice, our actions are proved or condemned, as they are founded on, or depart from, these eternal and immutable principles.

[16] There is an ingenious and simple method of proving that the area of a circle is equal to the rectangle of one-half the circumference, by one-half the diameter ; or in other words, is equal to that of a right angled parallellogram, two of whose sides are equal to one-half the diameter. Suppose a circle to be taken, and numerous radii to be drawn from its centre to its circumference at equal distances from each other ; then let the circle be divided into two parts, each a semicircle ; cut through the radial lines from the centre close to the circumference, and open each semicircle out so that the circumference of each part shall become a straight line ; the points of one piece will fit exactly into the spaces of the other, and the rectangle in question will be formed.

14*

several duties we owe to all men. And every man should be agreeable to this Square when perfectly finished.

For if it be allowed that no duty we owe to the Supreme Being should be omitted, and that we ought to be equally forward to the performance of every one; it will thence follow that this great duty, geometrically considered, may be as a right line. Again, if love to the Supreme Being be an animating principle, and if the love we owe to all men (when in its greatest perfection) flows directly (sincerely or right forward) from this principle, it will thence follow that our whole duty, geometrically considered, may be as a rectangular plane; and therefore ought perfectly to coincide with the perfect Square of theoretical duties.

This being premised, it will be no very hard thing even for an apprentice to handle the Gavel,[17] the Chisel, and the Square, with dexterity and judgment. For whatever is preferred before the greatest of duties, love to the Supreme Being will of consequence be projected beyond it, and therefore of necessity must be cut off.

Again, whatever is preferred before that great duty of equity we owe to all men, and as performed in uprightness and sincerity to the first great duty, love to the Deity is of consequence projected beyond it, and therefore of necessity must be cut off, in order that the Square may fit just and easy each way. When this is done, the Stone, or rough Ashlar,[18] is completely finished, and the Gavel and Chisel may be laid aside till the Square discovers some other irregularity.[19]

[17] With a small working tool the Master of a lodge governs the most numerous meetings. The blow of the Master's hammer commands industry, silence, or the close of labour, and every Brother respects and honours its sound. In so far, the gavel is a symbol of the power of the Master. It must never be lost sight of at the meeting of the lodge; and should the Master be unavoidably compelled to leave the lodge-room, he must deliver it to his deputy or Past Master, or some other skilful Brother. The Wardens do not govern the lodge with their gavels, they only direct attention by them to the commands of the W. M. (Freemasons' Lexicon.)

[18] The ancient savages of America had a perfect ashlar, which they applied to the most sacred purposes, although it was of a very diminutive size, being a cube of only three inches. It was composed of crystal, so very transparent that the grain of a man's skin might be seen through it; and, according to tradition, when placed in their temples, it became so very heavy that they were unable to move it.

[19] How wretchedly these symbolical references were wrested from their

Sincerity and uprightness are qualifications absolutely necessary in every member of a well-formed society. For as there is no medium betwixt sincerity and dissimulation, so of consequence he that is not a sincere man must be a deceitful one, than which none can be more pernicious to such a society. If mutual trust and confidence be necessary to its support, then of consequence that society must fall whose members want sincerity.

And certainly those who make no conscience wilfully to defeat that good-natured confidence which they have caused to be reposed in them by any other, have undoubtedly rotten hearts, and a very large share of dissimulation, impudence, and imposture.

It is possible that some such as these may value themselves on the Square; but let me ask, how do they look unless they stand upright in the building? Thus you plainly see the unfitness and absurdity of placing any trust or confidence in the weak supports of dissimulation and imposture. On the contrary, he that would be accounted a man, and worthy of trust, let him pursue the great qualifying virtue, sincerity, or let him not hypocritically assume that sacred title : neither let him think himself upright because he is sincere in a few particulars; for this would be a vain deception. Sincerity is an universal duty; neither can that man be said to be so who cannot stand the test of the true Plumb-line of gospel sincerity.[20] And he that is truly Square, well polished,

original purpose in the system of Illuminism, the following extract will show. The words are those of Weishaupt, the founder of the order, in a letter to his associate, Zwack. " The three conditions of human society are expressed by the rough, the split, and the polished stone. The rough stone, and the one that is split, express our condition under civil government; rough, by every fretting irregularity of condition ; and split, since we are no longer one family, and are farther divided by differences of government, rank, property. and religion ; but when reunited in one family, we are represented by the polished stone. G. is Grace; the Flaming Star is the Torch of Reason. Those who possess this knowledge are indeed Illuminati." ! ! !

[20] In the book from which I extracted the present lecture, I find the following curious memento :—

M—Magnitude, Moderation, Magnanimity.
A—Affability, Affection, Attention.
S—Silence, Secresy, Security.
O—Obedience, Order, Œconomy.
N—Noble, Natural, Neighbourly.
R—Rational, Reciprocative, Receptive.
Y—Yielding, Ypight (fixed), Yare (ready).

and thus uprightly fixed, is well qualified and fit to be a member of the most honourable society that ever existed.

He that trusteth such an one with any possible engagement, is freed from all trouble and anxiety about the performance of it; for his words are the breathings of his very heart; he promiseth, and is faithful to his trust, and is an utter stranger to things of a double meaning. And as he endeavoureth at all times to give satisfaction to others; so he is sure, as a reward for his constancy, to be admitted a member in that most amiable society, where every individual is perfectly square, perfectly polished, and perfectly upright.

The prophet David, who was a great lover of Masonry, expresseth himself excellently well to this purpose in the fifteenth Psalm : "Lord," says he, "who shall abide in Thy holy tabernacle? who shall dwell in Thy holy hill? he that walketh uprightly, and worketh righteousness, and speaketh the truth in his heart; he that backbiteth not with his tongue, nor doth evil to his neighbour, nor taketh up a reproach against his neighbour. In whose eyes a vile person is contemned, but he honoureth them that fear the Lord. He that sweareth to his own hurt and changeth not. He that putteth not out his money to usury, nor taketh reward against the innocent. He that doeth these things shall never be moved."

Which is explained thus :—

Masonry, of things, teaches how to attain their just	Magnitude.
To inordinate affections, the art of	Moderation.
It inspires the soul with true	Magnanimity.
It also teaches us	Affability.
To love each other with true	Affection.
And to pay to things sacred a just	Attention.
It instructs us how to keep	Silence.
To maintain	Secresy.
And preserve	Security.
Also, to whom it is due,	Obedience.
To observe good	Order.
And a commendable	Œconomy.
It likewise teaches us how to be worthily	Noble.
Truly	Natural.
And, without reserve.	Neighbourly.
It instils principles indisputably	Rational.
And forms in us a disposition	Reciprocative.
And	Receptive.
It makes us, to things indifferent,	Yielding.
To what is absolutely necessary, perfectly	Ypight.
And to do all that is truly good most willingly	Yare.

Whoever expects the kind assistance of others, should by all means endeavour to deserve it, by contributing all in his power to the happiness of all men.

He should put his hand to the Trowel of peace and beneficence, and not lay it by so long as he is able to join one stone to the building;[21] for beneficence, or active goodness, is the perfection of that good-will we owe to all mankind; not excepting those who differ from us either in rank, persuasion, or otherwise.

And though prejudice or partiality may prevail with some weak minds, stiffly to refuse doing good to those who cannot think or do as they do; yet let them remember that the Almighty Being has laid this injunction upon us, and therefore we should not withhold our hand when it is in our power to do good. But if prejudice must cavil, know then, that if we differ more from the infinitely great perfections of the Deity than we possibly can from one another, it will thence follow, that if we refuse to do good when it is in our power to do it, and because they differ from us, then the Almighty Being, for the same reason, may withhold his hand from us, the fatal consequence of which I leave you to consider. "As we have therefore opportunity, let us do good to all men."

Let us endeavour to reform the wicked and impenitent, and heartily desire the Almighty to turn their hearts. Let us assist the king in his lawful government, by paying his rightful dues and obeying his commands. Let us honour and reverence the ministers of the sacred word, and help to maintain them according to our abilities. Let us faithfully discharge every duty we owe to our parents, wives, children, and Brethren.

To every one let us speak the truth, and fulfil every engagement. Pay a suitable deference to superior merit,

---

[21] The trowel is appropriated to the Master's degree because, as the lectures say, it is as Master Masons only we constitute the recognized of the masonic family. Again, this implement is considered as the appropriate working tool of a Master Mason ; because, in operative masonry, while the E. A. P. prepares the materials, and the Fellowcraft places them in their proper situation, the Master Mason spreads the cement with the trowel, which binds them together. In speculative Masonry, the Master of the lodge is the cement which unites the the Brethren and binds them together in peace, harmony, and brotherly love.

and give honour to persons of quality. Let knowledge, comfort, counsel, advice, reproof, be dispensed where necessary. Let the poor and ignorant be assisted, and if you can conveniently, endeavour to reconcile those that are at variance with each other. Let the Plumb-line be applied, and you will have the true upright of this duty, " do good to them that hate you."[22]

The advantages arising from a conscientious discharge of these duties are many and various ; but what infinitely outweighs all other considerations is, that by so doing we shall be "the children of the Highest," and be received as such when it shall be said, " come ye blessed of my father, inherit the kingdom prepared for you from the foundation of the world."

[22] This lecture is an admirable illustration of the manner in which our ancient Brethren inculcated the duties of morality from the terms and propositions of geometry ; and I regret exceedingly that all my efforts to obtain the author's name have been unsuccessful.

LECTURE IX.

ON THE GOVERNMENT OF THE LODGE. DELIVERED BEFORE
THE BRETHREN OF ST. GEORGE'S LODGE, NO. 315, TAUN-
TON. BY JOHN WHITMASH, ESQ., W. M. 1765.

" In referring to the prosperous condition of the craft, and the accession which is daily making to its members, I would observe, that the
character of a lodge does not depend upon the number, but the respectability of its members. It is too often the case that a lodge manifests too
great anxiety to swell its numbers, under the erroneous idea that number
constitutes might. It should, however, be remembered, that the race is
not to the swift, nor the battle to the strong. So it is in Masonry—a
lodge of a dozen men of respectable standing in society, will exert more
influence upon the community, than five times the number of doubtful
reputation. The latter will be greater in numerical strength, but the
former in actual power. Guard, then, the portals of your temple against
the idle, the profligate, and the intemperate. Admit no man to the privileges of the Order whom you do not conscientiously believe will conform
to the rules of the Order."—TANNEHILL.

In every art two things seem peculiarly deserving of
attention, its origin and its design. And perhaps there
is none that can boast an origin more ancient and venerable, or a design more benevolent than that of Masonry.
When the Almighty fiat first bade this visible creation
exist, as the sacred page informs us, it was without form
and void, and darkness was upon the face of the deep: it
was yet a rude and shapeless chaos.[1] But the divine
Architect stretched out the line upon it, and reduced it

---

[1] It was in the darkness that God is said to have dwelt before the creation of our globe. The Manicheans adored the sun and the moon, under
the supposition that the *virtue* of God dwells in the sun, his *wisdom* in
the moon, and the Holy Ghost in the air ; and that the Deity dwelleth
alone in the light; forgetting that God said, " he would dwell in the thick
darkness." (2 Chron. vi. 1 ; 1 Kings viii. 12.) And again it is said,
" darkness was under his feet (Ps. xviii. 9); and he made darkness his
secret place ; his pavilion round about were dark waters and thick clouds."
(v. 11.)

to symmetry and order, so that we now behold the whole fabric stand confest, a stupendous monument of eternal wisdom—its pillars invested with strength and adorned with beauty. Executed with skill minute even below the sight of the philosophic eye, and vast beyond the bounds of imagination, it pronounceth its Author to be divine. Such was the original design of the eternal mind—and such we now behold the fair and magnificent fabric of the universe.[2]

But had the divine Architect here stopped short—had he not also given being to another system, namely, one of an intellectual kind, not only had the most glorious and excellent part of the divine workmanship been left unfinished, but even that which was created might have remained for ever unnoticed and unadmired. Though the fabric was beautiful and stupendous, it had been but like a deserted mansion, without inhabitants. Though the picture was fair, and the colours exquisite, yet none had been conscious of its beauty, but He alone who first designed and made it.

As an inhabitant, therefore, of this visible creation, and a witness of its beauty and magnificence, the great Author of nature gave being also to the intellectual system—He bade the human intelligence exist, and be conscious of good and evil, of beauty and deformity, of virtue and vice. As the former system was made the grand model of visible order, of measure and proportion; so was this last the subject of moral beauty and recti tude. The one is the object of science and the other of morality: and these, if I mistake not, are the two grand pillars of the masonic art.[3] On these its solid basis rests,

---

[2] The ancient Persians gave a curious account of the process of creation.—" The angels," say they, " are God's ministers, and assisted him at the creation—the completion of which occupied forty-five days. A dreadful darkness spread itself over the universe, at a considerable distance from the light. As soon as the Almighty perceived it, he was conscious that some powerful influence was at work, and that he had an enemy to encounter, who was at the head of a numerous army. He immediately appointed four of the most distinguished archangels to take command of the hosts of heaven. With these they attacked the evil spirit, and obtained a complete victory; and the powers of darkness were obliged to submit and surrender themselves to the clemency of the victors." It was from this legend, probably, that Milton took the hint of his great poem.

[3] This is a beautiful illustration of the origin of Masonry. The crea-

and hath ever rested unshaken and unimpaired. Thus,
it claims an origin coeval with the world; and its professed design is to promote civilization, and to adorn
human life with every scientific and moral accomplishment.

By what remote cause, or by what chain of causes or
accidents, mankind, originally formed for virtue and society, were led to pervert the intention of their nature,
and to lose the proper means of improvement—how they
were first divided amongst themselves, became rude in
their manners, hostile to their own species, ignorant and
unsociable, it is not our present business to inquire;[4]
suffice it here to observe that the fact itself is unquestionable, and that the immediate visible cause is the neglect of science and cultivation. Almost in every nation,
at some particular period of its history, men have been
found rude as the marble in the quarry; possessing
indeed a capacity of moral beauty, and of the fairest
proportions of virtue, but requiring the skilful hand of
art and culture to form and polish them. Such, we are
informed, were the ancient inhabitants of Greece (afterwards the most polished nation in the world) before its
savage tribes were tamed by the harmonious lyre of an

tion of this admirable structure in which we live, being the operative
division, and of the human intellect, the speculative. Nothing can better
mark the distinction which exists between thought and labour, design
and execution. And as the Almighty at the creation pronounced that
all was very good—so, to compare small things with great, the labour,
skill, and scientific knowledge exhibited by the three classes of Masons,
usually produce a piece of architecture which the best judges pronounce
perfect and complete.

[4] Some of the oriental nations, and particularly the Chinese, according
to their own historians, were in a very barbarous state. The Ouai-ki,
quoted in the Chinese annals, describes the manners of the people thus:
—"In the beginning," say these records, "men differed nothing from
other animals in their way of life. As they wandered up and down in
the woods, and women were in common, it so happened that children
never knew their own fathers, but only their mothers. They abandoned
themselves to every vice without shame, and had not the least idea of the
laws of decency. They thought of nothing but sleeping and snoring, and
then getting up and yawning. When hunger pressed them, they sought
for something to eat, and when they were glutted, they threw the rest
away. They eat the very feathers and hairs of animals, along with the
raw flesh, and drank their blood. They clothed themselves in skins un-
tanned. They dwelt in caves and dens; but Yoan-tsao taught them to
build dwellings. like the nests of birds, for the purpose of avoiding the
depredations of wild animals."

Orpheus.   And such are the inhabitants of every nation,
while yet unenlightened by science—untaught and unex-
perienced in the exalted virtue of benevolence—and un-
conscious of the sacred bonds of social union.[5]   Wild as
the woods in which they roam, and fierce as the animals
with which they herd—their clothing the spoils of the
chase, and dens their only shelter.   Such is the picture
of human life unenlightened by science, and unadorned
by art and cultivation.[6]

In the midst of this chaos of intellectual nature, behold
Masonry, whose task it is to enlighten and to adorn—behold the heaven-born virgin appear, bearing in her hand
the lamp of science, the mirror of truth, with the various
ensigns of art—joy smiling in her countenance, the fair
semblance of virtue and internal peace.   Steadily regarding the beauty and symmetry of the divine workmanship,
both in the visible and intellectual world, and fired with
a noble enthusiasm to examine and to imitate; from the
former she derives the various arts and ornaments of life,
and from the latter the rules of social duty.[7]   She teach-

[5] At this period of the world, political power and bodily strength went
hand in hand.   Whoever was able to encounter a fierce wild beast, and
clear the country of noxious animals, or in the day of battle to destroy
the greatest number of enemies, was looked up to by his companions as
a mighty chief.   Thus Nimrod, from being a successful hunter, became a
great monarch ; and, as it appears from history, most of his successors
copied his example.

[6] "When men are in a state of barbarity," says Laurie at the commencement of his History of Freemasonry, " and are scattered over the
surface of a country in small independent tribes, their wants are small in
magnitude, as they are few in number.   It is in the power, therefore, of
every individual to perform, for himself and his family, every work of labour which necessity or comfort requires ; and while, at one time, he
equips himself for the chase, or the combat, at another, he is rearing an
habitation for his offspring, or hollowing his canoe to surmount the dangers of the sea.   But as soon as these tribes associate together, for the
purposes of mutual protection and comfort, civilization advances apace ;
and, in the same proportion, the wants and desires of the community increase.   In order to gratify these, the ingenuity of individuals is called
forth ; and those who, from inability or indolence, cannot satisfy their
own wants, will immediately resort to the superior skill of their neighbours.   Those members of the community who can execute their work
with the greatest elegance and celerity, will be most frequently employed ;
and from this circumstance, combined with the principle of emulation and
other causes, that distinction of professions will arise. which is found only
among nations considerably advanced in civilization and refinement."

[7] Dr. Anderson, in the first edition of his Constitutions, said that

eth mankind to perceive that they were formed for
society, and that there their nature can reach the highest
perfection and happiness. She bids them lay aside the
fierceness of an hostile disposition ; and teacheth men of
every nation, of every different faith, and of every rank
in life, overlooking the prejudices and distinctions which
education or fortune may have established, to embrace
one another like Brethren, and to give the soul to harmony and love.

Union adds strength to enterprise, and fire to genius
and invention. Under the culture of her hand we, therefore, soon perceive the various arts and embellishments
of life improved and disseminated. Where lately all was
waste and deformity, we now behold the stately dome
arise, and display its magnificent ornaments. The rude
and shapeless marble assumes form and proportion, and
nature's fairest tints seem to live on the canvas. Lo !
music also, attended by soft poesy, her sister art, gives to
harmony the trembling strings, and wakes the soul to
ecstasy ; whilst the mighty tide of bold majestic verse
tames the savage breast, and forms it to humanity and
love. This is the labour, and this the pride of Masonry,
by such arts as these to adorn life, and to humanize the
temper.

Heaven, well pleased, first viewed the bold and generous design, with a look of soft complacency, then blessed
the enterprise, and bade the virgin proceed and prosper.
Attended by soft-eyed charity, her inseparable companion,
we now, therefore, behold her travelling down the vale

" though by sin Adam fell from his original happy state, and was expelled
from his lovely arbour and earthly paradise into the wide world, he still
retained knowledge, especially in geometry ; and its principles remaining
in the hearts of his offspring, have in process of time been drawn forth in
a convenient method of propositions, according to the laws of proportion
taken from mechanism. And as the mechanical arts gave occasion to the
learned to reduce the elements of geometry into method, so this noble
science, thus reduced and methodised, is now the foundation of all those
arts, especially of architecture, and the rule by which they are conducted
and finished. Adam, when expelled, resided in the most convenient natural abodes of the land of Eden, where he could be best sheltered from
colds and heats, from winds, rains, and tempests, and from wild beasts,
till his sons grew up to form a lodge, whom he taught geometry, and the
use of it in architecture, without which the children of men must have
lived like brutes, in woods, dens, and caves, or at best in poor huts of
mud, or arbours made of the branches of trees."

of time, hung round with the most venerable relics of
hoary antiquity, and crowned with the richest honours
of every preceding age, that with the same munificence,
and the same benevolent hand, she may yet bless and
adorn posterity.

This is but a faint and general outline of the origin
and design of the masonic art, which in all ages have
excited the curiosity of mankind ; and curiosity is one of
the most prevailing passions in the human breast.[8] The
mind of man is kept in a perpetual thirst after knowledge, nor can he bear to be ignorant of what he thinks
others know.   Anything secret or new immediately
excites an uneasy sensation, and becomes the proper fuel
of curiosity, which will be found stronger or weaker in
proportion to the time and opportunities that individuals
have for indulging it. It is observable further, that when
this passion is excited, and not instantly gratified, instead
of waiting for better intelligence, and using the proper
means of removing the darkness that envelops the object
of it, the mind precipitately forms ideas which are generally in the extremes.   If the object promote pleasure or
advantage, we receive it with commendations; if it appear in the opposite view, or if we are ignorant of it, we
then absurdly, as well as disingenuously, condemn, and
pretend at least to despise it.[9]   This has been the fate of

---

[8] Curiosity is certainly a very prevalent feeling in man ; and we owe to
its existence many of those vast and useful discoveries which have con
ferred such essential benefits on society. The use of machinery, which
has been applied to such a variety of uses, sprang from this principle ;
steam and gas may trace their origin to the same efficient cause ; the improvements in geology, chemistry, electricity, and other sciences, may be
attributed to the investigations of a laudable curiosity ; and it cannot be
denied but many masonic conversions had the same origin. A thirst for
knowledge has in all ages been attended with beneficial results. Necessity was the mother of architecture—rude, indeed, in its first essays, but
producing the most astonishing effects by the aid of geometry and its
wonder-working properties.   In speculative Masonry, curiosity ungrati-
fied has often led to uncompromising hostility ; and the severest attacks
on the institution have frequently had no other origin.

[9] The secresy of Freemasonry has been a fertile source of objection. It
has been urged—" If your institution has nothing in it disgraceful to
yourselves, or injurious to the world, if it really be that system of wisdom and virtue which you so loudly declare it to be, why do you confine
the knowledge of it to a few ? why do you not rather, like the real friends
of mankind, make it universally known, that its benefits may be universal ?"   The Grand Architect of the Universe locks up gold in the

our invaluable institution. Those who are acquainted with its nature and design, admire and espouse it; and if those who are in the dark, or whose minds are disposed to evil, should slight or speak disrespectfully of it, it is not considered a disgrace. When order shall produce confusion, when harmony shall give rise to discord, and proportion shall be the source of irregularity, then, and not till then, will Freemasonry be unworthy the patronage of the great, the wise, and good.

To love as Brethren, to be ready to communicate, to speak truth one to another, are the dictates of reason and revelation; and they are likewise the foundation and constituent parts of Freemasonry.

None, therefore, who believe the divine original of the sacred volume, and are influenced by a spirit of humanity, friendship, and benevolence, can with the least propriety object to our ancient and venerable institution.[10]

earth and pearls in the ocean; not to conceal them from human use, but to reward human industry for its search after them. It seems to be His fixed decree, that the improvement of the material world should depend on the combined efforts of human genius and labour; and that philosophy should be invoked for the melioration of the blessings of nature. And why do men lock up precious things, but to keep them from unhallowed hands? That secrecy is an important virtue, recommended in all ages by the wisest and best of men, cannot be contradicted; nor can it be denied, but that in in all ages there have been societies who have had secrets which they have not indiscriminately revealed, but have disclosed to those only whom they thought worthy to be associated with them. Do we not daily see corporations, secret committees, privy councils, &c., bind themselves to secresy, without censure or reproach? why, then, should not Freemasons enjoy the same liberty, without incurring illiberal reflections? It must be believed by all candid persons when they see it so zealously supported by the virtuous, the honourable and the wise, that Freemasonry contains nothing which is either disgraceful to individuals or injurious to the world. The door of Masonry is closed against the unworthy only. He, who does justly, loves mercy, and walks humbly with his God, will always find it open, and be received with fraternal affection.

[10] In fact, the morality of Masonry is Christian morality; and although the institution is universal, and admits to its secrets the Jew or the Mussulman, still there is no religion to which its moral precepts are so well adapted as Christianity. Our Saviour describes the Jewish morality in the strongest terms of reprobation, in the fifth chapter of St. Matthew, and the seventh chapter of St. Mark; and it is well known that the Mahometan morality consists in invoking the name of God even when performing the most flagrant acts of iniquity. But the morality of the gospel is quite another thing. It is unnecessary to describe it; for every Brother will find it in Freemasonry, embodied in the three theological and four

Every association of men, for the sake of order and harmony, must be regulated by certain laws, and for that purpose proper officers must be appointed, and empowered to carry those laws into execution, to preserve uniformity, and to restrain any irregularity that might reflect disgrace on the institution.[11]   For we may as reasonably suppose an army may be duly disciplined, well provided, and properly conducted, without generals or other officers, as that a society can be supported without governors and their subalterns, or (which is the same thing) without some form of civil government.[12]   And as such an arrangement must be revered, it becomes a necessary pre-requisite that a temper should be discovered in the several members adapted to the respective stations they are to fill.[13]

This thought will suggest to you, that those who are qualified to preside as officers in a lodge, will not be elated with that honour; but, losing sight of it, will have only in view, the service their office demands.   Their

cardinal virtues, made perfect by the requisitions of brotherly-love, relief, and truth.

[11] Because " actions, in the abstract, are right or wrong, according to their tendency ; the agent is virtuous or vicious, according to his design. Thus, if the question be, whether relieving common beggars be right or wrong, we inquire into the tendency of such a conduct to the public advantage or inconvenience.   If the question be whether a man, remarkable for this sort of bounty, is to be esteemed virtuous for that reason, we inquire into his design, whether his liberality springs from charity or from ostentation.   It is evident that our concern is with actions in the abstract." (Paley.)

[12] Thus the Constitutions of Masonry provide that " if any Brother behave in such a way as to disturb the harmony of the lodge, he shall be thrice formally admonished by the Master, and if he persists in his irregular conduct, he shall be punished according to the by-laws of the lodge, or the case may be reported to higher masonic authority.   But no member shall be excluded from his lodge without notice being given to him of the charge preferred against him, and of the time appointed for its consideration.   The name of every Brother so excluded, together with the cause for his exclusion, shall be sent to the grand secretary ; and, if a country lodge, also to the Provincial Grand Master, or his deputy."

[13] The duties of the masonic governments correspond with those of the civil governments of states ; they are to promote the peace, security, prosperity, and happiness of the people ; in times of danger to afford protection, by the wise application of their powers ; in periods of prosperity, to give the best direction to the current of activity in the lodges, by promoting the the cultivation of science, and elevating the standard of knowledge and virtue.

reproofs will be dictated by friendship, softened by candour, and enforced with mildness and affection; in the whole of their deportment they will preserve a degree of dignity tempered with affability and ease.[14]   This conduct, while it endears them to others, will not fail to raise their own reputation, and as envy should not be so much as once named among Freemasons, it will effectually prevent the growth of it, should it unfortunately ever appear.

Such is the nature of our constitution, that as some must of necessity rule and teach, so others must of course learn and obey.   Humility, therefore, in both becomes an essential duty; for pride and ambition, like a worm at the root of the tree, will prey on the vitals of our peace, harmony, and brotherly love.[15]

Had not this excellent temper prevailed, when the foundation of Solomon's temple was first laid, it is easy to see, that glorious edifice would never have risen to a height of splendour which astonished the world.   Had all employed in this work been masters, or superintendents, who must have prepared the timber in the forest, or hewn and marked the stone in the quarry?[16]   Yet,

[14] It is well to give rules for the good government of a lodge; but the best teacher is experience.   Points of minor importance, both in discipline and doctrine, are of constant occurrence, which have no precedent, and must be regulated by the judgment of the Master.   And on these trifling matters the welfare and prosperity of a lodge frequently depend; such as reconciling differences, and causing animosities to subside; applying—not only a remedy, but the proper remedy—to all irregularities *as they arise*, because, if they are suffered to acquire strength by time, they are sure to create, in the end, great confusion and difficulty.   In a word, he must unite the *suaviter in modo* with the *fortiter in re*.   His deportment should be serious; his temper uniform; and by striving to give general satisfaction to the Brethren, he will reap a rich reward in their approbation and respect.

[15] The most ancient Gothic charges provide against this baleful feeling. They direct that "none shall show envy at a Brother's prosperity, nor supplant him, nor put him out of his work, if capable to finish it.   Masons must avoid all ill language, calling each other Brother, or fellow, with much courtesy, both within and without the lodge.   They shall instruct a younger Brother to become *bright* and expert, that the Lord's materials may not be spoiled.   But Free and Accepted Masons shall not allow cowans to work with them; nor shall they be employed by cowans without an urgent necessity.   And even in that case, they must not teach cowans, but must have a separate communication."

[16] The preservation of this harmony may be attributed in a great measure to the system above alluded to, of dividing the men into lodges, and

though they were numbered and classed under different
denominations, as princes, rulers, provosts, comforters
of the people, stone-squares, sculptors, &c., such was
their unanimity, that they seemed actuated by one
spirit, and influenced by one principle.[17]

Merit alone then entitled to preferment; an indisputable instance of which we have in the deputy Grand
Master of that great undertaking, who, without either
wealth or power, without any other distinction, than
that of being the widow's son, was appointed by the
Grand Master, and approved by the people, for this
single reason, because he was a skilful artificer.

Let these considerations, my worthy Brethren, animate us in the pursuit of so noble a science, that we
may all be qualified to fill, in rotation, the most distin- .
guished places in the lodge, and keep the honours of the
craft (which are the just rewards of our labour) in a
regular circulation. And as none are less qualified to
govern than those who have not learned to obey, permit
me, in the warmest manner, to recommend to you all a
constant attendance in this place, a due obedience to
the laws of our institution, and a respectful submission
to the directions of your officers, that you may prove to

commanding that every carved stone shall be marked with the workman's
signature. This custom was carried by the Dionysiacs to every part of
the world, and was used both by heathen and Christian Freemasons
throughout all time. Such marks are found on heathen temples at the
farthest extremity of the world; and in all ancient Christian edifices of
any importance in every country where the gospel has been planted. See
the Freemasons' Quarterly Review for 1845, p. 319, 442; and Godwin's
Letters to Sir H. Ellis on Masons' Marks.

[17] This disposition of the lodges gave rise to a degree called "the Mark,"
and a Mark Master was appointed to rule over every fellowcraft's lodge.
It was, therefore, formerly the custom in England to connect this degree
with that of a fellowcraft; although at this time it is considered, to all
intents and purposes, a separate degree, and invested with a separate
colour. I can, however, find no good reason for this, unless it be supposed, by the multiplication of degrees, that the resources of the society
will increase in a corresponding ratio. Another reason may also be
given, applying in some instances to the fact, that by multiplying the
the number of degrees, persons who value their character, and wish their
associates to be select, could exclude from their intercourse in the lodge
all such persons as had been improvidently or improperly introduced into
the inferior degrees. But even in this view of the case, I can perceive
no cause for interposing the third degree between what were evidently,
at first, two consecutive sections of the same chapter in the science.

mankind the propriety of your election, and secure the establishment of this society to latest posterity.

To accomplish these desirable ends, let me entreat your strict attention to our by-laws, ever keeping in view the general regulations, constitutions and orders of our ancient and honourable society.[18] Let due regard be paid to your officers in their respective stations, whose duty it is to regulate the proceedings of the lodge, and to carry the laws into execution, and may the only contention amongst us be, a laudable emulation in cultivating the royal art, and endeavouring to excel each other in whatever is good and great. The moral and social duties of life we should make a principal subject of contemplation; for thereby we shall be enabled to subdue our passions, and cultivate fraternal affection, the glory and cement of this institution, laying aside all malice, and, all guile and hypocrisies, and envies, and all evil-speakings—manifesting our love one to another; for "love is of God, and he that loveth God, loveth his Brother also. And he that saith he is in the light, and hateth his Brother, is in darkness until now."

Suffer nothing to be heard within the sacred walls of this lodge, but the heavenly sounds of truth, peace, and concord, with a cheerful harmony of social and innocent mirth; and " be ye like minded, having the same love, being of one accord and of one mind; let nothing be done through strife or vain-glory, but in lowliness of mind, let each esteem other better than themselves." Never give cause for it to be said, that we who are solemnly connected by the strictest laws of amity, should ever omit the practice of forbearance, and allow our passions to control us, when one great end proposed by our meeting here, is to subdue them. Let us not sit down contented with the name only of a Mason, but walk worthy of that glorious profession, in constant conformity to its duties. To become Brethren worthy of our most ancient and honourable institution, we must devote ourselves to the study and discharge of the fol-

---

[18] This direction is of the utmost importance to Masonry, and has always constituted a principal feature in its laws. Its violation originated that unhappy schism which disunited the Freemasons of this country for eighty years; and the institution presented the anomalous appearance of two Grand Lodges, which mutually denounced each other.

lowing duties, which are more or less within the reach
of every capacity, viz., a knowledge of the mysterious
problems, hieroglyphics,[19] and symbolical customs and
ceremonies of the royal art, together with the origin,
nature, and design of the institution, its signs, tokens,
&c., whereby Masons are universally known to, and can
converse with each other, though born and bred in different countries and languages.[20]

A Freemason must likewise be a good man, one who
duly fears, loves, and serves his heavenly Master, and, in
imitation of the operative Mason, who erects a temporal
building according to the rules and designs laid down
for him by the Master Mason, on his tressel-board, raises
a spiritual building, according to the laws and injunctions laid down by the Supreme Architect of the Universe in the book of life, which may justly be considered
in this light as a spiritual tressel-board.

He must honour the king, and be subordinate to his
superiors, and ever ready to promote the deserving Brother in all his lawful employments and concerns.
These, my Brethren, are qualifications of a good Mason,
wherefore they merit our peculiar attention ; and, as it
is our duty, we should make it our pleasure to practise
them ; by so doing we shall let our light shine before

[19] One of the earliest methods of propagating knowledge was by the
use of symbols. Thus Clemens Alexandrinus, quoting from Dionysius
Thrax, an ancient grammarian, in his exposition of the symbol of the
wheels, says, that some persons made a representation of their acts to
others, not only by speech but by symbols also. (Strom. l. v.) Any one
who is conversant in the learning of ancient time, will have seen that this
was the chief way of communicating science ; as is evident in the hieroglyphics of Egypt ; and the custom of symbolical instruction, which the
Pythagoreans and other philosophers derived from thence.

[20] Wherever Brethren meet, in whatever part of the world it may be,
whether they can understand each other's language or not, if it be by day
or by night, if one be deaf and the other dumb, they can nevertheless recognize each other as Brothers. In this respect the recognition-signs are
a universal language, and they are communicated to every Mason at his
initiation. Signs and grips can be given so cautiously, that it is not possible to perceive, if they are surrounded by thousands who have not been
initiated. To give the word is somewhat more difficult. By the grip we
may make ourselves known to the blind, by the sign unto the deaf, and
by the word and grip by day or by night. Each degree has its sign, word,
and grip, as in many cases it is not sufficient to make ourselves generally
known as Freemasons. See the Freemasons' Lexicon in Voc. Erken-
nungszeichen oder Zeichen, Wort, Griff.

men, and prove ourselves worthy members of that institution, which ennobles all who conform to its most glorious precepts.

Finally, let me advise you to be very circumspect, and well guarded against the base attempts of pretenders, always setting a watch before your mouth. And with respect to any who may call themselves Masons, but (possessing refractory spirits) are at the same time enemies to all order, decency, and decorum, speaking and acting as rebels to the constitution of Masons in this kingdom; let me exhort you to have no connection with them, but, according to the advice of St. Paul to the Thessalonians, " withdraw yourselves from every Brother that walketh disorderly,"[21] leaving such to the natural consequence of their own bad conduct; being well assured, that the vain fabric which they mean to erect, having no other support than their own ignorance, debility and deformity, will of itself soon tumble to the ground, with shame and ruin on the builders' heads. On the other hand, let us live in strict amity and fraternal love with all just and upright Brethren, that we may say with the royal Psalmist: " Behold how good, and how pleasant it is, for Brethren to dwell together in unity."

Let God's holy word be the guide of our faith; and justice, charity, love, and mercy, our characteristics then we may reasonably hope to attain the celestial password, and gain admittance into the lodge of our Supreme Grand Master, where pleasures flow for evermore.[22] This

---

[21] It is often urged as an objection to our institution that many of its professors are vicious and immoral in their conduct, and consequently regardless of their obligations. They, who urge this objection, little think that they are passing a censure upon their own understanding. The abuse of a thing is no valid objection to its inherent goodness. How many break their baptismal vows! how many call themselves Christians who are a disgrace to Christianity, yet ultimately hurt not the gospel but themselves! In the best institutions on earth, worthless characters may occasionally be found. In the holy family itself, consisting but of twelve, one was a devil. Did that injure or impair the integrity of the eleven? very far from it. It rather added a lustre to their virtues.

[22] " These virtues would be totally inefficacious without the aid of Christianity. Mr. Hume, in his fourth appendix to his Principles of Morals, complains of the modern scheme of uniting ethics with the Christian theology. They who find themselves disposed to join in this complaint, will do well to observe what the author has been able to make of

is the fervent prayer of him who glories in the name of a faithful Mason, and has the honour to be Master of this right worshipful lodge.

morality without Christianity. And for that purpose, let them read the second part of the ninth section of the above essay, which contains the practical application of the whole treatise—a treatise which Mr. Hume declares to be incomparably the best he ever wrote. When they have read it over, let them consider whether any motives there proposed are likely to be found sufficient to withhold men from the gratification of lust, revenge, envy, ambition, avarice; or to prevent the existence of these passions. Unless they rise up from this celebrated essay with stronger impressions upon their minds than it ever left upon mine, they will acknowledge the necessity of additional sanctions. But the necessity of these sanctions is not now the question. If they be, in fact, established, if the rewards and punishments held forth in the gospel will actually come to pass, they must be considered. Such as reject the Christian religion, are to make the best shift they can to build up a system, and lay the foundation of morality without it. But it appears to me a great inconsistency in those who receive Christianity, and expect something to come of it, to endeavour to keep all such expectations out of sight, in their reasonings concerning human duty." (Paley.)

LECTURE X.

ON THE DESIGN OF MASONRY. DELIVERED IN THE UNION
LODGE, EXETER, NO. 370, BY JOHN CODP.NGTON, ESQ.,
D. P. G. M., 1770.

> Sermo oritur, non de regnis domibusve alienis ;
> ————— ————— —sed quod magis ad nos
> Pertinet, et nescire malum est agitamus ; utrumne
> Divitiis homines, an sint virtute beati ;
> Quidve ad amicitias, usus, rectumne trahat nos,
> Et quæ sit natura boni, summumq : quid ejus.
>
> HORACE.

BEING this day, by your choice, exalted into this chair,
it is the fervent wish of my heart to render myself as
little undeserving as possible of the distinguished honour.
Many important duties has a Master of a lodge to perform ; and though I despair performing all of them as I
ought, yet I shall always endeavour to do so.[1] To give
instruction is the business of the Master ; and I think it
incumbent upon me, on this occasion, to consider the
nature and design of our institution, and to remind you
of the duties it prescribes.

First, then, our Order instructs us in our duty to the
Great Artificer of the universe ; directs us to behave as
becomes creatures to their Creator ; to be satisfied with
his dispensations, and always to rely upon Him whose
wisdom cannot mistake our happiness, whose goodness
cannot contradict it.

---

[1] Some expressions, perhaps sentences, in this Charge, belong to different writers whose names are not mentioned. It was never intended to be
printed ; the author, therefore, at the time of writing it, never minuted
down to whom he was obliged for them, and he cannot now recollect. He
thinks it proper to say this, that it may not be thought he, in the smallest
degree, assumes to himself what belongs to another.

It directs us to be peaceable subjects, to give no umbrage to the civil powers, and never to be concerned in
plots and conspiracies against the well-being of the nation ; and as political matters have sown the seeds of
discord amongst the nearest relations and most intimate
friends, we are wisely enjoined in our assemblies never
to speak of them.

It instructs us in our duty to our neighbour; teaches
us to injure him in none of his connections, and in all our
dealings with him to act with justice and impartiality.
It discourages defamation ; it bids us not to circulate
any whispe.· of infamy, improve any hint of suspicion,
or publish any failure of conduct. It orders us to be
faithful to our trusts ; to deceive not him who relieth
upon us; to be above the meanness of dissimulation ;
to let the words of our mouths be the thoughts of our
hearts, and whatsoever we promise religiously to perform.

It teaches inviolable secresy; forbids us to discover
our mystic rites to the unenlightened, or to betray the
confidence of a Brother. It warms our hearts with true
philanthropy, with that philanthropy which directs us
never to permit a wretched fellow-creature to pass by
till we have presented him with the cup of consolation,
and have made him drink copious draughts of the heart-
reviving milk of human kindness. It makes us lovers
of order; stifles enmity, wrath, and dissension, and nou-
rishes love, peace, friendship, and every social virtue; it
tells us to seek our happiness in the happiness we bestow,
and to love our neighbour as ourselves.

It informs us that we are all children of one Father :
that man is an infirm, short-lived creature, who passes
away like a shadow : that he is hastening to that place
where human titles and distinctions are not considered ;
where the trappings of pride will be taken away, and
virtue alone have the pre-eminence ; and thus instructed,
we profess that merit is the only proper distinction. We
are not to vaunt ourselves upon our riches or our honours,
but to clothe ourselves with humility ; to condescend to
men of low estate ; to be the friends of merit in whatever
rank we find it. We are connected with men of the most
indigent circumstances, and in a lodge (though our Order
deprives no man of the honour due to his dignity or cha

ractei,) we rank as Brethren on a level;[2] and out of a lodge, the most abject wretch we behold belongs to the great fraternity of mankind ; and, therefore, when it is in our power, it is our duty to support the distressed, and patronize the neglected.

It directs us to divest ourselves of confined and bigot-- ed notions, (the source of so many cruel persecutions,) and teaches us that humanity is the soul of all religions. We never suffer any religious disputes in our lodges, (such disputes tend to disturb the tranquillity of the mind, and as Masons, we believe that in every nation he that feareth Him and worketh righteousness, is accepted of Him. All Masons, therefore, whether Christians, Jews, or Mahometans, who violate not the rule of right, written by the Almighty upon the tablets of the heart, who do fear Him, and work righteousness, we are to acknowledge as Brethren ; and though we take different roads, we are not to be angry with each other on that account; we mean all to travel to the same place ; we know that the end of our journey is the same ; and we are all affection- ately to hope to meet in the lodge of perfect happiness. How lovely is an institution fraught with sentiments like these ; how agreeable must it be to Him who is seated on a throne of everlasting mercy ; to that God who is no respecter of persons.

It instructs us likewise in our duty to ourselves ; it teaches us to set just bounds to our desires ; to put a curb upon our sensual appetites ; to walk uprightly.

Our Order excludes women ; not because it is unwil-

[2] The level is an emblem of equality ; because with God there is no respect of persons, and in His sight all men are equal ; liable to the same infirmities, redeemed by the same Saviour, subject to the same death and judgment. This is the sense in which Masons understand the equality of members in tyled lodges. They know nothing of that levelling equality which is the idol of the revolutionists of this world ; they are taught by their Constitutions to be "peaceable subjects, and obedient to the civil powers ;" and are enemies to that confusion and anarchy which is destructive of social happiness. Hence the level distinguishes the Senior Warden, to remind him that while he presides over the labours of the lodge, by command of the W. M., as the Junior Warden does over its re- freshments, it is his duty to see that every Brother meets upon the level, and that the principle of equality is preserved during the work, without which harmony, the chief support of our institution, could not be main- tained in its purity and usefulness

ling we should pay a proper regard to that lovely sex,[3]
the greatest, the most valuable gift that heaven has bestowed upon us, but it bids us enjoy their society in such
a manner as the laws of conscience, society, and temperance, permit.[4] It commands us for momentary gratifications not to destroy the peace of families; not to take

[3] Our ancient Brethren were not particularly complimentary to the
sex, if the following were really introduced, as we are told, amongst the
reasons for holding their lodges on the highest of hills or the lowest of
valleys. "Au sommet d'une grande montagne, et au fond d'une grande
vallée, où jamais coq n'a chanté, *femme n'a babillé*, lion n'a rugi ; en un
mot, où tout est tranquille comme dans la Vallée de Josaphat. Expressions figurées, pour marquer la concorde et la paix qui règnent dans les
assemblées Maçonniques, *et le soin que l'on prend d'en exclure les femmes.*"
After all, it is a question whether the onus of this satire ought to be
chargeable on the craft in general ; for we only find the expression in one
formula, and it appears to be an interpolation from Shakespeare. (Taming
of the Shrew, Act i.)

> Have I not in my time heard lions roar?
> Have I not heard the sea, puff'd up with winds,
> Rage like an angry boar chafed with sweat?
> Have I not heard great ordnance in the field,
> And heaven's artillery thunder in the skies?
> Have I not in a pitched battle heard
> Loud larums, neighing steeds, and trumpet's clang?
> And do you tell me of a woman's tongue?

And it is probable that Shakespeare used it as a parody on the brutal
dogma of Democritus, who taught his disciples, according to Laertius,
that "to speak little becomes a woman; plain attire adorns her. A woman is sharper-witted for mischief than a man. To obey a woman is the
greatest ignominy to a man."

[4] A writer in Moore's Freemasons' Magazine, published at Boston, in
the United States of America, says very truly, "never may an honest,
open-hearted Mason fear that the better part of the creation will urge
against his Order, to his detriment, the circumstance that the ladies are
not admitted to a membership among Free and Accepted Masons. Let
him tell what is the fact, that Minerva, the goddess of wisdom, presides
in the masonic lodges, in which she would have but a divided empire, if the
goddess of beauty were admitted along with her. We surely could not
trust Venus and Minerva together in our lodges, lest we should become
too much distracted with the blandishments of Beauty to hear at all the
severer teachings of Wisdom. But it will be high time to attempt a
laboured defence of this masonic usage when a lady shall complain of it, or
when she shall refuse to make a secret-keeping Mason the lord of her
affections; pillowing on her pure heart both the unlocked casket and the
secret which it contains. Could she make him a renegade to honour, how
would she loathe him? How unsafe in such hands, and in such keeping,
would she ever after consider her own fame, and those gems of affection
which woman never gives, save to the trusty, the brave, the unconquer-
able, and the inflexible in purpose."

away the happiness, (a happiness with which grandeur
and riches are not to be compared,) which those experience whose hearts are united by love; not to profane
the first and most holy institution of nature. To enjoy
the blessings sent by divine beneficence, it tells us, is
virtue and obedience; but it bids us avoid the allurements of intemperance, whose short hours of jollity are
followed by tedious days of pain and dejection; whose
joys turn to madness, and lead to diseases and to death.
Such are the duties which our Order teaches us, and Masonry (the heavenly genius!) seems now thus to address us:

" The Order I have established in every part of it
shows consummate wisdom; founded on moral and social
virtue, it is supported by strength; it is adorned by
beauty, for everything is found in it that can make society agreeable. In the most striking manner I teach you
to act with propriety in every station of life. The tools
and implements of architecture, and everything about .
you, I have contrived to be most expressive symbols to
convey to you the strongest moral truths. Let your improvement be proportionable to your instruction. Be
not contented with the name only of Freemasons. Invested with my ancient and honourable badge,[5] be Masons
indeed. Think not that it is to be so to meet together,
and to go through the ceremonies which I have appointed; these ceremonies, in such an Order as mine, are
necessary, but they are the most immaterial part of it,
and there are weightier matters which you must not
omit. To be Masons indeed, is to put in practice the
lessons of wisdom which I teach you. With reverential
gratitude, therefore, cheerfully worship the Eternal Providence; bow down yourselves in filial and submissive
obedience to the unerring direction of the Mighty Builder; work by his perfect plans, and your edifices shall be
beautiful and everlasting.

[5] The lambskin or white leather apron is the well-known badge of a
Mason, and is the first gift bestowed on the newly-initiated E. A. P.
The apron is worn by Operative Masons to preserve their garments from
spot or stain; but as Speculative Masons, we use it to promote the principles of morality. It is an emblem of innocence, and teaches us to preserve that purity of life and conduct which will not only increase our
happiness in this world, but exalt us ultimately to a house not made with
hands, eternal in the heavens.

15*

"I command you to love your neighbour; stretch forth the hand of relief to him if he be in necessity; if he be in danger, run to his assistance; tell him the truth if he be deceived; if he be unjustly reproached and neglected, comfort his soul, and soothe it to tranquillity You cannot show your gratitude to your Creator in a more amiable light than in your mutual regard for each other.

"Taught, as you are by me, to root out bigoted notions, have charity for the religious sentiments of all mankind; nor think the mercies of the Father of all the families of the earth, of that Being whom the heaven of heavens cannot contain, are confined within the narrow limits of any particular sect or religion.

"Pride not yourselves upon your birth, it is of no consequence of what parents any man is born, provided he be a man of merit; nor your honours, they are the objects of envy and impertinence, and must ere long be laid in the dust; nor your riches, they cannot gratify the wants they create; but be meek and lowly of heart. I reduce all conditions to a pleasing and rational equality; pride was not made for man, and he that humbleth himself shall be exalted.

"I am not gloomy and austere. I am a preacher of morality, but not a cruel and severe one; for I strive to render it lovely to you by the charms of pleasures which leave no sting behind; by moral music, rational joy, and harmless gaiety. I bid you not to abstain from the pleasures of society, or the innocent enjoyments of love or of wine: to abstain from them is to frustrate the intentions of Providence. I enjoin you not to consecrate your hours to solitude. Society is the true sphere of human virtue; and no life can be pleasing to God but what is useful to man. On this festival, in which well pleased, my sons, I see you assembled to honour me, be happy. Let no pensive look profane the general joy; let sorrow cease; let none be wretched; and let pleasure and her bosom friends attend this social board. Pleasure is a stranger to every malignant and unsocial passion, and is formed to expand, to exhilarate, to humanize the heart. But he is not to be met with at the table of turbulent festivity; he disclaims all connections with indecency and excess, and declines the society of riot roaring in the jollity of his heart.[6] A sense of the dignity of human nature always accompanies him, and he admits not of anything that degrades it. Temperance and cheerfulness are his bosom friends; and, at the social board, where he never refuses his presence, these friends are always placed on his right hand and on his left; during the time he generally addresses himself to cheerfulness, till temperance demands his attention. On this festival, I say be happy; but, remember now, and always remember, you are Masons, and act in such a manner that the eyes of the censorious, ever fixed upon you, may see nothing in your conduct worthy of reproof; that the tongue of the slanderer, always ready to revile you, may be put to silence. Be models of virtue to mankind. Examples profit more than precepts. Lead uncorrupt lives, do the thing which is right, and speak the truth from your hearts. Slander not your neighbour, and do no other evil unto him; and let your good actions convince the world of the wisdom and advantages of my institution. The unworthiness of some of those who have been initiated into my Order, but who have not made themselves acquainted with me, and who, because I am a friend to rational gaiety, have ignorantly thought excesses might be indulged in, has been disgraceful to themselves, and discreditable to me.

" Have I any occasion to mention charity to a lodge where no object of distress has ever applied without being relieved—to a lodge which has decreed that, on the festivals of St. John,[7] there should always be a collection

---

[6] An objection is frequently urged against Freemasonry on the ground that men, who, before they were Freemasons, were lovers of sobriety and domestic life, have afterwards been intemperate, and fond of resorting to places of public entertainment. If any real foundation were ever given to this objection, it must have been by men who have shut their ears to the earnest and repeated admonitions of their Order; which, though it indulges rational festivity, forbids, in the strongest manner, irregularity and intemperance. Thus, in the old Gothic charge of behaviour after the lodge is closed, the Brethren are permitted to " enjoy themselves with innocent mirth, treating one another according to their ability, but avoiding all excess; not forcing any Brother to eat or drink beyond his inclination, according to the old regulation of King Ahasuerus, (Esther, i. 5,) nor hindering him from going home when he pleases; for though, after lodge hours, Masons are like other men, yet the blame of their excess may be thrown upon the fraternity, though unjustly."

[7] One of the by-laws of the Union Lodge at Exeter, A. D. 1769,

made for charitable purposes, and that the Master or
Wardens should recommend the propriety of it. Whilst,
free from care, you are enjoying the blessings of Providence, you forget not to raise the drooping spirits, and
exhilarate the desponding hearts of indigent Brethren;
and whilst you know one worthy man is deprived of the
necessaries of life, you cannot enjoy its superfluities.
Ye have passed from death unto life, because ye love the
Brethren. With the chains of benevolence and social
affection, I link the welfare of every particular with that
of the whole. The chief foundation of my institution is
charity. I cry aloud to my children not to pass by on
the other side when they see objects of distress, but to
go to them, and have compassion upon them; to bind
up their wounds, pouring in oil and wine; to set them on
their own beasts; to carry them to a place of safety, and
take care of them. I bid them weep for those who are
in trouble; never to see any perish for want of clothing,
or suffer the stranger to lodge in the street, but to open
the door to the traveller. Never to cause the eyes of
the widow to fail, or eat the morsel by themselves alone,
and the fatherless not to be partakers thereof. I show
them the path which is perfumed by the breath of benediction, and which leads to the celestial lodge where the
merciful shall obtain mercy.

"But some might have inclination to assist the poor
in their trouble, and not to be able to do so without pre-
judicing themselves or their families. Remember that
when you are directed to be charitable, I direct you to
be so as far as you can without doing injury to yourselves
or your connections. But money is not the only thing
the unfortunate stand in need of. Compassion points
out many resources to those who are not rich for the
relief of the indigent; such as consolation, advice, protection, &c. The distressed often stand in need only of
a tongue to make known their complaints; they often
want no more than a word they cannot speak, a reason

---

directed "that the Master of a lodge or one of the Wardens, by his
Order, do take a proper opportunity soon after dinner, on every St. John's
Day, to recommend to the members, and visiting Brethren present, a
voluntary contribution towards increasing the fund for charity, and that
a collection be accordingly made by the treasurer for that purpose."

they are ashamed to give, or entrance at the door of a great man which they cannot obtain.

"Ye are connected by sacred ties; I warn you never to weaken, never to be forgetful of them. I have only to add, that I wish you happy. Virtue, my sons, confers peace of mind here, and happiness in the regions of immortality."[8]

Such would be the address of the genius of Masonry, were she to appear visibly amongst us. And none who are emulous to sustain the character of good and worthy Masons, could safely refuse to receive and obey her instructions. She thus teaches you that the qualifications necessary to form a worthy member of our Order are, a wise philanthropy, pure morality, inviolable secrecy, and a taste for the polite arts.

Lycurgus, Solon, Numa, and all other political legislators, could not make their establishments durable. How wise soever their laws might have been, they could not extend them into every country and every age. As these laws had in view only victories and conquests, military violence, and the elevation of one people above another, they could not become universal, nor agree with the taste, the genius, and the interests of every nation. Philanthropy was not their basis. The love of country, badly understood, and carried to an excess, often destroyed in those warlike republics the love of humanity in general. Men are not essentially distinguished by the difference of the languages they speak, the dresses they wear, or the dignities with which they are invested. The whole world is but one great republic, of which every nation is a family, and every particular person a child. To revive and spread abroad those ancient maxims drawn from the nature of man, is one of the ends of our establishment. We wish to unite all men of an agreeable humour and enlightened understanding, not only by the love of the polite arts, but still more by the great principles of virtue; and from such an union, the interest of the fraternity becomes that of all mankind. From such, every nation may draw solid knowledge,

---

[8] Or in the more expressive language of the old lectures, "Virtue is true nobility; wisdom is the channel by which virtue is directed; wisdom and virtue alone can distinguish us as Freemasons."

and all the subjects of different kingdoms may conspire without jealousy, live without discord, and mutually love one another without renouncing their country.[9]

Thus Masonry instructs us in our duty to the Supreme Architect of the universe, to our neighbours, and ourselves. It teaches truth, peace, and concord. It bids us open our ears to the cries of the unfortunate, and extend our hands to them with the cup of consolation; it unites men of all nations in one affectionate bond of Brotherhood; it shows us we are all upon a level, and that merit is the only just distinction. It orders us to live within compass, and always to act upon the square with the world, and with one another. It is not gloomy, but cheerful; it forbids intemperance, but encourages rational mirth and innocent pleasure; in short, it is a superstructure fixed with solid firmness on the broad basis of moral and social virtue.

Sound morality is also required in our society. Let a man's religion, or mode of it, be what it will, we do not exclude him from the benefits and advantages of our Order, provided he believes in the glorious Architect of heaven and earth, and practises the sacred duties of morality. We are directed to expand our hearts with the most generous sentiments, to root out bigotry, and stop the cruel hand of persecution. We are bid to unite with virtuous men of the most distant countries and opposite opinions; and to unite with them in the firm and pleasing bond of fraternal love. We therefore banish from our lodges every dispute which may tend to disturb the tranquillity of the mind and gentleness of the manners; or to destroy those sentiments of friendship, and that

---

[9] These happy results would always distinguish Freemasonry, if the lodges were influenced in the selection of their candidates by the three requisites which were enjoined by our ancient Brethren, denominated physical, mental, and moral. The physical qualifications are, that the candidate shall be a free man, born of a free woman, of mature age, and able body. The mental qualifications embrace sanity of mind; a capabilty of understanding the obligations and instructions of the Order, that he may be prepared to perform its duties The moral qualifications are, that he shall neither be an atheist, an infidel, nor an irreligious libertine; that he must obey the moral law, and practise the four cardinal and the three theological virtues; he must be an humble believer in the wisdom, power, and goodness of God, because this constitutes the religious creed of Freemasonry, and acts as a check upon vice, and a stimulus to virtue.

perfect harmony to be found only in the retrenching all indecent excesses and discordant passions.

The obligations that the Order lays upon its members, are to protect the Brethren by your authority : to enlighten them by your understanding; to edify them by your virtues; to sacrifice every personal resentment, and diligently to seek for everything which will best contribute to the peace, concord, and credit of the society. Let your heart be always ready to commiserate distress; your hand ever open to relieve it. Drop balm upon the wounds affliction has made, and bind up the hearts which sorrow has broken, and thus experience the exalted happiness of communicating happiness to others.

We have secrets amongst us, which compose a language, sometimes mute, and sometimes very eloquent, to be communicated at the greatest distance, and to know our Brethren by, let their country or their language be what it will.

What has scarcely happened to any other society, has happened to ours. Our lodges have been established in, and are now spread over, all polite nations; and yet, amongst so great a multitude of men, no Brother has ever yet betrayed our secrets.[10] Dispositions the most volatile, the most indiscreet, and the least trained up to secresy, learn this great science as soon as they enter amongst us. So great an empire over the mind has the idea of brotherly union! This inviolable secresy powerfully contributes to link together the subjects of different kingdoms, and to facilitate, and render mutual between them, the communication of benefits. We have many examples of it in the annals of our Order. Brethren

---

[10] It was one of the most ancient injunctions of Masonry to keep inviolate the secrets of the Order, although this appearance of mystery subjected the Brethren of the middle ages to many evil imputations. An old masonic MS. gives the following rule :—

> The thrydde poynt most be severele,
> With the prentes knowe hyt wele,
> His mayster cownsel he kepe and close,
> And hys felows by hys goode purpose ;
> The prevetyse of the chamber telle he no mon,
> Ny yn the logge whatsever they donn ;
> Whatsever thou horyst, or syste hem do.
> Telle yt no mon, whersever thou go ;
> The cownsel of halle, and yeke of bowre,
> Kepe hyt wel to gret honowre,
> Lest hyt wolde torne thyself to blame,
> And brynge the craft ynto gret schame.

travelling over the various nations of Europe, and finding
themselves distressed, have made themselves known to
our lodges, and immediately have they received all necessary assistance.[11]   We are connected by solemn promises.   If any one should fail in the solemn promises
which connect us, you know, Brethren, that there is no
greater punishment than the remorse of conscience, the
infamy of perfidy, and the exclusion from our society.

The famous feasts of Ceres at Eleusis, of Isis in Egypt,
of Minerva at Athens, of Urania amongst the Phœnicians,
and of Diana in Scythia, had some relation to our solemnities.   Mysteries were celebrated in them in which many
vestiges of the ancient religion of Noah and the patriarchs are to be met with.   They finished by repasts and
libations, but without the excesses, debaucheries, and
intemperance, which the pagans by degrees fell into.
The source of all these infamies, was the admission of
persons of both sexes to their nocturnal assemblies, contrary to their primitive institution.[12]   It is to prevent
such abuses that women are excluded from our Order.
It is not that we do not pay a natural and due regard to
that most beauteous part of the creation, or that we are
unjust enough to look upon them as incapable of secresy,

[11] The incident which induced Lord Ramsay, one of the Scottish Grand
Masters, to become a Mason, is a proof that this practice is not a vain
boast.   As this nobleman was walking with his tutor, before he became
of age, a wretched beggar, who appeared to be a foreigner, entreated his
charity.   The clergyman turned round to question the suppliant, and in
a moment grasped his hand with the most cordial kindness.   Lord Ramsay was surprised.   The stranger was a Freemason ; he was fed, clothed,
and supplied with the means of transport to the coast of Syria, from
whence he came.   This circumstance made such an impression upon Lord
Ramsay, that he determined, as soon as possible, to join an association so
pregnant with good works.

[12] The above observation is most true ; but the reasons for which the
custom was introduced appear plausible in theory, how revolting soever
they might prove in practice.   It was a received opinion amongst many
ancient nations, that some of their gods were propitious only to men,
and others only to women ; which made them sometimes prohibit the one,
and sometimes the other, from being present at their sacred rites and
solemnities.   The Lacedemonians took away this piece of superstition by
admitting both sexes to their most secret religious services.   Thus females were initiated into the most holy mysteries, as well as males, that
so by an early knowledge of each other, there might be a real love and
friendship established between them, which ever stood most firm upon the
basis of religion.

but because their presence might insensibly alter the purity of our maxims and our manners; we are afraid, nor groundless are our fears, that love would enter with them, and draw us to his flowery tempting paths, where jealousy too often would diffuse his venom through our hearts, and from affectionate Brethren, transform us into implacable rivals.

Another qualification necessary to enter into our Order, is a taste for useful sciences, and liberal arts of every kind. These improve the heart as much as the understanding; moderate the selfish affections; sweeten and harmonize the temper, and better fit men for social happiness—that happiness which Freemasonry most zealously endeavours to promote.

The name of Freemason ought not, then, to be taken in a literal, gross, and material sense, as if we were simple workmen in stone and marble. We do not consecrate our talents and our riches to the construction of external temples, but enlighten, edify, and protect the living temples of the Most High.

Thus have I given you some account of Masonry, and the qualifications necessary to make a worthy member of it; by which you see it is not a ridiculous and trifling, but a very serious and important institution; an institution founded on the most exalted principles of moral and social virtue.[13] May we ever keep in view its noble and real design, and catch the spirit of it. May it be our glory to practise the duties it prescribes. Moral architects as we are, may we build temples for every virtue; prisons and dungeons for vice, indecency, and immorality.[14] May we be disposed to every humane and friendly

---

[13] Addressed to a clergyman :—" You, Brother, are a preacher of that religion of which the distinguishing characteristics are universal benevolence and unbounded charity. You cannot, therefore, but be fond of the Order, and zealous of the interests of Freemasonry, which, in the strongest manner, inculcates the same charity and benevolence, and which, like that religion, encourages every moral and social virtue, which enforces the practice of all the softer virtues of humanity, which introduces peace and goodwill amongst mankind, and is the centre of union to those who otherwise might have remained at a perpetual distance ; and believe me, Brother, that whoever is warmed with the true spirit of Christianity, must esteem—must love Freemasonry."

[14] Addressed to a French gentleman :—" You, Brother, the native and subject of another, a great and enlightened kingdom, you, by entering

office, ever ready to pour oil and wine into the wounds of our distressed Brethren, and gently bind them up (it is one of the principal ends of our institution), so that when those who speak evil or lightly of us behold our conduct, and see by our means the hungry fed, the naked clothed, the sick sustained and cherished—shall see our light so usefully shine—their evil speaking may be silenced, their foolish prejudices removed, and they may be convinced that Masonry is an useful and a venerable structure, supported by the great and everlasting pillars of wisdom, strength, and beauty.

into our Order, have connected yourself by sacred and affectionate ties with thousands of Masons in this and other nations. Ever reflect that the Order you have entered into bids you always look upon the world as one great republic, of which every nation is a family, and every particular person a child. When, therefore, you are returned to, and settled in, your own country, take care that the progress of friendship be not confined to the narrow circle of national connections or particular religions, but let it be universal, and extend to every branch of the human race. At the same time, always consider that besides the common ties of humanity, you have this night entered into other obligations, which engage you to kind and friendly actions to your Brother Masons of all countries and religi●.

LECTURE XI.

ON THE MASONIC DUTIES. DELIVERED IN ST. NICHOLAS'S
LODGE, NO. 378, NEWCASTLE. BY THE REV. R. GREEN,
OF DURHAM, 1776.

" A Mason ought to be the most valiant warrior, the most just judge,
the kindest master, the most zealous servant, the tenderest father, the
most faithful husband, and the most obedient son ; for his duties as a
citizen in general have been strengthened and rendered sacred by the
voluntary masonic obligation ; and he, if ever he should neglect them, not
only would show a want of fortitude, but also be guilty of hypocrisy and
perjury."—EXHORTATIONS FROM THE GERMAN.

THE privileges which the members of a Freemasons'
lodge enjoy are too numerous, and of too exalted a character, to be comprised within the limits of a single address, and I shall, therefore, only mention one or two of
these on this occasion. Removed from that disagreeable
bustle, tumultuous confusion, and fortuitous intercom-
munity, which must unavoidably happen in houses of
public concourse, we are now, I hope, both in a commodious situation, and also a place of safe retirement,
where we may securely enjoy generous freedom, innocent
mirth, social friendship, and useful instruction ; with
many other privileges that might here be mentioned.
But, as there is no privilege which is of real use but
what is likewise subject to abuse, it therefore behoves
each of us to look carefully to ourselves, that none of us
be found guilty of any abuse whatever. Therefore, as
we have our refreshment under our own management,[1]

---

[1] It was frequently the custom of the Brethren in those days, who had
been prudent enough to erect a masonic hall for their exclusive use, to
furnish the vaults underneath their lodge room with a stock of wine, and
other necessaries, which made them totally independant as to the quality
and quantity of the refreshment which they thought proper to use.

and our time at our own disposal, I should think, that a moderate use of the one, and an useful improvement of the other, would stand in need of very few arguments to enforce the practice of either; more especially as we hold temperance, fortitude, justice, and prudence to be some of our first foundation-principles;[2] and, moreover, as meekness, temperance, moderation, and charity are so often recommended in the divine law, to which we pretend to pay the greatest deference. Let us, therefore, not be slothful in business, not wasters of time, but fervent in spirit, serving our Lord. And as we have this day dedicated and set apart this place for the worship of the true God, and the contemplation of his wonderful works, it would, therefore, be so much the more incongruous in any one of us, ever to make any other use thereof than that to which it is now destined, or to suffer any mean or unworthy practices, i. e. such as are unbecoming the Christian profession, ever to be exercised within these walls, at least so long as it is in our possession.

The better to attain these great ends, let us always, when we meet here, be moderate in our expenses, temperate in our regalements,[3] innocent in our amusements, and prudent in the length of time employed in each of these; and in all things so ordering our whole deportment, as to render due obedience to our Creator, perform real justice to our neighbour, and practise genuine virtue for ourselves.

---

[2] I am afraid, as society in the last century were *bons vivants*, the Masons did not escape censure on this point. The by-laws of the lodge at Lincoln, which existed in the early part of the last century, constitute a proof of the truth of this conjecture. Thus they provide that—"The lodge shall be opened and closed at the appointed hours, so that there may be one examination at least gone through every lodge night; and the person who neglects it shall forfeit *a bottle of wine*, to be drunk by the Brethren *after the lodge is closed*, to make them some part of amends. Not fewer than three leaves of the constitutions shall be read, &c., under the penalty of *one bottle of wine*, to be paid as aforesaid. No Brother made in another lodge shall be passed Master in this lodge under half-a guinea, to be paid *for the entertainment of the Masters present.*"

[3] The original Gothic charges were particularly applied to the preservation of temperance, in professed imitation of the old regulation of King Ahasuerus, in whose reign "the drinking was according to the law, none were compelled; for so the king had appointed to all the officers of his house, that they should do according to every man's pleasure." (Esther i. 8.)

There is one thing that I would earnestly desire to be practised in this lodge, and that is, that on all lodge nights every member thereof should keep good hours, and go soberly home ; and if he choose to indulge himself in staying a little later abroad, that he should do this at any other time, rather than on the lodge nights.[4] This would be one method, amongst several others, that might be used of making our friends and families, but especially the fair sex, to entertain a far better opinion of Freemasonry than they generally do. By this, and some similar methods, they would be induced to think, for instance, that we spent less money on account of Masonry than is generally thought ; that we were employed in more sober exercises than is frequently imagined ; and, in a word, that the strictest decorum in all things is always most scrupulously maintained in our society.

But when I reflect on our excellent by-laws, I find it almost needless for me to expatiate on this head, because they are in this article sufficiently explicit, if only they were but something more punctually adhered to. Besides this, I am agreeably prevented from enlarging on this topic, when I look round this assembly, and see all the offices of dignity supported by Brethren, who, I am firmly persuaded, want neither inclination nor abilities, both to recommend and to enforce whatever may be found necessary to maintain the universal reputation of the institution in general, and the true felicity of this lodge in particular.[5]

---

[4] A dissuasive from this indulgence altogether would have been better, because drunkenness is a social festive vice, apt, beyond any vice that can be mentioned, to draw in others by the example. The drinker collects his circle, the circle naturally spreads ; of those who are drawn within it, many become corrupters and centres of sets and circles of their own; every one countenancing, and, perhaps, emulating the rest, till a whole neighbourhood be infected from the contagion of a single example. This account is confirmed by what we often observe of drunkenness, that it is a local vice, found to prevail in certain countries, in certain districts of a country, or in particular towns, without any reason to be given for the fashion, but that it had been introduced by some popular example. (Paley.)

[5] The principal design of the laws of Masonry is to promote the harmony of its members, and by that means create a marked line of distinction between Freemasonry and every other existing society. The attributes of the several degrees were therefore distinctly characterized, that no mistake might occur in their application to the business of the

Only I would beg to be indulged a little in offering
you, my worthy Brethren, and the officers of this lodge,
one piece of sincere and friendly advice, which, I hope,
may not be altogether unseasonable. The advice is this,
that you, the officers, should have frequent meetings
among yourselves, in order to know and consult one
another,[6] concerning the good of the society ; that so,
when you come to appear in the lodge on any emergency
among the rest of the Brotherhood, you may all appear
to be of one heart, and of one mind, without any jarring
sentiment, or contradictory emotion, which must unavoidably be the case, if the foregoing method, or something similar thereto, be not put in practice.[7] And
opposition of sentiments, especially in those who are
previously supposed to be agreed, as managers and lead-

craft. The Brethren of the first degree were expected to distinguish
themselves by honour and probity ; the fellowcrafts by diligence, assiduity,
and a sincere love of scientific pursuits ; while the few, who by their
superior virtues attain to the third degree, recommended themselves to
notice by their truth, fidelity, and experience in the details and landmarks
of the Order.

  [6] Hence originated lodges of instruction, which are now become so
common, that the grand lodge has thought it necessary to issue a specific
law upon the subject ; although it appears to be rather vague. "No
general lodge of instruction shall be holden, unless under the sanction of
a regular warranted lodge, or by the special licence and authority of one
Grand Master. The lodge giving their sanction, or the Brethren to
whom such licence is granted, shall be answerable for the proceedings of
such lodge of instruction, and responsible that the mode of working there
adopted has received the sanction of the grand lodge." (Const. Lodges
of Instruction.)

  [7] In 1842 a singular case occurred in New York, in which the rights
and privileges of the Master of a lodge were placed in jeopardy by the
action of his lodge. After the lodge was opened, the Master had occasion to be absent for a short time, leaving the Senior Warden in the
chair. On his return to his seat, he found that charges had been preferred against him, and a committee appointed to try him, and the Senior
Warden refused to return to his hands the warrant and mallet of the
lodge ; complaint being made to the Grand Master by the Master, he
directed the Grand Secretary to inform the said Senior Warden, that it
was his direction that he should forthwith return the warrant to the hands
of the Master, and that the action of the lodge on that case must be suspended, and the members hold themselves in readiness to maintain their
charges before the Grand Stewards' lodge, which was all promptly complied with by the parties. The ground of his decision was, that the
Master of a lodge is only subject to impeachment and trial before his
peers, who are acquainted with his duties, but which the members of a
lodge cannot know until they are themselves seated in the oriental chair.
(See the Transactions of the Grand Lodge of New York, June 7. 1843.)

ers of the rest, must not only be derogatory to these officers themselves, disgustful to their Brethren, but likewise highly detrimental to the good order and harmony of this, or any other society. Therefore, as this disorder is attended with such pernicious consequences, and might be so easily remedied, it is to be hoped that the admonition will be so much the more readily complied with.[8] And further still, what would very much assist you in the honourable discharge of your duty as officers, would be, to get perfectly acquainted with our excellent book of constitutions, our regulations, and by-laws.

And as for the rest of you, my worthy Brethren, many of whom are yet but young Masons, I would also presume to offer you the following thoughts, viz., that you would give all diligence to become proficients in this our laudable profession, in order that you may know what is incumbent on you by being Masons, and how to discharge your duty in this particular, to your Creator, to your neighbour, and to your own consciences; for many, far too many, there are (with deep regret I utter the expression), who know nothing more of real Masonry than only the mere nominal appellation, to the great danger of their own peace of conscience while here, their eternal welfare hereafter, and likewise to the great detriment of our most ancient, honorable, and excellent society.[9] A knowledge of our duty, as far as we can possibly attain it, is an indispensable requisite. And the lodge is the only proper place, wherein we can expect to arrive at any proficiency in this our noble science; and by a con-

---

[8] In 1734 it was ordered by the grand lodge, that "if any Brother so far misbehave himself as to render his lodge uneasy, he shall be thrice admonished *by the Master and Wardens in a lodge formed;* and if he will not refrain his imprudence, nor obediently submit to the advice of his Brethren, he shall be dealt with according to the by-laws of that particular lodge, or else in such a manner as the quarterly communication shall in their prudence think fit."

[9] I am afraid there is much truth in this observation, even at the present day. Numbers of Brethren are satisfied with a knowledge of the signs, words, and tokens, and search after nothing further. And this is the reason why some of our Brethren, otherwise worthy men, are inclined to place Freemasonry on no higher scale than the ephemeral societies of the day. And it is to be feared that there are many intelligent men who have forsaken the Masonic institution, rather than be at the trouble of investigating its merits. All this is extremely unfortunate, but there are cogent reasons for believing it to be true.

stant and regular attendance there, we may reasonably
expect to become masters of this our royal art.[10]
   When I mention becoming masters in the art of Masonry, I would be understood not to extend this expression
to its utmost degree of latitude; because Masonry is one
one of the largest fields for speculation of any science or
profession whatever, Christianity only excepted; and,
therefore, to become complete masters of it, would require more time and pains than the lot or the capacity
of the general part of mankind can either afford, or put in
practice. But that knowledge which I would be understood to mean, is more or less within the reach of every
capacity, if cultivated with reflection and assiduity, viz.,
a knowledge of the mysterious problems, hieroglyphics,
symbolical customs and ceremonies of our royal art, together with the origin, nature, and design of the institution, its signs, words, tokens, &c.,[11] whereby Masons are

   [10] The gradual progression of the candidate to a competent knowledge
of the science of Masonry, has been clearly developed by a writer of the
last century. He enumerates the three classes as being perfectly distinct, and only to be attained by a perseverance in the practice of wisdom
and virtue. And he concludes his dissertation by saying, that the arrangement is so perfect as to promote friendship and hospitality, to reward industry, and to encourage ingenuity and scientific research. No one, who
has really given his mind to the study of the general principles of the
Order, can refuse his assent to so reasonable a proposition.
   [11] An intelligent Mason, Bro. Husenbeth, thus expresses himself on the
signs, words, and tokens of the Order:—" To found the universality of
Freemasonry upon the few traditional S. T. W., which we are taught in
the three initiatory degrees, is flying in the face of masonic experience,
and of our universally-spread doctrines, and is in opposition to the first
principles of the craft. The Jews, no doubt, had imbibed the principles
of secrecy from the Egyptians during their captivity; they continued,
under their great, learned, and inspired leader, those principles founded
upon the law of God. But as Freemasons we are only bound to believe
that the secret societies established amongst them were governed, guided,
and kept alive by the known principles of our Order, viz., charity to all
mankind, relief to the distressed, and truth in our relation with others.
But believing in those principles, so essential in all societies regularly
constituted, we are by no means bound to believe in all the idle tales of
S. T. and W. being the same now as they were at the time of the exit
of Moses; or in some silly and ridiculous traditions invented by fertile
brains, and so glaringly depicted in pretended masonic books, such as the
silly book called 'Jachin and Boaz,' and many others; for by whatever
exterior marks or signs the Brethren of the ancient secret societies knew
each other, matters little to the universality of our doctrines, provided
the grand principle be strictly observed. The Jews, for five hundred
years after their delivery from Egypt, have left us not a single masonic

universally known to, and can converse with, each other, though born and bred in different countries, and though they speak divers languages.[12]

Many are the encomiums and panegyrics which have been both spoken and written in praise of Freemasonry, and that by men of very great abilities, both in nature and literature. I have neither time, nor perhaps capacity, to come up to many that I have heard and seen on this subject, and therefore shall only say, that there is scarcely anything noble, anything desirable, or anything praiseworthy but what has been at some time or other applied to Masonry; and, indeed, it is no wonder, seeing that it is upheld by those excellent pillars, wisdom, strength, and beauty, which are three endowments the most desirable of any other in this life; and without which no regular science, nor mechanism, can either be put in execution, or carried on to any purpose; and though some may prefer riches to some one of these three, and indeed we must all allow that riches are good and desirable, if they are used for good ends, yet if they be desired, or preferred, for their own sake only, these are but mean and sordid sentiments, which no wise man or good Mason can possibly, with any consistency, be possessed of. See an instance in Solomon,[13] where we see that this wisest of men and best of Masons refused riches,

tradition beyond that recorded in the first degree; and as the second degree treats upon the arts and sciences, it certainly came from a different source than the first; for the ten commandments, and more especially the Talmudic explanation of the same, were a bar to the higher studies of the Jews." (Freemasons' Quarterly Review, 1836, p. 21.)

[12] Rabelais is very severe in his reprehension of this system in his account of the dispute between Thaumast, an English philosopher, and Panurge, the servant of Pantagruel. His commentator says:—" Our author's sole aim was to turn into ridicule the pretended science of signs and numbers, taught by the venerable Bede, and too much esteemed of by Thaumast, an Englishman, as well as Bede himself. Rabelais allots this task to the waggish Panurge, who, for one sign which the other makes to him, gives him two in return, and those the most out-of-the-way ones that could be. Accursius has enlivened his gloss De orig. Jurics with such another monkey-like scene, which he says did actually pass in ancient Rome, between a certain Greek philosopher and a fool, who was set up against him by the Romans. To all the Grecian mysterious signs, the fool returned very whimsical ones, which, in like manner as here by Thaumast, were taken by the philosopher for so many learned answers to all his doubts and objections."

[13] 2 Chron. i. 7—13.

16

wealth, and honour, and only chose wisdom, the better
to discharge the trust reposed in him. So, then, as these
three human endowments, and pillars of our science,
appear to be so laudable, useful, and desirable, therefore
let each of us endeavour, according to the utmost of our
power, to possess as much of them, or of those dispositions which follow from, or are indicated by them, as
possibly we can.

Again, Freemasonry deserves the highest applause,
because of its dignified principles, which are brotherly
love, relief, and truth ; principles the most noble, interesting, and sublime of any other in this sublunary state.
These, according to our blessed Lord and Saviour's own
words, are some of the main foundation principles upon
which he established both his gospel and his noble scheme
of Christianity. " On these two commandments (of the
love of God and of our neighbour) hang all the law and
the prophets." " What doth Jehovah require of thee,
but to do justly, to love mercy, and walk humbly with
thy God."[14] If these, and such like principles, were
really wanting in our science, it would not be worth the
least regard from the wise, the good, or the virtuous;
but since it is really possessed of these, and many of a
similar nature, it deserves to be cultivated with a far
more ardent affection, and a far greater assiduity, than
it at present seems to be, even by its most zealous votaries ;[15] and I am sorry to have it to say, that I am fully
persuaded it ought to be looked upon in quite a different
point of view, than it seems to be in our days, by too
many of the more remiss, and who yet go under the honourable designation of Free and Accepted Masons. These

---

[14] Matt. xxii. 40; Micah vi. 8.
[15] Bro. Frodsham, who presided over one of the old lodges in the
city of New York, A. D. 1762, thus describes Freemasonry :—" When I
consider the end of Masonry in general, when I reflect upon the noble-
ness of its original design, when I see it in its infancy rise with the sun
in the east, when I behold it in its meridian glory, spreading beams of
brightness around, then, when I view it struggling through the clouds
of superstition and oppression, and, here in the north, when I see it, notwithstanding the virulence of its foes, rising to its primeval state, it immediately occurs to me, that the institution came from heaven itself, that
it was ordained to stand against the tooth of time; and that firm and
collected in its own purity and integrity, it should for ever remain, that
in it there should be strength, and that God would establish it so firmly
that the gates shall never prevail against it."

grand principles ought never to depart from our views, but to be as it were engraven on our hearts, and to be as so many motives and incitements to our duty towards our Maker, our neighbour, and ourselves ; and I would add, that without we be duly impressed with a sense of these, we can never discharge our duty as we ought.

Need I mention that Masonry is connected with the four cardinal virtues, justice, fortitude, temperance, and prudence ; virtues which are the immediate hinges upon which all other virtues are said to turn, and to which every other virtue is some way related.

Again, there is no useful science, art, or mechanism with which Masonry is not closely connected. As for the seven liberal arts of grammar, rhetoric, logic, arithmetic, geometry, music, and astronomy, we know and are sure they all serve her in their turn, and yield to her their mutual assistance. Every sign, every token, every word in Masonry are so many different significant, comprehensive, and emphatic ways of a Freemason's expressing himself, which none but those who have served a sufficient time to the craft, so as to penetrate into these truly otherwise immense depths, can possibly understand or rightly comprehend.[16] Likewise our emblems of the square, level, plumb, compasses, and other moral jewels, each of which are so many well-contrived instruments suited to such an art, and so many silent monitors, teaching its moral and very instructive lessons to every one who has had the honour to come properly within a justly constituted Freemasons' lodge.

And now, my dear Brethren, seeing Freemasonry is upheld by such dignified supports, built upon such noble principles, and connected with so many useful, sublime, and laudable branches of sciences and virtues of different denominations, comprehending duties sacred, social, and

[16] The use of signs is carried to great perfection in the East ; for not only in private and domestic concerns, but also in those of public importance, on occasions of life and death, inferiors actually look *to the hands* of their superiors, and receive orders from them. The Orientals have a language by signs, and thus they give *silent orders* to their servants, who understand them perfectly. In the court of the grand seignior, the attendants, as we are told by Knolles, understand anything that is conveyed to them by signs ; and will themselves, by the gesture of their eyes, bodies, hands, and feet, deliver matters of great difficulty, to the great admiration of strangers.

civil ; how diligent ought we all to be, in order every one
to know his own duty, as also how to discharge it in a
becoming manner, each of us in our respective stations.[17]
For since Freemasonry is connected with so many various arts and sciences, it therefore requires a great deal
of time and attention, before we can possibly discharge
our duty even in any tolerable degree. But though this
may be difficult in respect to any perfect measure, yet
all that is essentially necessary may be known, if only
a tolerable degree of time, diligence, and application be
allotted for the attainment of what is so very requisite
for us to know.

Let us, therefore, not sit down contented with the bare
name of a Mason only, especially when a little time and
trouble would make us, in some degree, masters of the
science ; but let us devote ourselves to the study and discharge of those duties, the performance whereof is so very
incumbent on us ; let us walk worthy of that profession
which we have voluntarily entered into, and are strictly
bound to the faithful discharge of ; and let us be so much
the more punctual and constant in real conformity to all
the duties inculcated thereby. Because a contrary conduct, and a negligent attendance in the lodge, can produce
nothing but ignorance, error, and disaffection ; and, indeed, were these the only ill consequences of a wilful
or indolent absence, the craft might not suffer much by
such careless and lukewarm Brethren ; but I am sorry to
say, this is not all, the eye of the censurer is ever upon
us, and the tongues of those who hate us are ever ready
to lay hold of the least opportunity, in order to blaze
abroad what may be of the least disadvantage to our institution ; and, hence also it often happens, that Masons
themselves afford, to such as these, but too ample occasion to vent their spleen and rage in this respect.[18]

[17] To do this will equally promote the honour of Masonry and our own
individual benefit ; and to neglect it will cast a reproach upon the most
ancient and best of human institutions.

[18] "Amongst the various societies of men, few, if any, are wholly exempted from censure. Friendship, however valuable in itself, and however universal may be its pretensions, has seldom operated so powerfully
in general associations as to promote that sincere attachment to the welfare and prosperity of each other, which is necessary to constitute true
happiness. This may be ascribed to sundry causes, but to none with
more propriety than to the reprehensible motives which too frequently

For, whenever any member of our profession wilfully, or indolently, deserts the body, what can we expect from the unenlightened part of the world, but that the harmony and improvement of our society should be egregiously impeached; notwithstanding that we both profess and know that these valued privileges, an harmony of sentiment and improvement of the mind, are the inseparable companions of every well-regulated Freemasons' lodge, where virtue finds a real pleasure, and vice a just abhorrence.

Besides these several advantages of a regular attendance, I would beg leave to mention one more, and that is, that the frequent assembling of men in society has the greatest tendency of begetting in each of their breasts, besides a real love for each other, a kind of unity of sentiments; the great advantage of which, every one in our profession will readily apprehend; for when men often assemble together, and speak their minds freely to one another, as Freemasons are supposed to do, there may be an opportunity of regulating what may be amiss in any of our conducts—and who is there that is without his faults? There is an opportunity for the comfortless and needy to be relieved by the salutary councils and beneficent relief of those in capacity—there is an opportunity for the ignorant to be instructed by the learning and prudence of those who may be more advanced—an opportunity for the wise to display and use his talents to the best of purposes, viz., the real improvement of his companions and Brethren; so that all may

lead men to a participation of social entertainments. If to pass an idle hour, to oblige a friend, or probably to gratify an irregular indulgence, be the only inducement to mix in company, is it surprising that the important duties of society should be neglected, and that in the quick circulation of the cheerful glass, the noblest faculties should be sometimes buried in the cup of ebriety? But while the laws of the craft are properly supported, they will be proof against every attack. Men are not aware, that by decrying any laudable institution, they derogate from the dignity of human nature itself, and from that good order, and wise disposition of things, which the Almighty Author of the world has framed for the government of mankind, and established as the basis of the moral system. Friendship and social delights can never be the object of reproach; nor can that wisdom, which hoary time has sanctioned, be a subject for ridicule. Whoever attempts to censure what he does not comprehend, degrades himself; and the generous heart will pity the mistakes of such ignorant presumption." (Preston.)

mutually give and receive pleasure, improvement, and
satisfaction, and that grand principle of brotherly love
would immediately follow.[19]

To the neglect of frequently assembling together, I
think it may be fairly imputed, that so much dryness in
our outward deportment, so much distrust in our inward
conceptions, so little real regard for each other's welfare,
prevails amongst us. For by what means it has become
a kind of first principle in the human breast, I do not at
present intend to define; but this seems to be the real
case, that until one man be some way assured that another is of the same mind with himself in regard to
mutual acts of friendship, social duties, or relative obligations, they will one, if not both, very likely be rather
backward in the performance; but as soon as they come
to be possessed of something like an union of sentiments, then will they mutually perform their respective
duties, and that with the greatest cheerfulness and
alacrity.

But all this must spring from unity of sentiment; and,
therefore, the assiduous cultivation of this great Christian
principle of brotherly love cannot be too strictly inculcated; because the due improvement thereof would so
affect our hearts as to cure all those evils formerly mentioned, and change them into virtues; would produce all
those good effects which necessarily follow from well-

---

[19] " The uninformed world have ever been divided in their opinions of
the rites and origin of our Order. Philosophers have beheld in it an ano-
maly in the history of the earth. Without territorial possessions, its
moral dominion is almost universal; with no other arms than those of
prudence and fortitude, it hath conquered the persecutions of the superstitious, and survived the mighty fall of Israel, the vast empires of Egypt,
Babylon, Assyria, Media, Rome, and Greece, where alternately it was
honoured by the protection of kings and rulers, or exposed to the most
cruel hostility. In all the liberal states of Europe it is publicly honoured
and encouraged; monarchs are at its head, its ranks are adorned by men
eminent for their station and worth—by names illustrious in the annals
of science, benevolence, and virtue. In Italy, where formerly to have
been known as a member of the craft was to have been exposed to the
terrors of the stake, Masonry exists with scarcely more than the usual
precautions of secresy; active hostility has ceased, the thunders of the
Vatican are silent, opinion is making a sure though silent impression in
its favour; even these pages are written in a land where Castiglione
perished, where so many Brothers have sealed their devotion to the pure
principles of the Order in their blood." (Freemasons' Quarterly Review,
1836, p. 11.)

conducted causes, and operate so strongly on our constitutions, as to direct the very spring of our actions to the
best of events; then should we never be so happy as
when assembled together: then one unity of affections,
sentiment, and government, would most firmly subsist;
for whatever draws men into society, it is only the true
cultivation of these principles that can cement or keep
them in it.[20]

Now, my dear Brethren, let us endeavour to discharge
the duties incumbent on us as individuals, and then the
whole community will move in concord. Let us be
swift to hear, slow to speak, and candid in our whole deportment. Mankind are generally very sharp-sighted
and eagle-eyed towards their neighbours, and can readily
detect, reprehend, and find faults in the conduct of their
brethren; whereas they have seldom time, courage, or
ingenuity enough to look at home; where there may be
just as great faults, with regard to the union and good
agreement of society, in their own character, as those
they look upon to be of a more egregious nature. I have
seen the sour look and disdainful mien of one do more
prejudice to the true harmony of society, than the drunk-
en frolics of two or three. I have also seen the aspir-
ing airs and overbearing carriage of one have a much
worse tendency on society, than the inadvertent mis-
carriages and undesigned mistakes of several. Therefore,
when we see any of our Brethren overtaken in a fault,
let us judge of him with the utmost caution, and always
be ready to palliate and lessen his crime; if in a passion,
for instance, let us bear with him, and each seriously ask
ourselves, whether we have not given him some reason
for such behaviour. If overtaken in any fault, let us
never use any rough measures, where lenient ones will
work the effect.

[20] St. Paul in like manner says :—" Keep the unity of the spirt in the
bond of peace. There is one body, one spirit, one hope of yourcalling,
one Lord, one faith, one baptism." (Eph. iv. 5.) Again, to the Corin-
thians—" I beseech you, brethren, by the name of our Lord Jesus
Christ, that ye all speak the same thing, and that there be no divisions
among you; but that ye be perfectly joined together in the same mind
and in the same judgment." (1 Cor. i. 10.) The exhortations to unity,
both by Christ and his apostles, are always urged with becoming force
and energy. Hence, as one great object of the written revelation was to
promote unity amongst Christians, it dishonours the Almighty to rend

What I mean by all these injunctions is, that each of
us may be stirred up to act our own parts as individuals,
for the good government of the whole community, so
that true harmony may flow of its own accord; and in
order still to effect this so much the better, let no provo-
cation be amongst us, but each provoking one another to
love and good works; let no contention be amongst us,
but each contending for the truth; let there be no strife
amongst us, but each striving who can work best, and
love one another most; and hence will naturally spring,
of course, all those inestimable blessings to this society,
which I have been inculcating.

But suffer me here to add one piece of friendly advice,
which, I am persuaded, you will find no less advantageous
for the good government and welfare of this society, than
some of the foregoing; and that is, that all of us be exceeding careful in the admission of members; we have
all, perhaps, been hitherto too eager in this particular; I
would, therefore, recommend, that in our future choice
of a member, we seriously consider whether his conduct
and circumstances in life be such, as may not have the
least tendency to diminish the honour and credit of our
honourable society; nay, further, I would not only have
every member to be such, as that he may, negatively,
bring no discredit to the society, but, positively, that he
be such as may be some way useful and profitable thereto; as a good member of society, an agreeable companion,
and also have an ordinary measure of knowledge; so that
I think we ought not only to reject all who are not of
good report and sound morals, but likewise all those who
have not a competent measure of understanding; remembering that nothing contributes more to the dissolution of any society, especially a Freemasons' lodge, than
too great a number of members indiscriminately chosen.[21]

any moral institution into parties, divisions, and factions; or to dishonour
it by improper or vicious conduct.
  [21] Bro. Blanchard Powers, an aged American Brother, has some valuable observations on this subject in his prize essay, delivered in 1842,
which are worth quoting. He says:—"Let us remember the caution
which ought to be used in the admission of every candidate. Let it be
known to the world, that the character that would become a Mason must
undergo the strictest scrutiny. He must be a man of strict morality;
he must be humane, benevolent, and charitable to his fellow-creatures; he
must be no gambler, tippler, or profane swearer; he must be no railer

It being just as absurd to imagine that happiness is to be found in such a numerous lodge, as to think that true greatness consists in size or dimensions.

Hence, then, that we may be enabled to perform our respective duties with freedom, fervency, and zeal, let us unanimously concur in cultivating peace, harmony, and perfect friendship, striving who shall excel most in brotherly love, beneficence, and generosity; and then I make not the least doubt but that we may be enabled to conduct the business of the lodge, and discharge the duties incumbent on each, with universal approbation.

Let us consider that love is the new and greatest commandment, and that all others are comprehended in this one. This is said to be the fulfilling the whole law, and of consequence, a necessary qualification for the celestial lodge above, where universal love reigns and pervades through all the members, and where the Supreme Architect of the Universe presides alone, as Master over all, and whom the apostle John styles love itself. But remember that Faith, Hope, and Charity are the three principal graces by which we must be guided to those celestial mansions; there to enjoy the greatest felicity with immortality dwelling in light; and of these three, charity, or universal love, is the chief, for when faith shall be swallowed up in vision, and hope in enjoyment, then will true charity, or brotherly love, shine with the brightest lustre to all eternity. Or, in the words of the poet—

"Shall stand before the host of heaven confest,
For ever blessing, and for ever blest."

Further, let us take God's holy word for the only guide of our faith here, and let justice, charity, love, and mercy be our distinguishing characteristics; then may we rea-

against the religion of Christ, or the professors thereof; he must be a lover of decency and order; and he must be strictly honest, industrious, and upright in all his conduct; for such as delight in the practice of vice are a disgrace to civil society, and are seldom reformed by the most excellent instruction. Such retain their vices unchangeable, as the skin of the Ethiopian or the spots of the leopard. Such, indeed, would never apply for admission into our benign institution, were they acquainted with her solemn principles, who were not lovers of decency and order."

16*

sonably hope, by an humble dependence on divine grace, to attain the celestial pass-word for everlasting life, and so gain admittance into the lodge of our supreme Grand Master above, in whose blessed presence pleasures will most certainly flow for ever and for evermore.

LECTURE XII.

ON BROTHERLY LOVE. DELIVERED AT THE CONSTITUTION OF THE HARMONIC LODGE, NO. 369, DUDLEY. BY THE REV. JOHN HODGETS, A. M. 1784.

" Be not ashamed of an insignificant but honest man out of the Lodge, whom thou hast acknowledged a short time before as a Brother; the Order would then be ashamed of thee also, and send thee back to the profane theatre of the world, there to exercise thy pride. Is thy Brother in danger? Haste thou to his assistance, and hesitate not to endanger thy own life for him. Is he distressed? Open thy purse to him, and rejoice in having found an opportunity to make so benign a use of thy gold. Thy obligation compels thee to be benevolent to all mankind, but in particular to thy Brother."—FROM THE GERMAN.

IF we search into the constitution of the human mind, we find that God has planted within us two kinds of propensities very distinct from each other. One for the preservation of the individual, and the other for the union and mutual support of the whole species. Of the former kind are self-love, and the sensations of hunger, thirst, and fatigue, prompting us to refresh our beings; and if God had not designed us for social life, nature would have stopped here; we should not have been furnished with other necessary affections.[1] But as our natural

---

[1] And nothing can afford a greater proof that our ancient Brethren entertained this feeling than the establishment of our social institution. No matter how widely opinions may differ as to the date of this society, all are agreed on its moral and social tendency. To improve the good properties of the human mind, and to cultivate the liberal sciences, were the original intentions of those who first modelled the association into a specific form. But modern practice has far outstripped the primitive idea of moral benevolence. Charity amongst the ancient philosophers bore a very different signification to that which is attached to it amongst Christians, whether we understand it as a temporal propensity to relieve the distressed, or as an universal feeling of divine love. Amongst the former, charity was designated by three naked figures, which were termed

wants and weaknesses are such as render the assistance
of our fellow-creatures necessary to our well-being, and
this cannot be expected but from a mutual intercourse
and exchange of good offices, Providence has planted
in our hearts powerful incitements to promote the common good. Of this kind are love, conjugal, parental, and
filial; friendship, charity, and universal benevolence,
which are all natural sensations conspiring with the private affections to improve the general happiness; for
without this sympathy of nature, men would be greatly
deficient in those kind offices of charity, which, in the
vicissitudes of human affairs, are reciprocally wanted.[2]
All access would be denied to the indigent and miserable; they would have no advocate to plead for them;
but, being wretched, would remain so, with this aggravation of misery, that there would be no one to commiserate their unhappy case. It is the secret and invisible
tie of nature, which connects power with subjection,
wealth with poverty, and ease with affliction; for it
strengthen the client's dependance on the patron, gives
the necessitous an hold on the benefactor, and procures
the unhappy a friend in other bosoms. How kindly has

Graces. They were represented with joined hands, one turned from the
beholder, and the other with their faces towards him, to intimate that
when one act of charity is done, thanks are twice due. The Charities
were represented naked because kindness ought to be done in sincerity
and candour and without disguise. The joining of their hands symbolized that one good turn deserves another, and there ought to be a perpetual intercourse of kindness and assistance amongst friends. But with
us masonic charity builds hospitals and asylums for the distressed of every
grade; endows schools for training up destitute orphans to virtue and
religion; and makes the widow's heart to sing for joy. These good works
place Freemasonry in a high position amongst the philanthropic institutions of the world: which is augmented by its tendency to produce an
universal Brotherhood, and to promote the glory of God, peace on earth,
good will towards man.
   [2] A correspondent to the Sherborne Journal (August, 1835,) thus
plainly describes the object of true charity amongst Masons: " Merit
and virtue in distress; persons who are incapable of extricating themselves from misfortunes in their journey through life; industrious men
who, from inevitable accidents and acts of Providence, have fallen into
ruin; widows left survivors of their husbands, by whose labours they
subsisted; orphans in tender years left naked to the world; and the
aged, whose spirits are exhausted, whose arms are unbraced by time, and
thereby rendered unable to procure for themselves that sustenance they
could accomplish in their youthful days. Thus is charity the keystone
of our mystical fabric. '

nature provided against urgent distress, by planting even
in the breast of strangers so strong a compassion, that
they shall oftentimes step into the place of nearest relations and friends! You cannot here avoid recollecting
the good Samaritan, who, though an enemy to the unfortunate Jew that had fallen into the merciless hands
of robbers, yet knowing and feeling that the impressions
of humanity were not to be effaced by differences of religion, he has compassion on his fellow-creature, binds up
his wounds, pouring in oil and wine, sets him on his own
beast, brings him to an inn, and takes care of him.

We are not, like the Jews, to confine our affections,
and extend our liberality only to the narrow circle of a
particular family, tribe, or nation, and hate and persecute
the rest of mankind.[3] Go and ask the great Saviour and
Redeemer of the word, who is your neighbour and brother
He will show you, the relation of humanity entitles every
man to this character; that the obligations of justice,
the duties of friendship, the offices of kindness, are not
to be sacrified to that too selfish bigotry, which is so unhappily apt to whet men's passions, and alienate their
affections from one another.[4] His command to love our

[3] The above paragraph contains a very just view of the universality of
Masonry. Whatever be a man's creed, whatever his religion, if he be an
object of charity, relieve him—comfort him—restore him if you possibly
can. This was the teaching of Jesus Christ, and it is the teaching of
Freemasonry. When the daughter of the Canaanitess said to the Redeemer
of mankind : "Truth, Lord, but the dogs eat of the crumbs that fall from
their master's table," he healed her daughter, though she were of a hostile
and forbidding faith. And in like manner Masonry listens to the supplications of a distressed Jew or Mahometan, because they are of the same
blood with ourselves, and descended from a common parent. And nothing can be a greater evidence of the Christian application of Masonry ;
because no other religion that ever existed taught the sublime doctrines,
and practised the amiable precepts of universal charity.

[4] The blessed effects of Christian Brotherhood appeared most conspicuously in the first society of Christians, and forms an example worthy of
masonic imitation. They exhibited a total detachment from all perish-
able things. The earth became the image of heaven, the plaintive tone
of indigence was never heard ; the felicity of every individual was inseparable from the felicity of the whole ; and by this admirable concert
of parts, an august body was formed, in which all men, how unequal soever in rank, were rendered *equal* by their moderation, *great* by their
disinterestedness, and *happy* by their beneficence. " It is inconceivable,"
says a cotemporary writer, " what unremitting diligence those Christians
use to succour one another, since they have abandoned the true religion
to adore a crucified man. Their teachers have acquired *the wonderful*

neighbour is as extensive as his dominions, and reaches
to the poor heathen, his heritage, and to the utmost
parts of the earth, the boundaries of his possession. But
as the appetite may be depraved and lost by intemperance, so the affections may be altered, and even extinguished, by vicious habits.   A bad man may divest
himself even of his nature ; and he has effectually done
this who is not moved at another's misery.   He is no
longer of our species.   He may retain the outside form
and lineaments of a man, but within he is contrary to
nature—not having an heart of flesh, but of marble, unsus-
ceptible of tender impressions.[5]

But hitherto we have considered compassion as an animal affection.   This, under the conduct of judgment and
conscience, is a true principle of action ; but left entirely
to itself, like other passions, it may rather be called a
weakness than a perfection.   For how often do we see
the good-natured misled by the tenderness of this passion, to do things which they cannot approve of; but
reason points out the object, distinguishes the order, and
regulates the bounds ; discovers what compassion is due
to our country, parents, friends, families, relations, elected Brethren and acquaintance, to those who have particularly obliged us, or been of use and service to us ;

art of persuading them that they are all Brothers, in so much that the
whole of their possessions are given up for the general welfare."

[6] And the world can exhibit no other institutions which are distinguished by these beneficent principles, but Christianity and Masonry.   In the
earliest times the benevolence of Christians rose so far above the level of
ordinary conception, that the pagans attributed it to some secret spell or
charm that had the power of inspiring violent and irresistible attachment.
A bitter enemy to Christianity gives this testimony in its favour.   "Nothing," says he, "has contributed more to the progress of the Christian
superstition than their attention to the poor and friendless.   Let us even
exceed them in this way ; let us immediately establish hospitals and other
asylums for indigence and infirmity in every city ; for certainly it is no
small ground of reproach that we should be so glaringly deficient in
these things, whilst those impious Galileans cherish and relieve not only
the wretched of their own communion, but likewise of ours."   Eusebius,
in describing a plague that laid waste the interior of Egypt, has these
remarkable words :—" Multitudes of our Brethren, without distinction of
rank, were content to sacrifice their lives in carrying out the great principle of brotherly love.   They supported the loathsome and infected
bodies of the expiring in their arms ; and, after closing their eyes, carried
them on their shoulders to the grave, only living to receive, perhaps in
the course of a few minutes, the same prompt, generous, and intrepid office
of mercy from others."

shows what degree of pity is due to those who, by no
misconduct of their own, but by some of the unavoidable
accidents of human life, are reduced to distress; convincing us, by experience, that we are fellow-creatures,
liable to the same infirmities, to the same misfortunes,
and to the same wants; and therefore we have all of us
reason to exercise that compassion and tenderness which
no man knows but in the course of time he may stand in
need of himself.[6]

In the next place, religion comes in to the support of
reason, to strengthen the obligations of nature, by en-
forcing what is reasonable itself, with the positive
injunction of a Superior, who has an infinite authority
over us to command our obedience, for his having created, preserved, and redeemed us. As creatures, he has
made of one blood all nations of men, for to dwell together on all the face of the earth, and therefore commanded us not to hide ourselves from our own flesh; not
to shut up our bowels, but to show not merely justice,
equality, and integrity, but mercy and compassion every
man to his brother.[7] As our preserver, he is daily pour-

[6] When Coustos was imprisoned in the Inquisition, on the charge of
being a Freemason, in 1743, after having suffered various tortures to extort the secret from him, he thus truly described the design of the Order:—
"The works of charity which the fraternity think it incumbent on them
to exercise towards such as are real objects of compassion, and whereof I
have given your lordship some few instances, show that it is morally
impossible for a society so execrable as you have described that of the
Freemasons to be, to practise a virtue so generally neglected, and so
opposite to the love of riches, at this time the predominant vice, the root
of all evil. But Freemasons yield implicit obedience to the laws; and
revere, in the magistrates, the sacred person of the king, by whom they
were nominated; rooting up, to the utmost of their power, every seed of
sedition and rebellion; and are ready, at all times, to venture their lives
for the security of the prince and his government. They never quarrel
with the religious principles of any one; but live together in fraternal
love, which a difference of opinion can never lessen."
[7] These are symbolized in the lodge by the moveable jewels. It is a
singular fact that the application of these instruments of labour vary in
the systems of England and Scotland. In England the square is devoted
to the Master of a lodge, and the compasses to the Grand Master. In
Scotland the Brethren consider every Master of a lodge as the represent
ative of King Solomon, and therefore entitled to wear the same emblems
as the Grand Master. The jewels vary according to the wealth of the
lodge, although they generally consist of the compasses, square, rule,
quadrant, and the sun and moon with a stone in the centre to denote the
eye or blazing star. Indeed, the Brethren there look on the square and

ing down his benefits upon us, and laying us under infinite obligations; which debt of gratitude we have no clearer method of discharging, than by communicating the like benefits to our fellow-creatures. As our most gracious Redeemer has constituted a new relation among Christians; made us members of the same spiritual body, parts of each other, and inspired us with new life and affections in Christ Jesus our head. We have one Lord, one faith, one baptism, are one body, and one spirit, and have one hope of our calling; and in consequence of this most intimate relation, we are commanded to suffer with our fellow-members, to weep with them that weep, and to put on as the elect of God, holy and beloved, bowels of mercy and compassion, to be faithful, kind to one another, and tender-hearted. And these positive injunctions are supported by the strongest motives of fear and hope; it being declared on one side that he shall have judgment without mercy, who sheweth no mercy; and on the other that the minutest act of compassion, even a cup of cold water, given to a disciple for the sake of Christ, shall not lose its reward. And finally, to shew that our Lord requires herein nothing of us but what he practised himself, we frequently read of his being moved with compassion at the sight of the multitude having nothing to eat, to whom he gave food, lest they should faint by the way. On various other occasions at the sight of the lame, the blind, and the sick, to whom he gave limbs, eyes, and health. Even at the sight of the complicated misery of Jerusalem, when the measure of her iniquities being filled up, and his compassion could have no other effect, is dissolved into tears. Let the same mind then, my Brethren, be in you which was in Christ Jesus.

What has been hitherto delivered, is a true description

compasses combined as the *sine qua non* of the Master of a lodge. The moral jewels are the square, the level, and the plumb line. Perhaps this is the cause why in England the square is given to the Master. The Scotch Blue Grand Lodge, when established in 1736, instituted an officer called Substitute Master, which does not occur in any other country. When first this important office was created, he was very improperly invested with the jewel of the Senior Warden, while that officer used the square. But there is, I believe, scarcely one lodge in all Scotland, out of Edinburgh, that follows this system. They give, however, to the two deacons, one the square and the other the compasses.

of a good man, or a Christian. Suffer me, in the next place, to inform you, that it is the real basis on which Freemasonry is built.[8] To confute the aspersions of the illiberal and ungenerous on this our royal art, is not my intention; yet to descant a little on our noble and ancient Order will, I hope, neither expose me to censure nor displeasure. If our first parents had remained in their terrestrial paradise, they would have had no occasion for the mechanic arts, nor any of the sciences now in use; but having lost their innocence, they, in that unhappy moment, lost their supernatural ability and inspired knowledge. From that fatal æra we date the necessity and origin of the liberal arts and sciences. The royal art was, beyond all doubt, coeval with the above sciences, and so was carefully handed down by Methuselah to his grandson, Noah; and, passing through the Druids to the inhabitants of our island,[9] it has, and I hope ever will, been preserved with that veneration and esteem it justly merits, and none but the worthies of this, or any other nation, ever will be initiated in this our royal art.

Having briefly shown you the antiquity of Masonry,[10]

[8] On the Continent the requisites of an aspirant for Masonry are as follow. He is required to pass some hours in solitude, that he may have leisure to reflect on the qualities which have been recommended to him by the W. M., viz., on brotherly love, courage, and constancy; on temperance, fortitude, prudence, and justice. He must also meditate on the malign influence of those evil passions which produce disorders in society, that he may learn how to avoid them, viz., hatred, jealousy, avarice, ambition, &c. Moreover, he is recommended to reflect on the obligations of the divine law, and to examine himself respecting the errors of his past life, that he may not only be able to give an account of them if required so to do, but may also avoid them for the future. He is also expected to practise, during his probation, certain prescribed acts of charity to the poor and distressed.

[9] "In this country, under the Druids," says Hutchinson, "the first principles of our profession most assuredly were taught and exercised." Opposed to this assertion, we find in the Freemasons' Quarterly Review for 1840, p. 14, a clear argument to prove that the true Freemasonry and the Druidical mysteries were totally different and distinct from each other.

[10] The high antiquity of Freemasonry has been stoutly denied by its opponents. De Quincy boldly affirms, on the authority of Professor Buhle. that "before the beginning of the seventeenth century, no traces are to be met with of the Masonic Order." (London Magazine, 1824, p. 12.) Hammer, of Vienna, however, has condescended to carry it up as high as the crusades; which brought out an anonymous writer, who referred its origin to the building of Strasburgh church in the thirteenth century.

I shall, in a few words, point out its utility." As all
societies, without due regulations, must necessarily hasten
to ruin, so Freemasonry, unless accompanied with brotherly love, beneficence, and truth, will speedily rush
into discredit. By brotherly love we are to understand
a generous principle of the soul, which looks upon the
human species as one family, created by an All-wise
Being, and suffered to exist for the mutual assistance of
each other. Beneficence calls forth that generosity of
mind into action, and liberally alleviates the burdens and

He says:—"I defy all the Masons of England, France, Germany, or
Scotland—even those who have attained to the highest degrees in the
society—to prove that it was contemporary with the Knights Templars;
in spite of Hiram and the temple of Solomon; and in spite of Phaleg
and the tower of Babel. The cathedrals of Vienna, Cologne, and Lan-
shut, were all of them being built at the same time. I believe that the
tower of Strasburgh is a more sensible and certain monument of the origin of the society than the brazen columns of Jachin and Boaz." While
a periodical journal published at Leipsic carries its origin back to the
corporation of builders at Rome, mentioned by Vitruvius as "Corpora
Collegia;" and advances that no regular historical accounts of its origin
are to be found, owing to the unsettled state of the times, and the great
political events with which the earlier Masons were identified. The corporation of builders as Freemasons are here traced back to the reign of
Numa Pompilius, who built the temple of Janus, and divided the citizens
into classes and societies; those of the builders or masons he termed
"Collegia fabrorum—Collegia artificum." So conflicting are the state-
ments of the opponents of Freemasonry.
    " The lectures of the several degrees give more than one definition of
Masonry, agreeing perhaps in substance, but differing in terms. Thus,
in one instance, we find it explained as "the study of science blended with
the practice of virtue;" in another it is called "a peculiar system of morality, veiled in allegory, and illustrated by symbols;" and in a third "a
science which includes all others; teaching human and divine knowledge,
and the moral duties which are incumbent on all Masons, as members of
civil society." One of our ancient charges teaches that "though in ancient times Masons were charged in every country to be of the religion
of that country or nation, whatever it was, yet it is now thought more
expedient only to oblige them to that religion in which all men agree,
leaving their peculiar opinions to themselves." Another enjoins "that
we shall be good men and true to God and the holy church, and use no
error or heresy by our understanding or by other men's teaching." While
an ancient document, printed in Preston's Illustrations, defines Masonry
to be "the skylle of nature, the understondynge of the myghte that ys
hereynne, and its sondrye werkynges: sonderlyche, the skylle of recken-
ynges, of waightes and metynges, and the true manere of façonnynge al
thynges for manne's use; leadlye, dwellinges, and buyldynges of alle
kyndes, and all other thynges that make gudde to manne." Masonic
authors, in like manner, have varied the definition according to their
respective views.

miseries of the wretched.[12] Truth is a divine attribute, and the fountain of masonic virtues. This is an edifice founded upon a rock, which malice cannot shake, nor time destroy.[13]

What a secret satisfaction do we Freemasons enjoy, when in searching for truth, we find the first principle of useful science preserved among us, as we received it by oral tradition from the earliest ages; and this truth is also confirmed by the testimonies of the best and greatest men the world has produced. But this is not all, the sacred writings confirm what I assert, the sublime part of our mystery being there to be found; nor can any Christian Brother (let me speak it distinctly) be a good

---

[12] The most ancient charges and constitutions make Brotherly Love an indispensable duty in the craft. I subjoin a specimen of these injunctions form the ancient MS. published by Halliwell :

> At thys semblé were poyntes y-ordynt mo,
> Of grete lordys and maystrys also,
> That whose wol conne thys craft and com to astate,
> He must love wel God, and holy churche algate,
> And his mayster also that he ys wyth,
> Wheresever he go, yn fyld or fryth;
> And thy felows thou love also,
> For that thy craft wol that thou do.

[13] If the enquiry be pressed, "why has Masonry remained unmoved amid the convulsions which have agitated the political world?" I answer— all other institutions of human origin have trusted themselves to their own supposed excellence, or to their inherent value, being based alone upon the wisdom of man. Not so with Masonry. Conscious of man's impotency, and of the mutability of everything beneath the sun, Masonry has been based upon revelation, and places her trust on God. With heartfelt regret we are constrained to acknowledge, that there is too much recklessness in the deportment of some of her votaries. All her leading doctrines, however, are drawn from the Bible, which contains the only and sufficient rule, both of our faith and practice. As the inestimable gift of God to man, it is an all-important article in the furniture of every lodge. In that blessed volume only are we taught the relation we sustain to God. And Masonry, by her emblems, seeks constantly to illustrate and enforce its cheering truths, calling to her aid the collateral sciences. She tells man of his exalted origin, his present degraded and helpless condition, his ignorance, blindness, and bondage. She points out to him his high and immortal destination, and bids him ask, with the assurance that he shall receive. She regards sense, reason, and faith as progressive steps, by which the mind ascends to God. Appealing to his senses, she tells him that the great I AM is everywhere present; that the manifestations of his power are everywhere seen; that the light which shines upon his path at noonday, is an emblem of the divine purity; at the same time bidding him to walk in the light as he is in the light. (Slightly altered from an oration by the Rev. Bro. E. V. Levert, delivered before the Grand Lodge of Alabama, 1843.)

Mason, that does not make the word of God his first and
principal study.

To conclude : Masonry is the daughter of heaven ; the
patroness of the liberal arts and sciences, which polish
and adorn human nature ; thankful ought they to be who
have it in their power to embrace her, and happy are they
who do. She teaches the way to content, with fervency
and zeal unfeigned ; as sure of being unchangeable, as of
ending in felicity. Invested as we are with that ancient
and noble badge, which yields preference to no honour, or
order in the universe,[14] let us determine to abhor every
act that may lessen the dignity of a profession, which to
this hour is the glory of the greatest men on the face of
the globe. Let us conform our whole lives to that great
light, the law of God ; and let our actions convince the
world, that truth, brotherly-love, and a desire to afford
relief to the distressed, are the grand principles on which
we proceed. So that this life having passed in the dis-

---

[14] Johnson defines a badge as "a mark or cognizance worn to show the
relation of the wearer to any person or thing." The badge of a Mason is
his apron—an emblem of innocence and purity. It was originally a skin
of plain white leather. In 1730 it was regulated in grand lodge, that
the grand officers should wear " white leather aprons with blue silk ; and
that the Masters and Wardens of particular lodges may line their white
leather aprons with white silk, and may hang their jewels at white ribbons
about their necks." At present a Master Mason wears a lamb-skin apron
with sky-blue lining and edging, one inch and a half deep, with a rosette
on the fall or flap. No other colour or ornament is allowed, except to
officers or past officers of lodges, who may have the emblems of their offices
in silver or white, in the centre of the apron. The Masters and Past
Masters of lodges wear, in lieu of, and in the places of the three rosettes
on the Master Mason's apron, perpendicular lines upon horizontal lines,
thereby forming three several sets of two right angles, to be made of rib-
bon of the same colour as the edging of the apron. The Grand Stewards'
aprons are distinguished by crimson and silver, and other grand and provincial grand officers by purple and gold. In the spurious Freemasonry,
each nation had its peculiar badge of initiation. In the mysteries of
Bacchus, it was a sprig of ivy ; in those of Ceres, an ear of corn. Hence
the antiquity of badges. In more modern times heraldic badges were
placed on the banners, shields, and on the breast and shoulder of private
soldiers, servants, and attendants. They began to be used about the reign
of Edward I. The badge was placed on a wreath as an honorary distinction about the time of Henry V.; and no one was allowed to use this
symbol under the degree of a knight. It sometimes consists of a coil of
rope, or cable tow, twisted into some peculiar form called a knot ; as the
Stafford knot, Dacre's knot, Wake's knot, Harrington's knot, Boucher's
knot, &c. The badge was used in the stately liveries of our old English
gentlemen.

charge of our duty as men and Freemasons, we may at length, with all mankind, be received into the presence of our Supreme Grand Master, and rejoice in hearing him say, " Well done, good and faithful servants, enter ye into the joy of your Lord."

LECTURE XIII.

ON THE VALUE OF MASONIC SECRETS. BY THE REV
DANIEL TURNER, WOOLWICH. 1787.

" To heare discourses, and not to meditate thereon, is to receive water
into a sieve; to be an uncleane creature that chowes not the cudde; to
receive the seed upon the highway side, where it being unharrowed and
uncovered is, by the fowles of the ayre, that fowle spirit that raignes in
the ayre, and in the unsettled arts of aery and windy braines, to be
devoured. The lampe of true morality will not flame forth and burne in
holy fervency, if it be not fedde with the oyle of saving knowledge, being
pressed forth more copiously by the ventilation of errours and dissipation
of mystes, which would dampe and extinguish all."—HENRY BURTON.

A PANEGYRIC adequate to the honours of, and various
benefits flowing from the Craft, is no easy task.[1] It having, however, been so often attempted, by men of the first
erudition, shall apologize for my saying little on that
point; while I endeavour sincerely, though humbly, to
serve the science, by exposing the absurdity and weakness of the objections usually brought against it.

[1] One of the best panegyrics on Masonry was pronounced by Baron
Bielfield, secretary of legation to the late King of Prussia, when writing
to a lady of his acquaintance, who was angry with him for having become
a Mason. He said :—" You will not require, I am persuaded, that I should
explain to you our mysteries ; you are much too prudent. You would
entertain a passion for a man of honour, and not for a traitor or a monster. It is my interest to convince you of my discretion, and to make
you sensible that a man who can keep a secret from the woman he adores,
ought to be esteemed by her as worthy to have other secrets to keep.
You must, therefore, commend my discretion, and nourish my virtue. I
shall not, at the same time, keep from you any information concerning our
society that it is in my power to give; but for its mysteries, they are
sacred. One reflection that dissipated my scruples, and hastened my
reception was, that *I knew this Order to be composed of a great number
of very worthy men—men who, I was, sure would never have twice entered
a Lodge, if anything had passed there that was in the least incompatible with
a character of the strictest virtue.*"

Masonry I affirm to be a mystic science, wherein, under apt figures, select numbers, and choice emblems, solemn and important truths, naturally tending to improve the understanding, to mend the heart, and to bind us more closely to one another, are more expressly contained.[2] In proportion as the wise, the learned, and the good have studied it, they have loved it. But, like all other virtuous characters, or things, it hath met with persecution. Its enemies have been many; nor have its friends been few Mature reflection on the characters of its adversaries, in a great measure, destroys all they say; for, in the first place, no truly sensible man will ever speak against what he doth not understand.[3] There are some bigots in their opinions against it. It is, cry they, a bad thing—an unlawful thing—a sinful thing.—Why? Because we detest it, and abhor it. To pity such, is no mean part of Christian love; since, I am persuaded, that even in good hearts, the first emotions respecting them were those of scorn and contempt. Of what use is it to reason with bigots, whether in religion, morals, or politics?[4]

[2] This was a most ancient method of symbolizing, or expressing one thing by means of another. Thus the Lord gave to Noah the *rainbow* as a sign of his covenant (Gen. ix. 12, 13); and for the same purpose he appointed circumcision to Abraham (Gen. xvii. 11). In a word, action, as a system of indication, was familiar in the time of the patriarchs and prophets, as a method of communicating ideas. When Isaiah says, he and his children are for *signs;* when Jeremiah found his girdle marred, as a *sign;* when Ezekiel was a *sign* to the people, in not mourning for the dead; in his removing into captivity; in digging through a wall, &c.; these and similar actions were not only well understood, but they had the advantage of being in ordinary use among the people to whom they were addressed. (See Taylor's Calmet, in v. Eye.)

[3] And yet how very common it is to hear men eloquent in proof of a fallacy, knowing at the same time that everything they say is untrue. The withering rebuke of Bishop Watson to the author of the Age of Reason may well apply to such men :—" Prove this, and I will allow that Moses was the horrid monster you make him; prove this, and I will allow that the Bible is what you call it—a book of lies, wickedness and blasphemy; prove this, or excuse my warmth if I say to you, as Paul said to Elymas the sorcerer, who sought to turn away Surgius Paulus from the faith, ' O full of all subtlety, and all mischief, thou child of the devil, thou enemy of all righteousness, wilt thou not cease to pervert the right ways of the Lord?' "

[4] It will scarcely be believed that any bigotry could be so blind and savage in the nineteenth century of Christianity, as to denounce Freemasonry as a bloody and blasphemous institution. And yet a man, calling himself Major Allyn, did actually, a few years ago, publish a book in America, where, amongst a vast deal of impious verbiage, he cries out—

There are some who speak against it more from the
vanity of saying somewhat on the point, than that they
can urge a single rational objection. If it be good, say
they, why not tell it? But we apprehend, continue
these wise-acres, there is nothing in it. As for words,
signs, tokens—all stuff—depend upon it, there are no
such things. Now, what genuine son of Freemasonry
would hold converse with such people? Let them prat-
tle on; if it pleases any who hear, they must be as weak
as themselves, and it can never injure you.[5]

The weightiest objection is yet to come, nor will I
flinch from it. Many thinking, serious, and judicious
persons, argue thus: "The reason why we are enemies
to Masonry is, the effects which, from close observation,
we have repeatedly traced. We have seen those who
call themselves warm, zealous Masons, most regular in
their attendance on the Lodge—ready to go any lengths,
both as to distance of place, loss of time, and expenses,
in pursuit of Masonry, who never appeared at church,
and frequently left their families without bread. Others
we have remarked, apparently brimful of Masonry, and
vastly fond of each Brother, doubtless, in the Lodge,
according to their principles, who yet would cheat, deceive, and supplant those very Brethren in trade, and the

"Its bloody picture exhibits a combination of principles the most invete-
rate to free inquiry and individual rights that ever stained the annals of
infamy. You may search the blackened calendar of the holy vehme, or
invoke the knightly conclaves of the secret tribunals of Germany, where
torture yells and grinds her bloody teeth; but your exertions would be
vain, you could not find a case to match this master-piece. The Holy
Inquisition, that harbinger of hell's most malign attribute, vengeance,
alone may strive for the mastery—the struggle, how desperate!!" Poor
man—poor man—an asylum for the insane is the only safe retreat for
such a man as this.

[5] These frivolous evasions every Mason has heard, and answered in his
turn. I admit, with a writer of the last century—"That a man may be
very honest and very happy without being a Freemason; but this argument is equally applicable to every object that excites our curiosity, and
even to many of the most pleasant parts of learning. If we banish curiosity (the desire of increasing our knowledge) from the world, there is
at once an end of all improvement in science; the most ingenious, the
most pleasing inventions and discoveries would be lost in darkness. And
who can say how far the knowledge of those objects, of whose essence,
whose principles we are absolutely ignorant, may lead us? That which
at first appears frivolous, frequently becomes, in the hands of a skilful
man, highly useful."

ordinary transactions of society. They would defame them; and, were it practicable, we have beheld them attempting to take, as it were, the very bread out of their mouths. Instead of being friends to mankind, or one another, they are like wolves, preying with ferocity on whatever comes in their way."

In the first place, the abuse of a thing is no valid objection to its inherent goodness. How many call themselves Christians who are a disgrace to it, yet ultimately hurt not the gospel, but themselves?[6] Besides, a man's worth is not to be rated from his own exaggerated account of the matter, but from what he actually, uniformly, and absolutely is. The Apostle hath told us, that whosoever provideth not for his own, is an infidel; therefore, we conclude that no good Mason will ever be deficient in the due performance of all moral and relative duties. If a man is negligent in religious points, depend on it, he is good for little in the Lodge.[7]

As to the second part of the objection, viz., that they will backbite and injure one another, it is too true. But what does it prove? simply this—that in the best institutions upon earth, worthless characters may occasionally be found.[8] In the holy family itself, consisting but of

---

[6] How pure and unspotted soever the outline of a society may be, evil passions will occasionally intrude to deform the goodly fabric. There is an institution that promises to reward its members, if they be virtuous, with joy unspeakable and full of glory. Even this institution, though established by purity itself, has many unworthy members. Are not some Christians addicted to intemperance—others, dishonest in their dealings with their fellow-creatures—some, uncharitable, malicious, revengeful, filled with hypocrisy, deceit, and fraud—some, disobedient to parents, Sabbath-breakers, blasphemers, uncharitable—and others, guilty of crimes still more enormous and detestable? But can all these failings be attributed to the imperfection of the society into which they have been admitted by the common ceremony of baptism? Is Christianity to blame for the defection of some unworthy members? We answer, without hesitation, certainly not.

[7] No system can be justly condemned for the misconduct of individuals; nor can their evil practices cast any censure upon the institution into which they may have been qualified to establish a claim of fraternity. Freemasonry has a clear and legitimate title to the benefit of this reasoning. It includes a multitude of men of every rank, and every shade of moral and political feeling. And it would be highly favoured, indeed, if amongst such a diversity of members, there were none who were devoid of a sound and healthy tone of mind. Judah had her false prophets; and a Judas existed among the holy Apostles of Christ.

[8] The remedy for this appears to be easy, although, perhaps, its practi-

17

420 ON THE VALUE OF MASONIC SECRETS.

twelve, one was a devil. Did that hurt the integrity of
the eleven? far from it. Why lay the faults of a few at
the door of large, respectable bodies of men, who, by
assiduously working at the Craft, have done honour to
human nature? Where the heart is bad, what can you
expect from the tongue?[9] After all, is it more than
what happens in the most solemn duties of religion?
Have there not been wretches who could go to the table
of the Lord, and the very next day traduce the moral
character of the minister from whose hands they received
the holy sacrament? And if that was not making it to
themselves the cup of devils, I know not what the Apostle meant, when he made use of those terms.

Why need I multiply words to confirm it? Built on,
and drawn from revelation, must it not be of divine
original? Adorned by the beneficent actions and
amiable virtues of thousands, the first in point of rank
knowledge, and moral excellence, of every language, in
every age, and in every clime, must it not possess an
inherent worth?[10] Thou heaven-descended beam of light,

cal application may be difficult. No Lodge ought to admit any one as
a candidate for initiation, if he be not well known to be virtuous and
good; for the Brethren will certainly betray a most sacred trust, if any
person who is deficient in the performance of those duties which the con-
ventional usages of society require, in the character of parent or child,
friend or neighbour, magistrate or subject, be knowingly introduced into
the Lodge. The proposition of every candidate comes deliberately from
some member; and it is a personal disgrace to himself, as well as an
injury to the Order, if he recommends an improper person. The admission is afterwards submitted to the vote of the whole society, and no one
ought to give his consent to an improper candidate; because it would be
little better than an act of treachery and unfaithfulness to the community
at large; and the consequences would be dangerous to the institution,
and stamp it with a certain degradation in the opinion of mankind.

[9] St. James shall answer the question—" The tongue is a little member,
and boasteth great things. Behold how great a matter a little fire
kindleth. And the tongue is a fire, a world of iniquity; so is the tongue
amongst our members, that it defileth the whole body, and setteth on fire
the course of nature; and it is set on fire of hell. For every kind of beasts
and birds, and serpents, and things in the sea, is tamed, and hath been
tamed of mankind; but the tongue can no man tame; it is an unruly
evil, full of deadly poison." (James iii. 5—8.)

[10] The Masonic system exhibits a stupendous and beautiful fabric,
rounded on universal piety, unfolding its gates to receive, without prejudice or discrimination, the worthy professors of every description of
genuine religion; concentrating, as it were, in one body, the just tenets,
unincumbered by the disputable peculiarities, of all sects and persuasions.

beauty, and perfection! how oft hast thou been the means of saving life and property; reconciled the most jarring interests, and converted fiercest foes to dearest friends! On, on then, my dear Brethren, pursue the great lecture with alacrity and firmness, each moving on the square of truth, by the compass of God's word, according to your respective stations, in all the rules of symmetry, order, and proportion.[11] Nor dread when your earthly Lodge shall be dissolved; your jewels will still be safe, and you shall be admitted into a more glorious Lodge, even an house not made with hands, eternal in the heavens; where angels and saints shall be your fellowcrafts and companions; and the Supreme Architect of the Universe your ineffably great and glorious Grand Master—your light—your life—your joy—your all!

Need I tell you the honours of Masonry are as illustrious as they are ancient? You know it, and firmly believe it. Still do you not agree with me, they shine the brightest when they are grounded on real piety? In all sciences there have been pretenders, and perhaps of most secrets in the arts there have been counterfeits: yet, this neither tarnishes the beauty, nor weakens this tenet of our craft, that Masonry and brotherly love ought to go hand in hand. Diligently search the scriptures for the secrets of your art; and while you toil to pry into the covenant, the signs, and tokens, that subsisted and were communicated between the kings of Judah and of Tyre, O may the spirit of the widow's son be in you! filling you with a knowledge of the points on which all the above turned, even wisdom to design, strength to execute, and the beauties of holiness to

and storing up the most approved schemes of ethics adopted by the different nations of the world, where civilization has impressed her footsteps. (Masonic Miscellanies, No. 2.)

[11] In the lectures used by the ancient or Athol Masons in the last century, I find this illustration of virtue:—" Virtue is the highest exercise of the mind; the integrity, harmony, and just balance of affection; the health, strength, and beauty of the soul. The perfection of virtue is to give reason its full scope: to obey the authority of conscience with alacrity; to exercise the defensive passions with fortitude; the public with justice, and the private with temperance; i. e. in due proportion to each other. To love God with disinterested affection, and to acquiesce in his kind providence with calm resignation, is the surest step towards the test of virtue, and an approach to perfection and happiness; while a deviation therefrom is sure to produce vice and misery.

adorn.[12]   Remember that the same pages contain an inestimable pearl of great price, and that those individuals are the only wise and good who make that pearl their own. Numberless are the encouragements to do this. Ask, and ye shall receive; seek, and ye shall find; knock, and it shall be opened to you. In that case you lay hold on the right pillar in the temple, both of solid fame and spiritual wealth, whereby you shall be established; and then you may safely rest upon the left, a still higher column in your scientific line, since in that you will find strength. Another motive to this flows from the examples before you. In the various periods of society, the greatest—the most learned—and the very best of characters, have belonged to your fraternity.[13]

[12] This paragraph contains a reference to the great symbol of Masonry, the building of Solomon's temple ; which was effected by the architectural talent of the widow's son, under the exalted patronage of the kings of Israel and Tyre. The latter had been the friend and ally of David, and he now offered his assistance to Solomon in furtherance of this great and noble undertaking. The forest of cedars on the mountains of Lebanon could only supply timber for the work, and they were in possession of the Tyrians. Hiram therefore employed a great number of his subjects to cut down the trees and saw them into planks ; which being done, they brought the timber to the sea-side and passed it in floats to Joppa ; whence it might conveniently be conveyed to Jerusalem. The King of Tyre also furnished artificers of every description ; not only expert Masons, but also men who excelled in the working of gold, silver, and precious stones ; and also in dyeing scarlet, purple, and blue, in which the Tyrians greatly excelled. But the most valuable present he made to Solomon on the present occasion was, a divinely endowed architect and artist, who was a Tyrian by birth, but the son of a widow of the tribe of Naphtali. This man was a treasure to Solomon, and he constituted him Overseer of the work, and Grand Master over all the lodges of workmen wheresoever distributed, whether in the forest, the quarries, the plains of Zeredathah, or at Jerusalem.

[13] This is a most triumphant argument ; for that which has been honoured with the public sanction of wise and virtuous men throughout all time, cannot have an evil tendency. In fact, a Masons' lodge is the very seat of happiness and innocent enjoyment, which is the principle and end of all our actions and passions, our pleasures and our pains ; the common or universal centre to which all animated nature is hurried by a rapid and irresistible movement. Men are united in society only to procure it. The arts and sciences have been invented only to make it perfect. All states and professions are so many channels in which it is sought. The great and mean, the rich and poor, infancy and age, passions and talents, virtues and vices, pleasures and toils, are all engaged in an unremitting pursuit of it. In a word, from the people that inhabit the most civilized cities, to the savage that prowls in the bosom of the wilderness ; from the throne of the monarch to the hut of the most abject peasant, the

Whatever be your rank in life, on close observation, you will find those in a similar station who have dignified themselves, and been useful to mankind. The widow that threw in her mite was the most generous and compassionate of all who then entered the temple. Verbal love is but painted fire; therefore, let His example, who went about doing good, be the pillar so elegantly adorned with lily-work, kindly directing and inflaming your humanity towards the Brethren. Meet the very lowest of them on the level of condescension, nor venture to despise the man for whom, perhaps, a Saviour died; that so you may be able to hold up your heads when justice is laid to the line, and righteousness to the plummet. Let your pure benevolence spread every way, like the more than gem-studded arch of heaven, expanding even over your enemies when in distress, that you may prove yourselves to be the children of the Most High, who is benign to the unthankful, and to the evil. Philanthropy is not confined to name or sect, to climate or language. Like the power of attraction, which reaches from the largest to the smallest bodies in the universe, it unites men from the throne to the cottage. Whether your lodge meets on the high mountains of worldly grandeur, and is beheld from afar, or in the lowest vales of obscurity, and noticed but by a few; whether under Adoniram you hew on the tops of Lebanon, or, with Aholiab and Bezaleel,[14] are in distinguished

world is in labour to bring forth true peace and tranquillity of soul. I am inclined, however, to believe that if it has any existence upon this earth, it is probably in the person of a true Christian Mason. (Dean Kirwan.)

[14] The tabernacle built by these two worthy Brothers who constructed on the plan of the larger buildings of Egypt. "I believe really," says Goguet (vol. ii. p. 129), "that there must have been some relation between the taste which reigned in these edifices and the tabernacle. It is true, strictly speaking, this work ought not to be looked upon as a piece of architecture; it was only, to speak properly, a vast tent; this is the first idea it offers to the mind; but by reflecting on it more attentively, we shall perceive that the tabernacle had a great relation to architecture. We ought to look upon it as a representation of the temples and palaces of the East. Let us recollect the form of government of the Hebrews. The supreme Being was equally their God and king. The tabernacle was erected with a view to answer that double title. It served at once for the temple and palace. The Israelites went there sometimes to adore the Almighty and sometimes to receive the orders of their sovereign, present in a sensible manner in the midst of his people."

offices near the sanctum sanctorum, or with the sons of Levi serve at the altar, O sit not at a Brother's call; if he be in danger fly to his relief; if he be deceived tell him the truth ; if he be calumniated, justify his character —bear his burdens—allay his sorrows—and espouse his cause; nay, if in many things he hath erred, still recollect, that indiscretion in him ought not to destroy humanity in you.[15]

As the eastern magi opened their treasures, which, doubtless, were various, to the Redeemer of souls, so every Brother should be given to hospitality; ready to distribute, willing to communicate, and eager to employ his gift or power, whatever it may be, for the mutual good of each other, and the common benefit of all. Owing to the prevalency of this enduring munificence, the holy David, who collected so magnificently towards the building of the temple, aided by the spirit of inspiration, informs us in the book of Psalms, that the glorious head of the church, and Grand Master in Israel, of whom the whole family in heaven and on earth is called,[16] may, among other things, be found out by this,

---

[15] If the most determined opponent could make up his mind to devote himself quietly to the study of the true principles of Masonry, and if he would take the trouble to inquire into the operation of these principles, his objections would be undoubtedly removed. When he saw the cheering results of Masonic benevolence, when he saw the orphan clothed, and fed, and educated, when he saw the distressed Mason relieved, and the aged provided for, conviction could not fail to strike his senses, and he would feel inclined to say—" Let me assist in bearing your burden ; you are fulfilling the royal law of Christ ; and I am now anxious to have a share in this good work." Indeed, nothing can be more delightful than the practical operation of Masonry, in administering to the wants of others. In the performance of these duties we meet on the level ; we lay aside all party differences, and pursue the great work of benevolence in peace, harmony, and brotherly love.

[16] The divine personage here referred to by David was no other than the Messiah or Christ; and it is not improbable that the expectation which prevailed over all the East, that a deliverer should arise in Judea and rule over the whole world, was occasioned by this and similar prophecies in the Jewish writings ; particularly the star that was predicted by Jacob. This is further illustrated by the fact that an impostor arose in the reign of Adrian, who, taking advantage of this circumstance, endeavoured to convert the credulity of the Jews to his own benefit ; and therefore boldly gave out that he was the Messiah, and assumed the title of the Son of the Star, in allusion to this latter prophecy, that it might be believed that he was the star which Balaam saw afar off. And more than one of the Christian fathers affirm, that it was in consequence of Balaam's

that all his garments smell of myrrh, aloes, and cassia.[17]

Diminish not the value of your beneficence by the harshness of the manner, but be affable, be courteous, be kind, and so secret, lest you wound the sensibility of the receiver, that on many occasions you let not your right hand know what your left hand doth. Above all, be sincere, and, however powerful the enticements to the contrary, scorn dissimulation's winding path; for it inevitably leads to loss of character and future ruin. Joab and Judas could give good words, nay, kiss when they meant to kill. Equally treacherous are numbers in the present age, who never speak to you fairer than when they wish to undermine you; or, when they say that they pray for your success, would, nevertheless, inwardly rejoice at your misfortunes.

As light and science came from the East, may we, who by reason of mental darkness were once just in the opposite extreme, now quickened by the Spirit of God, and enlightened in the saving principles of true knowledge, be enabled to move according to the rules of order, in the nicest lines of symmetry, back to the source of perfect light. What improvements our science received among the magi of Persia, or the learned among the Egyptians, whether Pythagoras brought it to Greece,[18] and the silence imposed on his disciples was

prophecies, which were known and believed in the East, that the wise men on the appearance of a new star, concluding that this prince was born, came immediately to Jerusalem to inquire, where is he who is born King of the Jews?

[17] The cassia, or rather the acacia, was consecrated by the aborigines of America to the genius of chaste love. These fierce children of the prairies, whom nothing can subdue, conceive a sentiment full of delicacy, which they are unable to express by words. but which they understand by the symbol of a blooming branch of acacia. The young savage, like the civilized coquet, understands the offering, and accepts the homage thus delicately expressed. The acacia has also been made an emblem of domestic beauty. Thus a modern writer says:—"The acacia is found in the most retired places, and it blooms the fairest in the closeness of its own foliage. It loves the mossy rock and the solitary grove, but it pines away in the gay garden and crowded parterre. There can be no fitter emblem of a beautiful woman flourishing in the innocent retirement of her home, secluded from the vanities of crowded life, and adorning with her bloom the abode of domestic affection."

[18] It was late in life when he retired finally into Greece, to plant there his perfected system. Iamblichus says that he spent twenty-two years

analagous to our taciturnity about the mysteries of our
art to all but the Eklectoi, and how far it was preserved
and studied by the Druids in Britain, with many other
curious circumstances, we shall leave for the investiga
tion of more sequestered hours. Perhaps it employed
the solitary retirement, in some measure, of the Essenes,
the most particular and eremital sect among the Jews.
That some of its parts may have composed the abstruse
and impenetrable Sephiroth is not impossible.[19] Thus
far we can say, that if it did, it would be as rational an
interpretation of the ten circles, as any which Maimonides or the other cabalistical doctors have given.

Suffice it at present to note, that we are Free, because
no bondmen is permitted amongst us ; and Accepted,
seeing we have stood the test of several probationary
degrees with applause ; emulous to be found worthy of
the illustrious badges worn by those who hold the first
places there, where no atheist, no libertine, or reprobate
person, known to be such, ought ever to gain admission.
To guide us by the way, we have not one star, but many.
Let the Bible be the rule of our faith.[20] May we square
all our actions by the precepts of our Saviour, and set a
compass to our words, as relative to others, especially
those whom we know to be Brethren.

in Egypt, and acquired all the learning of that people ; that he was carried from thence by Cambyses, and spent twelve years in Babylon ; but
he did not go into Italy till the sixty-second Olympiad ; and, having
settled there, it was dignified by the name of Magna Grecia.

[19] The Sephiroth were ten in number ; the first seven of which were
supposed to occupy grades, like the steps of a ladder, crowned with the
remaining three, which represented the three divine hypostases of the
Godhead. The names of the inferior Sephiroth were. Strength, Mercy,
Beauty, Victory, Glory, Foundation, Kingdom. These represented the
seven heavens of the cabalistic Jews, which formed the dwelling of the
sacred Trinity.

[20] By the doctrines contained in that holy book, as the lectures of the
last century taught, we are induced to believe in the dispensations of
Providence, which strengthens our faith, and enables us to ascend the
first step of the theological ladder. This faith produces a hope that we
may share in the promises that are there recorded, which supports our
ascent to the second step. But the union of faith and hope cannot fail
to produce charity, which enables the Free and Accepted Mason to attain
the summit of the ladder. and to enjoy a glance into that ethereal mansion. which is veiled from mortal eye by the starry firmament, and depicted in a Masons' lodge by *seven stars ;* without which number of regular
Masons, no lodge can be perfect, neither can any person be legally initiated
therein.

As in our mundane system the sun rules by day, and the moon by night, with an inferior lustre, so may we fulfil our appointed duties; more particularly by yielding a cheerful obedience to those who in his providence the Architect of the Universe hath set over us, whether the more subordinate or the supreme.

Hail, mystic art! thou source of utility, as numbers have experienced; since if we were ever to be cast on an unknown shore, or obliged to travel through the most distant climes, however ignorant of their language, their customs, and apparently strange to their inhabitants, thou lendest thy unfeigned votaries a secret key to open the rudest bosoms, and to unlock the most concealed hoards of niggardly parsimony.

Then, my much-respected Brethren, foot to foot let us stand on the broad basis of rectitude, inscribed within the circle of harmony, to show that we are ready to move with and for a Brother in every just and laudable design. On bended knees let us join in each act of adoration and praise to the Grand Master of angels, saints, and men; humbly begging, through the merits of Christ Jesus, that his inexhaustible goodness would be pleased to confer what his infinite wisdom sees most conducive for the essential and permanent felicity of ourselves and all our genuine Brethren, whether in the present or future state of our existence. May we display the reciprocity of our esteem in imitation of the early Christians, who are said to have had but one heart; warmly pledging that, considering the instability in all the gifts of fortune, we are resolved, according to our ability and the necessities of a Brother, to be equally ready liberally to give, or, if our situation requires it, thankfully to receive.[21]

---

[21] Every Brother will see that the above observations bear a direct reference to the five points of fellowship; which were thus illustrated in the lectures used by the Athol Masons of the last century :—" 1. When the necessities of a Brother call for my support, I will be ever ready to lend him a helping hand, to save him from sinking, if I find him worthy thereof. 2. Indolence shall not cause my footsteps to halt, nor wrath to turn them aside; but, forgetting every selfish consideration, I will be ever swift of foot to save, help, and execute benevolence to a fellow-creature in distress; but more particularly to a Brother Mason. 3. When I offer up my ejaculations to Almighty God, I will remember my Brother's welfare, even as mine own ; for, as the voices of babes and sucklings ascend to the Throne of Grace, so, most assuredly, will the breathings of a fer-

17*

Thus acting, no human power can hurt you ; for your building, thus fitly and compactly framed together, must grow into an holy temple, both in and for the Lord. In order to maintain unsullied the honour of the Craft, be cautious whom ye admit to the knowledge of your far more exalted than Eleusinian mysteries ;[22] yet from the worshippers of Ceres be not ashamed to take a lesson of circumspection and vigilance. But zealous in the discharge of all the duties demanded of you, nor faint though it may fall to your lot to labour in the plains of Jordan, in the clayey ground between Succoth and Zeredathah.

Thus may your lodges appear beautiful as Thirzah, comely as Jerusalem, fair as the curtains of Solomon, and supported by workmen that need not be ashamed. May they be taught and ruled by Masters who comprehend the light of truth ; guarded by officers who will not remove the ancient landmarks which their fathers have set ; and may the watchmen upon the towers suffer every man to pass who can give proofs of his being a good Mason and a true, adorning by his life and conversation the secret tenets of the science, and, what is still more, the Gospel of our Lord and Saviour Jesus Christ, to which word of our salvation, unless we give earnest heed, and render all things sub-

vent heart ascend to the mansions of bliss. 4. A Brother's secrets, delivered to me as such, I will keep as I would my own ; because, if I betray the trust which has been reposed in me, I might do him an irreparable injury ; it would be like the villainy of an assassin, who lurks in darkness to stab his adversary when unarmed, and least prepared to meet an enemy. 5. A brother's character I will support in his absence, as I would in his presence. I will not revile him myself, nor suffer it to be done by others, if it is in my power to prevent it. Thus, by the five points of fellowship, we are linked together in one indivisible chain of sincere affection, brotherly love, relief, and truth."

[22] Stillingfleet thinks that the Eleusinian mysteries were derived from the Pelasgi. He says: "Without all question, the Samothracians had their names from thence, whence they derived their mysteries. And, to this purpose, it is farther observable, that, as the old Hetrurians were certainly a colony of the Pelasgi upon their removal out of Greece, so Vossius observes, that the old Hetruscan language hath almost all the sacred appellations from the Eastern tongues. For which purpose, it is further observable, which Grotius takes notice of, that the jus pontificum Romanorum was taken, a great part, from the Hetrusci, and the Hetrurians had it ab Hebræis, out of the eastern parts." (Orig. Sac. b. iii. c. 4.)

servient, we are but deceiving ourselves, and the truth is not in us.[23]

Can I conclude more emphatically than in the words of the apostle? Let all bitterness, and wrath, and anger, and clamour, and evil-speaking, be put away from you, with all malice. And be ye kind one to another, tenderhearted, forgiving one another, even as God for Christ's sake hath forgiven you.

[23] At the view of such a blessed scene who would not feel himself inclined to exclaim, like Balaam before the camp of the Israelites: "How goodly are thy tents, O Jacob, and thy tabernacles, O Israel!" This is what Freemasonry, universally known and practised, would produce. It would have an effect similar to that which was actually produced by Christianity on its earliest disciples. They were the friends of peace: they prayed for their persecutors; and were as much distinguished by their love to each other, as by the unequalled purity of their lives. There were riches and poverty amongst them, and yet they were nether rich nor poor. Brotherly love equalized everything. They had but one will, and that was the will of God; they had but one interest, and that was the universal interest of the whole community.

POPULAR WORKS ON FREEMASONRY

PUBLISHED BY THE

MASONIC PUBLISHING AND MANUFACTURING CO.

432 BROOME STREET, N. Y.

☞ Any book in this list sent by mail to any address in the United States, free of postage, on receipt of the price.

A CYCLOPEDIA OF FREEMASONRY; containing Definitions of the Technical Terms used by the Fraternity. With an account of the rise and progress of Freemasonry and its Kindred Associations—ancient and modern: embracing OLIVER'S DICTIONARY OF SYMBOLICAL MASONRY. Edited by ROBERT MACOY, 33d. *Illustrated with numerous Engravings.* Cloth, gilt side, $3 00. Half Morocco...............$4 00

GUIDE TO THE ROYAL ARCH CHAPTER; a complete Monitor for Royal Arch Masonry. With full instructions in the degrees of Mark Master, Past Master, Most Excellent Master, and Royal Arch, according to the text of the Manual of the Chapter. By JOHN SHEVILLE, P. G. H. P., of New Jersey, and JAS. L. GOULD, D. G. H. P., of Connecticut. Together with a Historical Introduction, Explanatory Notes, and Critical Emendations. To which are added Monitorial Instructions in the Holy Order of High-Priesthood in Royal Arch Masonry, with the Ceremonies of the Order. By JAS. L. GOULD, M. A., 33d. Cloth—gilt back and side............................ 1 50

THE MASONIC HARMONIA; a Collection of Music, Original and Selected, for the use of the Masonic Fraternity. By HENRY STEPHEN CUTLER, Doctor in Music, Director of the Cecilian Choir, etc. Published under the auspices of St. Cecile Lodge, No. 568, City of New York. Half-bound—cloth sides, $1 00...........per doz.10 00

THE GENERAL AHIMAN REZON AND FREEMASON'S GUIDE, containing Monitorial Instructions in the Degrees of Entered Apprentice, Fellow-Craft, and Master Mason, with Explanatory Notes, Emendations, and Lectures: together with the Ceremonies of Consecration and Dedication of New Lodges, Installation of Grand and Subordinate Officers, Laying Foundation Stones, Dedication of Masonic Halls, Grand Visitations, Burial Services, Regulations for Processions, Masonic Calendar, etc. To which are added a RITUAL for a LODGE OF SORROW and the Ceremonies of Consecrating Masonic Cemeteries; also an Appendix, with the Forms of Masonic Documents, Masonic Trials, etc. By DANIEL SICKELS, 33d. Embellished with nearly 300 Engravings and Portrait of the Author.
Bound in fine Cloth—extra—large 12mo........................... 1 50
"   "   Morocco, full gilt, for the W. Master's table, with appropriate insignia of the East.... .... 3 00

THE HISTORICAL LANDMARKS and other Evidences of Freemasonry, explained in a series of Practical Lectures, with copious Notes. By GEORGE OLIVER, D. D. 2 vols. Large duodecimo—with Portrait of the Author. Cloth, $5 00. Half Morocco................. 7 00

WASHINGTON AND HIS MASONIC COMPEERS. By SIDNEY HAYDEN, Past Master of Rural Amity Lodge, No. 70, Pennsylvania. Illustrated with a copy of a Masonic Portrait of Washington, *painted from life,* never before published, and numerous other engravings. Cloth—Uniform Style, $2 50. Cloth—full gilt—gilt edges, $3 50. Morocco—full gilt... 5 00

THE LIGHTS AND SHADOWS OF FREEMASONRY; consisting of
Masonic Tales, Songs, and Sentiments, never before published. By
ROB. MORRIS, K. T. Cloth, $1 75. Half Morocco....................$2 50

MANUAL OF THE ORDER OF THE EASTERN STAR, containing
Symbols, Scriptural Illustrations, Lectures, etc., adapted to the Ameri-
can system of Adoptive Masonry. By ROBT. MACOY, National Grand
Secretary. Beautifully Illustrated. Gilt Edges and Illuminated Cover 1 00

ANCIENT CONSTITUTIONS OF FREEMASONS. By JAMES AN-
DERSON. Verbatim copy of the original edition of 1723. Cloth, $1 00.
Half Morocco.. 2 00

ILLUSTRATIONS OF MASONRY. By WM. PRESTON. With
copious Notes and Additions. By REV. GEORGE OLIVER, D. D. Cloth,
$1 75. Half Morocco... 3 00

NEW YORK MASONIC CODE; containing the Old Charges,
compiled in 1720; Constitutions and General Regulations of the Grand
Lodge of New York, and the Resolutions and Decisions now in force
in that M. W. Grand Body. Collated by R. W. WILLIAM T. WOOD-
RUFF. Plain binding, 35 cents. Cloth, 50. Tuck.................... 1 00

THE USE AND ABUSE OF FREEMASONRY. A work of the
greatest utility to the Brethren of the Society, to mankind in general, and to the ladies in particular. By CAPT. GEO. SMITH. Cloth,
$1 25. Half Morocco.. 2 50

THE HISTORY OF INITIATION, in Twelve Lectures, comprising
a Detailed Account of the Rites and Ceremonies, Doctrines and Discipline of the Secret and Mysterious Institutions of the Ancient World.
By GEORGE OLIVER, D. D. Cloth, $1.50. Half Morocco............. 2 50

THE THEOCRATIC PHILOSOPHY OF FREEMASONRY, in Twelve
Lectures on its Speculative, Operative, and Spurious Branches. By
GEO. OLIVER, D.D. Cloth, $1 50. Half Morocco................... 2 50

FREEMASON'S MONITOR; containing the Degrees of Free-
masonry, embraced in the Lodge, Chapter, Council, and Commandery,
embellished with nearly 300 Symbolic Illustrations. Together with
Tactics and Drill of Masonic Knighthood. Also, Forms of Masonic
Documents, Notes, Songs, Masonic Dates, Installations, etc. By
DANIEL SICKELS, 33d. Tuck.. 1 50

TRADITIONS OF FREEMASONRY and its Coincidence with the
Ancient Mysteries. By A. T. C. PIERSON, 33d, Past Grand Master, Past
Grand High-Priest, etc. Illustrated. Large 12mo. Cloth........... 2 00

THE HISTORY OF MASONIC PERSECUTIONS, in different quar-
ters of the Globe. By VARIOUS AUTHORS. With an Introductory
Essay on the Usages and Customs of Symbolic Masonry. By REV.
GEO. OLIVER, D. D.
MASONIC INSTITUTES. By Various Authors. With an intro-
ductory Essay and Explanatory Notes. By Rev. GEO. OLIVER, D. D.
☞ Two useful works in one volume. Cloth, $2 00. Half Morocco, 3 00

THE TRUE MASONIC CHART; or, Hieroglyphic Monitor;
containing all the emblems explained in the degrees of Entered Apprentice, Fellow-Craft, and Master Mason. Designed and arranged
agreeably to the Lectures. By JEREMY L. Cross, Grand Lecturer.
With a Memoir and Portrait of the Author. Edited by DANIEL
SICKELS, 33d. 12mo. Cloth... 1 25

THE MYSTIC TIE; or, Facts and Opinions illustrative of the
Character and Tendency of Freemasonry. By A. G. MACKEY, M. D.
Cloth, $1 50. Half Morocco.. 2 50

THE SYMBOL OF GLORY, showing the Object and End of Freemasonry. By GEORGE OLIVER, D. D. Cloth, $1 50. Half Morocco.... 2 50

www.ingramcontent.com/pod-product-compliance
Lightning Source LLC
Chambersburg PA
CBHW022257280326
41932CB00010B/888